PARKS, POLITICS, and the PEOPLE

PARKS, POLITICS, and the PEOPLE

To: Rod Hellen 11/11/80
I was hoping to get down to see you in that sweat shop you are running befor I got fired. Ted even wrote my resignation so I didn't have a chance. Keep up the good work.
With best wishes
Connie

By Conrad L. Wirth

Conrad L. Wirth

FOREWORD BY MELVILLE BELL GROSVENOR

University of Oklahoma Press: Norman

Library of Congress Cataloging in Publication Data

Wirth, Conrad Louis, 1899–
Parks, politics, and the people.

1. National parks and reserves—United States—History. 2. Parks policy—United States—History. 3. Wirth, Conrad Louis, 1899– 4. United States. National Park Service—Officials and employees—Biography. I. Title.
SB482.A4W57 353.0086′32′0924 79-6709
ISBN 0-8061-1605-6

Dedication

It is with deep appreciation that we dedicate this book to those who have made possible the opportunities that have been ours down through the years:

Our Parents
Professor Frank A. Waugh
General U. S. Grant III
Mr. Horace M. Albright
Secretary Oscar L. Chapman
Mr. Laurance S. Rockefeller
Dr. Melville Bell Grosvenor

and

The National Park Service employees for their loyalty, hard work and devotion to the national park concept.

Conrad L. and Helen O. Wirth

Contents

Preface

The motivation to provide an account of my thirty-six years of experience in planning and administering national parks and other recreational areas grew out of the belief that such an account would be helpful to people who want to pursue careers in public service, particularly in the field of conservation of our natural and human resources.

It has been said that public servants live in a fishbowl. The public, Congress, and heads of government departments are constantly scrutinizing everything government employees do. Every letter they write, every document or plan they work on is the public's business. Public servants are subject to constant criticism, and they are often the victims of misrepresentation without benefit of any opportunity or means for rebuttal. Yet many of the best administrative, professional, and scientific people in the country are government employees. It is my belief that close observation by the public makes government employees more alert and proficient than they would be otherwise. Their skill and attitudes are thereby frequently adjusted and improved for better service to the country.

This is not to say that government service is all unrewarding drudgery. My point is simply that people should know as much as possible about the ups and downs of their proposed life's occupation and should select one they will enjoy, for if they do not enjoy their work they will not achieve success. Remember President Harry Truman's advice: "If you can't stand the heat, get out of the kitchen!" Although this statement was made in a political frame of reference, it can apply as well to any occupation, including working for the people at any level of government.

The event that crystallized my decision to write this, my first book, was the receipt of a letter dated January 5, 1957, from President Robert F. Goheen of Princeton University informing me that I, along with my counterpart and good friend in the United States Forest Service, Chief Forester Richard J. McArdle, had been selected to receive the Rockefeller Public Service Award for distinguished service to the nation in the field of conservation of resources. In his letter President Goheen said:

> The purpose of the University and of Mr. John D. Rockefeller, 3rd in establishing the program was to strengthen public service by giving recognition to distinguished

civilians in the federal government, to improve the public service as a career, and to make it possible for experienced men and women thus recognized to pass on to others some of the fruits of their career experience. Because of this last feature, the Trustees hope you will want to make some further contribution of your own, and to that end the University is prepared to provide financial assistance. . . . You have no obligation to the University nor to anyone else in connection with, or as a condition to receiving, the Award.

In my reply I stated:

I believe I understand fully the objective of the Princeton University and of Mr. John D. Rockefeller, 3rd in establishing the award, and the desirability of following certain procedures in order to obtain full benefits from its intended purpose. I am wholeheartedly in support of its purpose of creating in the public's mind an accurate picture of the scope and quality of work done by career public servants, which I hope will, at the same time, improve the quality of the career service.

I have been thinking about this book for a long time. When I retired from government service in 1964, I gave more thought to it, indicating in my retirement letter to my associates in the National Park Service that among the several things I was going to do in retirement was write a book, and a lot of people encouraged me to do so. I have tried to relate in an interesting way not only my own experiences but those of some of my associates and of the Park Service as a group, experiences that we have had as career public servants. Some of these episodes I think are quite interesting as illustrations of the problems that arise in public administration and of how they are approached and resolved. In telling of these experiences I hope to convey the overall importance of the human values in public service.

Although this book has turned out to be more about my own life in government than I originally intended, nevertheless that is perhaps the best way I can describe what government service is really like—its good points and its bad ones. Certainly it is the life I am best acquainted with, and I consider myself to be representative of thousands of other government employees. Much of the content of the book was assimilated from many years of association with National Park Service people in a common effort to serve our country as managers of the people's heritage, natural and man made. I thank each and every one of them for wonderful memories of the National Park Service of my time.

I am especially indebted to Horace M. Albright, one of the founders of the National Park Service and its director at the time the service's Civilian Conservation Corps organization and program were established in 1933. Mr. Albright read in draft the two chapters on the CCC, found them to be accurate and adequate, and suggested no corrections or revisions.

I must also say that had it not been for the succession of fine secretaries who kept me advised and helped in keeping my records straight during my years in the Park Service, I could not have attempted to write this book. To them—Florence Duncan, Lorraine Griffith, Virginia Ayres, Belva Brandon, Rita Matthews, and Helen Johnson—I owe a great deal.

Friends are a great asset and comfort, and they can keep one busy and on the right track. This book is as much the work of William S. Bahlman and James F. Kieley as it is mine. Bill spent hours on hours with me in the archives digging out material, setting up files, and being a general adviser. Jim has been my editor and must be given the credit for putting the entire manuscript in fine, readable condition. All three of us are retired National Park Service people, a part of the Steve Mather Park Service family.

CONRAD L. WIRTH

Montgomery County, Maryland

Foreword

Although I had known Connie Wirth for some years, I never realized the full measure of his devotion to his country and to the service of his people until we hiked together into the towering coastal redwood trees of California's Rockefeller Forest. It was 1958, and the graceful giants in the grove where we paused for a breather were then believed to be the world's tallest living things.

"Mel," said Connie, "suppose we lie on our backs and look up through the crowns of these trees into the sky. Not in this life, not even in a great cathedral, will you then feel closer to your Maker. For men built the cathedral, but God created the trees.

"And I am sure He created them for people—all the people of our country and of the earth, not just the few who want to cut them down for their personal profit. Now I am a servant of the people, and I think the best way to make sure these trees remain forever the property of the people is to get them into parks. Naturally, since I'm director of the national parks, I'd like to see as many redwoods as possible placed under the protection of the National Park Service."

Connie wasn't just talking. Just ten years later, Congress established Redwoods National Park. The National Geographic Society, I am proud to say, was able to help the legislators decide upon the size and boundaries of this important park by granting funds for a complete survey of the coastal redwood belt in northern California. The idea was born as Connie and I walked out of the Rockefeller Forest.

"Are these really the tallest trees in the world?" I remember asking.

"We don't really know," Connie said. "There's never been a thorough survey made, not even by the lumber companies. The Park Service has a little money we could use for the job. Do you think you could talk your Geographic trustees into putting up the rest?"

I did. The survey was duly made, concentrating on the broad question of what groves worthy of national park status were still available. Meanwhile, a *National Geographic Magazine* staffer, Dr. Paul Zahl, discovered the 367.8-foot giant that thus far holds the record as the world's tallest living thing. Hidden along the banks of isolated Redwood Creek, the tree and its neighbors were subsequently purchased from the lumber company that owned them, and the grove is now part of the national park.

The battle to establish Redwoods National Park was a bitter one. Without Connie Wirth to lead it, the cause could never have been won, and the American people he served would have been the losers. He cajoled congressmen. He browbeat people who could be swayed no other way. When he had to, he accepted insults with a smile. Loggers cursed him at public meetings, while lumber barons, in their plush offices, insulted him in more sophisticated terms.

But insults and other unpleasantries can be turned to advantage when one is a "magnificent bureaucarat," as a high federal official once called Connie Wirth. In his book Connie writes: "One should never forget his experiences, no matter how unpleasant, because experiences are the foundation of the road to the future." Sound advice for anyone, that, but especially for the public servant, the ready target of criticism from congressmen, from the top people in the executive branch of government, and from all the organizations and individuals with special interest in the public servant's field of jurisdiction. You can find this sort of advice, implicit or offered through example, throughout the book, making *Parks, Politics, and the People* a valuable manual for those who seek careers in government and for those already embarked upon them.

It is, in addition, a history. The exciting period during which the author served in government has been well documented by serious historians. Connie makes no attempt to duplicate their efforts but rather illuminates their accounts. He sheds light upon the government people at the working level who had much to do with shaping events for which the top brass received the credit but who drew little notice in the broad history of the era. This fleshing-out of history is a most valuable service.

Necessarily, the book is considerably autobiographical. The author describes the background that led him into government service: the influence of a father who, before there was a national park system, gained renown as a designer and administrator of local parks; Connie's venture into business as a landscape architect; and finally, his entry into a long career in the federal government.

Much of the book—again necessarily—concerns the National Park Service, in which the author served for thirty-three years. Of his many accomplishments in senior staff positions and as director of the service for twelve years, two were outstanding: his direction of Civilian Conservation Corps activities of his own and other bureaus of the Department of the Interior as departmental representative on the CCC Advisory Council and his initiation of the service's Mission 66 program through which our national parks were rehabilitated after years of unavoidable neglect during World War II.

Even when he was seconded to the Civilian Conservation Corps during the New Deal, Connie didn't leave parks entirely behind. His job was to build CCC camps, and many of these were in national and state parks. The work he did in the CCC was certainly one of his finest contributions to the welfare of the country. The CCC took city boys off the streets in the depression years, sent them into the wilds, and there built them into men sound in body and character. They planted trees, cut trails, fought fires, and built lasting structures. We are still reaping benefits from their work.

Perhaps the high point in Director Wirth's career was his inspiration and organization of Mission 66, a giant proposal to rejuvenate the parks. By 1956, the national parks had grown so numerous and become so run-down because appropriations had not kept up with growth that something dramatic, mammoth had to be done to restore them. It couldn't be a simple one-year appropriation but must be a long-term push. Connie proposed a ten-year effort, called Mission 66, whose culmination in 1966 would coincide with the fiftieth anniversary of the National Park Service. He kicked off the program with a huge banquet in the halls of the Department of the Interior and had rangers and others give illustrated talks that would dramatically point out the low condition of the parks and what ought to be done to bring them up to par for the millions of annual visitors.

Invited to the dinner were important members of Congress and all the committees that dealt with the parks, cabinet members, government officials, and distinguished friends from civilian life. The dinner was to be something different. From western parks Connie obtained surplus buffalo and elk, which were served as tempting roasts. Pictures flashed on the screen showing rangers' families living in squalor, poor facilities for tourists, congested and bumpy roads, and other defects. In contrast, architectural drawings conjured up villages of neat homes for park personnel and beautiful visitor centers designed to interpret the culture, history, and other information about the parks. Then Connie inveigled high-ranking government officials who were fond of the parks to give pep talks emphasizing the low state of the parks and what should be done. The whole program was dramatic, fast-moving, and enthusiastic. So well did Connie plan and carry out his project that he indeed accomplished everything he wanted, and in the fiftieth anniversary year the new wonders were dedicated with great ceremony and admiration.

Connie left the parks only once. Just after World War II the late Harold L. Ickes, then secretary of the interior, sent him to Europe to help work out a peace treaty with Austria. Then Connie returned to his beloved parks.

If *Parks, Politics, and the People* is largely the story of one man's service in the national parks, the fact does not diminish the value of the book as a public servant's guide. Except for the fields in which they function, one government bureau is much like another. Those who administer them face the same unrelenting pressures. If they are to be successful bureaucrats, they must employ the same techniques to find their way through the tortuous federal jungle.

Describing his methodology, Connie leaves out nothing. He tells of the battles he won and lists those he lost. He gives us full texts of the reprimands he received. He criticizes those he feels deserve criticism. But he tempers his barbs with kindness. When I first read his manuscript, I told him I couldn't understand why he was so temperate, since he was now out of government and not exposed to retaliation.

"Well," he replied, "it's like Voltaire is said to have put it: 'I may not agree with what you say, but I will defend to the death your right to say it.' So when a fellow bucked me, he was only exercising his right as a citizen of a democracy."

Democracy, American style, is really what *Parks, Politics, and the People* is all about—not democracy coldly defined, but democracy at work, serving the people under the skilled, devoted guidance of a "magnificent bureaucrat."

MELVILLE BELL GROSVENOR
Chairman Emeritus and
Editor Emeritus
National Geographic Society

PARKS, POLITICS, and the PEOPLE

1

An Overview

Civilized man has fortunately retained an instinct for holding on to the reality of his undisputed identity as an integral part of the universe. Colonel Richard Lieber, an ardent conservationist whose unstinting efforts gave Indiana its exceptional state park system, used to quote Francis Thompson: "Thou canst not stir a flower / without troubling of a star." An astute observation, certainly, projected to its not illogical conclusion. It is undoubtedly this feeling for the homogeneity of all creation that prompts so many of us to get outdoors and "back to nature" as a respite from the travail of everyday living. Henry David Thoreau succinctly explained his personal motivation: "I went to the woods because I wished to live deliberately, to front only the essential facts of life, and see if I could not learn what it had to teach, and not, when I came to die, discover that I had not lived."

The importance of reserving space for what we have come to call recreation has long been understood. The first American settlers provided their towns with commons or village greens, and as communities grew larger they included parks in their civic planning. As the nation's westward expansion proceeded in earnest after the Civil War, thoughtful people advocated conservation practices to insure the protection of suitable lands and waters for public enjoyment. Although their influence was initially only slight at a time when the store of such natural resources seemed inexhaustible, they scored a remarkable early success with the establishment of a state park in the Yosemite Valley of California in 1864, and with that the movement got well under way.

Congress acted as early as 1832 to reserve acreage in the Hot Springs region of Arkansas for public use, but the first area (first in the world, in fact) to be designated a national park was Yellowstone, in 1872. This was done at the urging of three men from Montana who had explored the region in the northwest corner of their neighboring Territory of Wyoming in 1870 to investigate the reports of fantastic natural phenomena—hot pools, geysers, and volcanoes—that had been circulated for over fifty years by hunters and trappers, who were the only white men to have visited the area. The Montanans not only confirmed these tales, which until then had been taken only lightly, but also described the awesome beauty of Yellowstone's canyons, waterfalls, and forests. Actual photographs of these natural treasures made the following year by a United States Geological Survey expedition helped to convince Congress that the area should be set aside and protected as a primeval wonderland.

In 1890, Congress designated Yosemite as a national park and added two others in California, namely Sequoia and General Grant National Parks. From these beginnings a large and diversified system of natural, historical, recreational, and cultural areas was developed which in 1972, a hundred years after the first national park came into being, totaled 284 units throughout the country.

In the early years of the national park movement, the parks were almost wholly inaccessible to visitors. The basic reason for establishing them was to prevent their unique resources from being exploited for profit by the lumber and mining industries which were then avidly seeking to penetrate remote parts of the West in anticipation of high returns on their investments. Gradually, however, railroad lines were built to serve park areas where practicable, and roads were extended or improved when the age of automobile travel arrived. In 1970, near the end of their first century, the national parks reported a year's total of 172,307,500 visitors.

With public use of all types of areas in the system increasing exponentially over the years, the main problem for park administrators became one of protecting them not simply from commercial exploitation, but rather from the erosive effect of heavy use by the park visitors themselves. This has continued to be a peculiarly baffling problem. The parks are for the people to use, and the people are encouraged to use them, but it has been aptly said that now the parks are literally being loved to death. How, then, can the irreplaceable resources of these areas be preserved for the very people whose intensive use of the parks threatens to destroy or at least impair them?

This is the challenge that led me into park planning and administration, for I had been cognizant of it throughout my childhood as I watched my father wrestle with the problem in developing and administering the municipal park systems of two large cities in the East and Middle West. I was actually born in a park and lived in parks until I left home to attend preparatory school and then college, where I majored in landscape architecture. Professionally, then, I am a landscape architect and planner—a land-use planner, that is—throughout a career that brought me major responsibilities in my professional field and in management.

My father, Theodore Wirth, a horticulturist, professional park planner, and administrator, immigrated to this country in the late 1880s from the oldest democracy in the world, Switzerland. According to the custom in those days, after getting his education in his home country he served an apprenticeship of four years in park work abroad, in Paris and London. When he arrived in

The Wirth brothers, Theodore, Walter, and Conrad, in Hartford, Connecticut, just before the family moved to Minneapolis, Minnesota.

America he got a job working as a tree trimmer in New York City's Central Park. Within two or three years he worked up to the position of sub-superintendent of Riverside Park, an area extending along the Hudson River for about a mile north of Seventy-second Street. A change of city government left practically all municipal employees without jobs. This abrupt unemployment came as a shock to Dad, who was inexperienced in the spoils system of New York City politics of that time, and he decided that working for the city was not for him. He found private employment on the Perkins estate at Glen Cove, Long Island, under a Frenchman, Felix Mense, a horticulturist who was head gardener, or manager, of the estate. The connection proved to be the most important of his life, because a few years later he proposed to the elder of the boss' two daughters, Leonie, and was accepted. Soon afterwards he accepted an offer to become superintendent of parks in Hartford, Connecticut, where he began his long and distinguished career.

In Hartford we lived in the superintendent's residence in Elizabeth Park. I always get a great deal of pleasure going back there to see the beautiful rose garden my father built, the first recorded municipal rose garden in the United States. It has changed very little and people by the thousands visit it every year.

Having established a sound reputation through his work in Hartford, Dad began to receive offers from other cities as early as 1903. He and Mother really had no desire to leave Hartford, where he had taken his bride and where their three sons had been born, but the die was cast after he accepted an invitation from Charles Loring, a prominent businessman in Minneapolis, Minnesota, and a member of the city's park commission, to come out and meet with them. He found the city very much to his liking. Minneapolis was then a small but growing town with great potential. It had very few parks but a lot of lakes, rivers, and other possibilities for park development. The park commission made him an attractive offer which included building a house of his own design in one of the parks as his official residence. In 1906 the Wirth family moved to Minneapolis and it was there that Dad thoroughly enhanced his reputation as a park planner and administrator.

Our house was built in a new park not far from Lake Harriet. It had a first floor at the level with the top of the hill it was built on. It had a second floor with four bedrooms and a big sleeping porch. The third floor had two bedrooms and a big storage room. In the basement level underneath the porch on the first floor, there was an office and a big drafting room with four drafting tables. The house was on the outskirts of Minneapolis and to get to school we had to cross farmlands in the winter but had to go around them in the summer. We went on skis in the winter and in the spring we played on the rubbery ice of a pond near the school. When the weather started to warm up, the ice would soften and some ten or twelve of us kids would link arms and run back and forth across the ice and watch it sort of wave in front of us. The more we did it the looser it became and then we'd have to gradually start cutting down the size of the gang. It was always exciting to see who could make the last run across without falling in.

Dad proved himself an imaginative planner and excellent designer and was one of the first park administrators to establish a professional recreation department as part of his organization. His plans provided for parks around all the natural waterways and lakes, a playground within a quarter mile of every child, and a complete recreation center within a half mile of every family. He was fortunate in having as his principal assistant Chris A. Bossen, who had served in this capacity in the Hartford days. I have fond recollections of Mr. Bossen and his family. Chris' administrative skill was a perfect match for Dad's creative ability. He succeeded Dad as superintendent of the Minneapolis park system when my father retired in 1936.

The park superintendent's house in Lyndale Park, Minneapolis, Minnesota.

With Dad settled for what proved to be the rest of his professional career, we were a happy family in an ideal setting in Minneapolis. Mother ran the household with the same deft, sure hand that Dad used in running the parks. In addition to three lusty, growing sons, she had a tempermental, intelligent, hardworking husband to handle—one with the old country notion that the father was really the head of the house. But Dad knew that not all the skills of his calling were in his sole possession, for Mother was no mean horticulturist herself. It was she who taught my brother Walt and me how to build and take care of a garden, even though at the time it did seem to us that she was merely trying to keep us occupied and out of mischief. We had to respect her expertise, for she was an active member, and several times president, of the Ladies' Horticultural Society.

Mother died in 1940 in her 65th year, and only Dad and Mother's sister, Aunt Juliette who had never married, were left in the family home. About two years later we three boys received wires from Dad stating that Juliette and he felt that the neighbors were beginning to talk and they had decided to get married if we didn't object. Within 24 hours Juliette and Dad received three wires from different parts of the world expressing our delight over the good news. I might say that the Swiss immigrant had not only had a successful

The Wirth family, about 1916, on a camping trip to Lake Itasca State Park, Minnesota. Conrad took the picture, with father and mother on the left, and brothers Walter and Ted.

career in his adopted country but had really hit the jackpot in marrying his boss' two daughters—the dearest mothers any boy ever had.

During the course of my father's long career in park management, he made considerable contributions to the field. He was one of a group of about a dozen park men who met in Boston in 1898 and formed an association of New England park superintendents, the first professional organization of its kind in the United States. At the time of his death, in 1949, he was the last surviving charter member of the organization that became the American Institute of Park Executives, which in turn was combined with other groups to form the National Recreation and Park Association. I have been a member of those organizations since 1924, and my brother Walter was a very active member from 1926 throughout the rest of his career, holding the office of president several times. I was president of the American Institute of Park Executives, as Dad had been, and I am still a member of the National Recreation and Park Association; my son Ted is also a member. My older brother, Theodore, ignored the family tradition of horticulture in favor of a career in the United States Navy, reaching the grade of Admiral. Walter, however, followed in Dad's footsteps, first in private practice with me in New Orleans, then on his own in the Tulsa, Oklahoma, park system, and later becoming superintendent of parks in New Haven, Connecticut; director of Pennsylvania State Parks; and superintendent of the Salem, Oregon, Regional Parks.

My brothers and I attended Saint John's Military Academy at Delafield, Wisconsin. At Saint John's they put each new cadet in one of the two clubs, the Kemper Club or the Dekoven Club, and he belonged to that club throughout his stay at the academy. The two clubs competed with one another both athletically and scholastically. I was a Dekoven and, in my last year, one of the five directors. Dr. Smythe, the headmaster and a Kemper, refereed some of the athletic events. I remember one of the last things before graduation was the shell race on Lake Nagawicka. The Dekovens felt certain that we had won both the heavyweight and lightweight shell races, but the headmaster's decision was in favor of the Kempers. Then in the cross-country race a Dekoven man came in first, but the headmaster ruled a foul on him, which gave first place to a Kemper. The Dekoven Club decided to make our feelings known to the headmaster, and I was detailed to do it. I was "officer of the day" and in full dress uniform. I went to the headmaster's office, saluted, and told him the Dekovens felt that the decisions on the boat race and the cross-country race were wrong and therefore unfair. He replied, "Is that all?" I said, "Yes, sir." And he said, "You are dismissed." I saluted and left. I was disturbed that he did not discuss the matter with me. The day after this incident was graduation day. In handing out the yearly awards they always left to last the most important one, the Delafield Medal for the most worthy cadet. I hadn't expected anything and was surprised when I was called up and

Cadets Wirth and James in rowing shell on Lake Nagawicka at Saint John's Military Academy, Delafield, Wisconsin.

Officer of the Day Wirth at Saint John's Military Academy, Delafield, Wisconsin.

presented with the medal. I was a little sorry about what I had said the day before, and I think maybe the headmaster realized that, because in passing me he stopped and said: "I want you to know you were awarded that medal before our interview the other day. And I also want you to know that when you came in and spoke your mind I realized that we had made the right choice." He further said his decisions were right, "however, you have a right to express an honest opinion and we admire you for it."

From Saint John's I proceeded to Massachusetts Agricultural College, now the University of Massachusetts. Here my preparation for a career in park and recreational work began with the business of earning the bachelor of science degree in what was then called landscape gardening. I studied under Professor Frank A. Waugh (known to the students as "Pinkie" when he was not around), who was my father's choice of teachers. He could not have selected a better one. Professor Waugh went into depth on the relationship between man and the natural environment. He and his assistant, Professor Harrison, an engineer, believed that man-made landscape developments, to be successful, must meet the needs of the people and that the the natural elements were a part of these needs. They proceeded on the principle that man's advanced culture and social development required certain modern conveniences but that these utilities should not be ugly or destructive of the needed natural environment. In fact, certain professional societies in those days would not recognize Waugh's graduates because of this conviction. The landscape profession then was oriented more toward the formal types of landscape design.

Professor Waugh felt that the term *landscape architecture* implied formal design and the destruction of the natural environment. He preferred the old term *landscape gardening* as more descriptive of the type of landscaping best suited for park and home improvements. Generally speaking, his concept has proven correct, and time has adjusted the meaning of the term *landscape architecture* to agree with the spirit of Professor Waugh's concept. Many landscape architects today, however, are using the term *land planner*, considering it more descriptive of the type of service provided. Really, the terms *land planner* and *landscape architect* are interchangeable with reference to the type of work these professionals are called upon to do. They are trained to provide plans for land uses that will best serve, over the long term, the environmental requirements of the people.

On arriving in Amherst, I stayed with the Waughs for a month before moving to a rented room in a home. Of course Professor Waugh had invited me, but I believe I stayed longer than he intended. When my father gave me the money I would need to pay for my room and board for the first month, he warned me to beware of gamblers and thieves on the train. But I had to learn the hard way. I got in a poker game on the train between Minneapolis and

Chicago on the invitation of a couple of seemingly very nice, friendly gentlemen. I guess the usual routine followed, and my money for room and board for September was soon gone.

I applied myself pretty thoroughly to my landscape studies, but I had trouble because of extracurriclar activities; in fact, I actually found myself below the average student. Actually, I wasn't a bad student in the subjects I liked: landscape architecture, planning, engineering, physics. Languages always gave me trouble and still do. We had to have two languages in addition to English in order to be graduated, and I never could fully understand why.

I made the freshman football and basketball teams and did a little track work. I never made any of the varsity teams, although in trying I lost two front teeth tackling somebody from the rear, had my Adam's apple stepped on good and hard, and broke my collarbone and my right leg. There were plenty of social activities at Mass Aggie, too. I was asked to join the Kappa Sigma fraternity, which I did. And there were two women's colleges nearby, each only a half-hour streetcar ride from Amherst: Smith College, at Northampton, and Holyoke College, near Holyoke. There were about a thousand male students in Amherst College and Massachusetts Agricultural College in Amherst and some four or five thousand women at Smith and Holyoke.

In the fall after my graduation from Massachusetts Agricultural College, I went to San Francisco to work for the firm of MacGrory & McLaren, Nurserymen and Landscape·Gardeners. I was the first and only professional landscape architect in the firm. The other members were interested primarily in selling nursery stock. They planned and developed some very fine estates, however, and it was a great experience for me. Donald McLaren, the only partner living at the time, was the only son of John McLaren, superintendent of the San Francisco park system and the creator of Golden Gate Park.

The elder McLaren was a close friend of my father's, and so the Donald McLaren family and I had dinner practically every Sunday at Golden Gate Lodge, the home of the superintendent. John McLaren was a canny Scotsman with the greenest thumb I have ever encountered. From the sand dunes of Golden Gate Park he created one of the finest large city parks in this country. He was a gentleman with a deep understanding of people and much political know-how, and he had a great knowledge of plants. He was so well thought of that the people of San Francisco passed a city ordinance making him superintendent of their park system for life or as long as he wanted to hold the office. He was in his nineties when he died, still superintendent of parks and very active to the end. To be treated as part of his family, as I was, was one of the finest experiences and lessons I could have had. I didn't fully realize at the time that he was getting from me the younger generation's attitude and thinking and at the same time letting me in on certain basic principles that he had learned the hard way through the years.

In the early spring of 1924, I had gotten jobs in the firm for two classmates of mine, Effy Buckley, a landscape architect of Natick, Massachusetts, and Willie Marshman, a pomologist of Springfield, Massachusetts. When Donald McLaren died in the spring of 1925, his widow and Mrs. MacGrory decided to dispose of their properties, and the nurseries in San Mateo were subdivided and sold. Buckley, Marshman, and I then decided to get a car and see the West, not knowing whether we would be there again. We wanted to see as much of it as we could and visit many of the national parks.

We got a canvas-top, four-door, secondhand Studebaker, put three folding canvas cots (World War I salvage) in the back of the car along with some cases of canned goods, and started out. We headed north to Seattle via Lassen Volcanic and Crater Lake national parks and crossed the states of Washington and Idaho, entering Montana and then Yellowstone National Park. We visited Mount Rainier and Glacier national parks en route. In Idaho we camped one night in a national forest. It was getting dark as we went into camp, and when we built our camp fire we saw the reflection of several pairs of eyes in the surrounding forest looking at us. We figured that those animals were interested in our supplies and that our fire was the best means of keeping them away. We took two-hour shifts staying awake to put wood on the fire.

We learned that the bears in Yellowstone will eat anything not locked up and that there is no way of locking an old canvas-top car. We camped one day at Madison Junction and set our three canvas cots in a row alongside the car, with the heads placed next to the running board. That night Willie was in the cot toward the front of the car, I was in the one toward the rear, and Effy was in the middle. It was a dark night. A little after midnight Willie was awakened by something tickling his face. He soon realized a bear was standing over him, its back feet on the ground and its forefeet on the running board. Willie didn't dare move and could hardly breathe. The bear stepped down and went around to the other side of the car. The park rangers had told us that if the bears bothered us at night we should turn on the car lights because these big animals don't like lights. Willie was too weak to get up, so he yelled, "Connie, turn on the lights!" I woke out of a sound sleep, climbed into the car, and reached over to turn on the lights. I felt something close by. When the lights came on, I found myself eyeball to eyeball with a black bear. Fortunately, he jumped out the far side of the car and ran off into the woods. I *fell* out of my side onto Effy and Willie. We lost only a loaf of bread and most of our night's sleep and were very glad to see the sun come up in the morning.

From Yellowstone we headed for Salt Lake City and then across Utah and Nevada and over Tioga Pass into Yosemite National Park. We did stop in Reno to try to replenish our supply of cash but finally had to wire home for a loan. It was late in the afternoon as we left Reno, and we did not go into camp until after dark. We found a good place near a stream among some rather large trees. When we woke up the next morning, we saw a sign stating that Kit Carson had camped there too. After a stay in Yosemite we went south to General Grant and Sequoia national parks. We decided to head home by way of Los Angeles, Mexicali, and the Grand Canyon. Going through Arizona on crushed stone roads, we had thirteen flat tires in one day, and those were the days of inner tubes! We then went east to Kansas and north to my home in Minneapolis. After a few days of rest Effy and Willie took the car back to their home in Massachusetts.

Back in Minneapolis I found two opportunities available to me: one to go to work with a firm in Chicago that manufactured architectural equipment, the other to enter into a partnership with Harold J. Neale in New Orleans. Harold Neale was also a landscape gardener from the Massachusetts Agricultural College, about ten years my senior, and, at that time, superintendent of Audubon Park in New Orleans. The plan was that we would form a partnership called Neale and Wirth, Landscape Architects and Town Planners, and he would stay on as superintendent of Audubon Park until we got our business going. Harold was a married man with three children, and he couldn't take too much of a chance. I decided to go to New Orleans.

We got off to a fine start. Harold learned that the Jonas Land Company had plans for development of a fairly large piece of land on the west bank of the Mississippi River in Jefferson Parish. We asked if we could lay out the subdivision for them. They answered that they had their own engineers, but after some discussion they did agree to let us submit a plan and to let their salesmen choose between our plan and the one their engineers woorked out. The land was flat, but we put in some curved roads anyway. We also set aside land that would be donated by the company for parks and playgrounds, schools and churches. The Jonas salesmen decided the developers could make more on our layout than on the engineers' rigid gridiron layout of fifty-foot by one-hundred-foot lots. We got all the company's work from then on.

We covered a territory from New Orleans to eastern Texas, plus eastern Oklahoma, parts of Tennessee, and the Mississippi Gulf Coast. In fact, we did so well that when I went home for Christmas of 1925, I proposed to Helen Olson, who was home for the holidays from Vassar College. Her father, Olaf J. Olson, was a good friend of my father. He was a partner in Holm and Olson, a florist and landscape firm in Saint Paul that had extensive greenhouses and nurseries. Because of my father's horticultural background, he and Mr. Olson had much in common, and as they became close so did the two families. The idea of an interfamily marriage made everyone happy. The wedding was set for June 30, which would be after Helen graduated. Business got better and better; we were happily married; and we were blessed with a son in the summer of 1927.

But soon the Great Depression began to be sorely felt all along the Gulf Coast, and by late fall of 1927 the partnership of Neale and Wirth was out of business. Harold was fortunate, for he had not given up his job as superintendent of Audubon Park. I worked long hours trying to earn a living, but our debts grew and grew.

One day in early March, 1928, I got a letter from my godfather, Gus Amrhyn, who was superintendent of parks in New Haven, Connecticut. He wrote that Frederick Law Olmsted, Jr., was wondering whether I would be interested in a job as landscape architect with the National Capital Park and Planning Commission. If so, I was to go to Washington and see Lieutenant Colonel U.S. Grant III, who was then the engineer officer in charge of the Office of Public Buildings and Grounds and executive officer of the National Capital Park and Planning Commission. My bank agreed to one more loan to finance the trip, and I went to Washington and landed the job. Then I went back to New Orleans and drove my family to Minneapolis, leaving them with my parents until I could provide suitable quarters in Washington. I entered on duty in Washington on May 11, 1928, and thus started a new career that was to extend over some thirty-six years.

My experiences in private business in San Francisco and New Orleans had lasting influence on me, short though they were. They helped give me insight into private enterprise and developed in me a better understanding of people's capabilities, their problems, and especially the feeling of helplessness that accompanies unemployment. Later in the thirties, when I helped administer the Civilian Conservation Corps program for the National Park Service, I remembered that feeling. If a person was out of work and really wanted a job, I would try my best to find a place for him. We built a very fine staff by putting well-qualified unemployed people into the low-level positions we had available and then promoting them as jobs more in keeping with their qualifications opened up. This group grew with the expanding National Park Service, and many of those hired in the depression were in the top positions that made Mission 66, in the fifties and sixties, a real success. This group of professionals furnished many of the plans and ideas and much of the administrative ability I shall describe in subsequent chapters.

Little did I know when I went to Washington that some day I would become a part of the National Park Service. It was Director Horace M. Albright who asked me in 1931 to transfer from the National Capital Park and Planning Commission to the National Park Service as assistant director in charge of the Branch of Land Planning. No one can really hope to do justice in describing Horace Albright. To know him, to say nothing of working for him,

Stephen T. Mather, first director of the National Park Service, served in that office from May 16, 1917, to January 8, 1929.

is an honor. Thinking back over the years to 1930, when I began to get well acquainted with Albright, I can't remember ever hearing anything but praise and admiration for him. Everyone still looks to him on national park matters.

Albright was a young lawyer working in the Department of the Interior when in 1914 he was assigned to help Stephen T. Mather manage the national parks and get legislation through Congress to establish the National Park Service. Mather, an influential and wealthy Chicago industrial leader, was dissatisfied with the way the parks were run and expressed that opinion to Secretary Franklin K. Lane. The secretary, a friend of Mather's, told him that if he didn't like the way they were run, he should come to Washington and "run them yourself." Mather did just that, giving up his business to come to Washington and lead the drive to establish the National Park Service and formulate the policy and organization to manage the national park system. The act establishing the National Park Service was passed by Congress and became law in August, 1916. Mather became the National Park Service's first director in 1917, and Albright became his assistant.

In 1919, Albright became superintendent of Yellowstone National Park while also serving as assistant to the director in the field. He was the first civilian superintendent of Yellowstone after the National Park Service took over administration of the park from the army. It is very possible that Albright was in Yellowstone when those three "upstate farmers," as we were called at Mass Aggie, went through the park in 1925.

Stephen T. Mather is considered the founder of the National Park Service and its basic policy, but the records of Mather and Albright and the relationship between these two stalwarts often cause them to be called co-founders. Shortly after Mather died in 1930, his friends and co-workers had bronze tablets made and placed in all the national parks. The tablets bear his profile in relief against a scenic mountain background and contain the following inscription:

> He laid the foundation of the National Park Service
> defining and establishing the policies under which its
> areas shall be developed and conserved unimpaired
> for future generations. There will never come an end
> to the good that he has done.

Any organization that had Mather and Albright could not help but get started in the right direction, and to have them as directors for the first seventeen years really gave the National Park Service a family feeling.

From 1872, when Yellowstone was established, until 1916, when the National Park Service was created, responsibility for the management and protection of national parks resided in the office of the Secretary of the Interior. Arrangements had been made with the army for the Corps of Engineers to handle the construction of roads and necessary park facilities and for the calvary to provide general administration and protection. When the National Park Service was established, there were twenty national monuments under the jurisdiction of the Department of the Interior and fourteen national parks, and together they constituted the National Park System. The parks had been established by separate acts of Congress, and the monuments under the Antiquities Act of 1906. The Antiquities Act authorized the president to set aside, by public proclamation, lands owned by the federal government containing "historic landmarks, historic and prehistoric structures, and other objects of historic or scientific interest. . . ." As lands in these categories were set aside as national monuments, they remained under the respective jurisdictions of the Departments of War, Agriculture, and the Interior. It is interesting to note that in 1916 all areas administered by the Interior Department were situated west of the Mississippi River.

The act of August 25, 1916, which established the National Park Service, states,

> . . . That there is hereby created in the Department of the Interior a service to be called the National Park Service, which shall be under the charge of a director, who shall be appointed by the Secretary, and who shall receive a salary of $4,500 per

annum. There shall also be appointed by the Secretary the following assistants and other employees at the salaries designated: One assistant director, at $2,500 per annum; one chief clerk, at $2,000 per annum; one draftsman, at $1,800 per annum; one messenger, at $600 per annum; and, in addition thereto, such other employees as the Secretary of the Interior shall deem necessary: *Provided,* that not more than $8,100 annually shall be expended for salaries of experts, assistants, and employees within the District of Columbia not herein specifically enumerated unless previously authorized by law.

The act provided for field responsibilities and did not limit the amount of funds or the number of people and their salaries. But the limitations put on the number of employees in Washington and on their salaries are an interesting commentary on the changing times. The total of $19,500 authorized in the 1916 act for the Washington office for all purposes is less than half the sum now set aside as salary for the director of the service and $500 less than I received as salary when I retired as director in 1964. The 1916 act set down the purpose of the service as follows:

... The service thus established shall promote and regulate the use of the Federal areas known as national parks, monuments and reservations hereinafter specified by such means and measures as conform to the fundamental purpose of the said parks, monuments, and reservations, which purpose is to conserve the scenery and the natural and historic objects and the wild life therein and to provide for the enjoyment of the same in such manner and by such means as will leave them unimpaired for the enjoyment of future generations.

Thus began the National Park Service. At the request of the director and the secretary, the calvary remained on duty in several of the large parks for several years until sufficient funds were appropriated by Congress to provide full management under civilian administration.

The young National Park Service struggled to become established during the First World War and began building up during the twenties, when it ran head on into the devastating depression. Fortunately, because of strong leadership in the Mather-Albright period, a sound policy had been formulated and basic principles established that were accepted by the administration, Congress, and the people in general. Just as the depression began to settle in, the service lost Mather, who was suffering poor health. Albright, young and vigorous, carried on through the greatest economic collapse this nation has experienced. He continued into the early part of the New Deal, a period of rehabilitation and adjustment to the economic and social changes that had been building over the years. The need and desire of the people to go to work in some cases resulted in needless make-work programs, which in turn threatened to uproot sound policies for the protection and preservation of our natural and historic resources.

Horace M. Albright, director of the National Park Service from January 12, 1929, to August 9, 1933.

After the first six months of President Franklin D. Roosevelt's administration, with the National Park Service well adjusted to the New Deal, Albright felt that it was time for him to leave the government and follow through on plans that he had set aside in the urgency of establishing the National Park Service. He accepted the offer of the United States Potash Company to become its vice-president and general manager. Over a period of sixteen years he had served the Park Service as assistant director, as superintendent of Yellowstone, and as director. Before leaving, he made arrangements for Arno B. Cammerer to become director and for Arthur E. Demaray to become associate director. Cammerer had been associate director under Albright, and both Cammerer and Demaray had worked under Mather.

The Park Service was on a sound basis and had the backing of a very strong secretary, Harold L. Ickes. It was a boom period for park and recreation activities of great magnitude, and the service was successful in getting what was needed for the national parks, while at the same time helping the states build up their state park systems. Overwork caused Cammerer to ask in 1940 to be relieved of the directorship and to be appointed regional director in Richmond, Virginia. His request was granted, but, because of the strain he had been under, he was compelled to retire in 1941, and he died about a year later.

Secretary Ickes selected a well-known and highly respected conservationist, Newton B. Drury, to be director. Drury took office on August 20, 1940. Demaray, a sturdy and sound administrator, stayed on as associate director. Director Drury was just getting well settled in his position when the Second World War arrived.

Within a couple of years all emergency recovery funds of the thirties were diverted to prepare for war, and the yearly appropriation for the Park Service dropped from the 1940 high of nearly thirty-five million dollars to a low of under five million dollars in 1945. All construction, of course, was stopped, maintenance was cut to the bone, and deterioration of facilities set in. Because of gas rationing, travel through the parks was cut to a mere trickle. Government agencies and private industry, with the cry of "national emergency" on their lips, looked at national park resources as free game. Drury, however, stood firm. For a time it was Drury's guts and fortitude alone that held the park policy and its principles intact. His final argument to a stubborn government agent would go something like this: "All right, if you will bring me a signed statement from your Secretary that what you propose is essential for the survival of the nation, I'll step aside." Nobody ever did.

As the war worked itself to a finish, more attention began to be directed to needs at home. But then our nation found itself in the middle of the cold war. Many felt it was necessary not only to keep ourselves well armed but to help arm other nations in the interest of insuring peace throughout the world. It was a period of many international compacts and defense agreements, and these activities required a great amount of money. It was exceedingly difficult, almost impossible, for the service to obtain funding for the rebuilding and refurbishing of park roads, buildings, and other facilities that had deteriorated from years of disuse and lack of maintenance.

In these trying times there were many changes in the department. Drury gave more and more thought to going back to his native California and his beloved Save-the-Redwoods League, in which he and his brother had worked very hard for many years to preserve the coastal redwoods. The thousands of acres of these groves that the Drury brothers played such an important part in saving are a monument to them and their loyal associates in the league. In the spring of 1951, Drury decided to accept appointment as head of the State Parks of California. The redwood groves that the Save-the-Redwoods League had purchased were a part of the state park system. Governor Earl Warren, later chief justice of the United States, had asked Drury to take the job. It is interesting to note that Warren, Albright, Mrs. Albright, and Drury were all classmates in the class of 1912 at the University of California. Mather was an earlier graduate.

At about the same time that Drury decided to return to California, Arthur Demaray notified Secretary of the Interior Oscar L. Chapman that he was going to retire, having been associate director since 1933. The secretary asked Demaray to stay on as director of the service. Demaray accepted on the condition that he could retire by the end of the year. He had a long and very significant career with the Park Service. Horace Albright, while serving as acting director during Mather's illness in 1917, had brought Demaray into the service, and Demaray was the last Mather man to be director.

From the time the National Park Service was organized in 1917, through to December 9, 1951, there had been five directors: Mather, Albright, Cammerer, Drury, and Demaray. Though it is true that Drury was not considered a Mather man, not having been in the Park Service at the time Mather was organizing it or through the initial period of administration, he was nevertheless of that vintage and a conservationist with many years of experience. I was the sixth, the first to become director after the service ran out of Mather men. I held the position the longest of any, from December 9, 1951, to January 8, 1964.

Nobody will ever convince me that there is a better agency in government or in private business than the National Park Service. We are, I believe, more fortunate than most organizations in that our job of preserving and managing the natural and historic heritage of the nation for the use and enjoyment of the poeple is so inspiring and personally rewarding. To do it properly, however, as with any other job, requires not only special training and hard work but also a certain sensitivity and aptitude. I believe I can best express what I have in mind by quoting from a letter I received in February, 1949, shortly after my father's death, from one of the nation's great landscape architects, the late Frederick Law Olmsted, Jr., the son of an equally famous landscape architect and planner. It was about my father, written in longhand, and it said in part:

When we can get together for a quiet chat, I want to talk with you about him and about something difficult to describe, which I think he and my father had very much in common and which was, I believe, largely responsible for the great accomplishment of both of them in park work. It is something to which my attention has been strongly drawn of late by reading certain old letters of my father's—and something of much more profound importance in park work than is generally recognized. At bottom, it depends on a deep-seated, constant and compelling interest in and sympathy with, the *people* using the parks—on finding one's chief satisfaction in appreciative friendly observation and study of the ways in which those people actually use, and derive pleasure and benefit from any given park, and in helping and guiding them by every available means to get the best values from their use of it, in the long run, that are made possible by the inherent characteristics of that particular park *and* by the widely various *personal characteristics of the people themselves.*

Unless a park man's interest in, and use of, the techniques of designing, constructing and operating parks are dominated and motivated by such a fundamental and absorbing interest in the *people* who use the parks and in all the details of *how* they use them and how they can be induced to use them with greater benefit to themselves in the long run—as was the case with my father and with yours—mere technical skill in any or all of those phases of park work tends to become academic and sterile, except so far as that man is used as a subordinate technician-assistant by a master-mind who has that broader human interest in the people as such, and can to some degree inspire his assistants with that same absorbing interest in them. Isn't that the most important thing that park-men ought to learn from your father's life work and that of my father?

Such sincere expressions of appreciation of my father's considerable contributions to his chosen field of endeavor have always served to substantiate what otherwise might seem an exaggerated estimate of his accomplishments on my own part.

As the sole surviving charter member, Dad attended the fiftieth anniversary of the American Institute of Park Executives in Boston in 1948. On his way there from San Diego, where he was living in retirement, he stopped in Minneapolis for a medical examination and learned that he had cancer. He went on to Boston, gave his scheduled address at the meeting, and on his return visited us in Washington as he had planned. He told us about his trouble and that he would undergo surgery when he got back to San Diego. He was 86, and seeing him off at the railroad station was a sad experience. He lived only a short time afterwards.

2

Introduction to Washington: The National Capital Park and Planning Commission

At the age of twenty-eight I placed my young wife and our ten-month-old boy with our parents in Minneapolis and Saint Paul and went to Washington to begin a career in the federal government. I had to leave my little family behind until I could afford to bring them east. I had been out of work for over nine months, we were broke, and our debts were staggering.

It was a rather warm but windy Tuesday in May, 1928, when I arrived in Washington on an early train. After checking the newspapers to see about a room, I decided to delay renting one until I had called at the National Capital Park and Planning Commission, since perhaps there I could get advice as to a suitable location. The offices were then in the World War I temporary Navy Building at Constitution Avenue and Eighteenth Street, N.W. Because I had more time than money, I checked my bag for ten cents in Union Station, walked the eighteen blocks to the Navy Building, and got there a half-hour before the offices were to open at 8:00.

I waited around a few minutes before Mrs. Nettie Benson arrived. Mrs. Benson was later to become secretary to two National Park Service directors and, in 1951, my administrative assistant. At that time she was secretary to Lieutenant Colonel U. S. Grant III, who then had three titles: vice-chairman and executive and disbursing officer of the National Capital Park and Planning Commission and engineer in charge of the Office of Public Buildings and Grounds of the National Capital. The latter agency built, operated, and maintained the federal parks and buildings in the city of Washington and the nearby region. Grant was one of the finest Corps of Engineers officers I have ever known, a man who was not only an excellent engineer but a fine administrative officer, a gentleman, and a strong conservationist of our natural environment, deeply involved in the preservation of our historic heritage. I was very fortunate to have the opportunity of working under his direction.

I had first met Colonel Grant some five weeks before, early in April. But I had not yet met the staffs of the planning commission and the Office of Public Buildings and Grounds. After a short talk Grant took me down to meet the staff of the planning commission, including Major Carey H. Brown, assistant executive officer to Grant, and Charles W. Eliot II, director of planning. I was to join Eliot's staff in the planning commission, but I soon learned that the colonel had assignments for me in connection with the operation of the parks of Washington as well. Therefore I was taken to meet Major Joseph C. Mehaffey, Grant's assistant in the Office of Public Buildings and Grounds. He in turn took me to meet the top-flight park people charged with responsibilities for the parks of Washington. I met Captain Kelly, chief of the park police; Frank Gartside, general manager of the parks; George Clark, the chief engineer; and John Nagel, who was the engineer responsible for such big construction projects as the Arlington Memorial Bridge. I also met Charles Peters, who was then in charge of the federal buildings and who through the years became a very dear friend. By his reorganization order (no. 6166) of June 10, 1933, President Franklin Delano Roosevelt transferred to the National Park Service the entire Office of Public Buildings and Grounds. So, the group of fine park people I met that morning in May, 1928, became National Park Service people.

After meeting my new colleagues, being assigned a drafting board and part of a desk, and having lunch in a cafeteria on the roof of the old Navy Building, I inquired about where I might look for a room on a weekly or monthly basis. I was told that there were fairly good and reasonable places in northwest Washington. I spent that afternoon looking for a room and found one that suited my strained financial situation, though the landlord required a down payment of one week's rent. That night I quickly discovered the bed was infested with bedbugs, and the next morning I packed my bags and left, reluctantly forfeiting my first week's rent.

It occurred to me that there were a couple of universities in Washington and that possibly one of them had a chapter of the Kappa Sigma fraternity, of which I was a member. Sure enough, there was a chapter at George Washington University, and they had a room for me. Apparently they needed a few paying guests, even though the state of my funds required that they wait until my first payday for the rent money.

On May 17, I received my appointment. The National Capital Park and Planning Commission was established by Congress in 1926, made up of several odd committees established in earlier years for special projects with no effective coordination to develop a sound comprehensive plan for the National Capital. Shortly after the federal government was established on April 30, 1789, and Congress started meeting, it was realized that it would be very difficult for the government to operate in any of the existing cities. President George Washington was authorized to proceed with the selection of a seat of government and the plans to develop the national capital. He employed Major Pierre Charles L'Enfant, of France, for the task. L'Enfant, working with the president and Secretary of State Thomas Jefferson, laid out a plan for the city of Washington and the District of Columbia. Construction was started shortly after 1791, and in 1800 Congress moved to Washington.

Major Pierre Charles L'Enfant, of France. *Courtesy National Capital Planning Commission.*

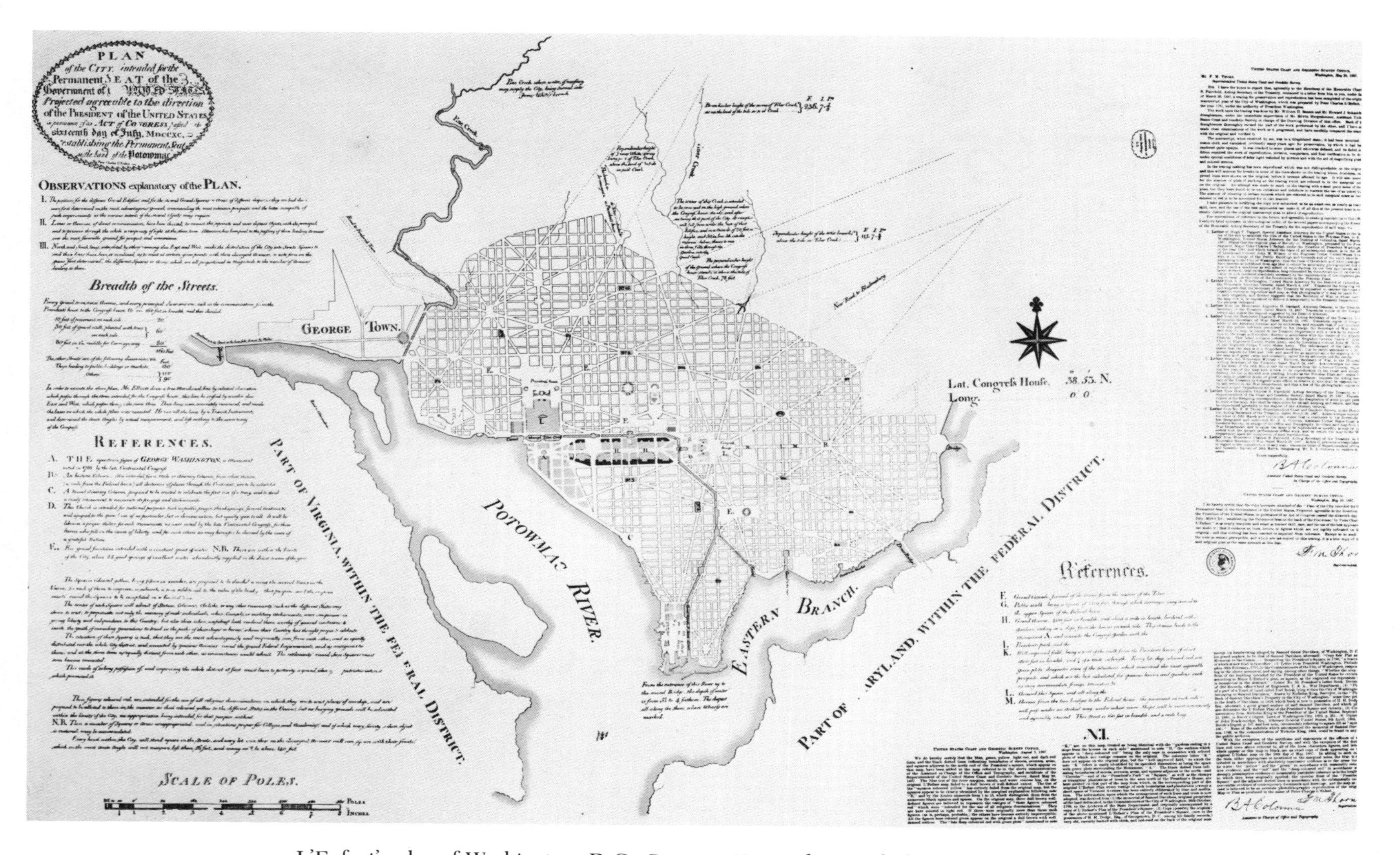

L'Enfant's plan of Washington, D.C. *Courtesy National Capital Planning Commission.*

While the plan prepared for the city of Washington in the late eighteenth century was a very good one, very advanced in relation to those of other cities in the United States at that time, a lack of continuous attention caused it to deteriorate during the nineteenth century. Alterations in the plan were made at times during the nineteenth century to satisfy political and personal interests. These changes more often than not were at odds with original concepts of Washington as the capital city of a great nation. Consequently, in late 1898, when the first hundred years had passed and an anniversary celebration was being planned, the central part of the city, especially the Mall area, was in sorry condition. Permits had been granted for buildings in the Mall, cattle and other livestock were grazed there, and Congress had approved the building of the railroad station at the foot of Capitol Hill.

The people of the District of Columbia worked hard making arrangements for the centennial, which naturally took on a national aspect. A joint committee of the two houses of Congress was appointed to act with the citizens' committee in planning the celebration. The celebration was very successful and was brought to a very satisfactory conclusion with a reception and banquet given by the Washington Board of Trade in honor of the congressional committee and distinguished guests. However, a good deal of dissatisfaction was expressed by people throughout the country with the conditions they found in Washington.

As a result Senator James McMillen, chairman of the Committee on the District of Columbia, introduced a resolution which, when passed on March 8, 1901, instructed his committee as follows:

> Resolved, that the Committee on the District of Columbia be, and it hereby is, directed to consider the subject and report to the Senate plans for the development and improvement of the entire park system of the District of Columbia. For the purpose of preparing such plans, the committee may sit during the recess of Congress, and may secure the services of such experts as may be necessary for a proper consideration of the subject. The expenses of such investigation shall be paid from the contingent fund of the Congress and reported to the Senate on the 15th day of January, 1902.

Senator McMillen and his committee selected Daniel H. Burham, a noted architect from Chicago, and Frederick Law Olmsted, Jr., a nationally recognized planner and landscape architect of Brookline, Massachusetts, and gave these two gentlemen the opportunity to add to their committee for the study as they saw fit. Burnham and Olmsted chose as their colleagues Charles F. McKim, a well-known and capable architect of New York, and one of America's great sculptors, Augustus Saint-Gaudens.

The report that resulted, often referred to as the McMillen Report, really stirred things up. On the front page of the second edition, dated March 14,

1903, a note by the Senate Committee on the District of Columbia states:

> The 57th Congress authorized the construction of the War College and the Engineering School of Application (page 117); the building of the Agriculture Department (page 44); a building for the national museum, to be located on the north side of the Mall (page 44); the Union Railroad Station, to be located at the intersection of Massachusetts Avenue and Delaware Avenue (page 29); a building for the use of the members of the House of Representatives, to be located on the square facing the Capitol grounds, East of New Jersey Avenue (page 38); a municipal building for the District of Columbia, to be located on the south side of Pennsylvania Avenue, between 13 1/2 and 14th Streets (page 70); and a Hall of Records, to be located on E Street between 18th and 19th Streets (page 29). The Daughters of the American Revolution have begun the erection of a Continental [Constitution] Hall, on the second square south of the Corcoran Museum of Art, and the restoration of the White House has been completed (page 65).

All these projects were recommended in the first edition of the McMillen Report. Within a little more than a year those actions had been taken. Thus did Congress eagerly begin carrying out the recommendations of the report and continued to do so in the first two decades of the century. An Act of Congress of May 17, 1910, established a permanent Commission of Fine Arts. A zoning law passed in 1920 provided the authority to control building setback and elevation of buildings in conformity with the overall city plan.

In 1924, Congress made provisions for the detailed planning of a public park and open space system, recognizing the failure to carry out the proposals of the 1901 plan for an open space system so important to the growing population of the city. Very soon the National Capital Park Commission and Congress came to the conclusion that a satisfactory park system could not be laid down without the full knowledge of the inter-relationship of parks, roads, zoning, building, and other elements of a comprehensive city plan. The authority of the commission was therefore broadened in 1926, when it was given its new title and responsibilites as the National Capital Park and Planning Commission. The authority of the presently named National Capital Planning Commission has been extended to regional responsibility, insofar as federal interests are concerned, which requires close cooperation with the authorities of Maryland and Virginia surrounding Washington.

After I had settled into my work in Washington, I found that one of the big things the commission, other governing agencies, civic groups, and Congress were working on was a proposed piece of legislation called the Cramton-Capper Bill. The sponsors of the bill were Representative Louis C. Cramton, from Michigan, and Senator Arthur Capper, from Kansas. Representative Cramton, one of my heroes, was chairman of the House Subcommittee on Appropriations, which handled the Park Service's as well as the Planning Commission's appropriations. He had been associated with many of my other

Members of the McMillen Commission working on a model of the Mall area. *Courtesy Fine Arts Commission.*

The National Capital Park and Planning Commission in the mid-1930s. *Left to right:* H. S. Settle, staff; J. A. Ryder, staff (behind Settle); Planner J. Nolen, Jr.; Commissioners Colonel Dan Sultan, William A. Delano, Norman Brown; Chairman Frederic A. Delano; J. C. Nichols; J. B. Gordon; Arno B. Cammerer; unidentified; H. V. Hubbard; T. C. Jeffers, staff; unidentified. *Courtesy National Capital Planning Commission.*

idols, such as Horace Albright, U. S. Grant III, J. Horace McFarland, Frederic Delano, Frederick Law Olmsted, Jr., and Miss Harlean James, secretary of the American Civic Association. Several of this group had worked for some ten years to establish the National Park Service and, joining with Mather and Albright, helped to get the legislation passed authorizing the service in 1916. This same group, along with others, were the backers of the establishment of the planning commission in 1926. Cramton was perhaps as much a Park Service man as he was a member of Congress. He befriended the service particularly when we greatly needed his help during the late twenties and early thirties.

The Cramton-Capper Bill called for an appropriation of some thirty-two million dollars for land acquisition for parks and for stream-valley protection within and adjacent to the District of Columbia. It included establishment of the George Washington Memorial Parkway on both sides of the Potomac River from just above Great Falls, upriver from Washington, to Mount Vernon on the Virginia side and to Fort Washington on the Maryland side, downriver. It also included acquisition of land for the city's park and recreation system and the development of a Fort-to-Fort Drive connecting the Civil War forts that ringed the capital. The growth of the city was such that by the time acquisition funds were available it was no longer practicable to build the Fort-to-Fort Drive, although practically all of the fort sites had been acquired and are now part of the city park system. The bill included aid to the counties in Virginia and Maryland bordering the District of Columbia on a matching-fund basis for the development of their park systems.

When I joined the staff of the National Capital Park and Planning Commission, it had four members from federal government agencies, two members from Congress, four members appointed by the president of the United States, and the District of Columbia engineer commissioner. The federal agencies were represented by the chief of the Corps of Engineers, the officer in charge of Public Buildings and Grounds, the director of the National Park Service, and the chief forester of the Forest Service. The members of Congress were the chairmen of the District of Columbia committees of the House and the Senate. The four then appointed by the president were Frederick Law Olmsted, Jr., the landscape architect from Massachusetts; Frederic A. Delano, of Washington, D.C., a businessman and uncle of Franklin Delano Roosevelt; Jesse C. Nichols, of Kansas City, an advanced thinker in the development of land for residential purposes; and Milton B. Medary, Jr., of Philadelphia, a well-known architect. Delano was designated chairman by the president, and Grant was vice-chairman. Nichols' development of the country club area of Kansas City was one of the early projects that brought into consideration the terrain, curved roads, odd-shaped lots, and open spaces for parks and schools. I think these members constituted a very well-balanced

Frederick Law Olmstead, one of the nation's foremost landscape architects. *Courtesy National Capital Planning Commission.*

commission. Most of them were in the business of managing the environment for human use and enjoyment. They worked long and hard, with excellent results, and commanded respect and admiration. They all served without compensation.

I want to include a word about some of my fellow commissioners. Frederick Law Olmsted, Jr., used to arrive several days in advance of commission meetings to study and review the staff plans and make whatever field investigations he thought necessary. I remember spending several days with him on the location plans for George Washington Memorial Parkway. He wanted to be sure the land to be included was adequate, that the parkway roads would take advantage of the vistas with the least possible damage to the rim of the Potomac River Gorge, and that it would provide necessary parking places with the least amount of damage to the scenic values. Olmsted would go into the field and walk the boundary lines. It was not enough for him to track them on the ground; he wanted to see from a height and would shinny up a tree to look in all directions. I would accompany him on these trips, carrying the plans. Climbing the trees, we had to carry the plans in our mouths, as a dog carries a bone. Olmsted was a very thorough and studious man, very perceptive, and a deep thinker. He often used long and involved sentences, which could become quite complicated; yet by attentive reading one would fully understand what was going through his mind (see, for example, his letter quoted at the end of Chapter 1).

Charles W. Eliot II, the commission's chief planner, had a tremendous capacity for work and was well versed in all planning matters. He had a fertile imagination fortified by sound facts. His writing was excellent, for he could combine fact and imagination in such a way that the completed composition was forceful and readily understood. To be a member of his staff was a pleasure and a very worthwhile experience. After several years on the planning commission and, during Franklin D. Roosevelt's administration, on National Planning Commission assignments, he returned to Harvard to teach.

Frederic A. Delano, affectionately referred to by the staff as "Uncle Freddy" (although never to his face), was a patient, thorough, determined, kind, and understanding individual. I don't recall his ever speaking a critical or harsh word about anyone. Everyone highly respected him and knew what he meant and wanted.

When I joined the staff of the planning commission, the member serving by virtue of his position as director of the National Park Service was Stephen T. Mather. I saw him only once, in the fall of 1928 before he left for Chicago, where he took sick in early November. He had a stroke and never did recover. He resigned his office on January 11, 1929, and died in a Boston Hospital on January 22, 1930. Horace M. Albright replaced him as director.

"Dusty" Lewis, National Park Service assistant director in charge of land planning, retired in August, 1930, because of illness and died shortly thereafter. In November, Albright asked me whether I would be willing to transfer to the National Park Service to fill the vacancy, and I readily agreed. Arno B. Cammerer, who was associate director of the service at the time, also spoke to me, and I looked forward eagerly to the transfer. Time passed without further word, however, and after the first of the year I ventured to ask Cammerer when my reassignment might take place. More time went by. Finally I saw Albright again and asked whether there had been any change in plans. His reply was unexpected: "No, but I never hire a person until I have had an opportunity to meet his wife, because the Park Service people are very close, a sort of family affair, and the wife is a very important part of the Park Service family."

Shortly afterwards, in April of 1931, Helen and I were invited by Mr. and Mrs. Albright to their home for dinner. The next day Albright told me that my papers were being processed for appointment as assistant director in charge of the branch of land planning. Women's liberation has been much in the news lately. All I can say is that Helen Wirth liberated me from the planning commission into the National Park Service, for which I have always been very, very grateful. I enjoyed my work with the planning commission, but I had a yearning to get into the park business. I felt that this should really

Grace and Horace Albright attending an annual meeting of the Forty-niners in Death Valley, California.

be my lifetime career, even though I never expected for a moment that I would eventually become director of the service.

Though I left the planning commission in 1931, I was to be a member twice afterwards: when I became director of the National Park Service and, again, by presidential appointment after I retired.

One National Capital Planning Commission member who deserves special mention is the lady who presided when I was representing the Park Service on the commission, Mrs. James H. Rowe, Jr., better known as "Lib." She made an excellent chairwoman and moved the commission agenda along very efficiently. She was all business but in a very pleasant way. Her husband, Jim, is a lawyer who was one of the New Dealers in the Roosevelt era. A rather unpleasant incident happened shortly after she took over the chair. The new chief planner of the commission got up and proceeded to lecture her on some matter, going on for two or three minutes while she said nothing. I finally interrupted to say that I had heard enough, that this was no way for a man in his position to talk to the chair or any commissioner, and that if I talked that way to my boss, the secretary of the interior, I'd be fired in a minute. I added that I felt the chairwoman was too much a lady even to enter into an argument with him. With that he got red in the face and sat down, and the commission went on with its business. About two or three weeks later he resigned.

My appointment as a citizen member of the commission came about in an interesting manner. I received a call one day asking whether I would accept a presidential appointment to the commission if it were offered to me. I personally felt that my past experience well qualified me, and the fact that I was asked this question by a person closely associated with the White House suggested that they thought so too. So my answer was yes. But a week or ten days later I received another call telling me that Walter Pozen, from the office of the secretary of the interior, had informed the White House that my appointment to the planning commission would be embarrassing to Secretary Stewart L. Udall. I do not think the secretary was consulted on the matter. What caused Pozen to do what he did I do not know, but his interference aroused my determination to go all out after the appointment. The caller asked whether I could get any congressional endorsement. I said I felt certain I could get a letter from Mike Kirwan, chairman of the House Subcommittee on Interior Appropriations and the second-ranking member on the powerful Committee on Appropriations of the House. I also named Representative Wayne Aspinall, chairman of the Public Lands Committee, which passes on all of the Interior Department's major legislation, and the Speaker of the House of Representatives McCormack. Before I could give some senators' names I was told that if I could get those already mentioned I had nothing to worry about.

I went up to Capitol Hill that afternoon and saw Mike Kirwan. When I told him my story he gave me some of his stationery and told me to write a letter to the president for his signature endorsing my selection. I then called on Wayne Aspinall, and he asked me when I needed a letter. I told him I needed it as soon as possible at his convenience, and he replied, "It will be on the president's desk in the morning." Speaker McCormack was not available. I went to the Interior Department and dictated the letter for Mike Kirwan to sign. The secretary who took it down told me that she could write a better one than I had dictated, and she did. The next morning I took the letter up to Mike, and he signed it and sent it off immediately to the president by messenger. I thanked him and told him I still needed to see the Speaker of the House, but he said that would not be necessary because he had already spoken to him, and the Speaker had promised he would send a recommendation to the president that day.

About ten days later in New York City I read in *The New York Times* that I had been appointed to the planning commission for the city of Washington by President Lyndon B. Johnson. When I returned to Washington I called the appointment clerk at the White House to confirm the newspaper story. He said an appointee was usually given advance notification of appointment, and he was surprised that I had not received it. He suggested that there must have been a slipup somewhere along the line but promised to send my appointment papers to me right away. I received them the next day. The appointment was for a regular six-year term. I was on the commission five years and nine months before I resigned. I had been vice-chairman for about four years.

During my final term on the planning commission I found that the apathy of the 1800s that resulted in the deterioration of the capital is recurring in our lifetime. One indication of the present decline is the near insanity of building highways of tremendous scale through the city itself and its great memorial areas, thus encroaching on our much needed open spaces. There is also a growing pressure to construct taller buildings and buildings out of character with established and accepted concepts and the master plans. Planes fly low over the city proper, polluting our memorials and ruining the use of our open spaces with their noise. I realize that these are rapidly changing times and that certain flexibility is necessary, but it must also be remembered that the nation's capital represents the culture and statesmanship of a great nation. Compare, for example, the architecture of the Federal Triangle between Pennsylvania Avenue and Constitution Avenue, N.W., with the mixed-up styles of architecture of the federal buildings in southwest Washington, and the trend becomes clear.

It becomes obvious to any thoughful person that the Washington plan is steadily being undermined. We are heading toward a mess such as Washington suffered in the nineteenth century or one even worse. We can't fully see it yet, but it is already here. The signs are particularly clear in the encroachments on the dignity of the great memorial areas. Even government agencies have misused these areas as bartering places or as places in which to carry on sideshows. These memorial areas contain monuments commemorating our greatest national heroes, the home of our presidents, and the Capitol itself, housing the nation's legislative body. On the long stem of the Mall, between the Capitol and the Washington Monument, are buildings containing our national artifacts that tell the history of our social, economic, and cultural development.

The most recent depredation was to bow to the egoism of a man who

The Hirshorn Museum of Modern Art. *Courtesy National Capital Planning Commission.*

insisted that his name be placed on a building the taxpayers paid for in return for the donation of his private collection of art—possibly as a tax credit procedure. True, the original idea of building a modern sculpture garden clear across the Mall, an even greater desecration, was scotched; but the Hirshorn Museum of Modern Art does nevertheless encroach on the tree panel of the Mall. Further, many architects agree with former Chairman of the Fine Arts Commission Gilmore Clarke that, from an architectural point of view, the building is a misfit and should not be on the nation's Mall. The Fine Arts Commission did approve the building (the architect was a member of that commission at the time). But the National Capital Planning Commission disapproved of the plans, even though construction had already begun before the plans were submitted for consideration. This verdict was overturned, however, when the professional people representing government agencies on the planning commission were instructed by their superiors to arrange for reconsideration and to change their vote to approval. Such divergent practice makes me feel that it would have been far better to let cattle graze on the Mall, as reported by Ripley in "Believe It or Not," than to permit profaning it by such an anomaly as the Hirshorn memorial. I resigned from the planning

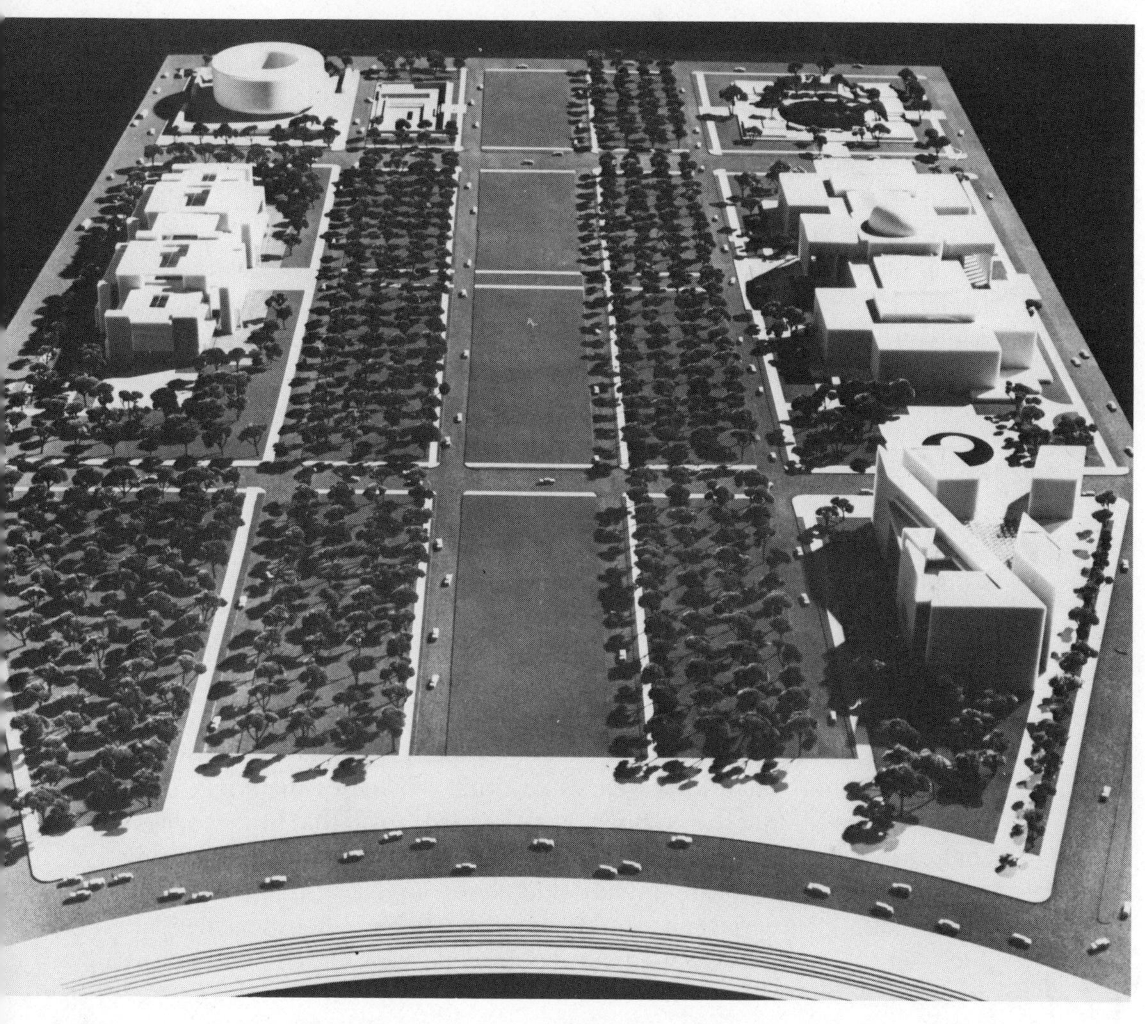

Model of the Mall as it looks today. Note intrusion of the Hirshorn Museum of Modern Art (*upper left corner*). *Courtesy National Capital Planning Commission.*

commission when, after disapproving the Hirshorn project at a morning meeting, the commission by afternoon decided to approve the museum by a one-vote margin. I did not want to be associated with this brand of planning for our nation's capital.

Such are the occurrences that I have witnessed personally. There are others, such as building highways and highway bridges, some of poor design and incompatible materials, across the Potomac River, where they destroy the purpose for which the land was purchased and given: to provide parks and scenic settings for our great national memorials. If all the plans of the Highway Department were carried out, the center of Washington would become a conglomerate of interstate highways, destructive to the economy, the quality of life, the business of government, and the cultural and scenic beauty of our nation's capital. If the department's plan to construct the inner loop of an interstate highway through the Mall and West Potomac Park is carried out, people gathered at the Jefferson Memorial and looking north to the Washington Monument and the White House will find the view blocked by an elevated interstate highway interchange on the north side of the Tidal Basin. This project certainly would not add to the beauty of the Japanese cherry blossoms, either.

Under the National Capital Park and Planning Commission of the late twenties and early thirties, planning moved forward on a sound basis and had great popular support as the wise and proper thing to do. The present National Capital Planning Commission is sound, but it is being bypassed by special-interest groups and one-purpose agencies whose high-powered political pressure is gradually depleting the commission's authority. The deplorable condition of Washington at the beginning of this century has been forgotten, and the commission is being deprived of its responsibility for planning the capital city of the United States.

I don't want to be critical of the planning commission, because I am well aware of the difficulties under which it worked while attempting to satisfy many different demands and expectations. I enjoyed working with the commission for more than forty years in various capacities including my membership as director of the National Park Service. In all that time we had never confronted anything comparable to the issue of the Hirshorn Museum.

I have gone into considerable detail about my background and how I got started on my career as a preamble to what follows. My experience with the planning commission seasoned me and gave me the training that I now realize was so important.

3

The National Park Service

I entered on duty in the National Park Service February 6, 1931, as an assistant director (grade CAF-13) at a yearly salary of $5,600, to head the Branch of Lands. The service at that time occupied the third floor of the east wing of the old Department of the Interior building, between Eighteenth and Nineteenth streets and E and F streets, N.W., in Washington. The next two years were interesting as a breaking-in and training period for me before the intensified activities of the New Deal period.

The National Park Service was then approaching its fifteenth anniversay. Its founder and first director, Stephen T. Mather, had retired in 1929. My father had been with Mather in 1921 when he, Horace Albright, and Secretary of the Interior John Barton Payne organized the National Conference on State Parks, in Des Moines, Iowa. Although I was too late to qualify as one of the devoted and capable group known as the "Mather men," once in the service I found myself surrounded by them. They were the core of about twenty-five people in the Washington office—a loyal, hard-working group. The thoroughness that Mather and Albright applied to insure a good, sound organization based on an equally sound policy, one constructed and documented to last through the years, quickly became apparent to a new staff member.

On May 13, 1918, Secretary of the Interior Franklin K. Lane wrote to Mather in some detail about the National Park Service and what he hoped it would become. In that letter Lane set forth the policy governing administration of the national park system by the new service:

> For the information of the public, an outline of the administrative policy to which the new Service will adhere may now be announced. This policy is based on three broad principles: First, that the national parks must be maintained in absolutely unimpaired form for the use of future generations as well as those of our own time; second, that they are set apart for the use, observation, health, and pleasure of the people; and third, that the national interest must dictate all decisions affecting public or private enterprise in the parks.

On March 11, 1925, Secretary of the Interior Hubert Work wrote Mather a similar letter:

> Owing to changed conditions since the establishment in 1917 of the National Park Service as an independent bureau of the Department of the Interior, I find it advisable to restate the policy governing the administration of the national park system to which the Service will adhere.
>
> This policy is based on three broad, accepted principles:
>
> First, that the national parks and national monuments must be maintained untouched by the inroads of modern civilization in order that unspoiled bits of the native America may be preserved to be enjoyed by future generations as well as our own;
>
> Second, that they are set apart, for the use, education, health and pleasure of all the people;
>
> Third, that the national interest must take precedence in all decisions affecting public or private enterprise in the parks and monuments.
>
> The duty imposed upon the National Park Service in the organic act creating it to faithfully preserve the parks and monuments for posterity in essentially their natural state is paramount to every other activity.
>
> The commercial use of these reservations, except as specifically authorized by law, or such as may be incidental to the accommodation and entertainment of visitors, is not to be permitted.

It is not too difficult to recognize that these letters were carefully prepared by the team of Mather and Albright and signed willingly and with pleasure by the secretaries of the Department of the Interior so as to establish firmly the administrative policy in conformity with the legislation. Secretary Lane was a Democrat, and Secretary Work a Republican.

Ronald F. Lee's *Family Tree of the National Park System*, a booklet published by the Eastern National Park and Monument Association, is valuable to an understanding of the history of the National Park Service. Early in the Civilian Conservation Corps period we brought Ronnie Lee to Washington as a young historian from one of the National Park Service CCC camps. He was a very imaginative, energetic, and intelligent person. After service in World War II he was gradually advanced to the position of chief historian of the National Park Service. He stimulated interest in the establishment of the National Trust for Historic Preservation, and he worked closely with Tom Vint in establishing the Federal Register for Historic Preservation. I hope that some day one of his associates will put all his accomplishments in print. In his *Family Tree* he traced seven categorical lines, or types of units, that made up the national park system as of 1972:

1. National Memorial Line, 1776
2. National Military Park Line, 1781
3. National Capital Parks Line, 1790
4. Mineral Springs Line, 1832
5. National Cemetery Line, 1867
6. National Park Line, 1872
7. National Monument Line, 1906

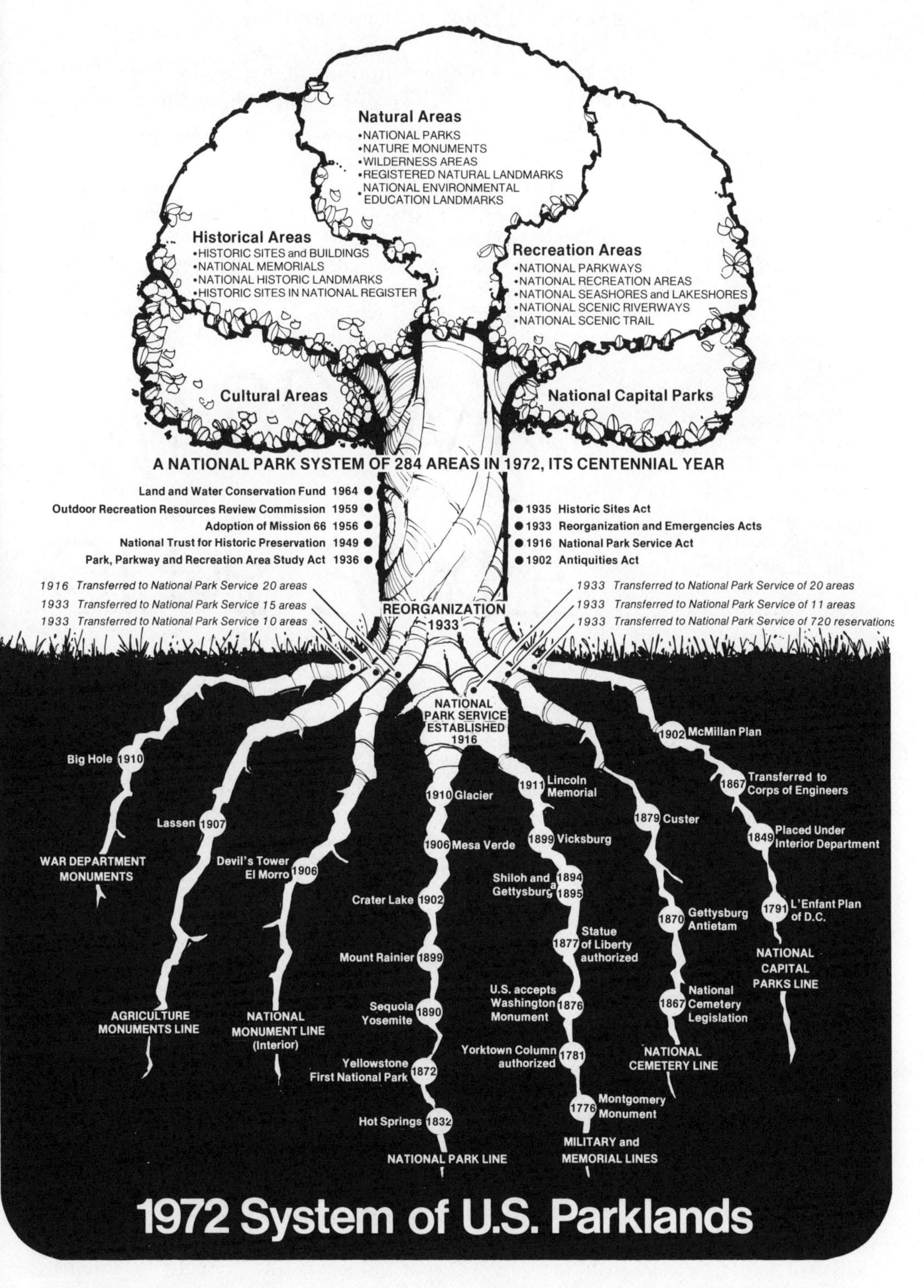

The family tree shows the growth and the different branches of the national park system. *From* Family Tree of the National Park System *by Ronald F. Lee (Eastern National Park and Monument Association).*

In Chapter 1, I briefly covered the founding and development of the National Park Service from the perspective of the individuals involved. Lee cogently outlined the evolution of the national park concept as it was set down in acts of Congress:

> Yellowstone National Park, established March 1, 1872, marks the beginning of the National Park line and the center of gravity of the chart. . . . Although Yosemite State Park, created by Federal cession in 1864 to protect Yosemite Valley and the Mariposa Big Tree Grove, was an important conservation milestone, Yellowstone was the first full and unfettered embodiment of the National Park idea—the world's first example of large-scale wilderness preservation for all the people. The United States has since exported the idea around the globe.
>
> The remarkable Yellowstone Act withdrew some two million acres of public land in Wyoming and Montana Territories from settlement, occupancy, or sale and dedicated it "as a public park or pleasure-ground for the benefit and enjoyment of the people." Furthermore, the law provided for preservation of all timber, mineral deposits, natural curiosities, and wonders within the park "in their natural condition." The twin purposes of preservation and use, so important and so susceptible to conflict, yet so eloquently reaffirmed by Congress when the National Park Service was established in 1916, were there from the beginning.
>
> Once invented—and Yellowstone National Park was an important social invention—the National Park idea was attacked by special interests, stoutly defended by friends in Congress, and refined and confirmed between 1872 and 1916. During this period fourteen more National Parks were created, most of them closely following the Yellowstone prototype. Their establishment extended the National Park concept throughout the West. . . .
>
> One milestone in this history is notable—the emergence of a distinction between National Parks and National Forests. Eighteen years elapsed after the Yellowstone Act before another scenic park was authorized, and then three—Sequoia, Yosemite, and General Grant—were created in the single year of 1890. Yosemite and General Grant were set aside as "reserved forest lands," but like Sequoia they were modeled after Yellowstone and named National Parks administratively by the Secretary of the Interior. The very next year, in the Forest Reserve Act of 1891, Congress separated the idea of forest conservation from the National Park idea. That act granted the President authority to create, by executive proclamation, permanent forest reserves on the public domain. Here is the fork in the road beyond which National Parks and National Forests proceeded by separate paths. Within sixteen years Presidents Cleveland, McKinley, and particularly Theodore Roosevelt established 159 National Forests containing more than 150 million acres. By 1916 Presidents Taft and Wilson had added another 26 million acres. During this same period each new National Park had to be created by individual Act of Congress, usually after many years of work. Nevertheless, by 1916 eleven National Parks including such superlative areas as Mount Rainier, Crater Lake, Mesa Verde, Glacier, Rocky Mountain, and Hawaii, had been added to the original four and Mackinac abolished, bringing the total number to fourteen and the acreage to approximately 4,750,000.
>
> Establishment of these first National Parks reflected in part changing American attitudes toward nature. The old colonial and pioneering emphasis on rapid exploitation of seemingly inexhaustible resources was at last giving way, among some influential Americans, to an awakened awareness of the beauty and wonder of nature. . . .

While the early National Parks were being created, a separate movement got under way to preserve the magnificent cliff dwellings, pueblo ruins, and early missions discovered by cowboys, army officers, ethnologists, and other explorers on the vast public lands of the Southwest from plunder and destruction by pot-hunters and vandals. The effort to secure protective legislation began early among historically minded scientists and civic leaders in Boston and spread to similar circles in Washington, New York, Denver, Santa Fe, and other centers during the 1880's and 1890's. Thus was born the National Monument idea. With important help from Rep. John Fletcher Lacey of Iowa and Senator Henry Cabot Lodge of Massachusetts, it was written into law in the Antiquities Act of 1906—with profound consequences for the National Park System.

The National Monument idea extended the principle of the Forest Reserve Act of 1891 to antiquities and objects of scientific interest on the public domain. It authorized the President, in his discretion, "to declare by public proclamation historic landmarks, historic and prehistoric structures, and other objects of historic or scientific interest" situated on lands owned or controlled by the United States to be National Monuments. The act also prohibited the excavation or appropriation of antiquities on Federal land without a permit. . . .

Between 1906 and 1933 three Federal agencies, the Departments of Interior, Agriculture and War, initiated and administered separate groups of National Monuments. In the *Family Tree*, these form three National Monument lines, one for each department. . . .

We conclude our presentation with the definition of the National Park System written into law in 1970 by the Congress of the United States. The General Authorities Act of that year, Public Law 91–383, signed by President Nixon on August 18, 1970, reads in part as follows:

"Be it enacted by the Senate and House of Representatives of the United States of America in Congress assembled, that Congress declares that the national park system, which began with establishment of Yellowstone National Park in 1872, has since grown to include superlative natural, historic, and recreation areas in every major region of the United States, its territories and island possessions; that these areas, though distinct in character, are united through their inter-related purposes and resources into one national park system as cumulative expressions of a single national heritage; that, individually and collectively, these areas derive increased national dignity and recognition of their superb environmental quality through their inclusion jointly with each other in one national park system preserved and managed for the benefit and inspiration of all the people of the United States; and that it is the purpose of this Act to include all such areas in the System and to clarify the authorities applicable to the System."

The title of Ron Lee's *Family Tree of the National Park System* is apt, for it suggests more than a genealogy. Through the years the people of the National Park Service have often been refereed to as the "Stephen T. Mather family," and they have, as Steve Mather did, devoted time and effort over and above their official duties to protect and manage the National Park System. (When I say "the people of the National Park Service," I include spouses and children as well as employees.) I am certain that they inherited this fondness for their assigned responsibilities as the protectors of the nation's great heritage of natural and human history from those who pioneered in the establishment of the first national park, Yellowstone, and those who subsequently developed a chain of such reservations for recreational use or cultural preservation throughout the country.

Mather contributed much of his private fortune and all of his energies the last eleven years of his life to organizing the Park Service, formulating policies, and developing the park system. There are several instances of other people with private means who followed his example. Among them was George Wright, a man of independent fortune and a dedicated worker in the service. He served without salary for a while and paid the salaries of some of his staff when Congress failed to make funds available. Another was Roger Toll, an engineer from Denver. He followed Horace Albright as superintendent of Yellowstone and field assistant to the director when Albright moved to Washington to devote his full time to assisting Mather. Both Toll and Wright met their tragic deaths in an automobile accident in the Southwest while studying proposed international park sites along the Mexican boundary.

Among the many others whose generosity benefited the Park Service, I should include George B. Dorr, superintendent of Acadia National Park in Maine, a man of considerable means who spent much of his own money buying land for the park. John D. Rockefeller, Jr., also spent a lot of money buying land for Acadia, and the joke of the time was that Superintendent Dorr was trying to outdo Rockefeller. When the time came for his retirement as superintendent of the park, he had spent all of his substantial fortune and had only two old family homes left. Representative Cramton, of Michigan, then chairman of the Subcommittee on Appropriations for the Department of the Interior, was apprised of Dorr's circumstances. He persuaded Congress to write into the appropriation act a specific amount each year for the salary of Superintendent Dorr of Acadia National Park. Dorr later willed his holdings to the government, and the old family home, with one-quarter mile of waterfront, became a part of Acadia National Park.

This deep feeling of concern and responsibility for the parks continues today, and while there may be no individuals of comparable wealth in the service at the present time, the Mather spirit prevails: complete dedication and devotion to the protection of the great scenic, historic, and scientific areas of the national park system for the use and enjoyment of the people.

Mather may not have originated the idea of providing park visitors with interpretation of what they saw in the national parks, but he believed in it strongly and adopted this public service as one of the cornerstones of his overall policy. The concept evolved over the years into the establishment of a strong ranger force responsible for the protection and informed use of the national parks. This force grew, and as conditions changed and gradually demanded new skills and specializations in protection and interpretation, its

The Washington office staff of the National Park Service in 1932. *Left to right:* Assistant Director Conrad L. Wirth, Associate Director Arno B. Cammerer, Chief Clerk R. H. Holmes, Director Horace M. Albright, Assistant Director Harold C. Bryant, Senior Assistant Director A. E. Demaray, Assistant Director G. T. Moskey, and Editor Isabelle F. Story.

members became classified as ranger naturalists, ranger historians, and a ranger protection force. The early park buildings contained what were called museums. These were gradually changed until, during Mission 66, they became focal points for all park activities and were named visitor centers. Today almost every area of the system has a visitor center where information concerning the area's indigenous features is available to the public.

Not all of these aids to park use are paid for by tax dollars. Since the beginning of the service the rangers, and to a great extent their families, have been on duty around the clock. In the Mather-Albright era the larger parks formed natural history associations that, under agreements with the service, undertook to prepare, print, and distribute literature for the park visitor.

They charged nothing for their time or efforts, and any profits from sales were used to prepare additional material and buy needed equipment for the interpretive program. Even the neighbors around the parks joined in and assisted these associations with their activities (see chapter seven).

The executive roster of the National Park Service at the beginning of the New Deal, March 4, 1933, was about the same as when I entered on duty in 1931. Director Albright's right-hand man was Arno Cammerer, assistant director from 1919 through January, 1926, and associate director from 1926 and 1933. Arthur Demaray was the senior assistant director in charge of general administrative matters, having under his jurisdiction personnel, finances, and so on. He had transferred to the National Park Service in the early twenties as a draftsman and went on to become the editor of publications, then assistant director, and then senior assistant director in 1929. George A. Moskey, assistant director, was the service's lawyer and handled legal matters, including legislation. In those days the bureaus had their own attorneys rather than having to depend on the solicitor of the Interior Department, as is now required. Harold C. Bryant, a naturalist, was the assistant director in charge of the Branch of Natural History and Interpretation. He had been in the field for a number of years and had transferred to the Washington office in 1930. Hillory A. Tolson was Moskey's assistant. In October, 1933, when Albright left to become vice-president and general manager of the U.S. Potash Company, Cammerer stepped up to be director, Demaray became associate director, and Tolson was promoted to assistant director in charge of the Branch of Administration. Isabelle F. Story was the editor for the National Park Service and supervised the preparation of informational bulletins and other printed material. Charles L. Gable was head of the Concessions Division, and R. M. Holmes was chief clerk.

As assistant director in charge of the Branch of Lands, I had responsibility for all land matters, including investigation, study, and reporting on proposed new areas for the park system, as well as land acquistion. Superintendent Roger Toll of Yellowstone was the principal pivot man for most of the field investigations of proposed new parks and monuments. I had a secretary and two draftsmen in my Branch of Lands, and besides land maps we prepared maps used in the publications issued for park visitors. The national highway system of the western states wasn't anything like it is today, and our *Park-to-Park Highway Map* of the western parks was always in demand.

Not long after I had entered on duty, Albright called me to his office and told me he had worked up a schedule for a trip I was to make to the West. It was designed primarily to give me a chance to get acquainted with some of the large parks and the field personnel and to learn about some of the land problems firsthand. I was delighted over the prospect of seeing the national parks in operation and of meeting some of the old-time park superintendents.

I started west by train in May, 1931, and my first stop was Grand Canyon National Park. Minor R. "Tilly" Tillotson was the superintendent. I had one of the real experiences of my life at the Grand Canyon, and I never let Tilly forget it. I did not realize it fully at the time, but I am convinced that Horace Albright was sending me around to some of his tried and true park people as a sort of test and also to give me a little "hazing," as if I were joining a fraternity. Tillotson met me at the station and had a very fine hotel room ready for me. I met several of the staff, and then Tilly turned me over to the chief ranger. He suggested that we go by muleback the next morning down to Phantom Ranch at the bottom of the canyon, spend the night there, and come back the following day. We'd have the rest of that day and a third day along the South Rim of the canyon to review some of their land needs. That sounded reasonable. Early the next day the chief ranger and I got on our mules and started down the Bright Angel Trail. We went all the way to the bottom, across the canyon, and about two-thirds of the trail up the North Rim Trail, then back down to the ranch, getting in late but in time for dinner. The chief ranger rode his mule all the way. I did not want him to outdo me, and so I rode mine all the way, too. Anyone who has ever ridden the steep Bright Angel Trail on a stiff-legged mule for some ten hours knows how I felt. I had a hard time sitting down that night. The next morning when we were about to start out, I told the chief ranger, "All right, now, I took it yesterday, and I think I took it in the spirit in which it was meant, but if something has to carry something out of this canyon, I'll carry the mule, he won't carry me." And so I walked practically the whole way up the canyon trail to the South Rim that morning. When we reached the top, Tilly met us with a grin on his face.

From the Grand Canyon I went on to Sequoia National Park, where I met the superintendent, Colonel John White, a man in his early fifties who had received his military rank during the Philippine engagements as one of the constabulary. He was pleasant yet very independent, a world traveler and soldier of fortune before he became a park superintendent. Apparently he was having some kind of running differences with Albright, although I didn't know that at the time. Colonel White ran his shop as a military man would; he was firm and decisive. He was quite a collector of surplus property, especially old military equipment from World War I. After a day in the field, a good part of it in the inspiring giant redwood forest, we spent most of the second day in the office and in his home. We talked nearly the whole day about various things that he was particularly interested in, and a lot of his statements took the form of questions though he never asked for approval of anything in particular. As the day went on I felt sure he had received a letter from the director covering several of the subjects he was bringing up, and so I took the precaution of not expressing outright agreement or opinions on anything. After all, the purpose of this trip was simply to get acquainted and to better understand some of the field problems.

On the third day I left for San Francisco, and on the train I got a little concerned about some of the things Colonel White had brought up. I decided to write a report to the director on both my Grand Canyon and Sequoia visits. I ended the letter saying that, while Colonel White had not asked for my approval of his ideas, the fact that I had not said much might have led him to believe I was in accord with his position. I wrote that I would report in more detail when I got back to Washington. Apparently as soon as I had left the park Colonel White also wrote to the director, telling him that I'd been there, that we'd gone over several matters in detail, that he thought very highly of me, and that I had approved this and that and that! The director, I understand, was about ready to summon me back to Washington—until he received my letter. I am certain he would not have fired me, but he certainly would have thought I was not very smart.

The Park Service had two staff groups based in the Bay Area. They were headed by Frank Kittredge, chief engineer, and Tom Vint, chief landscape architect, in San Francisco; and John J. Coffman, chief forester, in Berkeley. These were the main technical staffs, and their primary duty was to service the parks. I called first on Kittredge, since he was the senior officer. He introduced me to his staff, explained how they operated, and took me to visit some of the important people in the city, after which we were to attend a Park Service party at his home down the peninsula. The next day I visited with Chief Landscape Architect Vint. We had much in common and a lot to talk about. I really got my best insight into the service from Tom. We went out for dinner in Chinatown that night. The next day Tom and Frank took me to the ferry to Oakland, where I boarded the train. Those who have taken this ferry ride will agree, I think, that it gave one time to enjoy the skyline of San Francisco and the view of the hills beyond Oakland and Berkeley, sights worth more than the time now saved by driving across the Bay Bridge.

I had three days on the train to write up my notes. The trip had been an enjoyable and a very worthwhile experience. On the whole it gave me an essential understanding of how the National Park Service operated. I got acquainted with many of the front-line people—the ones who met the public, protected the parks, and planned and developed the facilities. They were my kind of people, and in my mind I felt that I had been accepted by them. They had given me a few hurdles to go over and had tested me to find out whether I was going to meet their standards and take my responsibilities in the Park Service family as seriously as they did.

San Francisco was the base of the Park Service's technical staffs because of the fifty-three areas in the national park system in 1929, amounting to about

8,273,835 acres, all but one, Acadia National Park, were west of the Mississippi River.

As a result of a study authorized by Congress February 21, 1925, to look into the possibility of national parks in the eastern part of the United States, Great Smoky Mountains National Park, in North Carolina and Tennessee, Shenandoah National Park, in Virginia, and Mammoth Cave National Park, in Kentucky, received congressional authorization in 1926. The authorization provided for the National Park Service to assume protection once certain lands were acquired and given to the federal government, but the areas could not be established as national parks until a majority of the land had come into federal ownership. Accordingly, Great Smoky was established for protection only on February 6, 1930, and established for full administration June 15, 1934; Mammoth Cave reached the minimum stage for protection on May 22, 1936, and full establishment on July 1, 1941; and Shenandoah was given protective status on February 16, 1928, and was fully established December 26, 1935.

All three of these areas required a great amount of negotiation and public-relations work. Shenandoah involved the acquisition of over 193,500 acres, and Great Smoky involved over 500,000 acres divided fairly evenly between North Carolina and Tennessee. Associate Director Cammerer spent a great part of his time on these projects, working with the states and individuals as the representative not only of the Park Service but also of John D. Rockefeller, Jr., who had committed himself to match the states' funds for land purchase up to five million dollars. As head of the Branch of Lands, I worked closely with Cammerer in carrying out these projects. He was the top man, and I was his "leg man." He personally handled most of the negotiations, even after he became director in 1933.

Shenandoah was the first of these three parks to materialize, although because of the depression progress was difficult. The Park Service, as with all federal agencies, was hard pressed for appropriations. Shortly after I came into the service, government salaries were cut 10 per cent across the board as a part of government economy under the great stress of the depression. President Herbert Hoover, a Republican, was having a very difficult time with a Congress that had a Republican Senate and a Democratic House of Representatives. He was able to get funds to begin a small public works program, however, including a start on construction of Skyline Drive in the authorized Shenandoah National Park, from Panorama, where U.S. highway 211 crossed the Blue Ridge Mountains, to Skyland, a distance of about twelve miles.

We had a planning meeting at Skyland. There was quite a summer cabin development there, but the only way to reach it was over a very steep, rocky dirt road up Kettle Canyon on the west side of the Blue Ridge Mountains.

Of all the areas of the national park system, Shenandoah National Park in the Blue Ridge Mountains of Virginia, with its Skyland and Stonyman Mountain, is the one the author goes back to year after year.

The meeting, which was attended by Secretary of the Interior Ray Lyman Wilbur, Arno Cammerer, and others, concerned the establishment of park boundary lines and an inspection of Skyland and Skyline Drive under construction.

The Blue Ridge, part of which is now Shenandoah National Park, had been settled in early colonial days by people with very meager funds on land given them by the more fortunate plantation owners down on the Piedmont Plateau. We found the people living there extremely poor and uneducated. They spoke a dialect that dated back to the late seventeenth-century English spoken by their forebears. Marriage within families had occurred often enough that inbreeding was a problem, and the incidence of mental retardation was high. The families all had small apple orchards and cornfields and made moonshine whiskey and applejack, though their market was greatly reduced when Prohibition went out in 1933. The people's houses were primarily one-room cabins, and their children were numerous. The property lines were handed down only by word of mouth; for example, "from the rock to the big oak tree over to the chestnut tree and back to the stream and up to the rock again." In many instances the rock or the tree or both had long since disappeared. The state bought the land, but the question of establishing acceptable boundary lines and good titles was most difficult. As a final solution, the state placed all its money into the courts of six counties, three on each side of the Blue Ridge Mountains, which Shenandoah National Park straddles. Through a special law enacted by the Virginia legislature, the courts put a blanket condemnation on all the property within the park boundary line and proceeded to use the funds to buy up the land according to appraisals based on property lines recognized and established by the courts. At the same time the people were allowed to continue living there. In condemning the land, the state took title to the property and then transferred it to the federal government. Only after the government received the titles could the work in the park begin.

The inhabitants posed another difficult problem. Their holdings had very little value, especially during the depression years. The amount the owners received for the land and so-called improvements did not provide anywhere near enough money for them to settle in a new location. The character and mentality of these people compounded the dilemma. It is hard to believe that people could be so poor and isolated in the twentieth century within a hundred miles of the capital of the United States. It was clear to Director Albright that, until a suitable solution was found, the service would have to let these people stay in their cabins. The opportunity to relocate them came several years later, in the mid-thirties, when the Resettlement Administration established farms in the valley, built reasonably comfortable houses, and moved the people there. But they were so used to the mountain country that after a few months they began to move back to their old homes. Finally, steps were taken to allow these people to live in the hollows until the older members of the family died. In the meantime the children were sent to school at government expense in order to fit them for reestablishment in the communities.

We had some of the same problems in establishing Great Smoky Mountains National Park, although not quite as bad or extensive. The mountaineers of that region were strong, intelligent, and in good health, with no apparent problems of inbreeding, and they possessed many basic skills. They had some problems similar to those of the Shenandoah mountain people, but most of them bargained for the sale of their homesteads, sold them, and left the mountains without much assistance from the government. Some sold subject to a life interest.

The Branch of Lands had a nearly continuous job of reviewing and changing the boundary lines of Great Smoky, Shenandoah, and Mammoth Cave national parks largely as a result of poor surveys and maps. The Shenandoah map was in three sections, and we could not get them on our drafting tables. We would spend Saturdays and Sundays with these maps stretched on the floor in the hall in the Interior Building trying to get them in shape for court and fieldwork.

There are only two ways in which areas of the national park system can be established: by congressional legislation or, in the case of nationally important historic, prehistoric, or scientific areas on government-owned land, by presidential proclamation. Both are often influenced by political circumstances. For instance, the approach of an election year has considerable influence on the actions of Congress and the administration. During the last days of a session of Congress there is a rush to get legislation enacted. The same urgency obtains towards the end of a president's term in office. The reason, of course, is that if a project to which expensive and time-consuming research and hearings have been devoted fails to receive final approval before the session or term ends, the whole process has to be repeated in order to present it to a new Congress or president.

Special circumstances surround the establishment of each new park area. Virgin Islands National Park is a good case in point. In the fall of 1955, Helen and I were in Grand Teton National Park. At Moose, where the Park Service headquarters is located, there was a log building that housed both the post office and a fishing tackle store. On a visit to the post office I noticed Laurance S. Rockefeller in the store buying fishing tackle. I stepped over to say hello to him, and he invited Helen and me to come up to his J Y Ranch the next morning and look over some maps of the Virgin Islands. He explained that he had been down to the islands in his boat some three or four years previously and had bought a piece of property called Caneel Bay Plantation, a depleted, unused tract with a fine beach. He had recently been down that way again, and a man named Frank Stick had given him a carbon copy of a report on a proposed national park on the Island of Saint Johns, in the Virgin Islands. It was dated 1939 and addressed to me as assistant director in charge of the Branch of Lands. I assured Laurance that I was still interested in the proposed national park. Frank Stick was an old friend of mine who had been of great help in the establishment of Cape Hatteras National Seashore, in North Carolina. The report he had given to Rockefeller was no doubt one I had asked Hal Hubler to prepare in 1939 when I was in the Virgin Islands in connection with the CCC program. Hubler, a landscape architect and superintendent of a local CCC camp at the time, had told CCC Director Fechner and me about Caneel Bay on Saint Johns Island and was so persuasive that we went over to see it and actually went swimming. However, the war came on before we could do anything about the proposed park.

Helen and I went up to the Rockefeller ranch the next morning and, while she and Mary Rockefeller took a walk, I joined Laurance in the recreation building, where he had at least a half-dozen maps and the report that Frank Stick had given him. I explained to Rockefeller that, while I was still in favor of a national park in the Virgin Islands, we could not proceed on the basis of the old report; it would have to be brought up to date. He wanted to know

Laurance E. Rockefeller (*third from right*) hands Secretary of the Interior Fred A. Seaton the deed to the land establishing Virgin Islands National Park on December 1, 1956. *On the left:* Representative O'Brien, of New York, and Director Wirth, *On the right:* Representative Wayne Aspinall, of Colorado, and Representative A. L. Miller, of Nebraska.

whether we could get on with a new study right away, and I told him that we had the necessary staff but were a little short of travel money. He readily helped us with that problem, and we came back with a report before the end of the calendar year and proceeded to draft legislation for consideration by the secretary of the interior and the Bureau of the Budget. The proposed bill was cleared and was introduced in Congress in early 1956.

In the meantime Laurance Rockefeller employed Frank Stick and proceeded to acquire land for the proposed national park. The legislation required that at least 50 per cent of the lands authorized within the boundary of the national park be in federal ownership before the park could be established. The bill was enacted by Congress and was signed into law on August 2, 1956, which was a very short time to get a bill processed into law. In that brief period Laurance Rockefeller had acquired more than 50 per cent of the land needed for the park, and the lawyers had already begun to get the titles in condition acceptable to the attorney general of the United States.

In due course all the details were cleared up, and success was celebrated with a big barbecue at Cruz Bay on Saint Johns Island December 1, 1956. Secretary of the Interior Fred Seaton and the governor of the Virgin Islands were there, and Rockefeller presented to the secretary the deeds to the lands he had bought for the Virgin Islands National Park. The park project, originally suggested seventeen years earlier, was started in earnest in the fall of 1955 and completed in a little more than a year's time.

The Rockefeller family for two generations has been most considerate and helpful in the development of the national park system. John D. Rockefeller, Jr., devoted much of his time making this country a better place to live in, certainly from the standpoint of conservation. His most heralded contribution was the restoration of colonial Williamsburg, in Virginia, and the establishment of the Williamsburg Foundation to operate it. Williamsburg is closely associated with Colonial National Historic Park, which includes Yorktown and Jamestown Island. The scope of Rockefeller's contributions to the national park system was broad and impressive. A large portion of the land for Acadia National Park, in Maine, was purchased by him and conveyed to the federal government. Grand Teton National Park, in Wyoming, is another example. Although a good bit of the land was in government ownership, a large amount remained in private ownership, notably some tracts in the valley on both sides of the Snake River. Grand Teton was established in 1929, but its original area included only the mountains. A proposal to extend the park boundary to include the valley was vigorously opposed, but the extension was finally settled by an act of Congress in 1950. At that time Rockefeller, who had been buying most of the private holdings in the disputed area, donated his land to the government for inclusion in the park. When Great Smoky Mountains National Park was established in 1934, Rockefeller matched the five million dollars provided by the states of North Carolina and Tennessee for land acquisition. Then, along the 450 miles of the Blue Ridge Parkway, he made other donations, including the Linville Falls area in North Carolina, giving part of the land to the U.S. Forest Service and the falls themselves for the parkway. In the West, he made contributions toward purchase of the redwoods, both the gigantia and the coastal redwoods, and also provided funds to buy and preserve the very fine western yellow pine stand as an addition to Yosemite National Park. Rockefeller also gave great assistance to the state parks of New York, especially Palisades Interstate Park, on the west side of the Hudson River in New Jersey and New York.

The daughter and five sons of John D. Rockefeller, Jr., are well known for their divergent interests, which include the conservation of our natural resources. Laurance S. Rockefeller in particular has a great interest in parks at all levels of government which brought me in direct contact with him long before I became director of the National Park Service in 1951. Since retirement I have been a consultant to him. As already described, Laurance S. Rockefeller gave his government the Virgin Islands National Park, and he has enlarged on his father's gifts of land at Teton and other national parks around the country. He and the various organizations that he belongs to have made many contributions to research that have advanced and will continue to advance the field of conservation, especially the park field. Laurance Rockefeller is a very imaginative person, vigorous, determined, and extremely generous. He's quick at grasping the essential points and relating them to the objective. One of Laurance's greatest contributions was his chairmanship of the Outdoor Recreation Resources Review Commission, which opened a new era in park development and led to the establishment of the Bureau of Outdoor Recreation. That bureau provides financial aid for the development of park and recreation facilities at all levels of government. He was also chairman and a member of the presidential Citizens' Advisory Committee on Environmental Quality. To these efforts he devoted a great deal of his time and resources.

While all the Rockefellers have pursued their individual interests, they nevertheless have worked together on joint enterprises, as for example, their several family foundations in which they and their children take part.

In this vein should be mentioned the shoreline projects with which Paul Mellon was so helpful. Cape Hatteras National Seashore, in North Carolina, was authorized for establishment as a national seashore area on August 17, 1937. The bill was introduced by Representative Lindsay Warren, a strong advocate of the protection of our seashores and of their use as parks. It authorized the assembling of ten thousand acres to comprise the seashore area and the transfer of certain lands under public ownership to the federal government. It also provided that the private lands within the boundary lines of the proposed area should be acquired by the National Park Service by means other than purchase with federal funds. In 1937 the state of North Carolina adopted legislation authorizing the purchase of private holdings in the area for transfer to the federal government, but this was not carried out. The state did have title to the land at the tip of the cape, which was administered as a state park, although this land was a small part of the total acreage required.

In the spring of 1952, I received a telephone call from Paul Mellon's office stating that there was a piece of land in North Carolina that was up for sale and asking whether the National Park Service would be interested in this acreage as a gift for park purposes. I was familiar with the land, and actually I didn't think we would be interested in it; however, I felt that I should have somebody take another look at it before I gave Mellon our answer. I told him I would look into it and get in touch with him a little later. A week went by and I got another call stating that the land in question was no longer available and wanting to know whether we were interested in any other land in that section of the country. I immediately replied that we were interested in Cape Hatteras seashore, which was authorized by Congress, and that since the state had not bought the land, we would like very much to interest Mellon in that. The office called me back a day later for an appointment with Mellon. Ben Thompson, head of the Branch of Lands, and I had lunch with Mellon at the Hay-Adams House. Mellon didn't ask very many questions, but I guess he didn't have a chance to, because Ben and I did most of the talking. The meeting adjourned and I didn't hear from Paul Mellon for about a week. I began to think that perhaps I had made the terrible mistake of talking too much. I was relieved to get a telephone call shortly thereafter inviting me to join Paul Mellon on a flight over Cape Hatteras; I accepted. A few days after that I got a call asking whether Mellon could come over to see me. I felt sure as we talked that he was going to offer to purchase land for us that we had estimated to cost about one and a quarter million dollars. But I thought that the state should help buy it, and I told Paul that I would like to go to North Carolina, talk to Governor Robert Scott, and find out whether the state would be willing to put in half the cost of the property if we could get some matching funds. I made an appointment to see the governor the following week.

In conversation with the conservation commissioner while waiting to see the governor, I solicited his support, and he offered to see the governor with me. He also told me that the balance in the governor's reserve fund was approximately $600,000. This money could go for the purchase of Cape Hatteras, if Governor Scott and his cabinet would approve it. I also was informed that the governor would most likely leave the talking to me and wouldn't say much himself. Most important of all, I was advised, if he pulled out his plug of tobacco and started chewing, it would mean he was interested, but if he didn't, I might just as well give up. I talked for some time to the governor with no movement on his part. Finally the conservation commissioner spoke up, but instead of supporting me, as he had led me to believe he would, he said he felt that if the state did anything, it should buy the land and keep it as a state park. This got me so irritated that I turned to him and demanded to know why he had reversed his stand since walking into the governor's office. With that the governor opened his desk drawer, picked up a plug of tobacco, and took a chew. Then in a rich southern drawl he asked me how much money I was talking about. I told him, and the governor rang for an assistant and asked him how much money they had in the "kitty." While the man went to find out, Scott gave me a plug of his chewing tobacco; although it was risky for me to do so, I took a bite and started chewing. The assistant came back in a few minutes and said, "You have slightly over $600,000." The governor looked at me and said, "Mr. Wirth, have you been looking at my books?" I answered, "I did know how much you had left, but our estimate was still

Cape Hatteras National Seashore was purchased with funds provided by the state of North Carolina and the Mellon family. Attending the dedication in 1958 were, *left to right:* Assistant Secretary of the Interior Roger Ernst, Representative Herbert Bonner, of North Carolina, Director Wirth, Paul Mellon, Governor Luther H. Hodges, of North Carolina, Comptroller General Lindsay Warren, and three representatives of the private landowners.

$1,250,000, and it just happens to match." He smiled and said, "Well, I'll tell you what I will do. My cabinet meets on Thursday of next week, and if they approve this I'll let you know."

On Friday of the next week I received a wire from the governor stating that the funds would be available if we could match them within ten days. I immediately called Paul Mellon and read the wire to him. On Monday morning a check for $600,000 was delivered to me to be deposited and held to match the state's $600,000. I sent a wire to the governor of North Carolina stating: "I've just received a donation of $600,000 to be held to match the state's funds. Where is your money?" Within a week I received a similar check from the state of North Carolina. We proceeded to buy the land. As it turned out, the $1.2 million was not enough, and we had to go back to Mellon and the state of North Carolina. Paul Mellon gave us an additional $200,000, and the state matched it. Cape Hatteras National Seashore was established on January 12, 1953, sixteen years after congressional authorization.

The money that came from the Mellons through Paul Mellon was actually from two foundations. Half was from Paul Mellon's Old Dominion Foundation, and the other half came from his sister's Avalon Foundation. Those two foundations have since been combined into one, the Richard Mellon Foundation. The Park Service had made a very thorough study of seashores in the thirties along the Atlantic and Gulf coasts as possible national and state seashore areas, and Cape Hatteras was the only one approved by Congress. Our negotiations with the Mellon foundations in 1952 and 1953 occurred almost twenty years after those studies were made. They showed great interest in the seashore projects at a time when the Park Service was suffering low budget problems that resulted from the costly cold war. At Paul Mellon's request we presented to the Old Dominion and Avalon foundations an estimate of the cost of making a restudy of not only the Atlantic and Gulf coasts but also the Pacific coast. The foundations provided the funds for this study and also for a study of the shores of the Great Lakes.

The acquisition of areas for the national park system and its administration are serious responsibilities that call for careful planning at a competent professional level. This fact was recognized early in the National Park Service, and the service takes credit for establishing and developing the master plan concept. The master plan as developed by the Park Service is a comprehensive land mass plan that contains all the basic known facts and needs for the protection, use, and development of a logical land mass set aside for a principal purpose or purposes, taking into consideration the potentialities for adjacent land uses and their effect on the area under study. A National Park Service master plan therefore consists of many maps and pages of written material covering every conceivable bit of information on an area, including its natural features, history and archaeology, engineering, road construction, developments of all kinds, forest-fire protection, maintenance, and nearly everything that must be considered in planning the protection and development of a piece of land for public use. The input comes from every professional and administrative person who has an interest in or information on the area and the surrounding related lands. Of course, the amount of written material and the number of maps vary from one master plan to another according to the areas' size, location, purpose, and related considerations. For instance, the forty acres of Arizona's Tuzigoot National Monument, containing a large Indian pueblo, did not require the twenty or thirty sheets, three feet by four feet, that Yellowstone National Park did, with its two and a quarter million acres. The Tuzigoot master plan does have four or five sheets, however, and was as thoroughly researched and prepared as the Yellowstone master plan was. The master plan covers all information necessary to fully

Western Office of Plans and Design staff reviewing master plans, which control the use, development, and management of national park system units and are prepared with the combined help of all those involved.

develop a park and maintain it for the use and enjoyment of the people in accordance with its basic legislation.

Obviously, master plans are not prepared overnight. In fact, the master plan is a living thing, constantly being altered and revised to meet changing conditions. Its sole purpose is to insure a sound, economical, and orderly development of each area of the national park system in accordance with the purpose for which the area was established. If the master plan concept had not been in existence at the time Mission 66 came into being in 1956, we would have been in great trouble. I don't mean to imply that it necessarily would have been impossible to carry out Mission 66 without the master plans. The Park Service was tired of seeing the parks gradually decay during World War II and the cold war as the result first of nonuse and then of a great increase in use, both coinciding with lack of funds for administration and maintenance. The service was ready and willing to tackle anything to get the job done, even under adverse conditions. But without master plans that job would have been much more difficult, more expensive, and less promising than it turned out to be. The whole purpose of Mission 66 was to update and carry out the National Park Service's master plans.

According to Major Owen A. Tomlinson, former superintendent of Mount

Rainier National Park, in Washington, and regional director of Region Four in San Francisco, the master plan had its origin at Mount Rainier in the late 1920s. The occasion was a meeting at the park called by Director Albright to review the concessioners' development programs. Chief Landscape Architect Tom Vint had been requested to bring plans to Mount Rainier for these discussions. There was a great rustling of tracing paper and pencils and many long hours of serious plan preparation in the design office in San Francisco, and they produced a package of plans they called the "Master Plan for Mount Rainier." While the master plan for Mount Rainier of the late twenties was not as comprehensive as such plans were by the time Mission 66 rolled around, it nevertheless had many of the full-scale master plan's basic ingredients. During the meetings, not only the concession proposals but also such other master plan subjects as park boundaries, land acquisition, roads, and Park Service facilities were reviewed. Albright was so impressed with Vint's master plan concept that before leaving the park he requested Tom to prepare similar master plans for each of the areas of the National Park System.

To carry out this directive, resident landscape architects were assigned to the major parks or groups of parks as funds became available, with the responsibility of developing and maintaining master plans. During the summer, while work progressed on approved construction projects, the long-range master plan would be reviewed with park staff and visiting officials from Washington and San Francisco. Major planning decisions in most cases were made in the park during these summer conferences. Late in the fall, after the weather had closed down most of the construction and field work, the park superintendents held staff meetings to review their master plans and the planning decisions of the past summer. With these data in hand the resident landscape architect would return to the San Francisco planning office for the winter. There the professional people in the central design office and the regional office would prepare the necessary plan revisions. As the revised plans were completed, copies were sent to the park and to the Washington office for review and approval. Upon completion of all revisions, the resident landscape architect would return to the park in the early spring to resume the master planning routine for the next season and supervise such developments as might be going on in the area.

In 1936, when four National Park Service regional offices were established, Tom Vint's planning staff was reassigned to the Washington office and the regional offices. Although most of the personnel of the division were now scattered throughout the regional offices, they were still under the professional control of the Central Design and Construction Division with Tom Vint in charge.

The following examples are but a few of many cases where the policies of protection and preservation of park values were applied through the master plan. In the early days of Yellowstone the explorer and his party could camp next to Old Faithful geyser without greatly harming the natural features because their requirements were very simple. The tents and log structures required later to accommodate the stage coach visitor needed permanent sites, and because they were few in number they were located adjacent to the points of interest. By the time the bus and automobile arrived on the scene, these overnight accommodations were well-established facilities, some located within the geyser area. The 1935 master plan for the Old Faithful area included recommendations for relocation of the main park road back of all the existing facilities and for removal of some of the buildings. Portions of this plan have been accomplished, and eventually, as conditions permit, other facilities will be eliminated or relocated. The new development at Grant Village, constructed under the Mission 66 program, is several miles removed from the West Thumb thermal activities. The master plan first recommended relocation of these facilities in 1936. It was twenty years later that the plan was implemented as one of the major projects of Mission 66. The master plan for Yellowstone contained other similar relocation projects, including those at the Canyon, Bridge Bay, and Madison Junction areas.

In nearby Grand Teton National Park a special master plan report prepared in 1936 recognized the dangers of continued expansion of facilities along the small lakes at the base of the mountains. The plan proposed relocation of the main highway on the east side of the Snake River and the development of visitor facilities along the north shore of Jackson Lake, far removed from the areas of greatest natural value. Stage coach access to the lakes and the mountain trails between the Snake River and the mountains was suggested. Except for the stage coach proposal, the development has followed the master plan recommendations.

In 1949 the master plan for Yosemite National Park proposed the development of the Big Meadows area, outside but overlooking the Yosemite Valley, for visitor accommodations. This would gradually phase out the overcrowding of overnight facilities in the valley. The proposal was based on the intent of reducing the visitor impact by gradually establishing day use for a major portion of the valley.

Before Mission 66 the master plans were loaded with projects of this type that needed financing. Mission 66 provided the momentum and resulted in a long list of completed projects that improved protection and the preservation of park values. Many of these projects involved major road construction, the engineering aspects of which were handled by the Bureau of Public Roads* under agreements dating back to the twenties. Over the years the Bureau of

*The functions of this bureau, formerly in the Department of Agriculture, were transferred to the Department of Transportation by act of Congress in 1966 and are assigned to the Federal Highway Administration.

Public Roads worked closely with the landscape architects of the design office and was very sympathetic to the policies of the service. It followed the approved priorities and recommendations outlined in the master plans. Differences of views regarding road standards and safety requirements admittedly caused some disagreements. The questions of location and design as well as final approval have always been the Park Service's responsibility. In the overall performance of its responsibilities, however, the bureau rendered outstanding service. It provided park visitors with excellent roads that brought a minimum of complaints.

The U.S. Public Health Service also has provided outstanding assistance to the national parks in maintaining high standards for the development and operation of sanitary facilities. Starting in the middle 1920s, Public Health Service sanitary engineers have been assigned to work with the design offices and the parks in a program for improving these facilities and establishing high standards of maintenance and operation.

In 1954, just before Mission 66, there was another reorganization of Tom Vint's planning staff that resulted in the establishment of the Western and Eastern Design and Construction offices. The planning personnel in the regions were transferred to these offices, located in San Francisco and Philadelphia. The two offices were headed by Red Hill, in the West, and Bob Hall, in the East, and here again were two outstanding professional men in the right place at the right time. Preparation and upkeep of master plans remained one of their primary responsibilities, although during Mission 66 the major portion of their duties was devoted to the design and supervision of construction projects.

The master plan concept was one of Tom Vint's finest contributions to the National Park System. He possessed the wonderful Scottish love of the natural landscape and was completely devoted to the protection and preservation of the parks. Through his planning leadership, recommendations of the master plans were always based on the preservation of natural features and the placing of required facilities in locations where they functioned effectively, blended into the natural landscape, and had minimum impact on the natural scene.

Many of Vint's staff also deserve special recognition for their contributions: particularly Bill Carnes, who was Tom's assistant for many years. Later, when Mission 66 was conceived, he was assigned to head a seven-man task force to develop the project. Every division of the service was represented on that task force, and its main job was to assemble a master plan of the National Park System itself, placing its various elements in a priority system and developing an orderly program. Bill Carnes's background made him the logical chairman of the task force, and he and his committee did an outstanding job.

The master plan as developed and practiced in the late twenties and re-

Tom Vint, chief landscape architect of the National Park Service for over forty years, caught at play when the director was away. *Photo by Abbie Rowe, courtesy National Park Service.*

fined with experience also exerted its influence for a well-conceived Civilian Conservation Corps program in the thirties. Its principles were applied to state and metropolitan parks. During the latter CCC days the National Park Service began a program called "Plans on the Shelf," which provided complete project plans to be used as soon as funds became available. It was only partially successful because of insufficient appropriations during World War II and the long subsequent delay before Mission 66 supplied adequate funds. In the meantime, changing conditions had required many plan revisions and, in some cases, a whole new master plan.

There may be some who claim that the master plans have led to overdevelopment in some of the parks, but there are very few instances, if any, where this has happened. In fact, the master plan helped prevent overdevelopment. Horace Albright, while in Washington to receive the Cosmos Club Award on April 15, 1974, stated that the areas of the National Park System were in better overall condition than they had ever been. Had the National Park Service maintained a more restrictive policy of visitor access, the national park idea would never have fulfilled its basic responsibility to preserve and maintain the parks "for the use and enjoyment of the people." The present so-called overcrowding is but a public expression that parks are essential to satisfy the people's needs.

4

The New Deal: The First Hundred Days

The first storm clouds of the Great Depression began to show themselves in 1927, if not earlier. But most people did not recognize them. In 1927–28 the bottom started falling out of the resort development business along the Mississippi and Alabama Gulf coast and in Florida, which had been experiencing one of the greatest land booms this country has known. By the time Hoover took office as president in 1929, the depression had begun to spread like wildfire, and it spared nobody. Even the biggest red plums on the trees of prosperity fell to the ground to rot. Land investors were trying to get back ten cents on the dollar, but there were no buyers. Private enterprise and government alike were letting employees go and cutting salaries. Contracts were being canceled, and resort to court action was useless. The stock market went bust. Everybody was trying to lift himself by his bootstraps.

These are my recollections. I was there, and my young family went broke and in debt to such a degree that I didn't think we would ever get ahead again. Those too young to have shared that experience can visualize it from a vivid description in *The New York Times Chronicle of American Life from the Crash to the Blitz, 1929–1939*, by Cabell Phillips:

> No new year ever dawned with less hope than 1933. The Great Depression, having grown progressively worse for three long years, had spread a pall of fear and desperation across the whole land. The new year brought no promise of abatement, only the prospect of more of the same. . . . The physical signs of distress were everywhere. You encountered them with wearying monotony day after day: clusters of hungry men and women waiting like docile peasants for food handouts at the relief stations; the smokeless chimneys and rusting sheds of factories standing mute and empty behind their locked gates; the abandoned shops and stores, their doorways littered with trash, their grime-streaked windows staring vacantly upon half empty streets; the drooping shoulders of a father, husband, brother, or friend whose pride had been battered into lethargy and dejection by months of fruitless job hunting; the panic and anger of the crowd milling before a bank entrance on whose door a typed note stated, "Closed until further notice by order of the Board of Directors."
>
> But even worse than this visible evidence of breakdown was the knowledge that it was everywhere—not just in your town or your state or your part of the country. The blight spread across the whole nation—big cities, small towns, and limitless countryside—like a deadly plague of the Middle Ages. Nor were its victims just certain kinds of people. They were farmers, bankers, carpenters, lawyers, factory

Symbol of the Great Depression of the 1930s: ". . . a father, husband, brother, or friend whose pride had been battered into lethargy and dejection by months of fruitless job hunting."

workers, preachers, chorus girls. Every class, it seemed, except the poor Negroes in the slums who had never known anything but hard times anyway, was stricken in some degree. But even those who still had jobs or income lived with a hot ball of fear in their gut that tomorrow their luck would run out. "What will I do then?" sprang equally from the tortured clerk behind the counter and the merchant behind his desk.

Worse still was the knowledge that there was nothing you or your boss or the governor of your state or the President of the United States could do about it. All the towers of wisdom and strength on which you were accustomed to lean had crumbled. The roots of your faith in the American way and even, perhaps, in the benevolence of God, had begun to wither like a vine too long deprived of rain. You felt trapped, like an animal in a cage, as some malevolent force that you could neither comprehend nor fend off inexorably worked to destroy your whole scheme of life. And in these early weeks of the new year 1933 you felt that the climax was approaching. Things were happening that seemed to warn, like thunderclaps in the hot night sky, that the storm was about to loose its furies.

Well, the storm was about to break, but it was a good storm. It went away, and the sun came out, brightening up homes throughout the country.

On March 4, 1933, a new president, Franklin Delano Roosevelt, took the oath of office. Every seat in the stands was taken on that inauguration day, and people by the thousands crowded in front of the platform and lined Pennsylvania Avenue. Americans throughout the land heard on the radio the words of the new president.

This is a day of national consecration, and I am certain that my fellow Americans expect that on my induction into the Presidency I will address them with a candor and a decision which the present situation of our nation impels.

This is preeminently the time to speak the truth, the whole truth, frankly and boldly, nor need we shrink from honestly facing the conditions in our country today. This great nation will endure as it has endured, will revive and will prosper.

So first of all let me assert my firm belief that the only thing we have to fear is fear itself—nameless, unreasoning, unjustified terror which paralyzes needed effort to convert retreat into advance. . . .

Phillips' *Chronicle* records the events and spirit that enlivened the government and the nation immediately after Franklin Delano Roosevelt's inauguration:

In the days that followed, the Washington scene was abruptly transformed from the quagmire of torpor and bewilderment that had gripped it for the past six months into an arena of spirited activity. . . . The Roosevelt Administration's fabled "Hundred Days"—probably as crucial a brief epoch as any in the nation's history—had started. They were to dissipate the panic of the Depression, even if they would not break the back of the Depression itself.

In virtually his first official act in office, initiated within hours of taking the oath, the President decreed a national bank holiday, shutting down every financial institu-

Franklin Delano Roosevelt and Eleanor Roosevelt on the way to the White House after the inaugural ceremony on March 4, 1933. *Courtesy National Archives.*

tion in the land, and called a special session of Congress to convene within four days. Simultaneously, a dozen task forces were at work drafting one of the most revolutionary legislative programs ever essayed by any President. Between March 9 and June 16, Roosevelt would propose and Congress would pass fifteen "emergency" acts, which, in their totality, would drastically affect the nation's social and political orientation far into the future. Some of these laws were temporary stopgaps, and some would in time be struck down by the courts, but fully half of these "emergency" enactments remain embedded in the statute books today. Never before had such a legislative miracle been wrought in so short a time.

"Whatever laws the President thinks he may need to end the Depression," Senator Burton K. Wheeler of Montana said on Inauguration Day, "Congress will jump through a hoop to put them through." His prophecy was fulfilled.

Whatever the causes and cures of the problems of the depression might have been, the immediate and most pressing responsibility of the government was to put men back to work. It was absolutely necessary to bring an end to idleness and to restore family incomes, even in a small measure, in order to strengthen the national morale, avert panic, and at the same time create a breathing spell that would permit the mobilization of the nation's forces for a systematic study and correction of the underlying causes of the depression.

The *Chronicle* continues with an account of Roosevelt's approach to these problems:

The broad outlines of the New Deal program had been spelled out by F.D.R. in his campaign, and he brought to Washington not only a sizable portfolio of policy papers and legislative proposals but also a crop of aides and experts capable of putting his plans into effect.

The nucleus of this corps was the "Brain Trust," a small team of scholars and technicians who had gravitated to Roosevelt during his 1932 campaign to help him formulate his program. The involvement of scholars instead of the familiar priesthood of business and finance on such a high political mission was, in itself, a significant innovation that would distinguish the New Deal from most Administrations of the past. . . .

That same night [of March 4], after the Cabinet had been sworn in, the new President sat down in the unfamiliar surroundings of the White House with Woodin, Moley, Cummings, and a handful of other advisors, and made a series of momentous decisions that were to set the Hundred Days off from any similar period in American history. . . . The first decision was to go through with the plan of declaring a national bank holiday; the second, to call Congress into special session to deal with the bank crisis; and third, to summon a group of leading bankers to Washington immediately for any advice they could give in the emergency. . . .

By 10:00 o'clock that night (Sunday) the necessary proclamation and orders were issued (thoughtfully postdated 1:00 AM Monday to avoid profaning the Sabbath). Effective immediately every bank in the nation was closed for four days, the shipment of gold and silver was embargoed . . . and Congress was under orders to convene at noon on Thursday, March 9th.

When Congress convened in special session on noon of Thursday, March 9, Secretary of the Treasury Woodin had ready for it the draft of an emergency banking bill. . . . There was not time enough to have the bill printed. The half-dozen typewritten copies that were rushed to the Capitol the morning of March 9 still bore marginal notes and corrections scribbled in pencil. In the House of Representatives there was no pretense of committee consideration. Only a few of the leaders had even seen the text. As the House reading clerk finished reading the one copy available in that chamber, cries went up from the floor. "Vote, vote, vote!" Thirty-eight minutes later the bill was passed by acclamation. The Senate was slightly more deliberate. It listened to three hours of debate . . . before passing the bill, 73 to 7. At 8:37 that night, F.D.R., with newsreel cameras focused on his desk in the White House, signed the first legislative enactment of the New Deal. . . .

It had originally been Roosevelt's intention to send Congress home once the emergency bank bill was passed, because he thought that his new Administration needed a chance to get the feel of the job and to devote a lot of care to the drafting of the legislative program. But the momentum and the good will generated by his swift handling of the banking crisis was too valuable an asset to be wasted. Tugwell urged him to rush for passage of the farm bill while he still had Congress in his hand, and Lew Douglas urged with equal vigor that now was the psychological moment to strike a blow for economy and fiscal "soundness." Roosevelt, aglow with optimism and impatience, said "Why not?" and picked up Senator Wheeler's option.

I won't go into details of the bills that passed and other actions taken in the famous "hundred days," but I will list the bills, the executive orders, and their dates: (1) We've seen that the bank bill became law on March 9, without congressional hearings. (2) The Agricultural Adjustment Act was introduced March 16 and enacted May 12. (3) The Civilian Conservation Corps Act was introduced March 21 and enacted March 31. The CCC was an original idea of FDR's, stimulated by his long interest in forestry and conservation in general. He proposed to take 250,000 unemployed young men off the streets and welfare rolls and give them jobs at thirty dollars a month, plus their keep, to do useful work primarily in the federal and state forests and parks. According to Phillips' *Chronicle*, "This work program of youths was the first and most widely approved of a variety of work relief programs that were to follow." Within a week after enactment boys were being enrolled by the thousands and the first CCC camp was being constructed near Luray, Virginia. (4) The Federal Emergency Relief Act was introduced March 21 and enacted May 12. (5) The Farm Credit Administration Act was introduced March 27 and enacted June 16. The FCA was initially established by executive order of the president. (6) The Truth in Securities Act was introduced March 29 and enacted May 27. (7) The Tennessee Valley Authority Act was introduced April 10 and enacted May 18. (8) The Home Owners Loan Act was introduced Arpil 13 and enacted June 13. (9) By an executive order of April 19 the gold standard was abandoned. (10) The Railroad Coordination Act was introduced May 4 and enacted June 16. (11) The National Industrial Recovery Act was introduced May 17 and enacted June 16. (12) The Glass-Steagall Banking Act was introduced May 17 and enacted June 16. (13) The Annulment of Gold Clause in Contract Act was introduced May 26 and enacted June 5.

The *Chronicle* states:

> The 73rd Congress, 1st session, adjourned in the early morning hours of June 16, bone weary but jubilant. In ninety-nine tumultuous days it had established a record such as no Congress before it or since has matched. In fifteen [Phillips cites only thirteen] major legislative enactments it had broken many bonds with the past, had set the nation on a revolutionary course toward new social and political goals, which could be perceived only dimly, and had subdued (though it had not wholly overcome) a crisis of confidence that had shaken the foundations of the Republic. . . .
>
> The tide turned with Roosevelt's swift and decisive action as he took office. Despair turned into hope and faith and confidence reached a peak as the Hundred Days came to an end.

The *Chronicle* goes into much greater detail, but the above should be enough to set the stage for a look at the National Park Service at the beginning of the New Deal. Size of staff was at a low ebb. Salaries were low; in 1932 they had been cut 10 per cent across the board. But we were all glad to have jobs and plenty of work to do. When the CCC and other New Deal programs began, we were happy to be a part of them and to put in long hours, far into the night, with a sandwich and coffee at our desk for dinner.

We got great satisfaction in providing jobs for others. Highly qualified professionals—architects, landscape architects, engineers—were available in all the fields needed to carry out our programs successfully. I remember one well-known landscape architect who wrote and said he was coming to Washington, hoping we could give him a job. Before we could reply he showed up in our office. We told him we could use him at the Richmond district office, which we were just setting up. He jumped at the chance, signed the necessary papers, and left the office to drive to Richmond so that he could start work the next day. In about fifteen minutes he was back with the sad story that somebody had broken into his car and stolen his suitcase and satchel, which contained all of his clothing and thirty dollars, the last money he had to keep him going until payday. We took up a collection and sent him on his way with about twenty dollars. He left an IOU and returned the money in sixty days.

The legislative accomplishments of Congress in its three-month session that marked the beginning of Roosevelt's New Deal were astounding, but the machinery to operate these programs still had to be organized by the administration and put to work. Of course, there was a lot of discussion of what might happen, whether the new secretary of the interior would want many changes, whether the whole department would be reorganized, or whether the old bureaus would be given additional responsibility. After the inaugural address on March 4 all agencies of government seemed to take on an aggressive

The Washington staff of the National Park Service in uniform in 1926. *Left to right:* Arno B. Cammerer, assistant director; Harry Karstens, superintendent of Mount McKinley National Park; Stephen T. Mather, director; Charles G. Thompson, superintendent of Crater Lake National Park; Horace M. Albright, superintendent of Yellowstone National Park; John R. White, superintendent of Sequoia National Park; Arthur E. Demaray, assistant director; Ernest Leavitt, assistant superintendent of Yosemite National Park; W. B. Lewis, superintendent of Yosemite National Park.

attitude, a feeling of "What's my job? Let me get on with it." Just listening to the president's fireside chats was an inspiration.

But if the fireside chats alone didn't turn us on, the CCC idea certainly did. The first official inkling I got of just what might happen was in a memorandum that Director Albright wrote to Senior Assistant Director Arthur Demaray on March 13, 1933:

> I was talking to Judge Finney last night and he told me that he was one of the men who drafted the $500,000,000 bond issue relief bill. He said that it is to be administered by the Secretaries of War, Interior and Agriculture. It contains authority for almost all kinds of public works, including road and trail building. He said the word "reforestation" will permit the cleaning up of old forests, removing dead and down timber, installation of protection facilities, as well as planting of young trees. I suggest that you wire Coffman to get up a reforestation or forest improvement budget for the Park Service, this is to include cleanup of construction areas, of timber around the west entrance of Glacier Park. It should also include cleanup of reservoirs such as Jackson Lake and Sherburne Lake in Glacier Park.
>
> There is no way of course of telling how much money will be allotted to the National Park Service. It will all depend upon the showing we make as to the need of the people in the neighborhood of the parks and the plans that we have for doing the work. Also we can point out that in Grand Canyon and Glacier we could use large numbers of Indians on roadside cleanup.

Obviously there was a lot of guesswork in Albright's memorandum, but he was out to get information in order to justify a good, sound park program should the funds suddenly become available.

The idea of creating a Civilian Conservation Corps wasn't an overnight decision. On at least four occasions before assuming the presidency, Roosevelt had outlined in public addresses certain ideas that appeared to presage his recommendations concerning the establishment of the CCC. In his acceptance speech in Chicago he stated that he had very definite plans for the conservation of human and natural resources on a national scale. Then in a speech he gave in Atlanta he gave his views concerning the conservation of forests. That was followed by a talk he gave in Boston in which he proposed a plan for employing men at public works that would benefit the nation. Finally, in his inaugural address he reiterated his views on putting the unemployed to work on projects that would be of value to the nation. Of course, we all knew that as governor of New York he had been very much interested in forest preserves.

On March 13, just nine days after Roosevelt was inaugurated, an unemployment bill that included work proposals similar to those finally assigned to the CCC was introduced in Congress, but because of considerable opposition it was withdrawn. Reintroduced on March 21, the act passed. It was signed on March 31, 1933. On March 14, the day after the first bill was introduced, however, the president had issued a memorandum for the secretary of war, secretary of the interior, secretary of agriculture, and secretary of labor:

> I am asking you to constitute yourselves an informal committee of the Cabinet to coordinate the plans for the proposed Civilian Conservation Corps. These plans include the necessity of checking up on all kinds of suggestions that are coming in relating to public works of various kinds. I suggest that the Secretary of the Interior act as a kind of clearing house to digest the suggestions and to discuss them with the other three members for this informal committee.

I have nothing in my records that would indicate just what this committee did; but I would assume, inasmuch as the first bill was introduced on March 13, withdrawn, and reintroduced on March 21, that the changes made in the bill during that week were the result of recommendations made by this committee of departmental secretaries. It actually took eighteen days for the CCC act to get through Congress; that is, eighteen days from the day the first bill was introduced on March 13 until March 31, when the president signed the act. Still, that was very fast in terms of legislative enactment.

Director Albright was prepared. By Thursday, the sixteenth, he had written a memorandum to all field officers informing them of the possibility of getting some of the $500 million fund for parks. He said that there was no way of telling from the Washington office just how much money we could use and that he was depending on the field for help. But, he said, he'd already compiled some estimates: about $7 million for major roads, $1 million for minor roads and trails, another $2 million for physical construction, or a total of around $10 million. He was going to direct Chief Forester John Coffman to set up a program on forest protection and cleanup. Without knowing anything about the CCC program at that time, he told the field officers to be sure to find out how many relief cases there were around the parks, both common laborers and skilled tradesmen, and to break the lists down to show those with families and those who were single. He also asked them to supply any other information on the conditions around the parks, because he felt that most likely we would be given money to do such jobs as we could do in the parks with the labor available in the vicinity.

Coffman wired back from the San Francisco office on the eighteenth saying that he was working on a forest cleanup program along park roads, with a lot of help from Chief Engineer Frank Kittredge and Chief Landscape Architect Tom Vint, but that the costs would run over one million dollars. He also stated that Kittredge was working on an estimate of the man-days required for other kinds of cleanup in all the parks. On March 28, Coffman advised the Washington office that his program was on the way in, that it was going to run over two million dollars, and that Kittredge's program was also being submitted. At the same time the director was getting a lot of mail from the parks wanting information and offering help. Finally, on April 1, Director Albright wired Kittredge in San Francisco that he wanted him and Coffman to be in the Washington office by Thursday, April 6, for a meeting.

Late on April 3, Director Albright reported to Secretary of the Interior Harold L. Ickes as follows:

> For the meetings today you asked me to represent you in the coordination of the forestry projects of the various bureaus of the department. This I have done and have attended two meetings at Colonel Howe's office at the White House, one at 12 o'clock noon and another at 3 o'clock this afternoon. There is to be another meeting tonight at 8 o'clock here in the Interior Department building.
>
> The head of the Civilian Conservation Corps is to be Mr. Robert Feckner (I am not sure of the spelling), who is to have an advisory group representing the Departments of Interior, Agriculture, Labor and War, one from each department. Col. Howe took the names of the representatives with him today and I explained that I was not sure that you intended me to represent you after today. The announcement of the organization will be made tomorrow at a press conference at noon. I will attend the meeting tonight.
>
> May I ask that you send word to Col. Howe before noon tomorrow of your wishes as to who will be your representative to assist Mr. Feckner in the formulation of the reforestation program? The meetings today were most interesting and I appreciate the opportunity very much.

Louis McHenry Howe, more often referred to as Colonel Howe, was a very close friend of the president. He had been a political adviser to FDR for years, dating back to the time Roosevelt went to Albany as a member of the New York state legislature and later as governor.

Albright also sent wires on April 3 to all the state park authorities telling them that the state parks would definitely come within the purview of the act that authorized the Civilian Conservation Corps and asking them to send representatives to a meeting in Washington on April 6. If they couldn't attend, because of distance or other reasons, he suggested that they authorize S. Herbert Evison to represent them. Evison was the secretary of the National Conference on State Parks.

The same day that the director sent his invitation to the state park authorities, he called a meeting in his office of several Park Service people, including myself. Up to this time I had been called upon now and then to help John Coffman and to do odd jobs, like everybody else in the office. These were the days when official job descriptions meant nothing. Everybody helped each other. But I remember distinctly the meeting called on April 3, because it marked the beginning of my association with the CCC program. At the meeting Albright told us that he would be the Interior Department's representative on the CCC Advisory Council. Coffman was told to get in touch with the bureaus of the departments that would have an interest in the CCC program and to ask them to designate the individuals who would handle the program for each bureau and who would comprise a small CCC council for the department.

The National Park Service's relationship with the state park systems had been one of informal, friendly interest, and we had no organization to carry out a work program. As we talked we began to realize that state park participation in the CCC would have to be administered apart from the going national park program. Each state had its own independent park organization, if it had a park organization at all.

Coffman was put in charge of National Park Service CCC work and was also designated coordinator of the other bureaus of the department, reporting directly to Albright and representing him at CCC Advisory Council meetings when he could not attend. The director then gave me the responsibility of organizing the state park program. I was to report my work to Coffman so that when he prepared the department's total program there would be uniformity in the presentations. Coffman immediately spoke up and said that he would like to have me go with him to the CCC Advisory Council meetings to supply details of the state park program if any questions came up.

Director Albright then suggested that I get in touch with Herb Evison and see whether he could give us part-time service because he was familiar with the conditions in the states. From our discussions there had emerged the idea of establishing districts for the state park CCC administration, which would bring many decision responsibilities closer to the field operations. It was decided to establish four districts: one on the West Coast, one in the Rocky Mountain region to include the Utah Basin to the southwest, one in the Mississippi River valley between the Alleghenies and the Rockies, and one on the East Coast. Albright suggested Lawrence C. Merriam, of San Francisco, as district officer for the western district, Herb Maier for the Rocky Mountain district, and Paul Brown for the midwestern district. Albright suggested that we invite the director of state parks for Pennsylvania to head the eastern district.

The rapidity with which the program took shape in one afternoon was most interesting. No doubt Albright had given the subject a great deal of thought and study, although when he opened the discussion one would have thought it was brand new.

Evison and I got together the next day and worked out an arrangement under which he would spend half of his time with us. That arrangement didn't last long, because within a few days he was spending the greater part of the day with us. Herb knew the state park people, he was a former newspaperman and a good writer, and to the Park Service he was a godsend.

Paul Brown, one of the four proposed district officers, was Colonel Richard Lieber's right-hand man in the Indiana state park system, one of the best in the country. Since he lived in Indianapolis, we decided that city was a good

S. Herbert Evison and Wirth stand before the power plant installed by the army for the CCC camp in the area known as the "basin" near the top of Chesos Mountain, at that time a Texas state park. Later it became a part of Big Bend National Park.

place for the midwestern district headquarters. Lawrence Merriam, a forester in private practice and a capable administrator, agreed to take the West Coast district, with offices in San Francisco. Herb Maier, an excellent architect who had done some work for the National Park Service, agreed to take the Rocky Mountain district, with headquarters in Denver. The director of state parks in Pennsylvania, J. M. Hoffman, took the eastern district temporarily and operated out of our Washington office. These four men stayed on for two or three days after the meeting to work out the details of setting up offices, allotment of funds, and so on. We had been given an advance of CCC funds for the purpose of organizing our part of the program.

As yet, the CCC was vague in the minds of many who would ultimately be very close to it. On April 4, Superintendent Eivind T. Scoyen of Glacier National Park wrote a letter to Director Albright. He, like all the other superintendents, had been doing a lot of thinking about the new program, and he had a lot of work laid out but very little money and equipment. He wrote in part:

> Yesterday, when we were planning our job on the basis of covering not only necessary but desirable reforestation work in the park, we were astounded to find that it would require 14,000 men to really reach all objectives. We were going on the assumption that these men will not be hired locally, but will be sent in from centers of population and on the average will not be experienced in woods work. Such a situation will cut down the output by at least half over lumberjack crews. To have such a force in the park will not be at all practical and we finally arrived at the figure of 2,500 men as the maximum we can handle but will be greatly surprised if we got that many.

It is clear that Scoyen was thinking of a short-term program that would operate just through the available workdays in Glacier National Park during the summer months. He went on as follows:

> The question which seems to be causing the most concern not only among ourselves, but others who may have some of this work in charge, is that of supervision. It would appear that the only practical solution would be to allow us to hire the foremen and other overhead at the going rates of pay. Unless this is done it is recommended that the crews be completely organized before they arrive in the park and that park officials will not be held responsible for the *amount* of work turned out. If we are to be responsible for this it would appear that it will not only be justice to let us hire the bosses, but to give us some authority to handle discipline. . . . Although we could equip a crew of about 600 men out of our warehouse with but little expense for some necessary items on which we are short, it will seriously cripple our future operations if this is not replaced as it will be worn out by the end of the year. If the Public Works program comes through later we will need this equipment on other projects.

Scoyen emphasized points that were unquestionably important, but little did he and others know how the CCC was going to be organized.

On April 5, as a result of the White House conference on April 3, an executive order by the president outlined the organization and administrative procedure for carrying out the provisions of the CCC act. This order provided for a director and fixed his salary; it established an advisory council, authorized the expenditure of funds, provided for supplies and materials, and determined the procedures for reimbursement.

On the same day, the new director of Emergency Conservation Work, Robert Fechner, called the first meeting of the CCC Advisory Council. The secretary of war appointed Colonel Duncan K. Major, Jr., as his representative on the council; the secretary of agriculture appointed R. Y. Stuart, chief forester of the Forest Service; the secretary of the interior appointed Horace M. Albright, director of the National Park Service; and the secretary of labor appointed W. Frank Persons. Nobody knew Bob Fechner or what he had

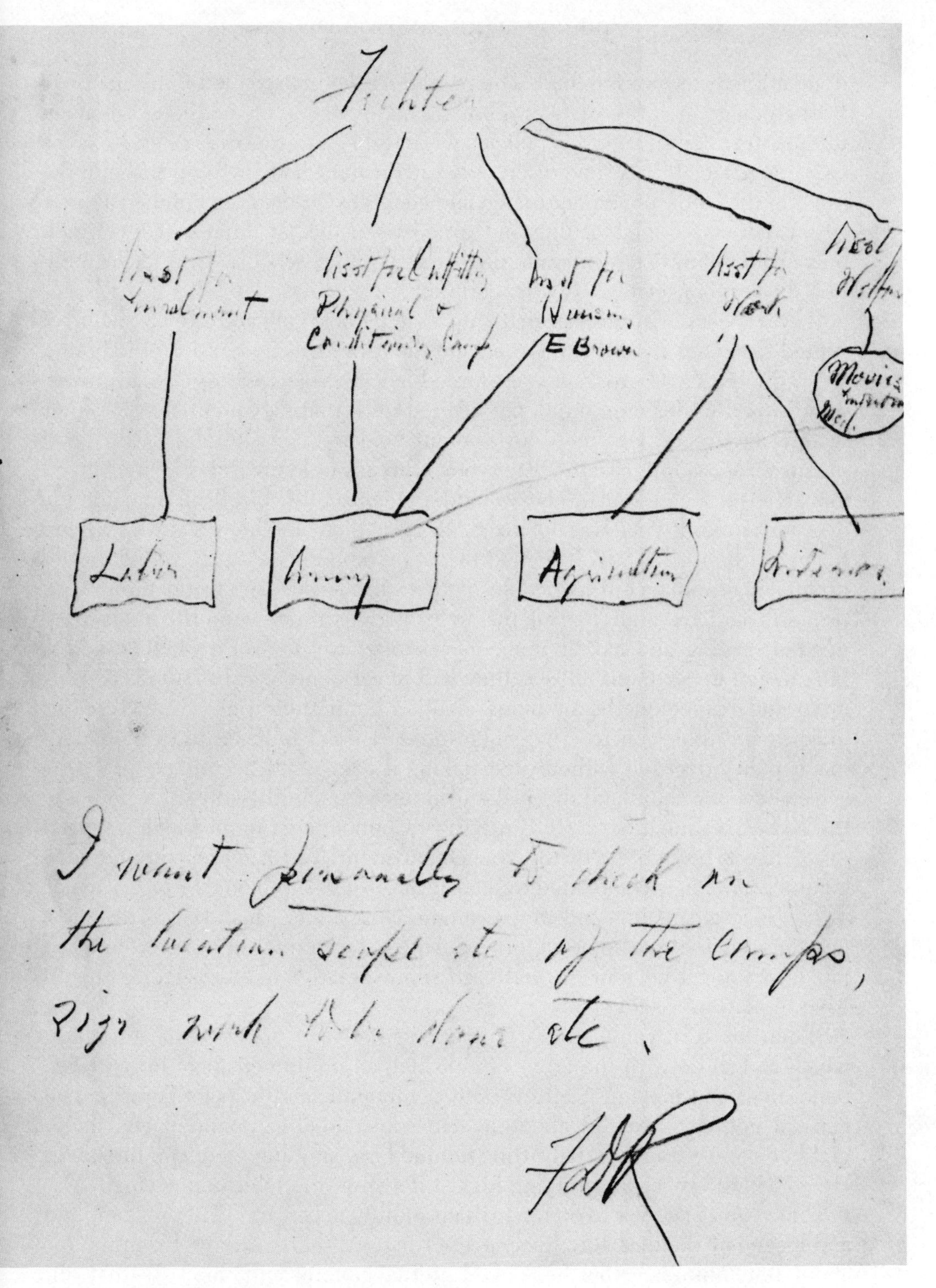

President Franklin D. Roosevelt quickly sketched this organization chart of the Civilian Conservation Corps during a meeting with the department representatives early in 1933.

done in the conservation field. The president even misspelled Bob's name on a rough diagram of the CCC proposal he had penciled on a desk pad, making it "Fechter." Yet he and his policies were the key to success or failure of the CCC program. It was soon disclosed that Fechner had come up through the ranks of the labor movement to become general vice-president of the International Association of Machinists. He had risen to that important level with only an elementary education in the Georgia public schools. He had a reputation for fairness, tact, and patience in all his dealings.

It was Fechner's fairness that impressed Roosevelt and Howe, who resented the attack by William Green and the American Federation of Labor on the proposed CCC program as a "forced labor" project whose "dollar a day" wage would undermine union pay scales. With that viewpoint Bob Fechner wholly disagreed. He knew little about conservation, but he was a good organizer and administrator. Everyone who got to know Bob Fechner loved him. He was a gentleman, always kind and courteous, but firm; he made his decisions promptly; he was not averse to discussion; and he was always willing to correct himself if he felt he had made a wrong decision. He relied on the professional and technical people of the various bureaus to do their work properly and devoted his talents to providing them with the tools they needed, urging and aiding them in a subtle way to work together across bureau and department lines as they had never done before. He was considerate and respected the opinions of others and their right to analyze his policies and offer constructive suggestions. I don't believe he ever made a major policy decision without first talking it over with the council.

Yet Fechner could and did make firm decisions on the spot, and he made them stick. I remember a CCC Advisory Council meeting in which a special problem was brought up by the War Department. The army representative, a general, came in accompanied by a fairly large staff—a colonel or two, a major or two, and a captain—and they brought along a lot of material. After a few opening remarks and some reports, Fechner started calling on us around the table, as was his custom, so that each representative of a department could have his say.

When his turn came, the army representative expounded his problem, which had to do with the army establishing an equipment pool for all CCC equipment and moving it into various compounds and forts for repairs. The general got very excited about it. He spoke loudly, pounded the table, grabbed papers from his staff sitting behind him, and flung them on the table. He concluded by again bringing his fist down on the table and saying, "Mr. Fechner, you have got to do this! It's absolutely necessary!" He then stopped and looked at the director. Bob Fechner had sat there, quietly listening, for about ten minutes. Now he looked at the general and said, "Is that all, General?" The general said, "Yes," and slammed the table again. Bob Fech-

Robert Fechner, director of the Civilian Conservation Corps, 1933 to 1939.

ner replied, "I ain't gonna do it!" Those words left the general dumbfounded.

Fechner turned to the representative of the Education Bureau and asked whether he had anything to bring up, and the reply was, "No, sir." He then went to the man from the Labor Department, who answered "No, sir." Then he came to Fred Morrell, of the Agriculture Department, and me. While we did have a few little things to discuss, we felt it best not to bring up anything, and both of us replied in the negative. With that, Bob Fechner took the gavel, pounded the table, and said, "Meeting adjourned." He got up and walked out, and so did we, leaving the military sitting there. It was a most startling performance, and a very effective one. As I recall, Fechner never did reconsider that subject.

Fechner was in his late fifties when he took the job, and I really believe he undertook the task primarily because he liked people, especially young people, and he felt that he could do something to help them. One of the things he wanted to do more than anything else was to inspect the camps, talk with the boys, and make sure that they were well taken care of. He believed they should work, but he also felt that they should get everything they possibly could out of the CCC experience. He strongly supported and encouraged education for the young men in the camps. He felt that the CCC, besides improving our natural resources, had a responsibility to teach the boys how to work and do a good job. He encouraged them to take pride in their accomplishments. He approved the employment in each camp of eight or ten "Local Experienced Men" (LEMs)—older, unemployed craftsmen who could guide the boys in doing skilled work such as carpentry, masonry, and the like.

Even though Bob had been an important labor figure, he objected when some union organizers attempted to move in on the CCC program in New England to form a union among the boys. The organizers got into two or three camps and met with the boys, but when word of this got to Fechner, he put a stop to it immediately. He didn't waste any words or even call a hearing. His decision was made on the premise that the government was doing everything that could possibly be done for these boys—they were happy; they were getting good food; they were sending money home to their parents; they were getting an education to the extent that was possible; and they were contributing in a good, healthy way to the conservation needs of the country and to their own well-being. There was no need for a union, as far as he was concerned. He sent orders to the camps to keep the union organizers out and gave instructions that if any of the boys joined a union they were to be sent home.

Often when he went on a trip to inspect the camps, he would take Mrs. Fechner along, together with her sister, and his secretary, Mrs. Holbrook. In the work-camp atmosphere—where there were anywhere from 150 to 200 young men working, day after day, month after month, under the management of men—it wasn't always the easiest situation to handle. Looking back at it, however, I believe that bringing these ladies into the camps was really a very nice thing to do. Their presence lent an air of dignity and a bit of homey atmosphere.

Fechner was very strict regarding the hours the boys were to work. He wanted them to have time off for study and for recreation. For the later, there was hardly a camp that didn't have facilities for volleyball, softball, and baseball. Boxing too was a popular sport. It was suprising to some of us that many of the young men who showed up in the camps were illiterate. Bob Fechner made it clear that he wanted the army and supervising forces to do everything possible to see that nobody left the CCC without mastering at least the fundamental elements of reading and writing.

A book entitled *The New Dealers,* published in 1934 by Simon and Schuster, which preserved the author's anonymity under the cognomen "Unofficial Observer," had the following to say about the Fechner character and personality:

At first the Army, which organized and officered the camps, tried to turn the CCC into a purely army project. It found that this quiet, stolid, friendly man, with his heavy spectacles and drooping head, could not be outwitted or bamboozled by even the highest-ranking generals. He is no policy-maker, no brain-truster, no administrative miracleman. He is simply one of the storm troopers who undertook an unprecedented job and did it well. The CCC experiment is one of the few completely successful emergency measures in our history.

The same day, April 5, that the CCC Advisory Council was established, the War Department informed the commanding generals of the corps areas that the Department of Labor would be responsible for the selection of the CCC candidates; that the initial national enrollment would be twenty-five thousand unmarried men ages eighteen to twenty-five with dependent immediate relatives, prorated among seven corps areas; that each corps area would be responsible for taking over the men from the selecting agency, making preliminary physical and mental examinations of the applicants, transporting accepted enrollees to designated camps, making further physical examination, and transporting rejectees back to points of acceptance; and that each corps area would control and allocate housing, food, clothing, equipment, medical care, and authorized allowances. It further stated that the primary mission of the army was to organize the members of the CCC into self-sustaining units for future work, to carry out physical conditioning, and to maintain high morale.

Also on April 5 a meeting of the representatives of established unemployment relief organizations in the sixteen cities from which the first twenty-five thousand men were to be selected was called by the Department of Labor to discuss organization plans and policies. These representatives agreed to assume the responsibility for selection and start such action the following day. On April 6 the first public announcement by the director of the CCC outlined the proposed program, and the selection process began in the designated cities. The press also stated that Horace Albright would be Secretary Ickes's representative on the council.

On April 8, R. Y. Stuart, chief of the U.S. Forest Service, sent a memorandum to Howe at the White House describing a method of operation, which he stated was concurred in by Albright of the Interior Department, that they felt would meet the president's desire to have certain activities of the camps handled by the army. The memorandum recommended that the army transport the men to the camps, feed them, clothe them, provide education, and take care of the incidental expenses of the operation of the camps, but that the agencies for which the camps worked be given full control over the boys during the workday. This arrangement would provide good training for a large number of army officers, especially in the junior grades up through the rank of major. Since the armed forces were very short of funds, the CCC would reimburse the army for their salaries.

On April 10 the secretary of the interior issued an order officially appointing Director Albright of the Park Service as the department's representative on the CCC Advisory Council. The associate director of the Park Service, Thomas Havell, of the General Land Office, and J. P. Kenney, director of forestry for the Indian Service, were designated alternates. The chief staff officer, as previously decided, was to be John Coffman. Just about this time the director of the CCC, Bob Fechner, in consultation with representatives of interior, agriculture, and war, established regional coordinators, using Forest Service people with headquarters established in the various army corps areas, to represent and coordinate the interests of all CCC agencies.

April 10 was the big day of reckoning between the representatives of the four departments on the CCC Advisory Council. Practically the whole day was taken up with meetings that lasted into the night. The morning was devoted to reviewing memorandums by the various bureaus of the departments in preparation for a meeting of the department representatives with Howe at the White House executive offices at three o'clock that afternoon. The purpose of that meeting was to try to straighten out many things that were in conflict between the departments, and it was very successful, although Fechner was ill and could not attend. It was understood that Howe was going to keep out of the picture as much as possible now and turn the full responsibility over to Fechner, who would report directly to the president. The technical agencies were going to run the work, and the army was going to run the camps.

The president had agreed, according to Howe, that a military officer would be normally the head of a camp. But there was to be no interference, direction, or suggestion from the military as to what work should be assigned the enrollees. Howe stated that when the work agencies took charge at the work hour the men were to be under the orders of the representatives of those agencies until they were back in camp. The technical agencies were to help the military in providing off-work activities for the boys and cooperate and help in every way they could. The money would be handled by the military, and the army paymaster would make all payments for both the technical agencies and the army through a voucher system. Howe also made it clear that the army could use some of the camps on their own reservations for forestry work but not for any other purpose. He announced that the president had approved, on the previous Saturday, April 8, some 107 camps located in the eastern part of the United States. The Forest Service people were also told that the president hoped that service would be able to get some of the money back for work done on state forests but nothing was mentioned about state parks. The Forest Service told Howe this was almost impossible to do, but he told them to try.

After the meeting the technical agencies adjourned to Fechner's hotel room and gave him a rundown on what had taken place. He informed us that he wanted to make all announcements of camps to be established so that there would be uniform procedure and no conflicts. That very day Fechner issued a press release to the effect that the first fifty camp sites had been selected and approved.

While these meetings were going on, Frank A. Kittredge and C. Duncan Montieth, of the National Park Service, were having discussions with Colonel Duncan Major, Jr., who was representing the secretary of war. They couldn't seem to get together on whose jurisdiction the men should be under while they were in the field. In fact the military, through Colonel Major, said there was no alternative but for the army to have full charge of the men at all times. The colonel's position was not in accordance with the understanding outlined by Stuart and Albright to Fechner, which had his approval, nor was it in conformity with what they understood Howe had agreed to when speaking for the president. A meeting was held that evening at eight o'clock with the chief of staff of the army and again this point could not be resolved. After meeting with the chief of staff, the technical people met again and went over their various procedures to see how they could eventually straighten out the army as to jurisdiction over the work program. The technical agencies began to feel that if they didn't have control of the men on the job it would be best for them not to have any camps.

On April 12, Chief Forester R. Y. Stuart wrote a memorandum to Colonel Major:

> In accordance with our conversation over the telephone this morning, I submit the following suggested paragraphs for insertion in the instructions prepared by you which were under discussion yesterday in Mr. Fechner's room. This language is believed preferable to that which you proposed last night in that we believe it defines more clearly the exact authority which will rest with the representatives of the Departments of Agriculture, Interior, and the States.
>
> The suggested language has been concurred in by the Interior Department through Mr. Kittredge, acting for Mr. Albright:
>
> The Representatives of the Department of Agriculture, the Department of the Interior, or the State, in charge of the conservation work to be done from the work camp shall fix the daily hours of work, subject to a maximum of eight hours per day, five days per week, except in cases of emergency such as forest fire suppression.
>
> The Departments of Agriculture and Interior, or the State, through their authorized representatives, shall furnish all necessary technical and supervisory force for the direction of the conservation work projects, shall plan and direct the work, and shall have complete and exclusive control of the enrolled men and hired personnel while on and going to and from the work except for such measures as the Army officer in charge of the camp may find it necessary to take in the event of serious breeches of discipline during working hours.

There's a note on the bottom of this memorandum that reads, "O.K.'d by Mr. McEntee for Mr. Fechner, and Col. Major says it coincides with their views (as changed!)." The initials, C.M.G., are those of Chris Granger, assistant chief forester of the U.S. Forest Service, the chief forester's alternate on the CCC Advisory Council and a very highly respected individual.

All during the time these meetings were going on, discussions were hot and heavy over details, many of which are not mentioned here. The information was being fed to the field; responses were coming back into the Washington office; contacts with the states were being established and maintained, offices set up for handling the state work, and staff appointed; and camp application forms were designed, sent to the field, returned with recommendations, and submitted to Fechner for approval. The president had very definite ideas about when he wanted the first camps in operation.

On April 13, in a long letter to the field, Albright pointed out that major changes would have to be made in the work program and consequently in camp locations in order to meet the president's requirements. The Emergency Conservation Work Camps would have two hundred men each, and the available money was to be spent establishing the greatest number of camps possible; therefore the program would have to be revised where necessary to restrict the purchase of expensive equipment in lieu of manpower. The camp size required dropping some projects and replacing them with projects that would require two hundred workers for at least a six-month period. It was realized that some trucks would be necessary to transfer workers, but if possible such equipment would be rented locally.

Albright explained that the purchases would be handled through the army paymaster and went on to say that it hadn't been determined whether we could buy our own tools or whether they'd be purchased through the army. What finally happened was that our request went in to the military, and the military did supply a certain amount of material and tools, such as shovels, from their warehouses. But the handles of the shovels and parts of other pieces of equipment they furnished were in a deteriorated condition—it turned out that the tools and equipment came out of the army stockpile left over from World War I—and the army replaced the items using funds from the CCC.

Director Albright's letter to the National Park Service's field people reflected the climate of the time and especially the spirit of the Park Service and those taking part in the CCC program. It conveyed the real underlying principle of the CCC concept.

> While this program involves hard work placed on the shoulders of every one of us, a large responsibility and a great deal of hard work, it also permits us to play a very important part in one of the greatest schemes ever devised for the relief of our fellow citizens in this present crisis and the rehabilitation of many young men of the nation

> who have as yet had no opportunity for decent occupation and have been the subjects of unfortunate attitude toward their native land and conditions in general. We therefore have a wonderful opportunity to play a leading part in the development of a wholesome and patriotic mental attitude in this younger generation.

In my opinion that defines the CCC. The effort was highly successful, and its by-product was one of the best conservation programs this country has ever had.

Albright wrote the secretary of the interior on April 17 urging him to sign a memorandum to the president informing him that compliance with the president's request to finish work at Shenandoah National Park was delayed because the land status had not been clarified. Albright also thought that the president should be informed that it would be almost impossible to continue any great amount of erosion repair work on the public domain land under the jurisdiction of what was known then as the General Land Office, because if erosion prevention structures were built they would need to be maintained. There was need for legislation, such as the Taylor Grazing Bill then before Congress, which would provide funds to undertake a program of this kind.

Another matter the Park Service director felt ought to be reported to the president was that the big coal fires in the public domain presented a very difficult problem. They were destroying vast amounts of good coal resources, but it was doubtful whether the crews of the CCC could successfully combat them. Rather than establishing a lot of camps to work on the fires, Albright proposed assigning a few camps to the coal fires as an experiment to see what could be done. We ended up putting a camp on the subsurface coal fire near Interior, North Dakota. Even with one camp working the entire CCC period, no dent was made in putting out the fire.

A fourth issue that the bureaus of the Interior Department wanted to have brought to the attention of the secretary and the president was their belief that the Indian problem in the CCC was a very difficult one under the program of alloting certain percentages of enrollees to the states. The Indian reservations are sparsely populated sections of the country, and therefore very few of the Indians could be reached under the state CCC quotas. Furthermore, there was a lot of unemployment among the Indians on the reservations, and the supervision of Indian camps ought to be under the Indian Service. To resolve this problem the Indian CCC program was turned over entirely to the Indian Service, which took charge of establishing camps, caring for the enrollees, and employing qualified Indians to plan and supervise the work. The Indian CCC also had its own quota of enrollees.

With the principal exception of those camps on Indian reservations and under the control of the Indian Service, each camp in the states had an officer of the army or navy in charge. He handled all camp matters and was responsible for the enrollees except when they were turned over to the representatives of the bureaus of the Departments of Interior and Agriculture for the purpose of carrying out work projects. The U.S. Forest Service administered the entire CCC program in Alaska and Puerto Rico, and the National Park Service administered it in Hawaii and the Virgin Islands.

One other exception was in effect for two years. Isle Royal National Park was authorized by Congress in March, 1931, and the state of Michigan agreed to acquire the necessary land and donate it to the federal government as a national park. In 1934 we placed two CCC camps there to clean up a lot of fallen trees and trash that had accumulated over the years from timber operations and had become a decided fire hazard. There were also a dozen or so old abandoned buildings left by the timber and fishing interests. The only time the material could be burned without the risk of starting a forest fire was in winter. Because of the difficulty of servicing them during the winter months, the army did not want to operate the Isle Royal camps, and so we asked CCC Director Fechner to turn them over to the National Park Service for two years. We used ski planes to bring in supplies when the ice made it impossible to use boats. The army helped by furnishing the normal supplies and certain services, such as medical care.

In organizing CCC activities in state parks, we had to have some guidance from the president as to how far we could go in cooperating with the states. The question was coming up constantly in that frantic spring of 1933, and it was time to get advice in writing. Therefore, on April 28 the secretary of the interior addressed a memorandum to the CCC director pointing out the importance of state parks, the type of work that would have to be done in them, and how they could contribute to conservation of our natural resources in the same way as the national parks. Then he proceeded to give a list of the proposals that he'd like to have approved. His recommendations were approved by Fechner and the president on April 29.

This approval was a go-ahead signal for the development of the state parks in the United States, something that Steve Mather and Horace Albright had long considered a national need and an objective that they fostered and dreamed of when they established the National Conference on State Parks in 1921. It resulted in creation of many new state parks, the enlargement of existing parks, and the establishment of state park organizations.

In the first part of May, Director Albright offered the services of the national park naturalists and other rangers to the military to help in the CCC training program and in the recreation activities, although as it turned out this help was limited almost entirely to national park camps.

The president had set June 30 as the deadline by which to have 250,000 boys in camps and working. That meant the recruiting, physical examination, and orientation of enrollees, the forming of two-hundred-men units, transporting the units to field location, building camps, employing supervisory personnel, planning work programs, preparing detailed construction plans where needed, and purchasing equipment for at least 1,250 camps scattered throughout the nation on federal, state, county, and metropolitan properties to work on various kinds of conservation projects. The U.S. Forest Service also assigned a considerable number of camps to privately owned forest lands in accordance with their long-range forest protection programs.

On May 5 the CCC Advisory Council met with Fechner in Howe's office. At that time the departmental representatives were worrying about meeting the president's deadline. Howe asked them to submit to Fechner the following day a memorandum of problems that were at the critical point and needed immediate solution. W. Frank Persons, the council member from the Department of Labor, pointed out in his memorandum that as of midnight, May 1, only 1,875 of the 40,486 men accepted at the conditioning camps had been transferred to work camps. He reported that the Labor Department had done its work, having gotten the states to register the prospective CCC enrollees. The states were now complaining that the men were not being called up by the army because their conditioning camps were slow in moving men out to the work camps. Persons wrote:

> You will recognize that the organization we have created for the selection of men is a mighty engine of public opinion. It embraces the influential citizens in every township in all of the 48 states. Without exception, so far as I know, these men and women have embraced the opportunity with enthusiasm, and are increasingly gratified that they may have a part in this plan. They are seeking the best available candidates. Naturally, they are interested in these boys. They are likely to manifest very actively any dissatisfaction that they feel is justified, because their implied promises that jobs are soon to be available for the men selected cannot be fulfilled.

He also pointed out that the president, when he submitted the legislation to Congress on March 21, had stated that if approval to go ahead was given within two weeks, he estimated that 250,000 men would be given temporary employment by early summer, meaning June 30. The legislation had been placed on the president's desk on March 31, well within the two-week limit.

The representatives of interior and agriculture wrote Fechner urging that the CCC meet the June 30 goal and stating that the two departments were ready to help the army in the construction of the camps. The army could send out advance cadres of twenty-five to thirty men to the parks and forests and, along with park and forest personnel, put up the camps.

On May 8 the president issued the following executive order on the "Administration of the Emergency Conservation Work":

> By virtue of the authority vested in me by the act of Congress entitled "AN ACT For the relief of unemployment through the performance of useful public work, and for other purposes," approved March 31, 1933 (Public, No. 5—73d Cong.), and

supplementing Executive Order No. 6101, dated April 5, 1933, it is hereby ordered that:

(1) In view of the limitation prescribed by the said act as to the time when the conservation work provided for therein must cease, the Director of the Emergency Conservation Work is hereby authorized, empowered, and directed within the limits of the allotment of funds made to him to complete the establishment of his office in the District of Columbia and to employ such civilian personnel as he may deem necessary for the efficient and economical discharge of his duties.

(2) The Director is also authorized to issue orders for such travel of the personnel of his office as he may deem necessary in connection with the Emergency Conservation Work, the travel orders issued to prescribe a per diem in lieu of subsistence at the rates authorized by the Standardized Government Travel Regulations.

(3) The Director is further authorized to purchase from the Emergency Conservation Fund such supplies, stationery, office fixtures, and equipment as may be required for his office whenever such articles cannot be issued or transferred for his use from stocks of other executive departments or Government establishments in the District of Columbia.

(4) Civilian and military personnel now in the service of the United States will be utilized to the greatest extent possible; but where absolutely necessary to the proper conduct of the work of the Emergency Conservation Corps the Director and the Secretaries of War, Interior, Agriculture, and Labor are hereby authorized, empowered, and directed within the limits of the allotment of funds made to them, to employ in the District of Columbia, or elsewhere, such additional personnel as they deem necessary in connection with the conservation work, without regard to the requirements of the civil-service laws and regulations and the Personnel Classification Act of 1923, as amended. The rates of compensation will be fixed by the Director and the heads of the departments concerned subject to the approval of the President, and subject to the reduction prescribed in the act approved March 20, 1933 (Public, No. 2—73d Cong.), and payment for all such civilian services and the pay and allowances of reserve officers of the Army, including their travel allowances authorized by law, called to active duty for service in connection with the conservation work, shall be made from the Emergency Conservation Fund. A weekly report of all such appointments must be made to the President, giving the rate of compensation in each case.

FRANKLIN D. ROOSEVELT

The White House
May 8, 1933

There were some "doubting Thomases" who questioned whether the program would be a success or whether it could meet the president's requirements of having all the camps established in accordance with his commitment to Congress; nevertheless spirit was high. There were more optimists than pessimists, and they prevailed.

The workdays were long; they started early in the morning and went late into the night. We had a coffeepot, and one person was detailed to keep it going. We'd take a few breaks and send out for sandwiches for dinner. Saturday was for working, just as any other day. Even Sunday was sometimes a

The National Park Service's field and Washington staff established to administer state, county, and metropolitan park CCC camps. *Left to right, front row:* E. A. Pesonen, M. B. Borgeson, C. L. Wirth, H. Evison, H. Maier, R. H. Reixach; *middle row:* D. B. Alexander, G. Gibbs, F. Hearon, J. H. Gadsby, L. C. Merriam; *back row:* A. T. Lindstrom, H. E. Weatherwax, P. Brown.

workday, primarily for discussion groups, and sixteen-hour sessions were not uncommon.

Fechner passed on to the agencies such responsibilities as were necessary for compliance with the executive order and requested in a memorandum of May 10 that they submit to him by May 12 a complete outline of their plans and requirements to accomplish their part of the Emergency Conservation Work goal of putting 274,375 men in camp and at work by July 1. Of special interest was the report Fechner received from the chief forester of the Forest Service, who stated in part:

> Mr. Howe has recently expressed disapproval of efforts of others than yourself to expedite essential action at the White House but I doubt whether he understands fully the extent to which delay there has measurable effect on slowing down the entire machinery. For example, the failure to get approval of the rules and regulations governing use of emergency conservation work funds on state and private land

The CCC caused the author a lot of travel but also gave him a chance to stop by home once in a while to see his father and mother. There was a metropolitan park CCC camp in Minneapolis.

projects prevents our expending any money whatever in behalf of the projects which have been approved for these classes of lands. Pennsylvania, which had its camps approved first, is now in the position of having its men in work camps but unable to go out and work because authority has not been extended to purchase tools and can not be extended until the White House acts.

Under the CCC legislation camps were set up on county and municipal properties at the discretion of the president. On May 8 the secretary of the interior asked the director of Emergency Conservation Work for the authority to put camps in the county parks that were closer than state parks to centers of population, where conservation and the development of recreation facilities were highly important. He referred particularly to the Westchester County parks of New York, the Cook County parks of Illinois, and the Milwaukee County parks of Wisconsin, as well as those in the vicinity of Boston, Cleveland, Akron, and other cities.

Just how many camps had been established by June 30 varies according to different reports; the program was on too large a scale and progressed too fast to allow such pinpointing. Fechner's report to the president for the period April 5 through June 30, 1933, is probably the most reliable. It stated:

> The selection and enrollment of 250,000 unmarried young men between the ages of 18 and 25 years was initiated at once. On April 7, 1933, the first man was selected and enrolled for C.C.C. work. Ten days later, on April 17, the first 200-man C.C.C. camp was established at Luray, Virginia. Within 3 months the 250,000 young men, together with an additional 25,000 war veterans and 25,000 experienced woodsmen, had been assembled and placed in 1,468 forest and park camps extending to every section of the Union. Since July 1, 1933, the strength of the C.C.C. has averaged about 300,000. The highest strength present on any given date has been 346,000 for the C.C.C. proper and 361,000 for all the forest camps, including Indians and camps allocated to Hawaii, Puerto Rico, Alaska, and the Virgin Islands.

5

The Civilian Conservation Corps

The War Department was proud of its part in getting the Civilian Conservation Corps started and had a right to be. In a letter to CCC Director Bob Fechner dated July 1, 1935, the department gave an interesting account of the first CCC enrollment:

> On May 16th [1933] enrollment jumped 5,890 to a total of 62,450, the next day added 8,100 men, the next 10,500 men. On June 1st a peak daily enrollment of 13,843 men was reached. The average daily gain in actual strength for this period was 8,700 men. During part of May 150,000 men were in reconditioning camps being organized and equipped for the field. By June 7th, 253,200 men had been enrolled, and by July 1, the enrollment of local men had increased this figure to 296,700. Of these, after deducting losses from all causes 270,000 men occupied 1,331 work camps in the forests of the country by June 29th. 55,000 men in 335 companies were transported from the eastern corps area to the far western states of the Ninth Corps area.
>
> A comparison with world war accomplishments is interesting. During the corresponding first three months of the world war, the War Department mobilized by July 1, 1917—117,000 men in the regular army, 58,000 in the National Guard, and 6,000 in the National Army, or a total of 181,000 men. By that date less than 16,000 men, mostly regular army units had embarked for France.

The processing of over 250,000 men in such a short time was no mean accomplishment. Before his enrollment each one of those young fellows was personally interviewed by welfare officials, who determined that the man needed employment and that his family was in need of substantial support from his earnings. The interviewers had to establish that the enrollee was a citizen of the United States, between seventeen and twenty-eight years old, and unmarried. They had to be satisfied that the enrollee, if finally accepted, could perform hard work without injury to himself and was free from communicable disease. They obtained a good record of his past experience, his interests, and his general character.

If the welfare officials felt the man met CCC standards and qualifications, they asked him to report for medical examination to make certain that his health would permit him to do hard work. Only after having passed the army's physical examination was the man formally enrolled in the Civilian

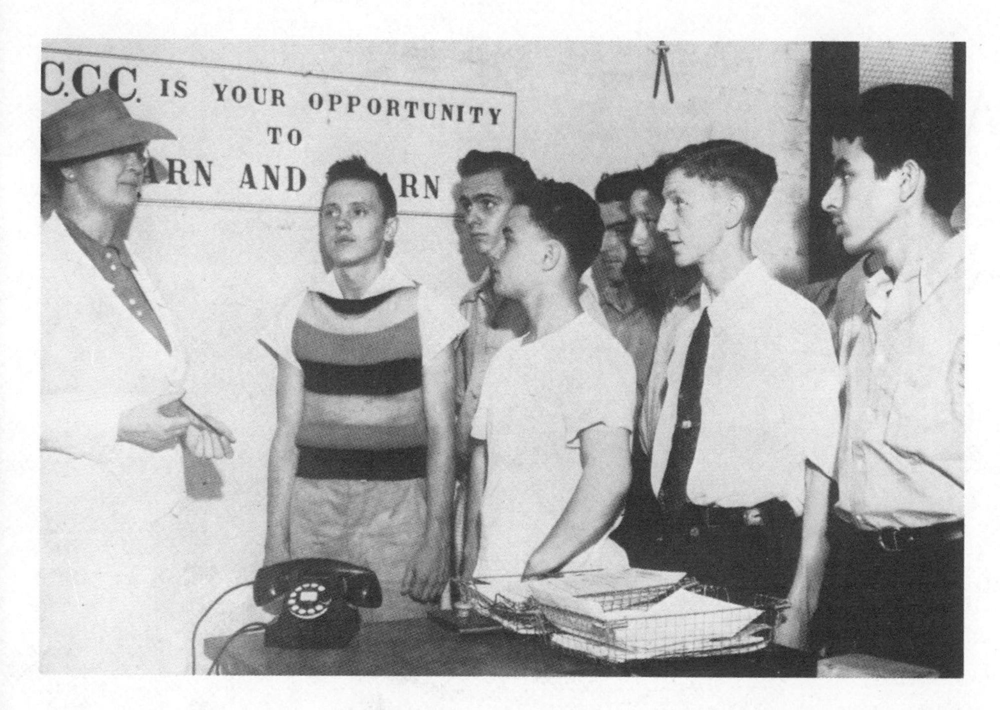

After personal interviews, CCC enrollees were given information and guidance by a welfare official.

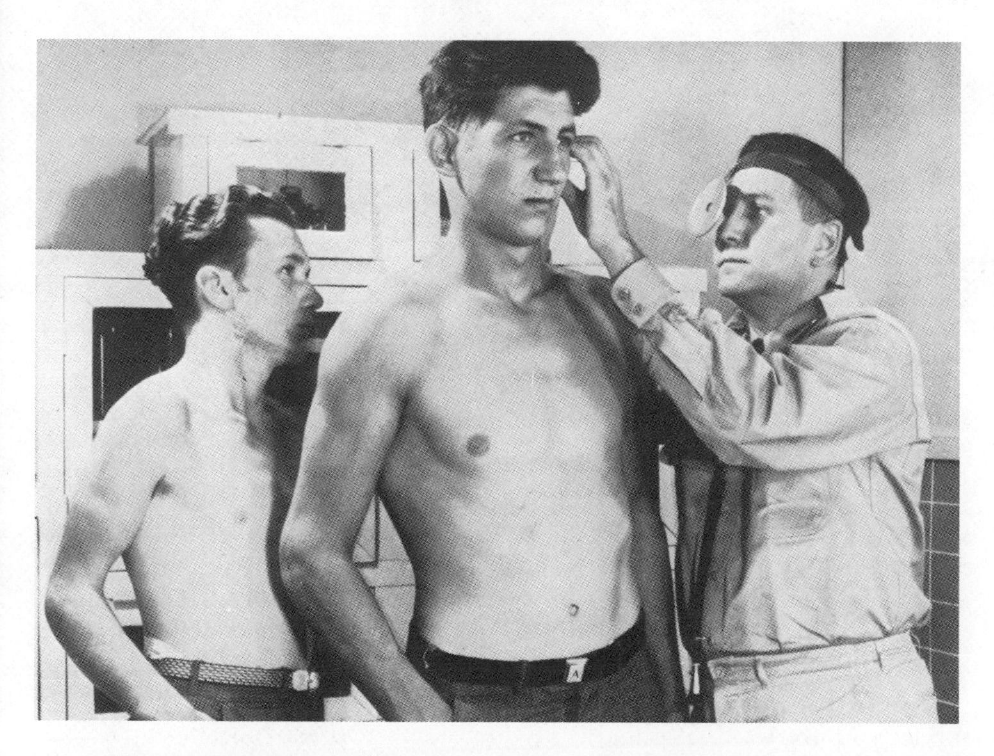

An important step for the CCC enrollee was his physical examination before entering on duty.

A typical CCC camp provided housing for two hundred enrollees, quarters for the military camp commander and staff and the supervising agency's superintendent and staff, medical services, recreation facilities, equipment storage and repair shops, and a mess hall.

Conservation Corps. He was then given a good meal and assigned to a group of young men who were sent with an officer or leader aboard a train or bus to a Civilian Conservation Corps camp.

When the young man arrived at camp he was furnished with complete outfits of work and off-duty clothes and was assigned a bed in one of the barracks. The clothes he wore on arrival were put away until he finished his service with the CCC. Within twenty-four hours after arriving at camp he was

All set to go to work, the new CCC enrollee totes away his issue of clothing and bedding.

vaccinated against smallpox and given his first anti-typhoid inoculation. He was also given a pneumonia inoculation if he volunteered for it. On the day the enrollee arrived at camp the company commander welcomed him and explained the general rules of the camp. Then the enrollee, depending on his individual need, was given one to three weeks of physical conditioning before joining the work crews. This conditioning was done under the camp commander's supervision and consisted of light duties around the camp along with good food, regular hours, sufficient sleep, and medical observation. In the beginning these conditioning periods were given at a military post. This

A CCC crew grading an overlook along a mountain road.

period provided an excellent time to instruct the enrollee in disease prevention and safety.

It is interesting to note some of the items that the military bought for the boys initially enrolled. About 1,061,000 pairs of service shoes were purchased for $2,824,000, or a little more than $2.66 per pair; approximately 295,000 raincoats, for about $953,000, or a little better than $3.16 each; and, the prize purchase, 3,600 motor vehicles, at a cost of a little more than $591 each. A sampling of some 15,000 boys showed that they gained an average of .277 inches in height and 7.23 pounds in weight in the first six months in the CCC.

When the enrollee got adjusted to camp routine, he was interviewed by the educational adviser, who encouraged him to discuss his personal problems, if any, his family background, and his amibitions. He was apprised of the opportunities in camp and in the adjacent community for attending various classes and also of job activities that might be available to him. He was urged to avail himself of these opportunities although given to understand that participation in any of the educational programs was entirely voluntary. The educational adviser and the supervisory personnel would also encourage the enrollee to participate in recreational activities at camp. Most of the camps organized teams for basketball, baseball, and other sports and were equipped with such facilities as a library, recreation hall, and usually a little camp store, where the enrollee could get supplies or refreshments.

Because these camps were doing conservation work, the enrollee had a wonderful opportunity to learn about nature, particularly plant and animal life, and the supervisory personnel were happy to help him learn. There is the story about a CCC boy, stationed at a camp somewhere in the Southwest, who had been "raised on the sidewalks of New York" and had little experience with wildlife in its many forms. One day, when he brought a rattlesnake's rattle into camp and showed it around, his foreman anxiously asked how he got it. "Off a woim," he said casually. No doubt he was set straight.

After a young man had gone through his conditioning period, he was assigned to work projects which, so far as practicable, were related to his special interests. It is surprising how many of the men turned out to be excellent mechanics. In one of Director Fechner's reports he had a table entitled "The Number of CCC Enrollees Classified According to the Kind of Work which the Civilian Conservation Corps Service and Training Has Fit Them to Do in Private Employment." Under the general category of agriculture, fishery, and forestry, there were 2,085 trained in landscaping and as agriculture foremen, overseers, and farmers. There were 1,294 foresters, forest rangers, and timber cruisers. Under manufacturing and mechanical industry, specifically the building and hand trades, there were 153 blacksmiths, 1,600 carpenters, 100 electricians, a few hundred machinists, 65 plumbers, and 1,323 other building and hand trades. There were over 2,000

A job that required learning new skills: CCC crew lining a drainage ditch with stones and cement.

brick and stone masons, over 3,000 foremen in building and general construction, over 2,700 machinists in automobile repair shops, and so on and on over several pages. There were 754 bakers, over 10,000 cooks, over 300 barbers, over 3,000 first-aid men, orderlies, and male nurses, over 5,500 shipping clerks, and over 3,500 stenographers and typists. I think this will give some idea of the human and educational values of the CCC over and above the

Many long, hard hours of CCC work were devoted to protecting forested areas from forest and grass fires.

The CCC was always willing and ready to help in times of public need.

work accomplished. The approach and attitude of all those associated with the CCC instilled confidence and a desire for excellence and progress.

The success of the War Department and Labor Department in the vast initial CCC mobilization effort in turn placed a tremendous burden on the Department of Agriculture and Department of the Interior. In a very short period those departments, through their various bureaus, had to organize a work program for the CCC, decide where the camps were to be located, employ some 10,276 foremen (7 to a camp) and familiarize them with the work to be done, employ mechanics to take care of the equipment, and buy and assemble automotive equipment and tools so that the boys could be put to work when they arrived in camp. Looking back, I have often wondered how we ever accomplished it all. The burden was fairly equally divided among all the bureaus, and though some were assigned more camps than others, they also had a larger organization to start with. The bureaus were all suffering from cuts in personnel and funds in 1933, and each bureau had its own particular problems. The problems we were faced with in the Park Service, however, were almost insurmountable, especially since we had to establish from scratch a working relationship with the state park people.

After the big rush to get camps in operation by June 30, things began to settle down. There were 1,477 camps working in 39 states by that date, 245 under the Department of the Interior, 1,211 under the Department of Agriculture, and 21 on military reservations. Under agriculture there were 597 camps in national forests, 315 on state and private forest properties, and 299 on areas of other bureaus of the department. The U.S. Forest Service and its related areas in the state forests took the bulk of the camps, since they controlled a great deal more land than the national and state parks; moreover, the Forest Service had been aiding state forests for a number of years. The 245 Interior Department camps were distributed as follows: 70 in the national parks, 102 in state parks, and 73 with other bureaus of the department.

Once the first camp was established and operating in Virginia, President Roosevelt wanted to visit it to see how things were getting along. He traveled from Washington to Harrisonburg, Virginia, by train. At Harrisonburg a large crowd was on hand to greet and cheer him. The Roosevelt image—the smile and the cigarette in its holder—was very much in evidence. From there he went up to George Washington National Forest in the Massanutten Mountain Range, where the first CCC camp had been established and named Camp Roosevelt in his honor. He spent some time there and then went over to Shenandoah National Park at Big Meadows, where the first Park Service camp, Camp Fechner, was in operation. He got there in time for lunch and chatted with the boys.

One of the newspaper photographers took a picture of the president having lunch, with the boys standing several rows deep on three sides of the table

President Franklin D. Roosevelt made his first visit to a CCC camp, at Big Meadows in Shenandoah National Park, Virginia, in early summer, 1933. Seated at the table are *left to right:* Major General Paul B. Malone, commanding general of the Third Corps Area; Louis Howe, secretary to the president; Secretary of the Interior Harold L. Ickes; CCC Director Robert Fechner; the president; Secretary of Agriculture Henry A. Wallace; and Assistant Secretary of Agriculture Rexford G. Tugwell.

(see p. 104). Fred Morrell, of the Forest Service (my counterpart in the Department of Agriculture), and I got copies and had all of the dignitaries, with the exception of the president, autograph them. We then asked Mike Reilly, of the White House secret service detail, if he could get the president to autograph our pictures. Mike took the two pictures to the White House and for some time we heard nothing from him. Finally he replied, saying that the president would not autograph them until we got a duplicate copy for him with all the signatures on it. Of course, we dug out another picture, got it autographed, and sent it to the president, and then we got our copies back with the president's signature. His copy is now in his library at Hyde Park, New York. I gave my copy to Superintendent Taylor Hoskins of Shenandoah National Park to put in the Harry F. Byrd Visitor Center, which looks out over Big Meadows and is not far from the CCC camp where the picture was taken.

The four districts set up to handle state park work began operations on May 15. By that time the states had received camp application forms, and some state areas had been cleared for establishing camps. Of course, the better-organized National Park Service had no real trouble putting 70 camps into full operation by June 30. The last half of the first six-month period, from July 1 to September 30, was a time for settling down and getting ready for the second CCC period, which was to begin October 1. The state parks used this time to organize and prepare acceptable applications, looking toward an increase in the number of camps at the beginning of the second period. The camp allotments for that period afforded a better balance between the Departments of Agriculture and the Interior, giving agriculture 993, interior 440, and the other agencies and the military, 35. This brought national park camps up from 70 to 102, and state park camps from 102 to 263. Allotments to the other bureaus of the department remained approximately the same as in the first period.

The reasons for selecting six-month periods was never explained, but perhaps it was related to the fact that the CCC was never considered a permanent program and depended on emergency and temporary legislation for its existence. Furthermore, it was felt that the CCC was a stopgap employment opportunity and that a period of six months would be long enough for some enrollees, who could then find regular work in their home communities. No enrollee was permitted to serve more than four terms, or two years, and very few stayed that long. Some of them did so well, however, that they were taken on as foremen or LEMs by the supervising technical agencies. Although the six-month periods applied also to the appointed supervisory personnel, there was no limit on reappointment.

The requirement of operating by periods necessitated the submission of proposed work programs every six months and the moving of camps to accommodate work programs. After the first period all programs had to be submitted at least two months in advance of the beginning of a period, which meant that the departments had to get together and determine how many camps each department would have for its bureaus. When that was decided it was necessary within the department to settle on the allotment of camps among the bureaus. It was not always possible for the Departments of the Interior and Agriculture to agree on camp allocations, but they both objected to putting camps on military reservations. The Interior Department felt that the Agriculture Department, on the first go-around, actually took more camps than they deserved, although the Department of Agriculture did already have basic legislation to cooperate with the states and also had authority to cooperate with the owners of timberland. In the periods that followed, beginning with the second period on October 1, 1933, adjustments between the two departments—interior and agriculture—were worked out to the satisfaction of both.

The table on page 107 shows distribution of the work camps among the bureaus and the personnel directly connected with them as of the end of September, 1933.

The last three colums of the table will give the reader an idea of the size of the camps and of the number of supervisory personnel in the camps at the end of the first six-month period. The military camps are separated from the rest in order to give a more accurate picture, since the military camps served as stopover points for enrollees on their way to other camps. Some 2,000 of the 3,554 enrollees included in the chart under military camps were actually being cleared for transportation to other work camps.

The CCC program was gradually being accepted by the entire country. At first some communities didn't want CCC "vagrants" in their neighborhoods. That is a harsh way to put it, but many people at first thought that these boys were being picked up off the streets and put in the camps as a sort of punitive relief measure, equated with the handling of delinquents. But this idea was unfounded. The boys did a wonderful job; they were on the whole good, clean, hard-working, and friendly young men, who became a part of the communities in which their camps were located. When the workday was over and they had time off to go into town, they changed into neat, good-looking dress uniforms that they were proud to wear. The CCC as an organization earned a fine reputation, and, with due respect to all of us behind the lines, the boys themselves deserve a large part of the credit for its success. The program's success showed me that there is nothing wrong with the younger generation in a country like ours, where they have the opportunity to prove themselves. Everybody knows that not every individual can be a top person or leader but that each one can be respected for contributing his best to his community.

A Breakdown of the Work Camps
September, 1933

	Number of Camps	Number of Enrollees	Number of Supervisors	Average Number of Enrollees per Camp	Average Number of Supervisors per Camp	Average Number of Enrollees per Supervisor
Department of the Interior						
National Park Service						
National Parks	70	11,487	731	164	10.4	15.8
State Parks	105	17,230	1,095	164	10.4	15.8
Total	175	28,717	1,826			
Bureau of Indian Affairs	67	13,069	798	195.1	11.9	16.4
Bureau of Land Management	1	193	13	193	13	14.8
Total Department of the Interior	243	41,979	2,637	172.7	10.8	16.0
Department of Agriculture						
U.S. Forest Service						
National Forest	599	93,415	5,782	156	9.6	16.3
State Forest	332	53,556	3,304	161.3	9.9	16.3
Private Forest	327	54,878	3,046	167.8	9.3	18.0
Other	7	869	83	124	11.9	10.4
Total	1,265	202,718	12,215			
Bureau of Biological Survey	3	489	29	163	9.7	16.8
Total Department of Agriculture	1,268	203,207	12,244	160	9.7	16.5
Total CCC, not including Military	1,511	245,186	14,881	162.3	9.8	16.7
Military Camps	9	3,554	34	394.9	3.8	103.9
Total CCC	1,520	248,740	14,915	163.6	9.8	16.7

I have often wondered what a big-city boy's reaction was to the CCC camp environment and what long-range effect the experience had on the boys. In my files I find an article written by a man who went all the way from New York City to a Forest Service camp in Idaho ten miles from the nearest town. It was a big change for him. He tells of a certain amount of razzing he got from the camp old-timers when he arrived. But then he goes on and tells how, after some of the boys left when their six months were up and new boys came in by train, he took part as an old-timer in razzing them. He especially notes that the scenery was absolutely gorgeous. Part of his time was spent in building a road. Later he was made an aide to an engineer staking out a new road location. He apparently finished his six-month tour toward the end of March, having spent the winter in the cold but beautiful mountains of Idaho. He concludes with the following paragraph:

> Now that I am home again and look back at those six months, there are certain things that come to mind, making it clear to me to understand the meaning of the Civilian Conservation Corps. I don't think I could have spent six months of my life more profitably anywhere. It's an indelible experience in a young man's life. The physical benefits alone were worth my enrollment. I emerged stronger, hardier and proud of a better body. I would never discourage anyone wishing to join the C's. It's no place for anyone without the determination to take it and benefit by it. It makes a man out of everybody with guts. The outdoor life is healthy and inspiring. A city boy learns that the world is larger than just the city. This contact with nature and association with other boys broadens the mind and gives a deeper insight into life. CC life teaches a person to be independent, and shows the value of money. It gives boys time to think and plan a career in their minds. The C's had its faults, too, but its virtues far outweighed them. I sincerely believe that the C's has done more to rehabilitate and restore confidence in American youth than any other organization ever existing. It is a young man's best friend when he is out of a job and low in spirits—America should thank President Roosevelt for the Civilian Conservation Corps.

This paragraph is taken from "The CCC, Six Months in Garden Valley," by Donald Tanasoca, edited by Elmo Richardson, published in the summer of 1967 in the magazine *Idaho Yesterdays*.

Long after the CCC was closed out, many groups of enrollees and supervisory personnel got together to talk over the CCC days. One such gathering took place at Fort Pulaski National Monument, Georgia. National Park Service Superintendent Ralston B. Lattimore had taken great interest in the boys, most of whom were from the Atlanta area. After their CCC and World War II military service, they had settled down as businessmen, bankers, insurance men, and so forth. Several of them got in touch with Superintendent Lattimore to arrange a reunion back at Pulaski. They had several reunions over the years. In his report on the reunion of 1950, Superintendent Lattimore described what had happened to some of the men who had been in the CCC ten to fifteen years earlier.

Years after their CCC experience, former enrollees get together for reunions, such as this one at Fort Pulaski National Monument, Georgia.

After luncheon, while everybody was still seated at the tables in the club, I led an informal talk fest. The first senior leader, R. B. Whitworth, who came down with the camp from Cornelia in 1934, is now postmaster of the City of Lawrenceville, Ga. He described the origin of the camp and told what his experiences in the camp had meant to him in molding his life. Homer Hawkins, one of our guides, now has a successful insurance agency in Augusta, Ga. Hawkins served with the paratroopers and was among the first troops dropped in Holland. He was also in the famous battle of the Bulge. Herbert Anderson of Scott, Ga., formerly one of our boatmen, now operates a farm equipment agency and runs a successful farm on the side. Henry A. Heath, Edgefield, S.C., who baked his way through the CCC and the jungles of New Guinea, now owns a bakery in Edgefield and lives happily with an Australian wife. Veteran Kilpatrick of Savannah reminded me that I had given him a letter of introduction to an engineer at the Union Bag and Paper Corporation. He has been with that outfit 12 years and now holds a responsible position. Veterans Whittle, Tryon, and Seekinger are all salesmen at the Savannah Coca Cola Company each making more than $500 a month. John Martin, who was formerly a LEM, entered the army

Director Wirth finds that a CCC cap still fits Representative Edward R. Roybal, of Los Angeles, California, a former CCC enrollee.

as a private, was made buck sergeant next day, and within 2 weeks was shipped to North Africa on the tail of the invasion. He is now employed by the Corps of Engineers.

We were told of three boys who were killed in action during the war, and of one who had died a few months ago from tuberculosis contracted as the result of exposure in the Navy.

The national and state park CCC organization outgrew the Interior Department's CCC office in Washington and needed additional space. During the second period, in the fall of 1933, offices were leased in the Bond Building at Fourteenth Street and New York Avenue, N.W. The department activities stayed in the Interior Building as did the Park Service's Branch of Lands. As assistant director in charge of the Branch of Lands, now called the Branch of Lands and State Cooperation, I divided my time between the two buildings, putting Herb Evison in charge of the activities in the Bond Building when I was not there.

The arrangement we had with the states was the simplest and most satisfactory we could devise. It was actually an extension of the understandings that were developed in 1921 when the National Conference on State Parks was organized. There was no sign of any sort in that organization that indicated a desire on the part of the federal park people to take over the states' responsibilities or even to tell them what to do. Both federal and state people realized there was a lot to be gained by the exchange of ideas. So when the CCC was started it was only natural to assume that we should continue this mutually advantageous relationship.

While the army finance officer paid the bills, we asked the state authorities to act as our procurement agents. The CCC camps were turned over to them, and, although the camp superintendents and the technical men who supervised the work were paid out of federal funds, they reported directly to the state park authorities. Each period we would divide our money among all the camps on an even basis. The state park authorities knew how much money they had for each camp. I'm sure there were some camps that over-expended, but there was enough savings at other camps within a park authority so that overall each state stayed within the total amount allotted. In fact, after the second year we found that 5 per cent of our funds were unexpended at the end of the fiscal year, while certain very important jobs were actually being held up because of lack of funds. So the next year, on the advice of our fiscal office, I allotted 5 per cent more money than we actually had for allotment. At the end of that fiscal year we still had a big reserve, and important projects delayed, so the next year I allotted 10 per cent more. That time we came out with a relatively small reserve at the end of the fiscal year—about 1 1/2 per cent.

As explained earlier, the four district offices for the state, county, and metropolitan parks CCC program were established on May 15, 1933. Their main purpose was to process applications and give careful review and general supervision to planning and carrying out the work. The state park offices prepared project plans and took care of employment and procurement. We reasoned that the district offices, later designated regional offices, should be limited in size to be closer to the work. Therefore, as the state, county, and metropolitan camps increased in number, we established additional regions so that each would be assigned about fifty camps. There were as many as eight regions at the height of the program, and as few as four. The chart on page 112 indicates, by years, the variation in the number of camps assigned to the Interior Department.

The camp inspectors we hired to supplement our regular staff were professional landscape architects, engineers, or foresters with considerable experience. Although many of them had very little direct experience in park and recreation planning, development, and management, it did not take them long to adjust to park and recreation principles and requirements. Neverthe-

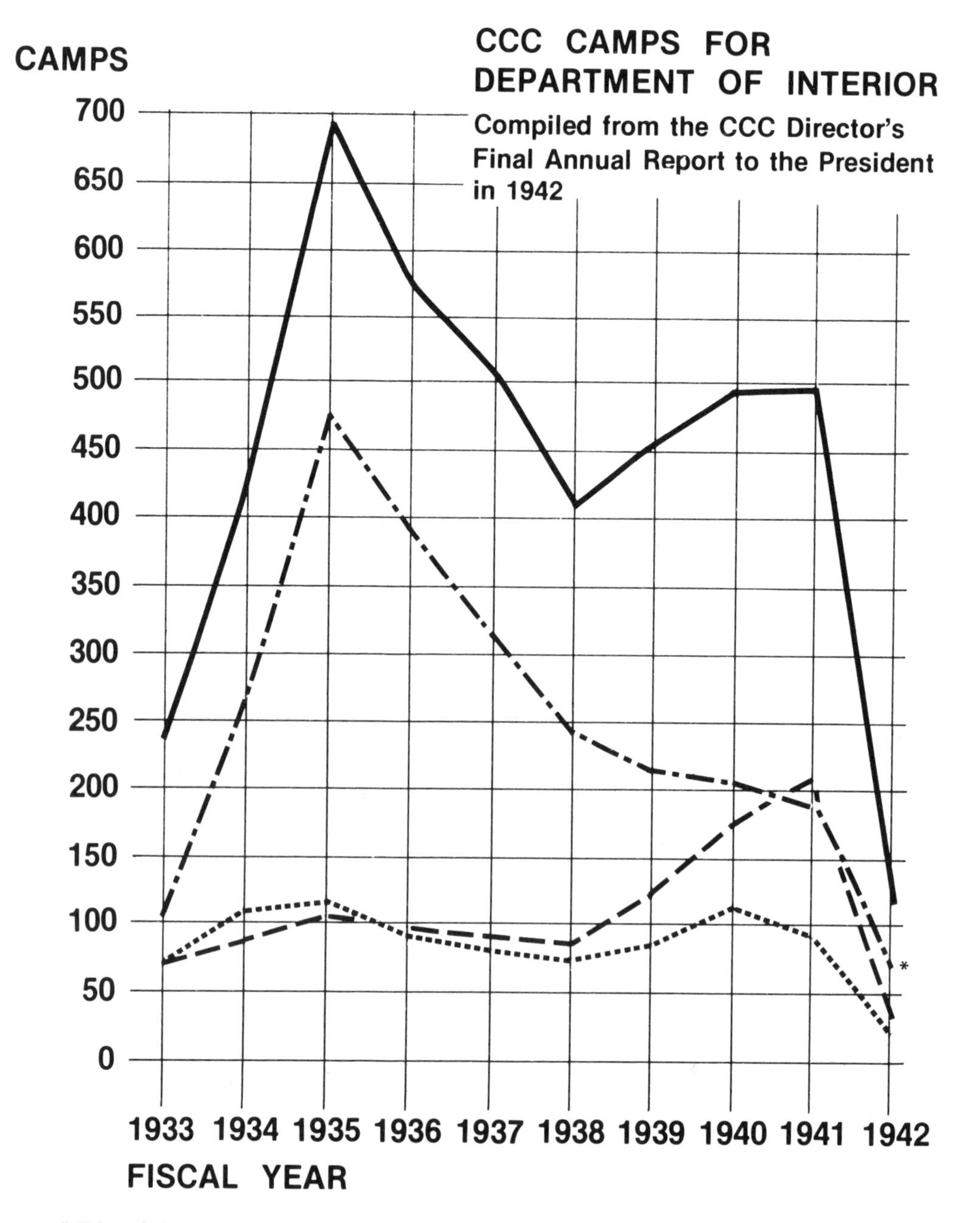

* Fifty of these camps were operated by the National Park Service on military reservations doing defense work.

TOTAL INTERIOR
STATE PARKS
NATIONAL PARKS
OTHER INTERIOR BUREAUS

less, it became necessary early in the state park program to call their attention to certain reports from several permanent Park Service field people, and from some inspectors, that the planning and development operation was not up to standard in the state parks. We were prompted to write a long letter to the regional officers and inspectors, and it proved very effective. They gave copies to the state authorities, who were eager to avoid losing any camps.

In the letter we stated that the park authorities in the states either hadn't understood or had failed to accept the fundamental principles of good land use planning and the problems of park development and sound management. Consequently large portions of the parks were being modified by unnecessary man-made intrusions that were costly and would needlessly increase maintenance and administrative costs in the future. We tried to point out that scattered, intensive uses meant increased costs in developing and maintaining roads, in water distribution, and in waste disposal. Such use would also increase fire hazards. We explained that the three basic essentials of a people's park are easy access, safe and abundant water supply, and adequate sanitary facilities. We clearly implied that if these essentials were not fully provided we would have to reassign the CCC camps. We also pointed out that many of the plans submitted for overnight accommodations looked like summer homes, whereas we were interested only in inexpensive accommodations, especially campgrounds. We discouraged construction of roads other than those that would provide access to points of intensive use, and we insisted that entrance roads be limited to the lowest possible number. We required that structures of long durability, such as those constructed of stone or masonry, be justified on a long-term basis and that all structures be designed to blend with the landscape. Further, we suggested that with a little thought the entrances to parks could be made unobtrusive and inviting rather than massive and forbidding. Although we did not say it in so many words, we strongly implied that these were the principles that would govern all future camp allotments, and the implication proved strong enough to improve all future applications for camps and to effect changes, where necessary, in the work programs of existing camps.

Twice a year we would call the procurement officers and regional directors into the Washington office for a week's seminar to discuss progress, new concepts, problems, and everything imaginable. Since our procurement officers were the state authorities, there were a lot of things we had to talk over besides the CCC—our recreational demonstration projects, state laws, nationwide studies, park management programs, methods of raising funds for land acquisition, to name a few. These discussions of major concepts looked toward the long-range evolvement of a nationwide system of parks for the American people.

At the request of various states, the National Park Service counseled them on drafting legislation to provide the necessary legal authority to plan, develop, and maintain state park systems. One state went so far as to include in its legislation a provision that the director of state parks be appointed by the governor subject to the approval of the director of the National Park Service. When the National Park Service learned of this, we immediately asked that the law be amended to rescind that provision and that the qualifications for the position be set forth in its place.

A couple of little instances in the summer and fall of 1933 helped to take some of the dreariness out of the workday and put a little spice and pleasure in its place. It was early in August, I believe, when a message came down to me via the secretary's office and John Coffman that President Roosevelt wanted to see me, but it gave no indication of what he wanted to see me about. Naturally I was somewhat apprehensive. I went to the White House at the appointed time and was ushered into the president's office. I was relieved to see him relaxed and smiling.

He asked about the CCC program in general, and then said, "By the way, I have a complaint from a congressman about a CCC work program in a state park in which you turned down the building of a road."

I said, "Yes, Mr. President, we turned it down, and did so in other state parks also." And I added, "At one of our meetings over here we were told that you would be quite insistent about not taking on big construction jobs like roads in the state park areas and even in the national parks and that the work of the CCC was supposed to be done with the least amount of equipment."

He smiled and said, "Well, that perhaps is so, but you can build fire trails, can't you?"

I replied, "Yes, sir, that's on the approved list of work."

He then looked at me and still smiling said, "I didn't say you couldn't build two fire lanes right next to one another did I?" And I said, "No, sir." We changed the subject and the road was built—as it should have been, because it was on the approved plan and really was needed. Our discussion opened the gate for more such projects, and from then on we did a complete job of park development.

In November, 1934, I made a swing through Georgia and Alabama with Fred Morrell of the Forest Service on an inspection trip with Director Fechner. We had received an invitation to the dedication of a state park in Georgia that was said to include an old Spanish fort. The park was being developed by a CCC camp, and the plantation owner who donated the land invited us to stay at his home. We accepted his offer and arrived there the day before the dedication. That evening our host asked whether anyone wanted to go deer hunting. He had thousands of acres that he kept as a game preserve used for hunting. Among the guests was Governor Eugene Talmadge, of Georgia, who

Director Fechner and his advisory council after lunching with the camp commander at a CCC camp.

said he would like to go. Since nobody else responded I spoke up saying I would like to join the governor. A guide took the governor, myself, and the governor's military aide in a car to a point a mile or so from the house where we started walking through the woods.

It wasn't long before we spotted a deer. Out of courtesy to the governor I held my gun in readiness but did not fire. The military aide handed the governor his gun; he fired and missed, and the deer ran off. We continued walking, and it wasn't long before we spotted a second deer. Again the gun was given to the governor; he fired and missed. We started off again, and before long we spotted a third deer. It occurred to me that perhaps I had extended all the courtesy required. The shot didn't look too hard, and so I raised my gun and fired. I hit the deer in a vital spot, and it dropped dead instantly. We carried it back to the car and took it to the house. This being my first deer hunt, Bob Fechner insisted on dashing a bit of the blood on both of my cheeks, which I was told was customary in Georgia. My shot was not all

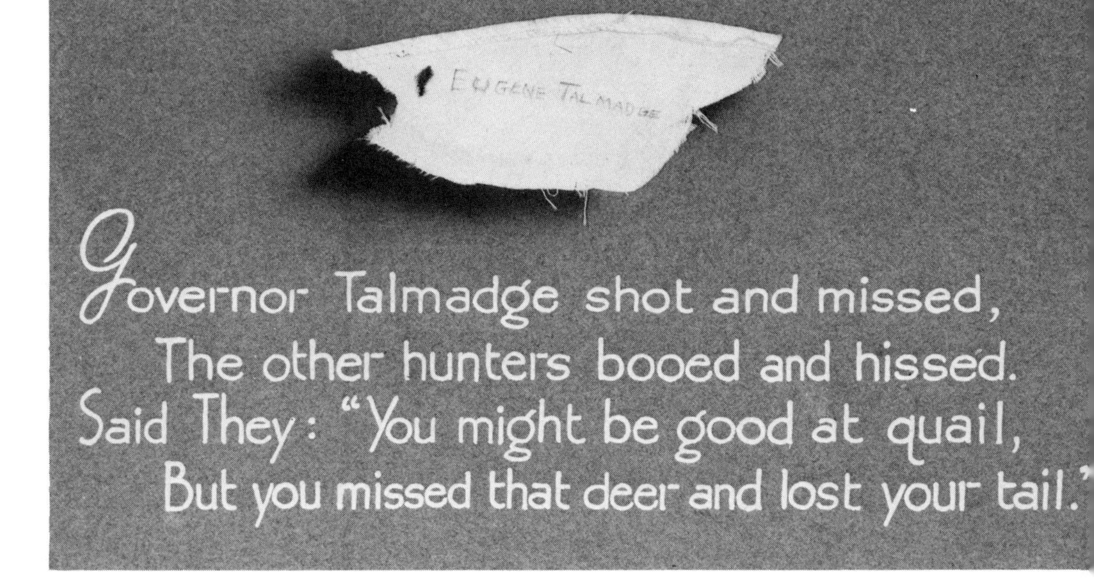

Piece of Governor Talmadge's shirttail.

luck, for I had earned a good rating on the rifle range at Saint John's Military Academy.

When he heard that the governor had missed two shots, Bob insisted that the governor cut off part of his shirttail and autograph it for me. Governor Talmadge said he would do that and send it to me, and he did. It arrived on the day I was going to a dinner of the American Planning and Civic Association, at which Frederic A. Delano, the uncle of President Roosevelt, was presiding as chairman of the board. Knowing that the president and Governor Talmadge had had a disagreement, I pulled the shirttail out of my pocket and showed it to "Uncle Freddy." I asked him how much he thought the president would pay to have the governor's autographed shirttail, and I told him the story. He laughed and asked to borrow it to show to the president.

The dedication of the old Spanish fort took place the morning after the hunt. There were a lot of nice people there, including one lady, a bit beyond middle age, who came up to me and said, "Mr. Wirth, there's a rumor going around here that you went hunting and shot a deer yesterday. I can't believe it! Please tell me it's not true." I realized I was in for a lecture, but I told the lady yes, I had gone hunting for the first time in my life and had shot a deer. With that, she said, "Mr. Wirth, I just can hardly believe that. If it didn't come from you, I would certainly not believe it. How could you, with your park background and love for wildlife and nature, shoot that poor deer with those lovely brown eyes!" If I managed to say anything I don't remember what it was, but she surely made me feel a little uneasy.

The dedication went off fine, but several months later our historian was doing some research in connection with this "Spanish fort" and called on me in Washington to tell me that the building we had solemnly dedicated was not an old Spanish fort but an old sugar mill. We said nothing publicly about the downgrading, but we informed the state. Anyway, the CCC did develop a very nice state park there, and it has served the people well.

The growth and diversification of the national park system between 1933 and 1936 caused the director considerable concern about just how to manage the system. This expansion was summarized very well in Ronald F. Lee's publication of 1972, *Family Tree of the National Park System,* put out by the Eastern National Park and Monument Association. As this account shows, the Park Service had grown right out of its nest of about fifty areas mostly in the West. It was rapidly reaching maturity and had to be prepared to carry its full responsibilities. Referring to President Roosevelt's reorganization of 1933, Lee wrote:

> The reorganization had three highly significant consequences: (1) it made the National Park Service the *sole* Federal agency responsible for all Federally owned public monuments and memorials; (2) it enlarged the *National Park System idea* to include at least four types of areas not clearly included in the System concept before 1933—National Memorials, like the Washington Monument and the Statue of Liberty; National Military Parks, like Gettysburg and Antietam with their adjoining National Cemeteries; National Capital Parks, a great urban park system as old as the nation itself; and the first recreation area—George Washington Memorial Parkway; (3) the reorganization substantially increased and diversified the holdings in the System by adding 12 natural areas located in 9 western states and Alaska and 57 historical areas located in 17 predominantly eastern states and the District of Columbia. The number of historic areas in the System thus quadrupled. The System became far more truly national than ever before.

In 1916, when the Park Service was established, there were 37 areas in the national park system. Before the reorganization by President Roosevelt in 1933, the system had grown to 67 areas. By transferring a large number of eastern historic areas from the War Department and some additional natural and historic areas from the Forest Service, the executive order more than doubled the total. According to Lee's book, the national park system then consisted of 58 natural areas, 77 historic areas, 1 recreation area, and the park system of the nation's capital, which consisted of many recreation areas scattered among residential neighborhoods, the Mall, the White House grounds, and all federally owned public buildings in Washington (by 1936 these buildings were transferred to the Public Buildings Administration). As a result of investigation of proposed areas to be included in the national park system, by 1936 there were 4 additional natural areas, 9 nationally important historic areas, and 4 national recreation areas either established or in the process of being established as part of the national park system. So it can be said that the park system in 1936 consisted of 154 areas scattered throughout the United States, each with a superintendent reporting directly to the Washington office. Further, there were favorable reports in the office on 17 additional proposed areas and the national seashore studies were going full force.

Another development that had to be considered was the enactment of the 1935 Historic Sites Act, the basic legislation in support of the preservation of our historic heritage, which set forth duties and responsibilities for the National Park Service in the field of historic preservation. This act started a whole field of study and classificiation of historic sites, buildings, and objects. The act also created the Advisory Board on National Parks, Historic Sites, Buildings, and Monuments. At this point the service felt that cooperation with the states needed a much stronger basic authority than that for emergency work. Such authority was provided in the 1936 Park, Parkway and Recreational-Area Study Act, the main purpose of which was to help the states plan their park systems. Under that act we used funds from CCC allotments to assist forty-five of the forty-eight states in drafting comprehensive plans for their state park systems. The National Park Service was a cooperating agency only, and we reviewed and supervised the planning.

In 1935, Director Cammerer began to consider the feasibility of regionalizing the entire National Park Service. Coffman was getting more and more concerned about his forestry responsibilities, and he felt besides that the administration of two CCC programs by a single bureau—one for national parks and one for state parks—was not economical. It had not been the intent of Director Albright, when he assigned me the responsibility of the state parks CCC program, that it should be separated from the national park CCC program. But the whole thing had grown tremendously, and, although there was close coordination through Coffman as the man in charge, for all intents and purposes the two programs were separate.

By 1936, Coffman was devoting his entire time to forestry work in the national parks, the director had designated me as his acting alternate, and Coffman's national park CCC staff was turned over to me. Unless I made some changes I would in effect be running two CCC programs. I had to consolidate the national and state park programs, which was not going to be easy. As we started consolidating the CCC program, the regional inspectors started dropping by the national parks to carry out the same duties that they performed for the state parks—assisting in getting things that were needed, handling contacts in the corps areas, and the like. The superintendents didn't like it. A park superintendent is an important person in the National Park Service, a key man. He and his rangers are the troops out front, and he has a lot of responsibility and authority. The regional inspectors were doing no more than Coffman's men had been doing coming out of the Washington office, but they were not old-line Park Service men, and the whole idea went against the superintendents' grain a little bit. Finally, Director Cammerer called many of the key people from the field to Washington to discuss the problem of complete regionalization of the service.

Director Cammerer scheduled a conference of field people in the fall of 1936 to present a regionalization plan. The director was very busy and could not be with us constantly. At one meeting, on a Tuesday, he opened up the session and then departed. Because I had organized the CCC, on a regional basis he left me there to talk to the superintendents on the touchy subject. In the annals of the National Park Service that day became known as "bloody Tuesday." The superintendents did not want regionalization; they were adamant. I think they were prejudiced primarily because they were afraid it would interfere with the authority of the park superintendent; also they didn't want anybody between them and the director, least of all a lot of temporary people brought in for the CCC program. During the discussion, however, it was made clear to them that if the National Park Service became regionalized it would be only logical and natural for the director to appoint new regional directors from the permanent personnel who would be thoroughly informed on the principles and policies of the National Park System as a whole. I emphasized that the regional office setup would be oriented and adjusted to the basic requirements of the National Park System. I also pointed out that the superintendents would be in a much better position in justifying their financial requirements when dealing through somebody more familiar with the Washington office than when 150 superintendents were trying to get the special attention of one man, the director. Regionalization eventually became a fact.

A few weeks after the director's reorganization meeting, I went on another field trip with CCC Director Fechner and Fred Morrell of the Forest Service. I was glad to get out of Washington for a while, and I don't think that Bob Fechner ever forgot the visit we made to Big Bend State Park, in Texas. I know Morrell and I never did. On this occasion we also visited Hot Springs National Park, in Arkansas, where we had two camps. We intended to spend the afternoon there, fly on to Dallas, Texas, for the night, the next day fly to El Paso, and from there drive to Big Bend State Park south of Alpine. The state park later became a part of the present Big Bend National Park.

There was a commercial plane leaving Hot Springs for Dallas about six o'clock in the evening. When we arrived at Hot Springs in the morning we found that the national park superintendent had made arrangements with the chamber of commerce for a banquet that night, at which Fechner was to speak. This was not on our schedule, and the flight we intended to take to Dallas was the last one that day. Fechner didn't seem to be disturbed, and he asked us to arrange some way to get to Dallas after the talk so as not to disrupt his trip. We chartered a plane that would take off when we got through with the banquet that night and get us to Dallas, where we could pick up our scheduled flight in the morning. But when it came time to board the plane, thick fog had set in. The airport at Hot Springs was not at that time fully lighted, and the pilot said takeoff would be dangerous, but he'd try to make it if we wanted to. We decided not to fly. We then arranged for two government cars with four good ranger drivers, two to a car, that would drive us to Dallas. Herb Maier, the Park Service regional director for the southwestern region, was with us. We got to Dallas the next morning just in time to catch the plane on which we had reservations to El Paso.

It just happened that Herb Maier and I had a very important question to ask Fechner, and we were trying to find the right time to do it. Although we felt he would not turn us down, we needed his specific approval. About a half hour after taking off Fechner was dozing and nodding. I told him we had plans for constructing a building in Santa Fe as the regional office for the Park Service. The CCC boys would make the adobe bricks and would do a good part of the construction, but we had some Public Works Administration funds for materials and skilled labor. We told him that a museum in Santa Fe would give us the property on condition that the building would be for the National Park Service regional office. He said, "That sounds reasonable." I continued, "Bob, I think we need your approval of it—it's a fairly good-sized project, and I have the plans here." You could tell that Bob Fechner was not too anxious to get into much of a discussion; he was more in the mood for a nap. He said, "Well, if it meets the legal requirements and you think it's all right, Connie, go ahead. It will be all right with me." Herb Maier must have called Santa Fe as soon as we reached El Paso and told them to go ahead, or perhaps he had even started before we had Fechner's approval, because when we arrived in Santa Fe about five days later the foundations were being dug.

By the way, Herb Maier was I believe the only person in the Park Service group who could boast of being officially investigated by the Department of the Interior. Somebody had made some kind of charge against Herb. It never was clear to me what these charges were, but the department sent a man out from Washington to tail him. Herb found out about it and told me that he felt somebody was following him everywhere he went. One day when I was eating lunch in the Executive Dining room in the Interior Building I found myself sitting across from one of the secretarial investigators. I finally told him that I had heard there was somebody investigating one of our CCC employees and that if he ever got orders to investigate me, I'd appreciate it if he'd let me know. I informed him that I would tell him things he could never find out otherwise. Then, about six months later this man sent me a report on Herb Maier with a note asking for my recommendations. The report was an inch thick. I turned to the "Summary and Recommendations" in the back of the book and found that the only charge against Herb was that he was probably an inactive Republican. I sent the report back to the investigator and recommended that it be put in "file 13." That was the last either Herb or I ever heard of the investigation.

We had one interesting experience before we got to Santa Fe. About halfway to the top of the Chisos Mountains there was a state park of about 640 acres in a small valley in what was called "the window." There was a camp there, and most of the men were of Hispanic descent. It was early in December, and they wanted to put on a Christmas party before we left. They arranged a very hospitable gathering. Having heard that eggnog was appropriate at Christmastime, they had to have eggnog for their party. We drank some of it, but it wasn't too easy to do! We finally found out that it was made from goat milk, the only milk they could scare up on short notice, and tequila. The spirit was right, but I've tasted better eggnog. The cocktail hour was in the officers' and supervisory personnel quarters, after which we joined the boys for an extra fine Christmas dinner.

The high-water mark in the growth of the CCC was reached with a total of 2,916 camps on June 30, 1935. It became evident early in the period, however, that there would not be enough enrollees to keep that number of camps up to reasonable strength. The average strength per camp shortly after the beginning of the 1936 fiscal year, that is, around August, 1935, was 210 men, and by the last day of the fiscal year, June 30, 1936, it was 134 men. The chart on page 149 gives a summary of the camps by the odd periods. Each period lasted six months, April 1 to September 31 and October 1 to March 31. The years shown on the chart are fiscal years, which then ended on June 30, or in the middle of the CCC six-month period. It should be pointed out that at that time the fiscal year for the federal government began on July 1 and ended on June 30 of the following calendar year. All reports to the president and to Congress on such programs as the CCC were made at the end of the fiscal year, June 30. Consequently the reports referred to money spent for a twelve-month fiscal year that included one-half of two CCC periods and all of another period. The charts simply show all information as of a given day, June 30. The basic records, however, show the location of every camp, the date it was established, and the date it was deactivated.

By January, 1936, it had become obvious that some reduction in the number of camps would be necessary at the beginning of the next period, starting April 1. These shifts did not come easy; people and their families were involved. A quick buildup is not devastating, but a quick reduction is. The total number of camps was reduced to 2,405 by June 30, 1936. The shortage of enrollees was caused by better paying jobs cutting into the availability of recruits. By September, 1937, the average number of men per camp had climbed back to 186, but by June, 1938, it had dropped to 142. The size of the CCC program was reduced by 1939 to its original total of 1,500

The entrance to Longhorn Cavern State Park, Texas, built by the CCC.

The entrance and checking station in Turner Falls State Park, Oklahoma, built by the CCC.

The administration building in Zion National Park, Utah, built by the CCC.

The custodian's dwelling in Silver Creek Falls State Park, Oregon, built by the CCC.

The custodian's cabin in Douthat State Park, Virginia, built by the CCC.

The wood and ice house in Scenic State Park, Minnesota, built by the CCC.

The storage and work shop in Pilot Knob State Park, Iowa, built by the CCC.

A comfort station in Lake Murray State Park, Oklahoma, built by the CCC.

A foot bridge in Deception Pass State Park, Washington, built by the CCC.

camps. It was maintained at this level for the next three years with an average camp enrollment of 190. By 1941 the war was coming on, and drastic steps were taken to cut down the CCC and eventually eliminate it.

The emergency legislation enacted during the first hundred days of the New Deal provided the National Park Service with the opportunity to launch several worthwhile programs that were of tremendous importance to the National Park System and especially to state and county park systems. Furthermore, the conservation trend introduced many federal agencies that had large land holdings to the desirability of making their lands available for public recreation. It certainly established the Park Service as the federal agency primarily responsible for nationwide park, historic, and recreation programs. Of greatest importance, of course, was the liberal funding of emergency conservation work assigned to the service. Although expansion during the thirties was financed primarily with emergency funds, the base for our regular appropriations remained about the same. Consequently, as the war came on and the emergency funds were cut off, the base for the National Park Service was extremely low compared with the service's enlarged responsibilities.

Number of CCC Camps by Fiscal Years
Compiled from the CCC Director's Final Annual Report to the President in 1942

Fiscal Year	National Parks	State Parks	Other Interior Bureaus	Total Interior	National Forests	State and Private Forests	Other Agriculture Bureaus	Total Agriculture	Other Agencies	Total CCC
1933	70	102	73	245	597	315	299	1,211	21	1,477
1934	102	263	75	440	431	296	266	993	35	1,468
1935	115	475	104	694	747	409	911	2,067	155	2,916
1936	92	393	94	579	577	336	816	1,729	97	2,405
1937	83	337	85	505	479	282	729	1,490	74	2,069
1938	77	245	82	404	370	196	605	1,171	48	1,623
1939	83	227	131	441	329	178	551	1,058	1	1,500
1940	109	201	175	485	323	177	515	1,015	—	1,500
1941	91	194	207	492	329	175	512	1,016	—	1,508
1942	19	70*	29	118	104	—	265	369	—	487
Total Camp Years	841	2,507	1,055	4,403	4,286	2,364	5,469	12,119	431	16,953

*Fifty of these camps were operated by the National Park Service on military reservations doing defense work.

6

The CCC: Accomplishments and Demise

By August 1, 1937, the total number of CCC camps had gone down to 2,029 and a year later to only 1,623. The National Park Service had gone back to a four-region setup with 83 national park camps and 337 state park camps. Director Arno B. Cammerer had made his move in January to regionalize the National Park Service, effective August 1.

The eastern region, Region I, had offices in Richmond, Virginia, and Dr. Carl P. Russell was its director. Russell had many years of service as an administrator and naturalist in the field as well as in the Washington office.

Region II included the states of the northern Midwest. Its headquarters were in Omaha, Nebraska, and Thomas J. Allen served as regional director. Allen was a Mather man whose experience went a long way back. He started as a ranger and advanced through all the steps, including assignments as superintendent of Bryce Canyon, Hawaii Volcanoes, Hot Springs, and Rocky Mountain national parks.

Region III included Arizona, New Mexico, Texas, Oklahoma, and Arkansas, with the regional office in Santa Fe. Herbert Maier, the regional director during the CCC program, was made acting regional director. Maier had been with the service from the beginning of the CCC program. He was an excellent architect and exerted a strong influence on the style of park architecture that still persists. The first Region III director was Assistant Director Hillory Tolson of the Washington Office, who took up the assignment on May 1, 1939.

It was Secretary Ickes' idea to send Hillory Tolson to Santa Fe. He also suggested that I be sent to Yellowstone as superintendent for a year, but then I got word that my move had been called off. E. K. Burlew, assistant to the secretary, asked that I not be reassigned because it would be difficult to get somebody to handle the emergency programs in which I had become so deeply involved. Instead, they made me the secretary's representative on the CCC Advisory Council in place of Director Cammerer.

Region IV included California, Oregon, Washington, Idaho, Nevada, and Utah. Chief Engineer Frank A. Kittredge was regional director with offices in San Francisco. The members of Kittredge's engineer staff were moved to the regional offices and to Tom Vint's new office, the Branch of Plans and Design.

Arno B. Cammerer, director of the National Park Service from August 10, 1933, to August 9, 1940. The service was regionalized under his leadership.

This move put engineers, architects, and landscape architects all in one organization.

The year 1937 was one of the roughest years of the CCC as far as I personally was concerned. Although we got a great deal of satisfaction and pleasure out of the CCC because it was such a good program, there were difficult times—times of disappointment, times of concern, times when one wished to have a little more opportunity for meditation. My new designation as the secretary's representative on the CCC Advisory Council didn't really change my activities very much. I had already gone through a consolidation of the national park and the state park CCC. I had been attending all the council meetings, and practically all of Coffman's responsibilities had already been turned over to me and my staff. I had been in direct contact with E. K. Burlew and Mrs. J. Atwood Maulding, who were Secretary Harold Ickes' closest working associates. Practically everything was known to them, and they took on a lot of hard work.

But nobody in the department worked any harder than did Secretary Ickes himself. He practically lived in his office, a circumstance that more than likely had something to do with the planning of the secretary's suite in the present Department of the Interior Building. The construction of a new Interior

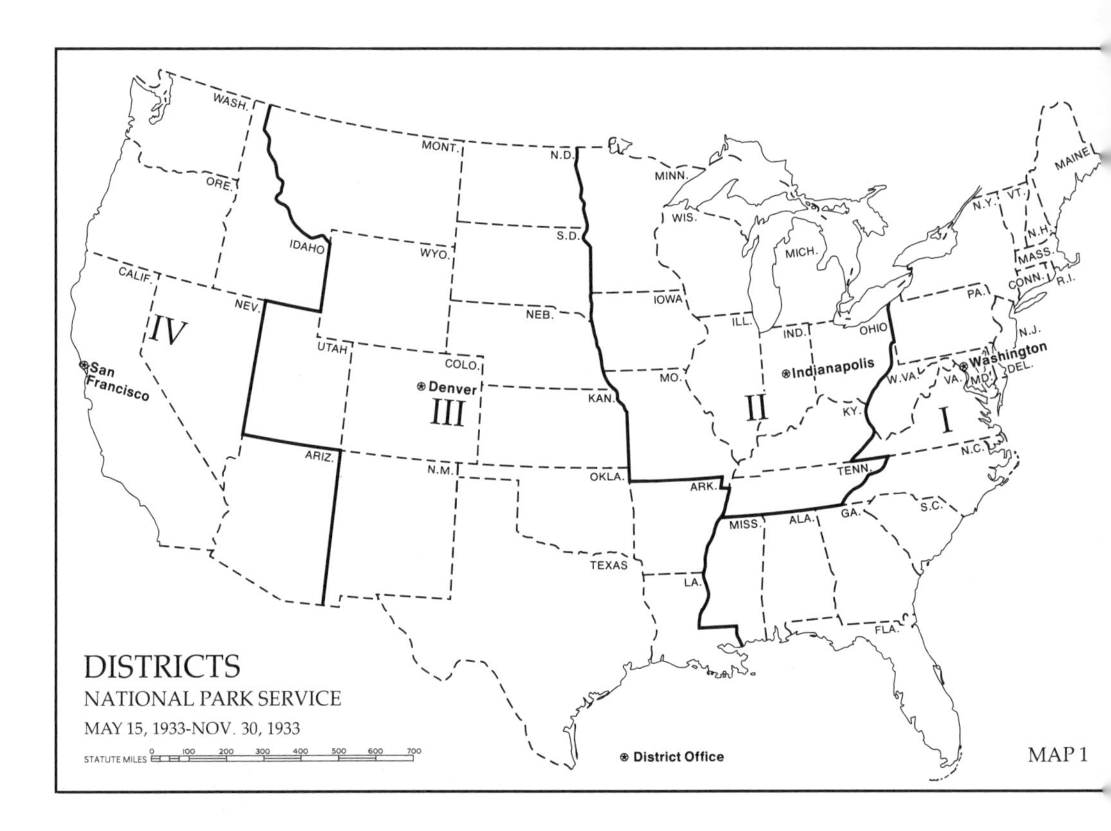
WASH.
MONT.
N.D.
MINN.
MAINE
ORE.
N.Y.
VT.
WIS.
S.D.
N.H.
IDAHO
WYO.
MICH.
MASS.
CONN.
R.I.
CALIF.
NEV.
IOWA
PA.
IV
NEB.
ILL.
IND.
OHIO
N.J.
UTAH
COLO.
Indianapolis
Washington
DEL.
San Francisco
Denver
MO.
W.VA.
VA.
MD.
III
KAN.
II
KY.
I
ARIZ.
N.M.
OKLA.
ARK.
TENN.
N.C.
MISS.
ALA.
GA.
S.C.
TEXAS
LA.
FLA.
DISTRICTS
NATIONAL PARK SERVICE
MAY 15, 1933-NOV. 30, 1933
STATUTE MILES 0 100 200 300 400 500 600 700
District Office
MAP 1

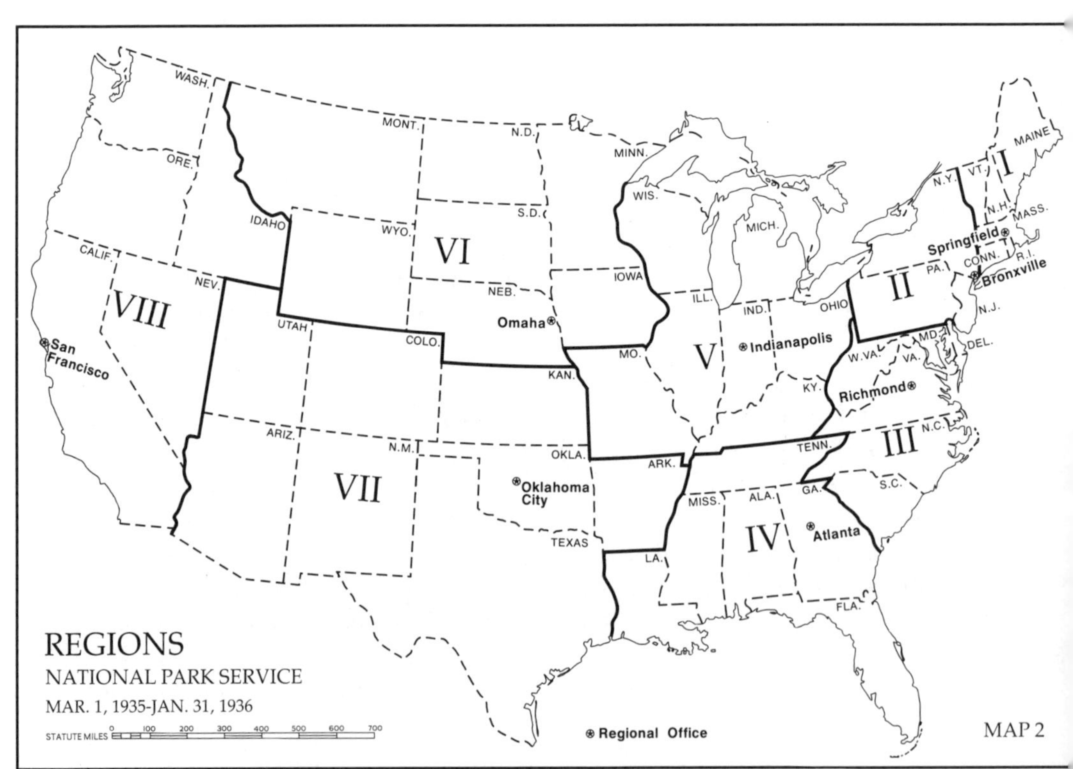
WASH.
MONT.
N.D.
MINN.
MAINE
ORE.
N.Y.
VT.
I
WIS.
S.D.
N.H.
MASS.
IDAHO
WYO.
VI
MICH.
Springfield
CALIF.
NEV.
IOWA
CONN.
R.I.
PA.
Bronxville
VIII
NEB.
ILL.
II
Omaha
IND.
OHIO
N.J.
UTAH
COLO.
Indianapolis
San Francisco
MO.
V
W.VA.
MD.
DEL.
KAN.
VA.
KY.
Richmond
ARIZ.
N.M.
OKLA.
TENN.
III
N.C.
ARK.
VII
Oklahoma City
GA.
S.C.
MISS.
ALA.
IV
Atlanta
TEXAS
LA.
FLA.
REGIONS
NATIONAL PARK SERVICE
MAR. 1, 1935-JAN. 31, 1936
STATUTE MILES 0 100 200 300 400 500 600 700
Regional Office
MAP 2

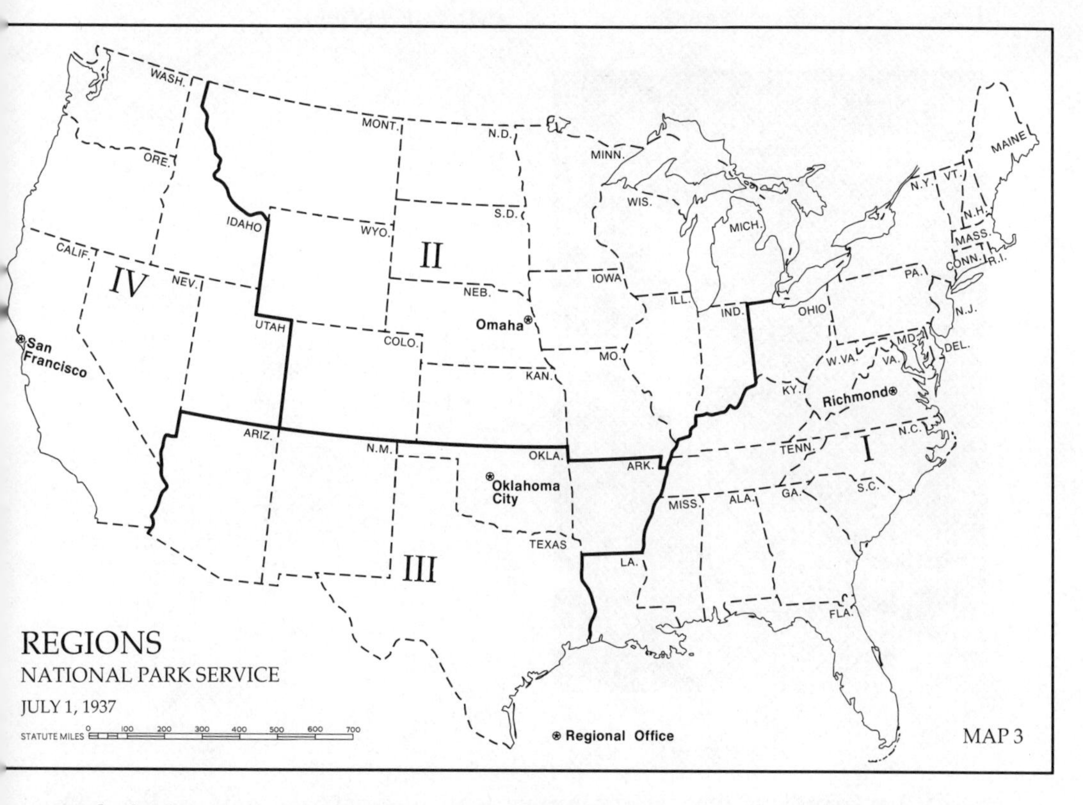

With the beginning of the Civilian Conservation Corps, the National Park Service established four district offices to administer the state park CCC program, as shown on Map 1. At that time there were 100 camps assigned to this work.

By 1935 the number of camps assigned to state and metropolitan parks had reached 475. Under the Park, Parkway, and Recreational-Area Study Act of 1936, federal aid to the states for planning park and recreation activities and to certain federal agencies for similar purposes was greatly increased. The districts were increased to eight and were redesignated regions (Map 2).

By July 1, 1937, the camps administered by the National Park Service had decreased to 325 as the CCC program began to taper off. At that time the National Park Service as a whole was regionalized in four areas, as shown on Map 3.

Building was one of the early projects he authorized as administrator of the Public Works Administration, a position he held simultaneously with his service as secretary of the interior. Although the National Park Service, which then was responsible for all public buildings in Washington, was in charge of this project, the secretary kept close watch over the planning and

Harold L. Ickes was secretary of the interior from 1933 to 1945—longer than any other head of the department.

actual construction. One of the rooms in the secretary's suite in the new building was equipped with furniture that could be converted to bedroom use, and adjoining it was a bathroom complete with tub and shower. Nearby was the official dining room. There was quite a bit to do about all this in the newspapers at the time, but I know Ickes spent many nights in his office working very late, and I have no doubt that he often slept there, because his home was several miles away in the vicinity of Olney, Maryland.

Ickes served as secretary under Presidents Roosevelt and Truman for twelve consecutive years, which I believe is a record for a secretary of the interior and possibly for secretary of any federal department. He wasn't a person one could get very close to, yet he was a hard worker who believed thoroughly in what the Park Service was doing, and he had the reputation of being a strong conservationist. I didn't have much contact with him when he first came to office and Horace Albright was director. But as I became involved with the CCC, and particularly after I was designated Ickes's representative on the CCC Advisory Council in 1937, I got to know the secretary well. He was a gruff sort of a person, but I enjoyed working for him very much. He was unequivocal in his instructions and could be depended upon to back up an employee who got in trouble carrying out his orders.

One case in point was an embezzlement in the CCC, concerning a camp that never existed. Bob Jennings was the head of our fiscal division, handling both regular appropriations and CCC allotments. One day the army finance officer telephoned and asked for one of Jennings' men. Jennings informed him that the man was on sick leave. The finance officer then wanted to know who was going to pick up the payroll. Jennings was startled but quickly said, "Well, I'll come down and get it very shortly." The finance officer gave him the copies of the receipted payroll together with the salary checks. This procedure was irregular, but Jennings accepted them and returned to his office. The standard procedure for handling the payroll for the camps was for the superintendent to send it to the army finance officer, who would check it over, make out the checks, send them directly to the individuals through the mail, mark the payroll "paid," and send one copy of it to the superintendent and another copy to the office of the bureau that had jurisdiction over the camp. In this case there was no camp. The man in Jennings' office was taking the checks, forging the payee endorsements, and getting them cashed at stores and banks in Washington. Jennings reported the embezzlement to me immediately. He found that it had been going on for over a year. In order to maintain a semblance of authenticity, the man had actually "fired" certain foremen, "hired" additional ones, given promotions, and relocated the fictitious camp.

Just as this matter was being checked into, one of the ambitious young clerks in our fiscal office managed to slip upstairs to the secretary's investigation division and give them an oral report of what was happening down in the Park Service. The investigators immediately informed the secretary, and I got a telephone summons to the secretary's office. When I went into his office, Ickes was working at his desk, coat off as usual, shirt sleeves rolled up, and without looking up he said, "You are in charge of the CCC program, aren't you?" I said, "Yes." He then said that he understood there had been a payroll issued for a camp that never existed. I said, "Yes, we've just discovered the embezzlement, we're getting all the details and our report will be up very shortly." He said, "Well, then, it actually happened?" And I said, "Yes." He said, "You are in charge." And I replied, "Yes." He said, "Well you're through as of now." There was little I could do. I turned around, walked out, and returned to our office. The director was not there, and so I reported the incident to Arthur Demaray, the associate director. He knew that our investigation was in progress and told me to go back to my office and act as though nothing had happened. He said everything would be straightened out. I tried to keep busy, but naturally I was disturbed.

About three days later I was called back to the secretary's office. I tried to get hold of Demaray to accompany me, but he was not in the building and so I went alone. The secretary was in the same position—coat off, sleeves rolled up—and, again without looking up, he said he thought that I was carrying too much work. I replied that I was doing only the jobs that he and the director of the Park Service had assigned to me. He talked a little more, never looking up, and finally said, "Well, I'll have to see what I can do to shift some of your work load." I waited a few minutes, nothing more was said, and so I turned around and walked out. He said nothing about having fired me three days before, and I certainly saw no reason why I should bring it up. A month later I received written notice assigning me additional duties and responsibilities.

Secretary Ickes did seem to have a penchant for premature judgments, as illustrated by my sudden firing and also by the following letters.

THE SECRETARY OF THE INTERIOR
WASHINGTON

January 25, 1937

Mr. Conrad L. Wirth,
Assistant Director,
National Park Service

My dear Mr. Wirth:

Your memorandum of January 18 sent to Mr. Blossom has been brought to my attention.

I regret that your action in serving notices of separation on five employees in the Recreational Branch of your office is cause for reprimand. You are fully informed of personnel procedure and your explanation that the action you took conformed to procedure in effect in the State Park Emergency Conservation Work and in other emergency activities for at least several years is untrue. This is another example of the unsatisfactory handling of personnel matters in the activities under your supervision and, unless marked improvement is shown immediately, it will be necessary to reorganize your office and separate from the service the offending employees.

Sincerely yours,
H. Ickes
Secretary of the Interior

UNITED STATES
DEPARTMENT OF THE INTERIOR
NATIONAL PARK SERVICE

February 2, 1937

The Honorable
The Secretary of the Interior

My dear Mr. Secretary:

It is with sincere regret that I acknowledge your letter of reprimand dated January 25. To the best of my ability, I have devoted my entire efforts to the carrying out of what I honestly believe to be your wishes and policies. The most disturbing part of the reprimand is the reference to my memorandum as being untrue. I am not given to falsifying nor would I knowingly permit any one in an organization, which I might be given to manage, to be untruthful. If my statement is untrue, may I assure you it is due to misunderstanding, and I respectfully request that other members of the

National Park Service dealing with personnel be questioned as to their understanding of that particular part of the personnel procedure which I have violated.

With reference to the handling of personnel matters in the activities under my supervision, definite steps have been undertaken to correct this situation. By the time the entire Park Service is together in one building, all personnel procedure will be handled through the regular national park personnel division, and my office will retain only administrative matters such as selections, organization, etc.

I sincerely hope that my future efforts will prove to be satisfactory and that you will be convinced that my foregoing statements are my honest convictions.

Sincerely yours,
Conrad L. Wirth
Assistant Director

I do not intend this as a criticism of Secretary Ickes, for this was not the only time I got fired or reprimanded. Other letters by other secretaries will appear in later pages. I have never failed to answer such letters, but my answers have never been acknowledged. While this silence leads me to believe that my answers were found to be correct and that the secretaries were willing to let the record rest, I believe they should have acknowledged my replies. Again I emphasize that my direct contacts with Secretary Ickes were very rewarding, and I have a very deep feeling of gratitude for the support, understanding, and backing of Secretary Ickes, Director Cammerer, Associate Director Demaray, Senior Assistant to the Secretary Burlew, and his very efficient and understanding assistant, Mrs. Maulding.

In the same vein I must also relate an incident, concerning a silver bowl, that grew out of a simple park dedication ceremony in Virginia. Will Carson, who had the big house on the hill in the relatively small town of Riverton near Front Royal at the north entrance of Shenandoah National Park, was conservation commissioner of the state of Virginia in the early CCC days and held the office until the state made it a salaried job in the late thirties. The Carsons lost their only son in the First World War, and in memory of this boy they had given to Riverton some forty acres of land along the Shenandoah River for a park. The town of Riverton applied for a spike camp of forty CCC boys for one year to develop park facilities for the community and offered to pay for all materials. This was a normal request and well within the regulations; we had undertaken such projects many times in other places throughout the country. This spike camp came from a CCC camp some fifteen miles away, in Shenandoah National Park.

After the job was completed the local committee decided to have a dedication as an expression of thanks to the Carsons. They invited Mrs. Wirth and me and asked me to say a few words. I spoke for about five minutes along with four or five local people. Then Will Carson got up and responded, and at the end of his talk he turned, picked up a package, and presented it to me. In it was a good-sized, engraved Paul Revere silver bowl. I knew I should not accept it, but it would have been terrible to refuse at that moment—so I thanked them. The next day I sent a memo to the director telling him what had happened and asking for instructions on what to do. Cammerer sent my memo to the secretary, recommending that I be allowed to keep the gift. In about two days word came back telling me to return it. I wrote the Riverton committee that I was not allowed to keep the gift and asked whether I should send it to them or return it to the store in Washington where they had bought it. About two weeks later Will Carson called to say that the committee was undecided just how to handle the matter, that they didn't want to embarrass me any further, and that if it was agreeable with Mrs. Wirth they would appreciate it if she would hold the bowl for them until they worked the matter out. I reported this development to Director Cammerer, and he sent my memo on to the secretary, who approved it. A few days later I received the following letter from Will Carson. A copy of this letter was sent to the secretary, without eliciting any comment. Helen is still holding the bowl for the Riverton citizens.

WILLIAM E. CARSON
RIVERTON, VIRGINIA

September 9, 1938

Dear Mr. Wirth:

This is to own your letter in which you advise me that due to a ruling in the U.S. Code, Section 66, Title 5, you had to return the silver bowl that was presented to you by the citizens of this community.

Of course we had no information of the ruling and are sorry that we put you in such an embarrassing position. However, you will realize that the presentation of the bowl by the citizens of this community was made out of the fullness of feeling of the good work you had done, and was a way to acknowledge to you and to the Department our gratitude.

This letter also acknowledges the return of the bowl.

Yours very sincerely,
Wm. E. Carson

Mr. Conrad L. Wirth
National Park Service
Washington, D.C.

As the silver-bowl incident showed, things often happen when they are least expected to; "Chic-Chat" provided another of those happenings. At the CCC camp in Chickamauga and Chattanooga National Military Park in Georgia and Tennessee, there was a disagreement over the location of a park entrance road. The argument was between the superintendent and our technical people, but the local community took sides. It began to be a hot issue, and no plan could be approved. Finally, Director Cammerer asked me to go there to try to arrange a solution. I indicated to Cammerer that I would be glad to go but would like to have the authority to make a decision on the spot and get construction under way at once. This he readily gave me. When I arrived representatives of the state highway department, our park superintendent, and our technical people were all present, and we spent a whole morning examining plans and going over the proposed locations in the field. Finally, I reached a decision and told them that we would start construction that afternoon. I asked the superintendent to get in touch with the mayor in the nearby community and announce that we were going to have a brief ground-breaking ceremony at three o'clock that afternoon. Then I told the CCC camp superintendent to have two or three trucks and some twenty or thirty CCC boys there with shovels so we could break ground.

About a quarter to three a couple of dozen CCC boys and a couple of trucks showed up, and then the mayor arrived with seventy-five or one hundred local citizens to witness the beginning of the road. Among those present were two elderly ladies who carried small Confederate flags. I saw them talking to a member of the mayor's staff and then to the mayor. They made several trips back and forth. Finally, the mayor's assistant came to me and asked, "Mr. Wirth, where are you from?" I said, "I'm from Washington, D.C." He said, "I realize that, but in what part of the nation did you live before you went to Washington?" I said, "Well, I was born in Hartford, Connecticut, raised in Minneapolis, and went to school in Massachusetts." That settled it. He explained, "These two ladies always take part in our celebrations and dedications. There is a problem concerning whom they are to be photographed with. Would you mind if they were photographed with the mayor during the ground breaking, and then we'll have a picture of you and the mayor after they have been photographed?" It seems they were unwilling to have a Yankee in the picture with them. I understood, and I told the aide to assure them there was no harm done and I just hoped they were pleased with the location of the road. He assured me that they were. I never really had a chance to talk to them. The mayor expressed his concern over the attitude of the ladies but was very appreciative of getting the work under way. I told him there wasn't any reason to be concerned, that the project was started, which made me happy, and that my feelings were not hurt nor was I embarrassed.

In the last week of 1939 while out west I got the news that Fechner had died. He had been sick for some time, but apparently death was quite sudden. James McEntee, Bob Fechner's assistant director, was, of course, the logical person to take over, and though his attitudes were opposite from Fechner's in several ways, he had made a good second man for him. Jim had seen that the office was always in order and that business was handled on time. He believed in centralizing many of the activities of the agencies, and he began at once to transfer things around.

King George VI and Queen Elizabeth visited Fort Hunt, near Washington, D.C., in 1939 to view an exhibition of pictures of CCC work. Walking with the king are the company commander and CCC Director Robert Fechner.

McEntee established a system of central repair shops for automotive equipment and operated it out of his office. Some of these shops were three, four, or five hundred miles away from the camps they served. Any major repair jobs would require towing broken-down trucks to the central repair shop. No matter how much we discussed this matter with him and pointed out irrefutable facts—how much it was going to cost and how it would tie up our personnel and equipment for a much longer time—none of our arguments seemed to have any effect on him. The effect of the central repair shop activities on the morale of the technical agencies can be judged when one considers a specific instance: under the new system a truck from a camp near Yakima, Washington, in need of ordinary repairs had to be sent through a mountain pass in the Cascades to the central shop in Olympia, a distance of 220 miles. The technical agency's shop at Yakima could have accomplished all

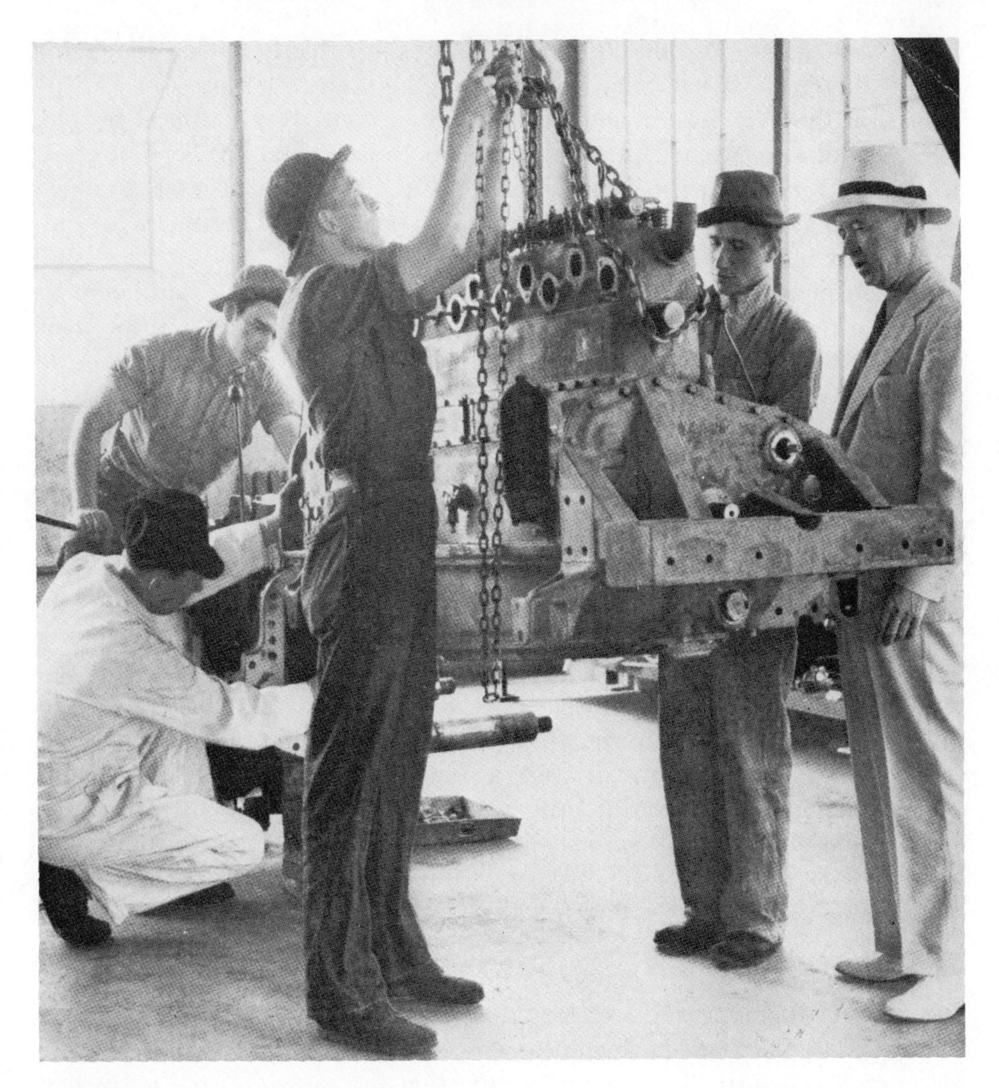

CCC Director James McEntee, *right*, inspecting a CCC training and repair shop.

but major repairs, and good commercial shops were available locally for the more difficult jobs.

One of the policies of the CCC under Fechner had been to contract with the local firms for help with problems we could not take care of ourselves. We also purchased as much of our materials and supplies locally as we could. This practice was a great help to the local communities, disseminating money in the grass roots where it was needed and fostering good public relations as well. McEntee proceeded to do away with many such arrangements. As a result we began to lose the local community spirit that had been so much a part of the CCC. It had been common for the boys to go into town to the movies in the evenings or on weekends when invited by the local people. They would also attend church services in the neighboring communities. Some CCC men went to local night schools, and a few schools arranged courses especially for them. Many of these activities were sacrificed to comply with the new policy.

Certain people like Bob Fechner can instill an indefinable sentiment or spirit that really makes an organization go. Others, proceeding in accordance with a restricted organization chart and rigid policies, instill a harsh, cold approach that kills the spirit and morale of an organization. It is entirely possible that Fechner, without the braking effect of McEntee's control, might have been too lenient, for the interaction of these two personalities was very productive. I just don't know how much influence Jim McEntee actually exerted on Bob Fechner, but as far as I know he was loyal to the director and carried out Fechner's wishes apparently to the director's full satisfaction. I am certain, however, that the CCC would not have been as highly regarded by the technical agencies, the boys, and the public as a whole if McEntee's policies had been in effect from the beginning or if the program had continued much longer than the few years he was director. It seems to be human nature that when there is a change made in the head administrative office of an organization the new man feels he has to make changes—and these changes often go far beyond improvement of existing operations. The question of central control versus dispersed operations had received long and intense discussion in the CCC Advisory Council, and, as I recall, we were all in accord with the policies and practices originally established by Director Fechner.

What McEntee was trying to do finally became so evident that it was necessary to report to the secretary of the interior the state of the Civilian Conservation Corps as the technical agencies saw it. On November 22 the secretary was informed by memorandum that the morale of the corps had deteriorated and that this condition was definitely the result of an increased number of functions being taken over by the office of the director of the CCC. He was told of complications and duplications resulting from this change. It was explained that the mutual understandings essential to the coordination of such an enterprise were being destroyed because the functions of the CCC Advisory Council had been abandoned. We stated that our understanding of the original intent of the president was that cooperation among the several departments should be the fundamental basis of the CCC undertaking and that, contrary to this, the director's office had extended its activities far beyond its original functions of policy making and coordination: that it was making field inspection of work programs, operating an expanding and excessively costly system of central equipment repair shops, insisting on giving prior approval to all automotive and construction equipment purchases and to all purchases of items in excess of $2,500 even when justified and approved in the budget and controlled by law and regular department procedures, and requiring the submission of regulations governing purely departmental CCC functions for review and approval by the director. The report to the secretary further stated that the expanded activities of the office of the CCC director had necessitated an increase of personnel in that office from some seventy-six employees during the fiscal year 1938 to a total of 1,876 positions requested of the Bureau of the Budget for the fiscal year 1942. That increase in staff had produced no noticeable improvement in the situation of the three cooperating departments, nor had it improved central administration of the corps in any way whatsoever; rather, it had slowed down the efficient operation of the corps to a considerable degree. Besides this increase in personnel there had been additional expenses incurred in connection with the construction of buildings for central repair shops, rental of office space for division offices, travel, and other incidental expenses. The secretary was told that these expenditures had not necessarily increased the budget of the corps but represented unsound and uneconomic uses of funds badly needed for the purchase of equipment and supplies to carry out CCC projects.

The secretary was further advised that there had been a gradual movement by the office of CCC director toward complete operation of the corps. There had been only eight CCC Advisory Council meetings in the calendar year October 1, 1939, to September 30, 1940. In the earlier stages of the CCC, under the guidance of Director Fechner and before his illness, meetings had been held frequently, and all matters affecting the departments were discussed before any policy was adopted. In contrast, under the new director practically the only time the council was called together was when McEntee desired to issue instructions to its members. The council had virtually ceased to function as an advisory body.

In a letter to Harold D. Smith, director of the Bureau of the Budget, Secretary Ickes restated our case, consolidating some of the points made in the memorandum of November 22, and proposed a solution:

The proper solution seems to be to revert to the early idea of the President of placing in the old line Departments the full responsibility of carrying out the functions of the CCC. I recommend the following reorganization:

That the office of the Director, CCC, be abolished.

That the War Department be relieved of its duties in connection with the CCC.

That the duties of the Army Finance Office be transferred to the United States Treasury.

That there be established a CCC Coordinating Committee consisting of one of the

Executive Assistants to the President, a Representative of the Department of the Interior, and a Representative of the Department of Agriculture, with the power to determine major policies and to provide uniformity of operation.

That the Departments of Interior and Agriculture be given full authority to carry out the activities of the CCC, including housing and welfare, as well as the work program under the general policies established by the CCC Coordinating Committee.

This recommended reorganization would provide savings sufficient to permit the operation of 1,350 camps instead of 1,227 now planned with the fiscal 1941 estimate of 230 million dollars.

I would not suggest this reorganization if Mr. Fechner were still alive because of his contribution to the CCC. His death is a distinct loss and his illness of the last year and a half has been felt in the functioning of the Corps. If consideration is to be given to the reorganization of the CCC on a more economical and permanent basis, the proper time to do it is now.

The CCC Coordinating Committee should be set up immediately and given the duty to reorganize the CCC on the basis outlined above so as to become fully effective by July 1, 1940.

On the same date, January 4, 1940, Secretary Henry A. Wallace of the Department of Agriculture wrote to Smith at the Bureau of the Budget expressing his "complete concurrence" with Secretary Ickes's recommendations. Smith brought these two letters to the president's attention. There followed two years of memorandums, proposed plans for reorganization, and what not. In the meantime McEntee's office and the CCC were placed under the Federal Security Agency. Because the CCC military officers were being withdrawn for active war duty, careful study was given to the possibility of training the CCC for various war-connected activities and for management of the camps.

On January 9, First Assistant Secretary Burlew wrote a letter to the president on behalf of Secretary Ickes outlining the same suggestions for reorganizing the CCC that the secretary had submitted to the Bureau of the Budget. The president's reply of January 25 directed to the secretary was at least diplomatic.

My dear Mr. Secretary:

I have received First Assistant Secretary Burlew's letter of January 9, 1940, concerning the proposed reorganization of the Civilian Conservation Corps.

While I recognize that the proposal has for its purpose economy in operations and perhaps more efficient administration, it is my belief that the Corps should not lose its identity and that it should be continued as a policy making body with a Director responsible for its general functions.

I am particularly interested in many of the economies mentioned. It seems to me, however, that it would be possible to accomplish a number of these under the present organization. I am therefore asking the Director of the Bureau of the Budget to undertake a study of the Corps' activities in the near future in order to determine what savings can be made and if any practical advantages would result from the changes suggested in Mr. Burlew's letter.

Sincerely yours,
Franklin D. Roosevelt

Nothing really was done, and the corps faded out of the picture as the war came on. The staffs of the many organizations involved in the CCC program seemed to disappear almost overnight. The following list shows the directors of the Civilian Conservation Corps and the members of the CCC Advisory Council from the establishment of the corps until its dissolution:

DIRECTORS

	Fiscal years
Robert Fechner	1933–39
James J. McEntee	1940–43

ADVISORY COUNCIL

War Department	
Colonel Duncan K. Major, Jr.	1933–36
Brigadier General George P. Tyner	1936–39
Major General James A. Ulio	1940–43
Department of the Interior	
Horace M. Albright	1933
Arno B. Cammerer	1933–37
Conrad L. Wirth	1937–43
Department of Agriculture	
R. Y. Stuart	1933–34
Frank A. Silcox	1934–38
Fred Morrell	1938–43
Department of Labor	
W. Frank Persons	1933–38
Veterans' Administration	
C. W. Bailey	1937–43

It was just nine years and three months after the creation of the Civilian Conservation Corps on March 31, 1933, that the corps ceased active operation. The final decision to liquidate the CCC was made on June 30, 1942, when Congress enacted the Labor-Federal Security Administration Appropriation Act for the fiscal year 1943. Enacting that supply bill, Congress voted to terminate the CCC and set aside eight million dollars to defray the cost of liquidation. As soon as the bill was signed by the president, directives went out to the Departments of the Interior, Agriculture, and War, and to the Veterans' Administration to proceed as rapidly as possible and complete the process by July 1, 1943. All during the fiscal year 1942 the CCC had been cut back; camps were abandoned when the jobs begun earlier were completed. By the close of the fiscal year, June 30, 1942, there were only about 350 camps left in operation.

But the CCC was still in charge of some 1,400 closed camps, each containing an average of 20 buildings. It also owned over 35,000 pieces of automotive equipment, mostly trucks and tractors, and vast quantities of other materials including large stocks of woolens, cotten, foodstuffs, portable buildings, motor equipment, replacement parts, tires—in fact nearly everything needed to run a program the size of the CCC. The congressional act that terminated the CCC stipulated that the War Department, the Navy Department, and the Civil Aeronatutics Administration had first choice of all CCC properties and materials. The worst part of the liquidation process was that the men who were in charge of all this equipment and material were leaving so rapidly. The armed services were organizing and expanding for the war effort, and many of the CCC men were answering the call to duty. Not only were the officers being recalled from their assignments as camp commanders, but many of the technical work supervisors were being offered commissions. The CCC boys who had been well trained in automotive equipment were, upon entering the services, made specialists in the noncommissioned ranks.

Some time in December, 1941, in response to a request from the military, the CCC director approved assigning national-defense projects to camps on military reservations. By the first of the year 70 of the camps assigned to the various technical agencies either had relocated on military reservations or had their manpower there. The technical agencies continued to perform management functions in order to relieve the military of that additional work. Later the director, with the approval of the president, established a CCC victory war program whereby all CCC agencies cooperated with the army in every way possible. By the end of May, 1942, there were approximately 175 camps located on military reservations, and by late June the CCC was devoted completely to war-related projects. Whole camp companies and their heavy equipment were taken over by the army and sent to Canada and Alaska to work on construction of the Alcan Highway. Later the secretary of war publicly complimented the CCC on the part it played in the prosecution of the war effort, stating that the enrollees were "hardened physically, have learned to live together as a Company in barracks, have respect for authority, and are potential soldiers of high caliber."

Thus ended one of the great conservation programs in the history of the United States. The National Park Service had directed the work programs of

CCC camps on areas administered by the service; it also had been in charge of recreation-oriented camps on Tennessee Valley Authority lands, in state, county, and metropolitan parks throughout the continental United States, and in Hawaii and the Virgin Islands. The work projects were designed primarily to protect and conserve exceptional natural resources and to develop park and recreation areas for public benefit.

During the entire period of the program—from April, 1933, through June, 1942—work was undertaken by the National Park Service on a total of 655 parks and related types of recreation areas, broken down as follows: national park areas, 71; recreational demonstration areas, 23; TVA areas, 8; federal defense areas, 29; state parks, 405; county parks, 42; metropolitan parks, 75; and 2 areas not classified above, on the West Point Military Academy reservation, in New York, and on Battery Cove Federal Reservation, in Virginia. The service supervised a total of approximately 3,350 camp years, or some 580,000 man years (including camp foremen) of work. Of this work about 25 per cent was on National Park Service areas and 75 per cent on other park and recreation areas. At the peak of the program, in 1935, there were 115 camps assigned to national park areas and 475 to other areas.

In the following table are statistics on a few of the types of work projects undertaken by the CCC from 1933 to 1943.

Item	Unit	National Parks	State Parks and Related Areas	Total
Bathhouses	Number	13	152	165
Cabins	Number	14	1,463	1,477
Large dams	Number	0	197	197
Telephone lines	Miles	1,850	1,707	3,557
Water lines	Miles	188	635	823
Roads and truck trails	Miles	2,186	5,246	7,432
Campground development	Acres	5,310	11,587	16,897
Picnic ground development	Acres	404	5,370	5,774
Fighting forest fires	Man days	250,000	408,276	658,276
Fire presuppression	Man days	414,000	436,823	850,823

The amount of money expended by the service totaled $130,504,000. It must be kept in mind, however, that the overhead expenditures reflected only about 25 per cent of the total, because housing, feeding, medical care, clothing, and education of the enrollees and army officers' salaries were expenditures paid from CCC funds allotted to the army. Consequently, the total expenditures for camps under National Park Service supervision amounted to approximately $467,100,000. Of this amount, $132,100,000 went to camps on national park system properties; the balance of

Cost of the CCC for the Fiscal Year 1939

Agency	Funds	% of Total	Camps
Director's Office	$ 237,319	.07	1,500*
War Department	215,173,270	77.40	1,500*
Interior Department	18,492,645	6.70	450
Agriculture Department	43,905,114	15.80	1,050
Labor Department	30,567		1,500*
Commerce Department	26,691	.03	1,500*
Public Health Service	29,871		1,500*
Total	$277,895,477	100	1,500

*These agencies provided services to all camps.

$335,000,000 went to camps working on state and metropolitan parks and other recreation areas under National Park Service supervision.

How much did the CCC program cost, and how many boys went through the CCC? On the basis of the CCC director's report for one fiscal year, 1939, I'll try to give a reasonable answer.

The average daily strength of the camps for fiscal year 1939 was 156 boys, giving a total strength of 234,000 boys (156 × 1,500). The table on page 127 shows a total of 16,935 camp years, or 203,220 camp months, for the entire CCC program. The records show that the average enrollment of a CCC boy was nine months, and the overall average number of enrollees per camp was 160. So, by dividing the 203,220 camp months by 9 × 160, we find that the total enrollment was in the neighborhood of 3,612,800 men. My records show the total cost to be around $2,780,000,000 or about $770 per average nine-month enrollee, or $1,025 per enrollment year. The actual cost in the beginning was a little less than $900 per enrollee year, but by the time the program was closing out the cost was in the neighborhood of $1,400 per enrollment year.

On June 30, 1942, the Department of the Interior was operating 114 active CCC camps in the continental United States, in addition to 41 CCC projects on 80 Indian reservations and camps in Hawaii and the Virgin Islands, and

Cost Per Camp and Enrollee, Fiscal Year 1939

Agency	Per Camp	Per Enrollee
Army	$143,450	$ 920.00
Interior Department Agriculture Department	41,454	266.00
Director and others	216	1.40
	$185,120	$1,187.40

had on hand approximately $17 million worth of construction and other operating equipment. The closing of camps involved leaving the unfinished work projects in the best possible shape; terminating around 1,800 employees; transferring CCC property to the army, navy, and other agencies; and preparing final accountability records. By June 30, 1943, the liquidation of the CCC was virtually completed. The Interior Department had approximately $1.5 million left of the $8 million appropriated for terminating the program. In order to take care of the final stages of CCC liquidation, Congress appropriated $20,000 to the Federal Security Agency for the 1944 fiscal year. No funds from this appropriation were alloted to the Department of the Interior. I informed the secretary that there was still work to be done and that I was planning to continue discharging the duties of deparmental representative until June 30, 1944, but would submit my final report on the interior CCC program by January, 1944.

Included in my report was a statement of the accomplishments of the CCC camps prepared by each bureau of the department that had camps assigned to it, and all the bureaus preferred to tell in their own way the accomplishments of their camps. Although the statements of the several bureaus are not included here, the tables on pages 148 and 149 show the extent of their participation and how the distribution of camps in the Interior Department compared with that in the Agriculture Department.

For the National Park Service I reported in part as follows:

> The Civilian Conservation Corps advanced park development by many years. It made possible the development of many protective facilities on the areas that comprise the National Park System, and also provided, for the first time, a Federal aid program for State park systems through which the National Park Service gave technical assistance and administrative guidance for immediate park developments and long-range planning. . . .
>
> The National Park System benefited immeasurably by the Civilian Conservation Corps, principally through the building of many greatly needed fire trails and other forest fire-preventional facilities such as lookout towers and ranger cabins. During the life of the CCC, the areas received the best fire protection in the history of the Service. . . .
>
> The CCC also provided the manpower and materials to construct many administrative and public-use facilities such as utility buildings, sanitation and water systems, housing for its employees, service roads, campground improvement, and museums and exhibits; to do reforestation and work relating to insect and disease control; to improve the roadsides; to restore historic sites and buildings; to perform erosion control, and sand fixation research and work; to make various travel and use studies; and to do many other developmental and administrative tasks that are so important to the proper protection and use of the National Park System.
>
> The CCC made available to the superintendents of the national parks, for the first time, a certain amount of manpower that allowed them to do many important jobs when and as they arose. Many of these jobs made the difference between a well-managed park and one "just getting along." If the CCC or a similar organization is

Civilian Conservation Corps, Department of the Interior—Number of Appointive Personnel Employed

	Bureau of Reclamation	Fish and Wildlife Service [1]	General Land Office	Grazing Service	National Park Service	Office of Indian Affairs
On June 30:						
1933	—	—	9	—	44+	—
1934	—	—	14	—	4,731	829
1935	50	—	14	98	7,031	1,180
1936	227	—	25	601	5,890	986
1937	284	—	27	600	6,203	806
1938	295	—	18	631	4,303	782
1939	346	463	50	889	3,506	609
1940	362	387	67	950	3,400	646
1941	379	369	62	898	3,228	613
1942	155	209	44	305	1,219	534
1943	—	—	1	—	30	5

[1]Does not include employees on CCC rolls prior to consolidation of the Bureau of Biological Survey of the Department of Agriculture with the Bureau of Fisheries of the Department of Commerce to form the Fish and Wildlife Service, and its transfer to the Department of the Interior.

Civilian Conservation Corps, Department of the Interior—Total Camp Months of CCC Operations

Fiscal year	Bureau of Reclamation	Fish and Wildlife Service [1]	General Land Office	Grazing Service	National Park Service [2]	Office of Indian Affairs
1933	—	—	1	—	99	—
1934	—	—	12	—	3,274	804
1935	83	—	12	14	5,184	900
1936	377	—	22	486	5,928	852
1937	431	—	24	535	5,210	792
1938	449	—	16	546	3,981	828
1939	527	63	60	964	3,822	840
1940	555	408	69	1,108	3,832	852
1941	550	433	72	1,045	3,769	852
1942	372	325	48	546	2,268	840
Total	3,344	1,229	336	5,244	37,367	7,560

[1]Does not include operations prior to consolidation of the Bureau of Biological Survey of the Department of Agriculture with the Bureau of Fisheries of the Department of Commerce to form the Fish and Wildlife Service, and its transfer to the Department of the Interior.

[2]Includes operations in Hawaii, Alaska, and the Virgin Islands.

Distributions of Standard CCC Camps in Continental United States

CCC period	Dates embraced by CCC period [1]	Bureau of Recla-mation	Fish and Wildlife Service [2]	General Land Office	Grazing Service	National Park Service	Others under Interior Depart-ment	Total Interior	Total Agri-culture	Total others [3]	Grand total
1	June 1, 1933, to Sept. 30, 1933	—	—	1	—	172	—	173	1,264	31	1,468
2	Oct. 1, 1933, to Mar. 31, 1934	—	—	1	—	304	—	305	1,128	35	1,468
3	Apr. 1, 1934, to Sept. 30, 1934	8	—	1	—	428	[4]34	471	1,135	34	1,640
4	Oct. 1, 1934, to Mar. 31, 1935	9	—	1	—	429	[4]51	490	1,125	25	1,640
5	Apr. 1, 1935, to Sept. 30, 1935	30	—	2	31	561	—	624	1,907	104	2,635
6	Oct. 1, 1935, to Mar. 31, 1936	37	—	2	45	489	—	573	1,751	103	2,427
7	Apr. 1, 1936, to Sept. 30, 1936	34	—	2	45	430	—	511	1,524	76	2,111
8	Oct. 1, 1936, to Mar. 31, 1937	34	—	2	45	426	—	507	1,505	78	2,090
9	Apr. 1, 1937, to Sept. 30, 1937	34	—	2	45	379	—	460	1,335	54	1,849
10	Oct. 1, 1937, to Mar. 31, 1938	34	—	1	45	320	—	400	1,157	47	1,604
11	Apr. 1, 1938, to Sept. 30, 1938	40	—	4	72	305	—	421	1,073	6	1,500
12	Oct. 1, 1938, to Mar. 31, 1939	42	—	4	87	311	—	444	1,056	—	1,500
13	Apr. 1, 1939, to Sept. 30, 1939	44	—	5	90	311	—	450	1,050	—	1,500
14	Oct. 1, 1939, to Mar. 31, 1940	44	34	6	91	310	—	485	1,015		1,500
15	Apr. 1, 1940, to Sept. 30, 1940	44	36	6	89	310	—	485	1,012	3	1,500
16	Oct. 1, 1940, to Mar. 31, 1941	44	36	6	89	308	—	483	1,008	9	1,500
17	Apr. 1, 1941, to Sept. 30, 1941	36	29	4	53	223	[5]23	368	[6]730	5	1,103
18	Oct. 1, 1941, to Mar. 31, 1942	26	20	4	34	78	[5]36	198	[7]397	5	600
19	Apr. 1, 1942, to June 30, 1942	7	5	3	3	39	[5]57	114	[8]250	5	369

[1] In some instances program changed within the period.

[2] Prior to 14th period, the Bureau of Biological Survey, (now integrated with the Fish and Wildlife Service) received camps under quota of the Department of Agriculture.

[3] Army and Navy.

[4] Soil Erosion Service.

[5] National Defense.

[6] Includes 27 on National Defense.

[7] Includes 55 on National Defense.

[8] Includes 92 on National Defense.

NOTE.—Office of Indian Affairs not included because its camps were not standard-type camps.

established in the future, a more flexible use of the men assigned to National Park System areas would increase its value to them.

The State park program received a tremendous impetus through the CCC. Without having had any previous official relationship with State park organizations, the National Park Service was asked to supervise CCC work on non-Federal park areas. This required the setting up of a supplementary organization on a regional basis. Many States were not prepared to utilize effectively the manpower and materials that were suddenly available to them—in fact, the majority of them had practically no State park system or organization.

The CCC was not just a pick-and-shovel project. It contributed tremendously to the Nation's thought on parks and recreation. It was soon realized that one of the first requirements for adequate programs, both immediate and long range, was a comprehensive survey and study of the entire park and recreational problem on a Nation-wide basis. In 1936, Congress enacted the Park, Parkway, and Recreation Study Act (49 Stat. 1894), and pursuant to this act, 46 of the States and the Territory of Hawaii participated in the conduct of State-wide studies. Thirty-seven of the States completed reports on their studies and 21 published them. In 1941, the National Park Service published its report, "A Study of the Park and Recreation Problem of the United States." Between 1936 and 1942, the National Park Service responded to the requests of 18 States in helping to rewrite their general conservation laws, which placed parks and recreation in a stronger position. During the 10 years of CCC, the National Park Service issued the following publications relating to park work—all made possible by the CCC:

A Study of the Park and Recreation Problem of the United States
Park Structures and Facilities
Park and Recreation Structures
Park Use Studies and Demonstrations
Fees and Charges for Public Recreation
Yearbook—Park and Recreation Progress, 1937, 1938, 1940, 1941
Tree Preservation Bulletin, Series 1–9, incl.
Digest of Laws Relating to State Parks
Digest of Laws Affecting Organized Camping
Digest of Laws Relating to Local Parks and Recreation
Municipal and County Parks in the United States—1935

The above mentioned work was fundamental and essential to insure proper physical improvements on the State park and recreational areas throughout the country. Although Congress authorized this work under the CCC, an emergency organization, and again in the Park, Parkway, and Recreation Study Act of 1936, it never appropriated any funds specifically for it. Virtually all of this planning performed by the National Park Service was carried out by personnel employed with CCC funds. While this work was being conducted, the CCC camps were proceeding with the development of more than 561 non-Federal park areas throughout the country. The work included every conceivable type of project necessary to develop well-rounded park and recreational areas. To enumerate the work accomplished, State by State, would take too much space in this report. As an example, however, the State of Virginia in 1933 had only Matoaka State Park, and the Richmond Battlefield which was acquired by the State for transfer to the Federal Government for inclusion in the National Park System. By June 1942 the State had developed, principally with the aid of the CCC (78-1/2 camp-years) 11 areas with a total of 19,367 acres, well distributed throughout the State from the coast to the mountains. The CCC provided each of its six principal State parks with a road system, water supply and sewage disposal systems, telephone lines, power lines, and necessary utility and administrative structures and facilities. It built three recreational dams and one swimming pool; it provided bathhouses and necessary appurtenances in each park, and beach facilities in five of them; it constructed hundreds of other buildings for public use; and it provided recreation and protection by the construction of many miles of trails. In short, with the aid of CCC, the State has given its citizens a system of parks with most of the recreation activities for their leisure-time use. In the 1942 fiscal year, their largest attendance year, 486,376 visitors used the State park system.

With the liquidation of the CCC work forces in July 1942, aid to the States was terminated, and planning assistance authorized by the Park, Parkway, and Recreation Study Act virtually ceased. For insurance of the success of any future Federal aid program, regardless of what agency administers it, or the methods used, the provisions of the Recreation Study Act should continue to be carried out, at least to the extent of assisting the States in keeping the studies and plans alive and abreast with the developments of the time. This would permit rapid resumption of development work on a sound basis, either with or without Federal assistance.

Because of the accomplishments and the success of the original CCC, I felt that a similar type of organization should be authorized on a permanent basis, and I enumerated my reasons as follows: (1) There was in the thirties, and still is, a need to give nationwide attention to the conservation of our natural resources. The natural resources are so vital to our existence and progress that it seems reasonable to give them continual attention and protection. (2) The general type of program as planned and executed by the CCC was well received by all. Perhaps one of the greatest accomplishments of the civilian Conservation Corps was that it made the people of this country aware of the value of an active conservation program. (3) The CCC not only taught the youth of our nation in a very practical way the meaning and value of our natural resources but helped to strengthen the nation's human resources. (4) The CCC program was looked on by many as a relief program rather than a conservation program, and that view was justified to a certain extent. A good conservation program can do much toward the relief of the unemployed, although its main and most important objective is conservation. (5) The CCC program brought together many subdivisions of government in such a way as to help them realize that the protection of natural resources was a problem common to all. (6) Learning how to handle heavy equipment proved to be of great value to the boys when the time came for them to leave camp. Men with experience in handling and repairing equipment were in demand by private business concerns and government agencies, including the armed services. (7) Standard and attractive CCC uniforms created and maintained a fine organization spirit. (8) The two-year limit of service impressed upon the boys that they must progress and that the CCC was a place to learn how to work and to prepare themselves for better jobs. (9) Work outdoors, regular hours, and plenty of wholesome food did wonders for the health of the boys at one of the most critical growing periods of their lives. (10) Camp life and recreation programs taught cooperation and team play to a very high degree. Brigadier General George P. Tyner, a representative of the War Department on the CCC Advisory Council, stated before a committee of Congress that he felt the training of the boys in the CCC camps was equal to 75 per cent of the type of training required of the soldiers in the army.

I concluded by saying that the CCC had been deficient in several respects and that, if a similar organization was to be established, those faults should first be carefully examined. I attributed the CCC's deficiencies and lack of effectiveness to the following: (1) The CCC director's office superimposed controls over the departments' management and development of federal properties. General policies and controls were necessary for a unified CCC program, but they must not interfere with the primary functions of the departments. The director of the CCC assumed more and more administrative control over the camp programs, and towards the end he was interfering with the responsibilities of the departments in the management of their properties. This interference became worse with the addition of the administrative controls of the Federal Security Agency. (2) While the relationship between the army and the technical services in the field and in Washington was very good, many administrative officers felt that simplification and consolidation of control in the camps would remove excessive overhead. For instance, the use of two finance agencies—the Treasury Department for regular functions and the Finance Office of the War Department for the CCC—caused unnecessary additional work for the technical agencies. While the army finance officer did an excellent job, two procedures and two different sets of records and forms were required on each area where CCC and regular funds were being spent, frequently on the same general work project. (3) Many work projects could have been undertaken more economically with smaller camps. The two-hundred-man camp was considered the smallest unit that could be used to justify the dual overhead cost of the army and technical agency. But the financial loss in an overmanned work project more than offsets the increased man-unit overhead cost of a smaller camp. Further, if more than two hundred men were needed, the addition had to be a multiple of the two-hundred-man unit, and by this rigid procedure the man-unit overhead cost could not be reduced much below the two-hundred-man unit camp. (4) The trend to build up a classroom type of educational program in the camps with impractical (and unpopular) academic courses confused the understanding of the purposes of the corps. Practically everybody believed it to be reasonable and desirable to teach the boys reading and writing; first aid and safety measures; and how to advance themselves in the type of work to which they seemed best adapted. Many could not understand, however, why the boys were urged and even pressured to take a foreign language, or other regular classroom courses, after a hard day's work in the field.

While the CCC operation had faults, none was serious enough to nullify the good it did for the boys and the country. Minor adjustments in organization and policy would provide an adequate solution.

I strongly believe that the United States should establish an organization similar to the Civilian Conservation Corps on a permanent basis and that such an organization should be a joint enterprise of the federal departments and agencies that now administer and protect the natural resources of the nation. The natural resources that make up the livable environment of the world do not conform to political or jurisdictional bounday lines, and an environmental conservation program must therefore be a joint interagency program. The main objectives of the proposed corps should be: (1) Development and protection of the natural resources of the country for the use and enjoyment of present and future generations; (2) Teaching the workers and others the necessity and the importance of proper use of the natural resources; (3) The coordination and integration of a nationally planned program through a uniform and respected work organization that does not interfere with the existing objectives and responsibilities of the various member agencies; and (4) Cooperation with and aid to the states and their political subdivisions and the owners of private holdings in matters of conservation.

Under this proposed system the president of the United States would appoint the director. Each of the departments or independent agencies using the resources of the corps would appoint two members to the policy council. One of these members would be the department's administrator of the corps activities within the department he represented. The other member would be the representative of the head of the department and the senior high policy representative. Each department would have one vote. The two appointees from each department and the director appointed by the president would constitute the policy council of the corps. The policy and regulations governing the operation of the corps would, in all cases, be made or approved by the policy council. The director would be the chairman of the council. It would take a majority vote of the council, plus one additional vote, to approve regulations or to establish policy.

The director would have direct charge of certain functions of the corps. These functions would be decided upon and approved by the policy council. Generally speaking, these functions would be only those that are common to all operating agencies, that would help to unify the corps, and that would be more economically handled by central organization. It would also be the director's responsibility, acting through the administrators of the departments or agencies, to see that all policies and regulations of the corps are properly and promptly carried out. Some of the functions that might logically

PROPOSED ORGANIZATION DIAGRAM
CONSERVATION CORPS

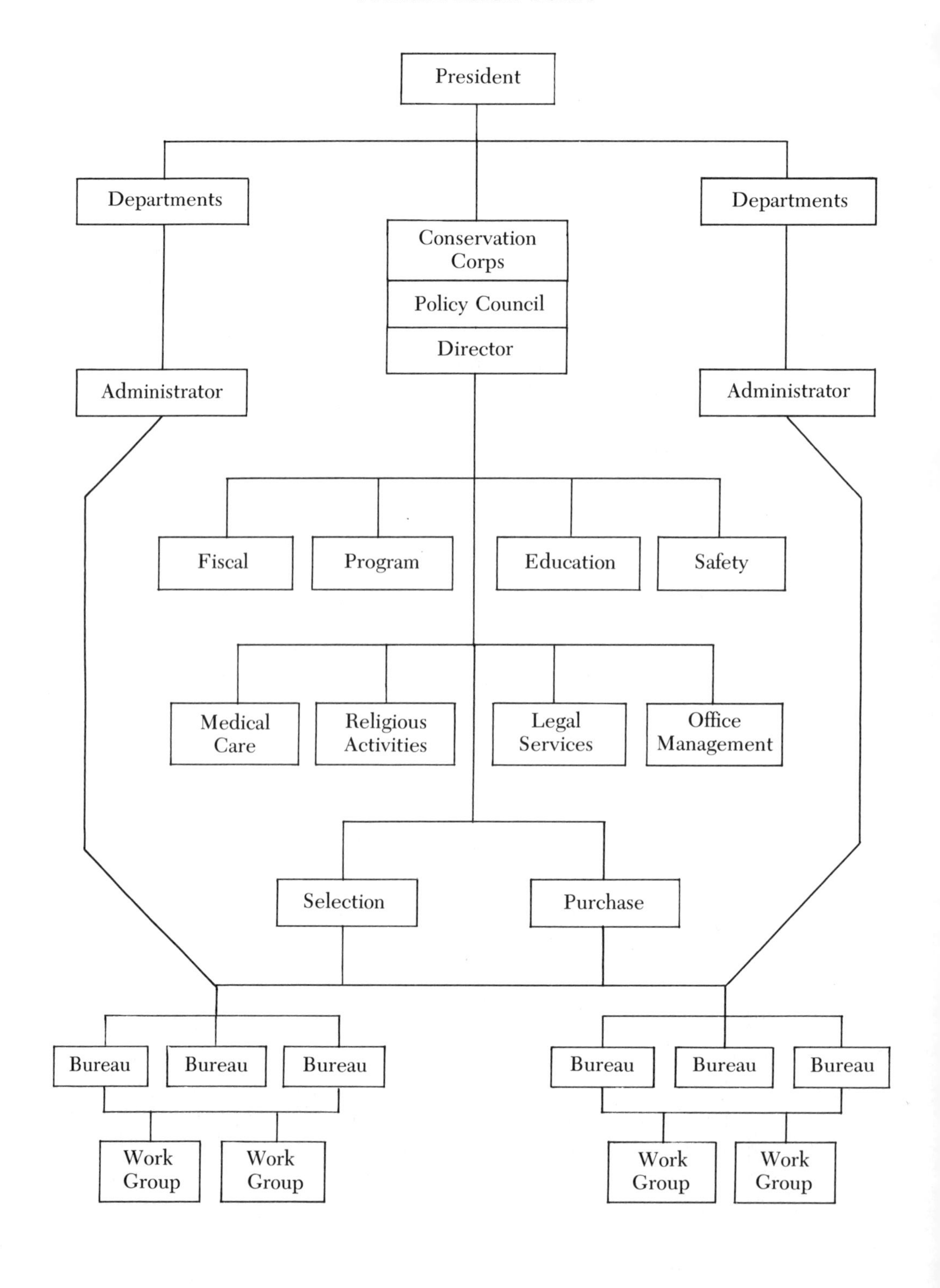

be placed in the director's office are:

Fiscal. It would be necessary to assemble in one place the budget requirements for all activities of the corps for presentation to the Bureau of Management and Budget and the Congress. After the funds have been appropriated it would be necessary to allot them to the departments and keep certain limited financial records.

Program. The operating agencies would, from time to time, submit their requirements for camps or men, and these requests would have to be assembled and presented to the council through the director for approval. Records of the decisions would have to be kept, and orders would have to be issued to the departments or agencies to carry into effect the decisions of the council.

Education. A basic education program should be adopted. Such a program would be limited in the camps to job training and the teaching of reading and writing. It would be necessary to have, in a central location, a division that would see that a unified program was maintained for the corps and that would make reports and recommendations for the policy council's consideration.

Purchase. It would be economical for one office to purchase and warehouse items that are required for the member departments or agencies, and to ship out, on requisition, items such as clothing, shoes, bedding, cooking and camp equipment, and certain staple foods. It also would be the duty of this division to collect and recondition such items as clothing and shoes wherever practical and to warehouse them for reissuing.

The bureaus would have full control of all phases of the work projects in their areas and would be held directly responsible for adherence to the policies and regulations of the corps. Appointment of personnel would be in accordance with civil service and department procedures. In selection of personnel under this procedure, special consideration should be given to their qualifications as leaders of young men.

Development and protection programs would be undertaken either by camps or by small groups of men, not less than ten or more than forty. In cases where small groups of men were supplied, the bureau would have to meet all basic responsibilities of the corps—supervision, health care, housing, and so forth. Camps would range in size from a fifty-man unit up, in multiples of fifty. A superintendent would be in charge of a camp and all its activities. This proposed system of organization has several advantages. The departments and agencies most concerned with the development, protection, and use of natural resources would have a definite hand in formulating the policies affecting the work program on the areas under their administrative control. The director, as the president's appointee, could make such reports to the president as were found necessary. The value of a uniform organization of young men working on conservation projects would be maintained. Setting up a strong administrative office within each department would provide the controls necessary to insure adherence to the regulations that make the corps a uniform organization. The bureaus would have the full responsibility for all of the activities of the corps on the areas under their administrative jurisdiction, including camp management, which they did not have under CCC. This arrangement would eliminate the conflict that existed under the old setup between the army and the technical services as to camp location, campground development, division and release of men, and the like. It should also reduce the general overhead costs and permit the use of smaller camps at a reasonable man-month cost. Moreover, it would make possible the use of small groups of men without the establishment of camps, where the area to which they were assigned had the facilities available to take care of them. Besides these general advantages, such an organization would be flexible and would fit into changing and varying conditions.

The complete text of my final report to the secretary of the interior of the department's Civilian Conservation Corps program for the period March, 1933, to June, 1943, was inserted in the *Congressional Record* by Senator Henry M. ("Scoop") Jackson, of Washington, in support of a bill (S. 1595) that he introduced in the Ninety-second Congress proposing to establish a permanent organization along the lines of the CCC (*Congressional Record*, 92d Congress, 1st sess., April 20, 1971, vol. 117, #54, pp. S5155–5165). Other similar bills have been introduced from time to time, but Senator Jackson has been one of the strongest advocates of this proposal.

A lot of the good things said about the CCC have been said best by some of the people who were associated with it in one capacity or another. In 1954, during a period when an effort was being made outside of government to form an organization to sponsor legislation for the establishment of a permanent conservation corps organization, a former CCC staff man—an educational adviser—wrote as follows:

> In the very dark, depressed years of the thirties, when farmers had lost their farms, when industries and commercial establishments, small and large, had collapsed, when banks were closed, when millions of American people, jobless, homeless, malnourished, frustrated, hopeless, sat in their homes, losing confidence in themselves, in their government, in our way of life, the Civilian Conservation Corps was born and I was a CCC Camp Educational Adviser located in the Huron National Forest, Michigan.
>
> We who were in the CCC camps, millions of us, in general, youth in their late teens and twenties, were humanity uprooted. We were boxcar barnacles. We were knights of the highway. From the city streets, from rural areas, from the transient centers, from the hobo jungles, thru the Civilian Conservation Corps, we found homes on mountain tops, in isolated valleys, on the plateaus, in the desert, in the marshlands.
>
> Tall boys, short boys; fat and lean; black and white, brown and red; illiterates,

half-educated, well educated; talentless and talentful; friendly and friendless; hopeful and hopeless; we lived in a world that we had not created, in a world that others had created for us.

Under the blistering hot sun of summer, in the bitter cold of winter, when snow-bound, we went on "emergency rations," when Springtime's raging rivers swept all before them, when the crack of hunters' guns beset us, we were CCC men, alert in our country's service.

In 1954, look about you! These CC men are among our finest citizens.

There are highways (Virginia's Skyline Drive, for example) bridges, dams, fish hatcheries, levees, swimming beaches, parks, forests, productive farms, free-flowing lakes and rivers, full of fish, enjoyed by millions of people.

These are the nation's wealth! These are the nation's pride!

Each year the contribution of CC men grows esthetically more beautiful, economically more valuable, used and enjoyed by millions of people!

How did all this happen? The full story has yet to be written!

It is regrettable that legislation establishing a permanent conservation corps was not enacted while the success of the CCC and its great accomplishments were foremost in people's minds. Many believed that if the cold war had not followed World War II the CCC would have been reestablished and on a permanent basis. Several similar work programs have been considered. In fact, in 1972 a test program was authorized by Congress and instituted by the Departments of Interior and Agriculture. This trial period proved very successful, and in 1975 Congress considered legislation to enlarge and extend the program for a five-year period. Representative Lloyd Meeds, of Washington, asked me to come up and start the hearing off with a recommendation made by the Department of the Interior. Although I did not have enough time to study the bill in detail, I accepted the invitation and made remarks in connection with the value of the CCC program as I knew it. A Forest Service man spoke after me at the hearing. The next day in a Washington, D.C., newspaper I read that he was there to oppose the bill on behalf of the administration because the White House believed that it would be inflationary and that it was up to private enterprise to hire the unemployed, not the government.

The main trouble with most of the programs that have been considered and tried so far is that everyone wants to make a complete study of overhead, classification of personnel, and what not, before even putting anybody to work. One of the beauties of the 1933 operation was that the laws went through with a purpose in mind, and it was left to the administrators to carry out that purpose. It is true that some of the laws passed in the first hundred days of the New Deal were found unconstitutional and had to be changed or done away with, but nevertheless for the periods they were in effect many served a very good purpose.

7

Other Emergency Period Programs

This chapter describes major programs and activities related to the full scope of National Park Service responsibility, as differentiated from programs of relatively short duration and limited scale. These emergency programs are treated under the following subheadings:

Natural History and History Associations
Historic Sites Act of 1935
Park, Parkway, and Recreational-Area Study Act of 1936
Recreational Demonstration Areas
Historic American Buildings Survey
Seashore and Lakeshore Studies
Shangri-La
Park Structures and Facilities
Digest of Laws Relating to Local Parks and Recreation

NATURAL HISTORY AND HISTORY ASSOCIATIONS

One of the most efficacious and gratifying aspects of the administration of our National Park System has been the cooperation received from voluntary groups in developing a wide range of services to park visitors. This movement came about primarily through the concern of our field operations people in the parks and of people living close to parks who helped provide or supplement services not supplied in adequate measure by the limited government funding. These groups formed nonprofit distributing associations to assist and extend the historical, scientific, educational, and interpretive activities of the National Park Service. Some sixty-six cooperating associations have been established, and all of them engage in one or more of the following activities: (1) publishing and making available relevant literature; (2) selling souvenirs; (3) acquiring materials pertaining to the history or natural history of an area; (4) developing a suitable park library; (5) helping improve interpretive programs, including signs, markers, and museums; and (6) acquiring lands needed to protect significant features of a park.

Where local resources have not been sufficient to support separate cooperative programs, regional associations have been formed to give mutual support to groups serving individual park needs. An outstanding example is

Glass House Point, a part of Jamestown National Historic Site, Virginia, is the site of the first industry of the colonial period. The glass industry, under the leadership of Carl Guskey, financed the study and development of colonial-design furnaces, now operated by the Eastern National Park and Monument Association. *Photo by Richard Frear, courtesy National Park Service.*

the Eastern National Park and Monument Association, which was organized to encompass the many small, historic sites along the east coast. This arrangement has demonstrated how an association operating profitably for larger parks can upgrade visitor services of all parks in a region by underwriting the operations of smaller cooperating groups.

At this point it will be helpful to quote from the annual report of the Eastern National Park and Monument Association for 1972:

> The Eastern National Park and Monument Association was formed in response to a recommendation made at the National Park Service Interpretive Personnel Conference in Gettysburg in May 1947. Incorporated on May 2, 1948, under the laws of the Commonwealth of Virginia, by Roy E. Appleman, Edward A. Hummel and Elbert Cox, the charter of the corporation was issued by the State Corporation Commission in Virginia on May 18, 1948 in Richmond, Virginia.

The new organization encompassed associations that had served individual large parks since the thirties and a few even older groups.

Donations to the Eastern National Park and Monument Association financed a study of the kind of clothing worn by Abraham Lincoln's family and other early settlers in Indiana. These women wear costumes made at Lincoln Boyhood National Memorial, Lincoln City, Indiana, as they dye material for other costumes to be worn by the interpretive staff. In the background is a smokehouse used in curing meat. *Photo by Richard Frear, courtesy National Park Service.*

Roy Appleman, who was regional historian of the Park Service's eastern region, was designated executive secretary and did outstanding work in launching the association. He drafted the articles of incorporation, beat the bushes for memberships, and set up the first six outlets, or agencies. When he resigned in 1951, the association was well established. James W. Holland was appointed his successor and moved ahead with vigor. Within ten years the association had grown to thirty-five agencies, had gross annual sales of $129,000, and had donated $109,000 to the service.

The procedure for allocating funds to a park is relatively simple. Any park or monument with an approved educational or interpretive program may apply for financial assistance by submitting a request through the regional director to the board of the association. The board at its January meeting considers all worthy requests. Its aim is to put funds to productive use.

The rapid growth of the Eastern National Park and Monument Association made it apparent that the work load could no longer be supported on a volunteer basis by the executive secretary and the chairman. In 1964 the board decided to hire a full-time professional executive secretary, and Herbert E. Kahler was offered the job. Herb had served as chairman of the association since it was organized in 1948. With this offer in hand he retired from the National Park Service, where he had served as chief historian. With a full-time executive secretary to give guidance and direction, the services to park visitors, as well as sales, increased manyfold, In a nine-year period (1964–72) sales skyrocketed from $368,000 to $1.4 million per annum, and the accumulated donations to the service totaled $1 million.

Leslie T. Arnberger, chairman of the board of directors, in 1972 wrote in his annual report:

> We have gotten so used to success that we sometimes take it for granted. Success does not just happen. It takes teamwork from dedicated, enthusiastic people throughout the organization—from the field areas, through central office to the Executive Director at the top.
>
> Your Association has had this kind of teamwork for years. From my experience during the past three years I have learned that this stems principally from the tireless and devoted work of one man—Executive Secretary Herb Kahler.
>
> Your Association has been in operation for 24 years and has had spectacular success. In 1948 gross sales were $997, and in 1972 they were over one and a quarter million dollars. We have served more people than ever this year, and sales have exceeded any previous year.
>
> All who have participated in the growth of the Association can draw real satisfaction from its accomplishments and feel their efforts have been well spent. In supplying visitors with selected interpretive items at nominal cost, the Association has brought many benefits to the interpretive program; in supplying funds to the National Park Service, it has helped to improve the Interpretive Program. . . .
>
> The primary purpose of the Association is to assist the Service in the interpretive field. The more we meet the visitors' needs in the interpretive program, the more funds we have to help the Service improve its Interpretive Program. . . . For the year 1972 the Association honored requests totaling $168,223.50.

The Eastern National Park and Monument Association has a total of 73 agents. An agent is a man or a group that runs the operation in an area. The association's 73 areas of operation are located in 26 different states and in Puerto Rico and the Virgin Islands. The association has 509 paying members—people who are interested in the work and support it with membership dues. Members do not necessarily have to be from any of the parks in which the association is operating.

Interpretive merchandise is attractively displayed for visitors in the refurbished sales center in the West Wing of Independence Hall, a part of Independence National Historic Park, Philadelphia, Pennsylvania. *Photo by Clyde Lockwood, courtesy National Park Service.*

In 1972 the smallest total sales of an agency that had been in existence more than one year were at Saint Gaudens National Historic Site ($1,057), and the largest were at Independence National Historic Park in Philadelphia ($187,380). The assets of the association at the end of the fiscal year 1972 totaled $1,260,035.

I've gone to considerable length on this subject primarily to show what people can do to improve their product by "pulling themselves up by their bootstraps." There are other associations in the national park system that have similar records, but Eastern is the largest and the one that tackled the toughest job, for it took in all the small areas in the eastern part of the United States that wanted to join. Without that help the small areas could do little or nothing toward developing satisfactory programs.

There has been a spin-off from the success of organizations of this kind. At the beginning of the Kennedy administration Jacqueline Kennedy took a great deal of interest in refurbishing the White House, and of course that took money. The National Park Service maintains the White House grounds, which are the number one reservation of the National Capital Parks, and the White House is classified as a historic building. In a conversation with Mrs. Kennedy we suggested that a historical association similar to the Eastern National Park and Monument Association be established that would prepare a booklet about the White House to be sold only in the White House as a souvenir for those making the guided tour. The White House Historical Association was established in 1961. The National Geographic Society gave the association a loan of noninterest money to get started and also donated editorial services and pictures for the booklet. The booklet was published by the association and went on sale at the beginning of 1962. It has undergone several revisions and reprintings, and several companion publications, such as *The Living White House* and *The Book of the Presidents*, have been issued. The revenue from the sale of its books enabled the White House Historical Association to pay back the loan and, as of December, 1978, to contribute close to $3.5 million to the White House to refurbish the interior of the building, provide funds for the painting of portraits of the presidents and first ladies, and give assistance to the White House library. This is a remarkable record, and it was made possible through the donation of thousands of hours of professional time and other resources by the National Geographic Society.

Similar associations have since been formed for the Capitol and the Supreme Court. The Washington Monument Association has issued a historic booklet on the Washington Monument, which has also been very successful. They too have taken advantage of the generosity of the National Geographic Society and several trustees of the society have memberships on one or more of these four associations.

HISTORIC SITES ACT OF 1935

The first section of the Historic Sites Act of 1935 reads, "That it is hereby declared that it is a national policy to preserve for public use historic sites, buildings and objects of national significance for the inspiration and benefit of the people of the United States." It is hard to figure how a policy could be written any simpler and yet cover such a broad, all inclusive purpose.

The second section describes the duties to be performed by the secretary of the interior, through the National Park Service, in effectuating the policy expressed in the act. These duties are: collating data, surveys, etc. that illustrate United States history; carrying out investigations and research; acquiring property; protecting religious groups; providing for funds; and mak-

The home of the founder of the American Red Cross, now preserved as Clara Barton National Historic Site, Maryland, was the organization's headquarters for seven years. *Courtesy National Park Service.*

ing cooperative agreements with other organizations and political bodies to restore, reconstruct, rehabilitate, preserve, and maintain historic or prehistoric sites, buildings, and objects. It further gives the secretary authority to provide tablets and markers, operate buildings, make contracts with concessionaires, conduct educational programs, establish rules and regulations, and define penalities for violations. Although the National Park Service had acquired historic sites and objects under the 1906 Antiquities Act, and the 1916 act establishing the National Park Service, the Historic Sites Act of 1935 spelled out and assigned definite responsibility for protecting and interpreting the history of man on this continent.

Section three provides for the establishment of the Advisory Board on National Parks, Historic Sites, Buildings, and Monuments to be composed of not more than eleven citizens of the United States, including representatives competent in the fields of history, archaeology, architecture, and human

The Advisory Board on National Parks, Historic Sites, Buildings and Monuments at a meeting in Grand Teton National Park, September 7–9, 1955. *Left to right:* Walter L. Huber, California; Horace M. Albright, California; Harold S. Wagner, Ohio; Conrad L. Wirth, director, National Park Service; Alfred A. Knopf, chairman, New York; Dr. Turpin C. Bannister, Illinois; Dr. John O. Brew, Massachusetts; Dr. E. Raymond Hall, Kansas; Dr. Charles G. Woodbury, Washington, D.C.; John B. Oakes, New York.

geography. They are appointed by the secretary. Shortly after the act became law a very talented group of people in various professional fields were appointed to the advisory board by the secretary. They had no set terms and they stayed on until they resigned or were replaced. It wasn't until the late forties that Secretary Oscar Chapman established staggered terms of six years for the members. The original board served the secretary and the National Park Service with distinction, and the committees of Congress depended to a great extent on its recommendations.

I believe Congress still relies on the board's advice, but, I am informed, to a lesser degree than formerly. In my opinion the reason is that people have been appointed who do not have the qualifications to make sound professional recommendations in accordance with the intent of the law. In fact, there have been several appointed for political reasons or for their contributions to political parties, possibly as a form of personal recognition for there is no salary attached to these appointments. I see no objection to politically oriented appointees as long as they are professionals qualified to fulfill the responsibilities of the office.

	Natural Areas	Historic Areas	Recreation Areas	Other Areas	Total
1916	26	8	0	1	35
1933					
Before reorganization	46	20	0	0	66
After reorganization	38	77	1	1	137
1964	65	144	16	1	226
1972	74	172	36	2	284
1978	84	184	51	1	320

From Ronald F. Lee, *Family Tree of the National Park System* (Philadelphia: Eastern National Park and Monument Association, 1972), p. 88.

The Historic Sites act is of tremendous importance to the nation, and a good deal of credit is due to the National Park Service chief historian of that time, Dr. Verne E. Chatelain, for its effectiveness. I must make clear that while the act is referred to as the *Historic* Sites Act, the board's responsibility applied to the Park Service as a whole, not just to historic areas. Keep in mind that when the National Park Service was established, in 1916, there were fourteen national parks and twenty-one national monuments, seven of which dealt with history, three each in Arizona and New Mexico and one in Alaska. By 1933, before reorganization, the system had grown to sixty-six areas, of which forty-six were classified as natural areas and twenty as historic areas. The preceding table shows the increase in the number of areas in the national park system before and since the 1933 reorganization.

The big expansion in the national park system and in state parks initiated in the CCC period was further encouraged by Mission 66; this program stimulated federal legislation for the preservation of natural and historic sites and promoted the development at all levels of government of historic, recreational, and natural areas.

PARK, PARKWAY, AND RECREATIONAL-AREA STUDY ACT OF 1936

At the request of the National Park Service through the Department of the Interior, the Seventy-fourth Congress enacted legislation whereby the service was empowered to continue on a permanent basis the cooperation with the states it had established during the CCC period. A nationwide study was then made to secure basic data so that the service and the states and their civil divisions could develop integrated park and recreation systems based on the best experience in the nation. Success depended on the mutual efforts of all agencies concerned with the public park and recreation movement.

The importance of comprehensive park, parkway, and recreational-area planning has long been recognized and was repeatedly demonstrated during the emergency programs, particularly in selecting and developing additional park and recreation areas to round out park systems. But in the spring of 1933 when the National Park Service, through its Branch of Land Planning and State Cooperation, began collaborating with the states and their divisions in emergency programs, planning information for such programs was extremely meager on the state level. Recreational programs had been in operation for some years in a number of states, but only in a few cases had long-range plans been formulated on the basis of in-depth studies of land uses and recreation needs. It is a well-known fact that leisure time needs increase with economic growth and social advances as well as with population growth. Before the opportunities to fulfill these needs can be provided, however, recreational resources must be appraised and recreational needs estimated, and only on the basis of comprehensive surveys is it possible to establish and maintain standards that are both adequate and feasible in terms of available resources. It was this lack of planning information and the increasing need for recreational facilities that led to enactment of the 1936 law. The national study would have to include an inventory and analysis of existing park, parkway, and recreational facilities, whether federal, state, county, municipal, or private. It would also have to bring together the plans or proposals for future park development that had been drawn up at these various levels, including areas studied for possible acquisition or development, an analysis and appraisal of findings, and recommendations.

The Park, Parkway, and Recreational-Area Study Act plays a key role in the history of parks in the United States, and for this reason I have included the complete text of the act below:

An Act to authorize a study of the park, parkway, and recreational-area programs in the United States, and for other purposes, approved June 23, 1936 (49 Stat. 1894).

Be it enacted by the Senate and House of Representatives of the United States of America in Congress assembled, that the Secretary of the Interior (hereinafter referred to as the "Secretary") is authorized and directed to cause the National Park Service to make a comprehensive study, other than on lands under the jurisdiction of the Department of Agriculture, of the public park, parkway, and recreational-area programs of the United States, and of the several States and political subdivisions thereof, and of the lands throughout the United States which are or may be chiefly valuable as such areas, but no such study shall be made in any State without the consent and approval of the State officials, boards, or departments having jurisdiction over such lands and park areas. The said study shall be such as, in the judgment of the Secretary, will provide data helpful in developing a plan for coordinated and adequate public park, parkway, and recreational-area facilities for the people of the United States. In making the said study and in accomplishing any of the purposes of this Act, the Secretary is authorized and directed, through the National Park Service, to seek and accept the cooperation and assistance of Federal departments or agencies having jurisdiction of lands belonging to the United States, and may cooperate and make agreements with and seek and accept the assistance of other Federal agencies and instrumentalities, and of States and political subdivisions thereof and the agencies and instrumentalities of either of them. (16 U.S.C. sec. 17k.)

Sec. 2. For the purpose of developing coordinated and adequate public park, parkway, and recreational-area facilities for the people of the United States, the Secretary is authorized to aid the several States and political subdivisions thereof in planning such areas therein, and in cooperating with one another to accomplish these ends. Such aid shall be made available through the National Park Service acting in cooperation with such State agencies or agencies of political subdivisions of States as the Secretary deems best. (16 U.S.C. sec. 17L.)

Sec. 3. The consent of Congress is hereby given to any two or more States to negotiate and enter into compacts or agreements with one another with reference to planning, establishing, developing, improving, and maintaining any park, parkway, or recreational area. No such compact or agreement shall be effective until approved by the legislatures of the several States which are parties thereto and by the Congress of the United States. (16 U.S.C. sec. 17m.)

Sec. 4. As used in sections 1 and 2 of this Act the term "State" shall be deemed to include Hawaii, Alaska, Puerto Rico, the Virgin Islands, and the District of Columbia. (16 U.S.C. sec. 17n.)

Shortly after approval of the 1936 act Secretary Ickes addressed the following letter to the governors of the states:

I am enclosing for your consideration a copy of "An act to authorize a study of the park, parkway, and recreational-area programs in the United States, and for other purposes" approved June 23, 1936. You will note that the Act provides for cooperation between the Federal Government, through the National Park Service, of this Department, and the several States and local civil divisions thereof, in making comprehensive studies as a basis for State and local planning for park, parkway, and recreational-areas and facilities and in aiding in the planning of such areas.

Prior to the passage of this Act, many of the States, through various agencies, such as planning boards and commissions, had initiated studies for the purpose of establishing and extending State park and recreational systems.

Now that there is definite authority for a closer cooperation between the Federal Government and the several States, it is expected that State and local park, parkway, and recreational-area planning will receive greater consideration and that the work will be systematized and correlated on a State, regional, and Nation-wide basis.

Plans are now being made to carry out the provisions of the Act, and I shall appreciate knowing whether your State wishes to avail itself of the cooperative assistance of the National Park Service in studying and planning park, parkway, and recreational-area facilities within the State, and in coordination with similar facilities in the other States. Approval by the State of —— of such cooperation with the Federal Government will aid in the development of a coordinated plan for the Nation.

Sincerely yours,
Harold L. Ickes
Secretary of the Interior

Retired Justice William O. Douglas of the United States Supreme Court, *left*, lunches with a boy scout troop and Park Service officials at Great Falls in Chesapeake and Ohio Canal National Historic Park. Douglas has hiked the entire 184 miles of the canal between Washington, D.C., and Cumberland, Maryland, in the interest of preserving the canal.

The secretary received a favorable response from all the states, and in January, 1937, the Park Service issued a brochure on how this program with the states would be carried out.

The Park Service brochure informed the states that the service was in the process of making several related studies that would be of help in the cooperative effort authorized by the act. First, there was state legislation for parks and recreation to be considered. The Park Service had been making a compilation of laws pertaining to park conservation and recreation and had announced that when that study was completed it would be made available for wide distribution (see the final section of this chapter). Second, the service was studying areas proposed as additions to the national park system, and the results indicated that some of the lands studied would be more suitable for state park systems. That information would be turned over to the sponsors of the appropriate state recreational studies. It was hoped that any areas that the states found in their park studies to be more suitable for the national system, particularly historic sites, would be made available to the National Park Service. The third study was of municipal and metropolitan parks. It was reported that an inventory of municipal, metropolitan, and county parks and recreation areas and facilities was being conducted jointly by the National Park Service and the National Recreation Association and that the tabulation was expected to be ready for publication in early 1937. This information would be available in manuscript form before then, for use by the states in connection with their studies under the Park, Parkway, and Recreational-Area Study Act.

The service's brochure discussed the problem of land use in a comprehensive study. It observed that conservation could be defined as the dedication of particular natural resources to the use for which they were best suited and that lands put to recreational use were part of the general conservation program. As the study of these lands indicated, recreation may be the highest or the only use that should be made of some areas, but it may be only one of several concurrent uses of other areas. It went on to say that as the need for park, parkway, and recreational areas becomes more widely recognized, the recreational uses will tend to supersede other uses in many cases.

The brochure gave a brief history of America's public land use. In 1641 the Boston Bay Colony decreed that the great parks were to be forever open and free to the public for fowling and fishing. This was a forerunner of land conservation by the states for recreation purposes. Toward the end of the eighteenth century plans for the national capital city set a new standard for parks and open spaces. At the close of the colonial period and toward the first part of the nineteenth century, interest in the recreational use of natural resources lapsed and commercial exploitation of resources became the order of the day. The demand for open space for recreational use by city populations was not revived until the middle of the nineteenth century, coincident with the period of rapid urban growth. Central Park was established in New York City in 1852. and the park movement spread to other cities. But it wasn't until 1872 that the federal government began to take an interest in the conservation of natural resources for recreational purposes. In that year it established the first national park in the world, Yellowstone. Several states, notably New York, Michigan, and Minnesota, had established state park systems during the twenty-year period ending in 1890, but this movement had been slow.

At the time the brochure was published in 1937 there were eighty-one areas in the national park system, which, along with the National Capital Parks, totaled approximately sixteen million acres. With the beginning of the

CCC program in 1933, several of the states, including Arizona, Louisiana, Mississippi, Montana, Nevada, New Mexico, Oklahoma, South Carolina, Utah, Virginia, and West Virginia, established state park systems and acquired park areas. By 1937 practically every state had a state park program.

It is interesting to note that, between the beginning of the CCC and the time the brochure was written, the number of acres of land in state park systems, exclusive of the Adirondack and Catskill Mountains in New York (which were really part of the state preserve and contained some 2,373,000 acres), had grown from 887,000 to 1,486,000 acres, an increase of approximately 600,000 acres, or better than 67½ per cent. The impetus provided by the CCC program was responsible for much of this growth. A good part of the 600,000 acres was donated by public-minded citizens who wanted CCC camps to turn the land into parks in the interest of conservation and community improvement.

The brochure briefly listed the types of recreational activity that should be considered in parks: (1) *Physical:* sports of all kinds—hiking, riding, etc. (2) *Aesthetic:* appreciation of beauty as manifested in nature, art music, drama, etc. (3) *Creative:* self-expression through handicraft, writing, painting, etc. (4) *Intellectual:* avocational pursuits such as study of history, archaeology, geology, etc. (5) *Social:* group or family gatherings, games, and the like.

The classification of recreational areas was next described. The customary designation of recreational areas in terms of administrative jurisdiction—national parks, state parks, etc.—had led to some confusion in the real meaning of the term *park.* In order to provide an adequate classification of recreational areas on the basis of use, a special subcommittee of the National Resources Committee was appointed to study the question. After reviewing the terms and definitions in use by federal and other agencies, the committee proposed the classification of recreational areas under four principal headings: primitive, modified, developed, and scientific.

The first part of the Park Service's brochure had set forth the basic approach and the need for a comprehensive study of the nationwide system of parks. It concluded with a look at the necessary data that study would have to consider: climatic, economic, biological, historic, archaeological, social, and other factors.

The second part of the brochure went into considerable detail on organization and procedure. That part of the booklet was devoted to forms, enumeration of considerations, graphics, and all the tools necessary to carry out the plan to develop state park systems and tie them together into a nationwide system.

The Park, Parkway, and Recreational-Area Study Act, though weak in many respects, became very effective through mutual understanding and cooperation between all the agencies involved. This team spirit was undoubtedly inspired by Secretary Ickes's letter to the states. In the thirties no regularly appropriated funds were allotted to the Park, Parkway, and Recreational-Area Study by the federal government. But the study was felt to be so important to the implementation of a successful emergency program, especially the CCC program, that most of the study was financed with federal CCC funds. Some forty-six states completed comprehensive state park system plans. Technicians were either assigned to them from the National Park Service or employed with CCC funds allotted to the states through the service. The comprehensive plans and the states' written reports (not federal government reports) were products of state and federal collaboration. The allotment of CCC camps to the states also influenced the development of the state park systems, for if a state park was not part of an overall state park system, in accordance with the study, there were grave questions raised as to whether that park could be allotted a camp.

Because of its great interest and experience in planning and developing recreational lands, the National Park Service had been asked by the National Resources Board to prepare a report on "Recreational Use of Lands in the United States." This 1934 report, published as part of the board's report on land planning, was an attempt to produce on very short notice an overall picture of recreational land use and the problems that must be faced in providing land to satisfy the needs of the people. It got us started on a second report, which was printed in 1941. By the time we were assembling and writing the 1941 report, over thirty-four states had completed detailed studies that showed not only what provisions were currently available for nonurban recreation in various land categories but also what was still needed.

The term *recreation* was very rarely used in the 1934 report. In contrast, the 1941 report endeavored to use the word consistently in its broad sense rather than in the narrow sense of mere physical exertion. The dictionary defines recreation as "the act of recreating, or the state of being recreated; refreshment of body or mind after toil; diversion; amusement." There is justification within that broad definition to classify national parks and monuments as recreation areas. The act of 1916 creating the National Park Service states that such areas are to be conserved for enjoyment, which surely includes refreshment not only of body and mind but of the spirit as well. The service has consistently maintained that its dominant purpose has been to stimulate refreshment of mind and spirit; that this purpose can be fulfilled only if the inspirational qualities of the areas it administers, whether based on natural scenery or on scientific, historic, or prehistoric values, are safeguarded to the utmost; and that provisions for physical recreation should be limited so that they do not impair inspirational qualities.

The 1941 report was comprehensive, covering the recreational habits and needs of the people; aspects of recreational planning; existing public outdoor recreational facilities on city, county, state, and federal lands; administration, including organization, operations, personnel, budget, public relations, and so on; finance, including the history and current situation of financing recreation and park work, cooperative financing, nonprofit corporations, and so forth; and legislation at all levels of government. The report also had a brief description and a map of each state, giving physical characteristics and indicating the existing condition of the state parks. And it proposed developments and additions to state park systems.

Secretary Ickes wrote the foreword, which stated in part:

> The proper use of leisure time is a fundamental problem of modern society. The industrial age has given the people of the United States more free time and greater opportunities for employing it to good purpose than any previous era, but the very circumstances which shorten working hours also speed up production, intensify the strain of present-day living, and create a need for periodic relief. Outdoor recreation answers this need.

Although this report was finished in 1941, it didn't get off the press until after we got involved in war. And so the secretary inserted a supplemental foreword, dated February 10, 1942, which is very interesting because it leads on to another principle.

> The accompanying report is presented at a time when our energies and resources are centered in one objective—victory in war. Although it was prepared and printed prior to our involvement, it is timely with respect to the Nation's immediate recreational needs and its value with respect to long-range problems remains pertinent.
>
> While our present war effort must take precedence over all other activities, planning to meet our park and recreational requirements must continue to receive consideration. The inspiration experienced through visiting the Nation's scenic wonders and historic shrines instills a love of country and maintains morale, and participation in recreational activities is vital to the welfare of the people, both military and civilian.

The war was on and money was in short supply as far as the Park Service was concerned. But with what we had we kept on working in close relationship with the states, mostly thinking and planning for the future. We had hopes that we could review our plan of 1941 and bring it up to date every five years. There was definitely a joint effort between the states and the federal government to present a comprehensive plan that required implementation—a program of detailed land planning, land acquisition, development, administration, and maintenance.

We also felt that there should be a definite grant-in-aid program by the federal government to the states and, through the states, to their political subdivisions. Such a program required additional legislation. By 1945 we had worked up a draft of a bill that Representative J. Hardin Peterson of Florida, chairman of the Public Lands Committee, introduced on October 16, 1945, as H.R. 4395 of the Seventy-ninth Congress, first session. Its title was "To provide that the United States shall aid the States in the acquisition and development of systems of State parks, and for other purposes." The first section of that bill read as follows:

Be it enacted by the Senate and House of Representatives of the United States of America in Congress assembled, That in order to aid in the acquisition and development of systems of State parks for use by the people of the States of the Union, and in the construction and improvement of facilities in such parks the Secretary of the Interior (hereinafter referred to as the Secretary), acting through the National Park Service, is hereby authorized to cooperate with the States through the respective State park agencies, by making grant-in-aid of projects as hereinafter set forth in this Act.

I was the principal advocate of the bill in the National Park Service, but twelve days after the bill was introduced I left for Vienna, Austria, on an assignment by Secretary Ickes. Nothing really happened to that piece of legislation after my departure.

Twenty years later the pressures for open spaces, parks, and recreational areas, as well as for the preservation of wilderness areas, became so great that the president of the United States recommended and Congress authorized establishment of the Outdoor Recreation Resources Review Commission. Its broad concept was similar to that of the Park, Parkway, and Recreational-Area Study Act of 1936, except that it required the full cooperation of all federal agencies. The ORRRC spent the better part of four years making a very full and well-organized analysis of our open space needs. Among its main recommendations were the establishment of the Bureau of Outdoor Recreation as an agency of the Interior Department distinct from the National Park Service and passage of the Land and Water Bill, an authorization act that would provide for funding certain items for federal, state, and local park systems. The bureau allots funds for planning, land purchase, and development of state and local park systems and for land purchase by federal bureaus. We in the National Park Service were disappointed that BOR was set up as a separate agency in the department but pleased to know that finally the nationwide park and recreation requirements were receiving proper attention and that federal aid was being provided. The disappointment became even harder to bear when the new bureau was established on the authority of the Park, Parkway, and Recreational-Area Study Act of 1936, before it got its own basic legislation. The National Park Service was obliged to transfer its personnel who were then cooperating with the state park people along with $1.5 million in funds to the new agency.

It is only right that I clarify the record about the so-called final report of the National Park Service in the series that was started at the request of the National Resources Board in 1934. The first report was entitled "Recreational Use of Lands in the United States." The second, called "A Study of the Park and Recreation Problem of the United States," came off the press early in 1942 but had actually been completed in 1941 before we got involved in the war. Both were financed with CCC funds. The third, the "service's last report," was a Mission 66 project started in 1957 and completed in the spring of 1961. The Department of the Interior, however, refused to let it be released pending the report of the Outdoor Recreation Resources Review Commission, which came out in January, 1962. "Parks for America," finally released in 1964, had input from every state in the union.

It had a foreword by Secretary Stewart Udall that was anything but favorable. Nowhere in his foreword did the secretary say a good thing about the report. He did say it might be a tool that BOR could use. His foreword was a slur on the Park Service and the states that helped, over a period of six years, to put the report together. It was disconcerting that a new bureau was established to do the work that the service had been doing since 1921, especially since we hadn't even been consulted on the matter. We were further upset to learn that a man who had no park and recreation planning experience was appointed its director, though he was well qualified as a career forester.

Despite all this, it was my most sincere hope that BOR would provide the grant-in-aid help that is so necessary for the nation's open spaces to be preserved and developed for the benefit of the people. Perhaps the best way to indicate my true feelings on this matter is to quote from a letter I wrote to some two dozen senators in 1964 in support of BOR.

> The Land and Water Bill, H.R. 3846, has passed the House and is now before the Senate. There is no question but that this bill, if it becomes law, will be one of the most important pieces of permanent legislation that have been enacted in the field of conservation of our natural resources, for the benefit of our human resources, and for the enjoyment of a fuller life, for years to come, by the people in all the communities of our country. Further, never in our history has it been so important to give serious and profound attention to this matter. To delay further will be not only more costly in a monetary way, but could deal a blow to the nation's welfare from which we may not be able to recover fully for years to come.
>
> This may sound like strong language—it is intended to be just that. But it is no stronger than the language used by the Supreme Court of the State of Washington in one of its decisions made over thirty years ago, when it said: "An unwritten compact between the dead, the living, and the unborn requires that we leave the unborn something more than debts and depleted natural resources." Some of the "unborn" then referred to have since been born, and more unborn are still to come, but we continue merrily along our way, with no definite comprehensive program devoted to caring for people and their God-given right to understand, enjoy, and obtain inspiration and healthful benefits from the very land, water, and air from whence all have sprung. . . .
>
> H.R. 3846, if it becomes law—and I pray that it will—will be a real advance, providing the first step toward setting up the necessary machinery around which all governmental agencies can work hand-in-hand, to rid ourselves of the cancerous

disease of self-destruction. Congress provided the funds and incentive through the Outdoor Recreation Resources Review Commission, chaired by Laurance S. Rockefeller, to check into what was recognized as a national problem and to recommend a solution. Congress took the first step by establishing the Bureau of Outdoor Recreation. H.R. 3846 would give the Bureau the tools necessary to start carrying out the findings of ORRRC, which I understand is the intent of Congress.

There is little doubt in my mind but that additional legislation will be needed as time goes on and as experience dictates. Perhaps this legislation is not perfect, but at least it will give, to the agency to which Congress has assigned the responsibility, a chance to carry out that responsibility, and to report back to Congress, with recommendations, the results of its efforts.

. . . The nation must provide its people with a means to insure a fuller, more enjoyable life, and one that will provide satisfying outdoor recreation opportunity for all. If we don't, our troubles will forever increase.

Unless somebody has a better idea, I believe that a park and recreation program for the entire nation is our best solution. I felt that way when Congress enacted the Park, Parkway and Recreation Study Act in 1936. I feel that way now, except that it is presently many times more important. However, now we have H.R. 3846 under consideration, which, if it becomes law, will give the B.O.R. some real tools to work with, tools which were not provided under the 1936 Act. . . .

My closing remarks are: *Please pass this legislation (H.R. 3846) during this session of Congress.* To delay another year or two will gain us nothing but a deeper rut out of which to climb. . . .

RECREATIONAL DEMONSTRATION AREAS

One of the really successful New Deal programs was the Recreational Demonstration Area (RDA) Program. In the thirties the CCC, WPA, PWA, and several other federal work programs were available for the development of national, state, and metropolitan parks. Generally speaking, however, their funds could not be used for the acquisition of land. In the case of state parks most of the lands were donated. These areas were usually some distance from communities, but they added greatly to satisyfing the recreational needs of the people.

At the same time there were farmlands relatively close to centers of population that were of poor soil, or abused, eroded, or otherwise submarginal from the standpoint of agricultural production. With the advent of the New Deal the whole question of land use and upkeep became a national topic. Studies revealed that the cost of maintaining schools, roads, and other governmental services for such poor farming areas generally exceeded the total income derived from these submarginal lands. During the depression most of the people on these lands were on relief. Before the Roosevelt administration little had been done to try to solve these problems. There were a few exceptions: Michigan had initiated a program of buying up submarginal land and turning it into state forests, and Maine had large areas outside local government jurisdiction reserved for private and public forests.

When he was governor of New York, Roosevelt had become very much concerned with the problem of land utilization. It was only natural, therefore, that his recovery program should provide a solution for the problem of submarginal farmland. In January, 1934, the president set up a Land Planning Committee consisting of Secretary of the Interior Harold L. Ickes, Secretary of Agriculture Henry A. Wallace, WPA Administrator Harry L. Hopkins, and the governor of the Farm Credit Administration, W. I. Myers, to develop a program of land utilization. This committee worked through coordinators appointed by the cooperating agencies, somewhat as was done in establishing the CCC. I was designated the Interior Department coordinator, and Matt Huppuch of the National Park Service staff was my alternate.

The general program was liberal enough to be available to nearly every land-using bureau of the government. Of course, in interior we needed additional lands for the national park system—not so much for new areas as for rounding out existing areas—and there were several other bureaus in the department that had land needs. For example, the Fish and Wildlife Service was being organized at this time, and one of the great conservation leaders of the nation, the well-known cartoonist Ding Darling, was appointed to head it. One of its most urgent problems involved preserving marshlands as nesting grounds and as rest stops along the flyways for migratory birds.

The Park Service came forward with a definite program for acquiring lands that were no longer suitable for agriculture but that, if returned to natural condition and if within a reasonable distance of metropolitan areas, would provide a much needed recreation facility for large numbers of people. Most of the existing state parks were highly scenic areas situated at considerable distances from centers of population. Our studies indicated an urgent need for natural areas relatively close to population centers and available to large numbers of people for weekend and even day use. These were, in fact, the most needed links in the nation's park and recreation programs. Such areas would have to be large enough to provide natural campsite spots as well as group campsites, hiking trails, swimming, and picnic facilities. The studies also indicated that many private groups—especially such social organizations as police boys' clubs—could provide for the operation and maintenance of group camps but could not afford the necessary capital investments for such essentials as sufficient land, sanitary facilities, recreation facilities, and so forth. The early provisions of the New Deal law authorized manpower and materials for improvement and development of such areas. Land acquisition was the big problem.

A program was prepared to provide land for four types of development projects: (1) Areas eligible for and worthy of inclusion in existing or proposed national parks and monuments and historic areas. (2) Wayside areas along existing or proposed highways as demonstrations of needed rest areas. (3)

Principal federal officials who were working together on conservation and park development programs inspected a wayside area at Quantico, Virginia, south of Washington, D.C., in 1936. *Left to right:* Robert Fechner, director, Civilian Conservation Corps; Theodore A. Walters, assistant secretary, Department of the Interior; Wally Richards, assistant director, Emergency Relief Administration Land Program; Conrad L. Wirth, chief, Branch of Recreation, Land Planning and State Cooperation, National Park Service; John Lansill, director, Land Program, ERA; Marshall Finnan, director National Capital Parks, National Park Service; Mr. Jacobs, administrative assistant to Harry L. Hopkins, director of Federal Emergency Relief and the Civil Works program. *Courtesy James F. Kieley.*

State scenic area extensions. (4) Vacation or recreation areas near urban communities, which became known as Recreational Demonstration Areas.

Early in 1934, as a result of the recommendations of the Land Planning Committee, the Public Works Administration allocated twenty-five million dollars to the Federal Surplus Relief Administration for the purchase of submarginal agricultural lands. In July the Land Planning Committee formulated a program of recreational, general agricultural, biological, and Indian projects. This program was approved by the special Board of Public Works, and the previously allocated twenty-five million dollars was transferred to the newly organized Land Program of the Federal Emergency Relief Administration. All agencies of the government interested in rural land utilization were advised to submit their programs of land use adjustment to the Land Planning Committee.

John S. Lansill, of Kentucky, was appointed director of the Land Program, and Wallace Richards was assistant director. Fortunately for us they both

Group camp checking station at Beach Pond, a 1,620-acre Recreational Demonstration Area in Rhode Island. *Courtesy National Park Service.*

Picnic shelter in Silver Creek State Park, a 3,390-acre RDA in Oregon. *Courtesy National Park Service.*

A rest period during a game of checkers at Hard Labor Creek, a 5,815-acre RDA in Georgia. *Courtesy National Park Service.*

A group sleeping cabin for six at Montgomery Bell, a 3,820-acre RDA in Tennessee. *Courtesy National Park Service.*

A unit lodge in Lake Murray State Park, a 2,230-acre RDA in Oklahoma. *Courtesy National Park Service.*

Schoolgirl campers using the swimming pool in Blue Knob State Park, a 5,565-acre RDA in Pennsylvania. *Courtesy National Park Service.*

Lake of the Ozarks State Park, a 16,025-acre RDA in Missouri, contains general park facilities and group camps. *Courtesy National Park Service.*

Pine Mountain State Park Extension, a 3,025-acre RDA in Georgia, aids in the protection of FDR's Georgia White House, which is in the park. *Courtesy National Park Service.*

Swimming lessons in a lake created by a dam that was built through RDA efforts in Crabtree Creek State Park, a 4,985-acre RDA in North Carolina. *Courtesy National Park Service.*

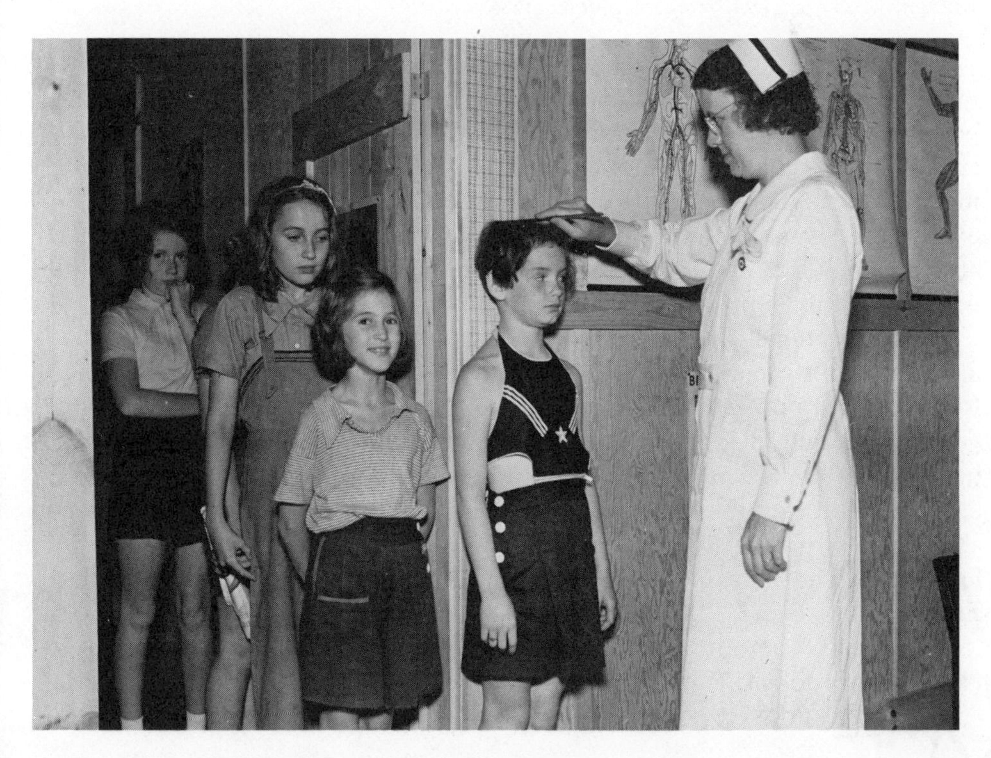

Children check in at a RDA group camp in Bear Brook State Park, a 6,345-acre RDA in New Hampshire. *Courtesy National Park Service.*

A campfire program at one of the group camps in Montserrat State Park, a 3,445-acre RDA in Missouri. *Courtesy National Park Service.*

were very interested in vacation areas and in the need for them near heavily populated areas. Wally Richards had traveled extensively in Europe. He strongly favored acquisition of sizable areas of submarginal land within fifty miles of population centers to provide camping, hiking, and swimming for children, adults, and families. Matt Huppuch was aware that in Switzerland all school children had opportunities to spend time in a nature camp, and he wholeheartedly approved of the practice.

The Recreational Demonstration Areas got under way with the unanimous approval and support of the National Park Service and the Land Planning Committee of the Federal Emergency Relief Administration. In less than a year the National Park Service—its emergency personnel paid from various funds—investigated over four hundred areas, and twenty-five projects were approved and were in various stages of planning and development. Eventually there were forty-six RDAs and several miscellaneous projects in twenty-four states. The following tables give an overall picture of the complete Land Program.

Two sites became new areas to the park system. At Theodore Roosevelt National Memorial Park, in North Dakota, we bought over sixty-three

National Park System Areas Established

Name	State	Approximate Acreage
Theodore Roosevelt National Memorial Park	North Dakota	63,483
Hopewell Village National Historic Site	Pennsylvania	848
		64,331

thousand acres of land at an average cost of slightly over two dollars an acre. This land borders the little Missouri River and is in two units. It is the location of Theodore Roosevelt's Elk Horn Ranch, where he went to regain his health and where he recruited and organized the Rough Riders of the Spanish-American War. It is northern prairie grass country, rich in the history of the early settlers and cowboys.

Hopewell Village National Historic Site was a discovery we stumbled upon in buying the French Creek Recreation Area for the state of Pennsylvania. We discovered an old foundry, several buildings with some twenty old carriages in them, and a blacksmith shop. The blacksmith shop was practically all covered over with dirt. When we dug our way into it we found that it contained all the old blacksmith tools used in the days of the Revolution. A study revealed that this area had manufactured a lot of hardware for the Continental army—cannon balls and the like. Because its history was certainly of national importance, we kept some 848 acres in federal ownership to establish a historic site and turned the rest—about 5,125 acres—over to the state for its park system.

The Blue Ridge Parkway was being built on land given to the federal government by the states and on right-of-way provided by the United States Forest Service where the parkway went through several national forests. In addition, some 10,000 acres in five different locations were purchased with funds provided by the Land Program Committee. The parkway is 469 miles long, along the ridge of the Blue Ridge Mountains, and connects Shenandoah and Great Smoky Mountains national parks. There are now services of various kinds along this parkway, including parking areas and campgrounds.

Kings Mountain National Military Park, commemorating a revolutionary war engagement, was established by the military in 1931 and transferred to the National Park Service in 1933. The military hadn't obtained much more than the site for a memorial. We purchased additional land in order to tell the full story of the battle.

The other areas that extended national parks included private lands that were within the authorized boundaries and that qualified under the Land Planning Committee's regulations, but that had not been purchased because regular funds were not available.

National Park System Area Extensions

Name	State	Approximate Acreage
Acadia National Park	Maine	5,691
White Sands National Monument	New Mexico	1,718
Manassas National Battlefield Park	Virginia	1,475
Shenandoah National Park	Virginia	10,294
Badlands National Monument	South Dakota	43,452
Kings Mountain National Military Park	South Carolina	4,079
Blue Ridge Parkway	Virginia and North Carolina	10,585
		77,294

Waysides is the title we gave to lands purchased to provide rest and picnic areas along main highways. South Carolina and Virginia were the two states that offered to cooperate on this experiment. We were not in a position to spend much money on this program; furthermore, most of the land along highways cost more than we were willing to spend. Back in the thirties the only state I know of that did anything like this of its own accord was Michigan. The states had their limitations and had to spend most of their money on rights-of-way, and construction and maintenance were a problem. Many interstate and United States highways now have rest areas, though our term *waysides* was not adopted. We would like to believe that the waysides program we started was the beginning of a movement toward providing such stopping accommodations along highways.

The Recreational Demonstration Areas were the main purpose of the larger program. On these areas we proposed to build campsites primarily for group camping but also to provide year-round camping and recreation for individuals, small groups, and families. Our general objective was to provide quality outdoor recreation facilities at the lowest possible cost for the benefit of people of lower and middle incomes. One of the initial requirements—and we stuck to them very closely—was that the area should be from two to ten thousand acres and within a radius of approximately fifty miles of a population

Waysides

State	Number	Approximate Acreage
Virginia	7 areas	203
South Carolina	6 areas	239
		442

State Park Extensions

Name	State	Approximate Acreage
Alex H. Stephens	Georgia	985
Pine Mountain	Georgia	3,023
Custer Park	South Dakota	20,168
Falls Creek Falls	Tennessee	15,785
Lake Guernsey	Wyoming	1,880
		41,841

Recreational Demonstration Areas Transferred to the States as Part of Their State Park Systems

Name	State	Approximate Acreage
Oak Mountain	Alabama	7,802
Mendocino	California	5,425
Hard Labor Creek	Georgia	5,816
Pere Marquette	Illinois	2,205
Versailles	Indiana	5,345
Winamac	Indiana	6,250
Otter Creek	Kentucky	2,455
Camden	Maine	5,153
Catoctin [1]	Maryland	9,988
Waterloo	Michigan	12,105
Yankee Springs	Michigan	4,217
Saint Croix	Minnesota	18,483
Lake of the Ozarks	Missouri	16,023
Cuivre River	Missouri	5,751
Montserrat	Missouri	3,444
Bear Brook	New Hampshire	6,347
Crabtree Creek	North Carolina	4,986
Lake Murray	Oklahoma	2,230
Silver Creek	Oregon	3,391
Raccoon Creek	Pennsylvania	5,066
French Creek [2]	Pennsylvania	5,971
Laurel Hill	Pennsylvania	4,025
Blue Knob	Pennsylvania	5,565
Hickory Run	Pennsylvania	12,907
Beach Pond	Rhode Island	1,619
Cheraw	South Carolina	6,930
Kings Mountain	South Carolina	6,069
Montgomery Bell	Tennessee	3,821
Shelby Forest	Tennessee	12,478
Swift Creek	Virginia	7,548
Chopawamsic [3]	Virginia	14,414
	Total	213,829

[1]A tract of 5,659 acres was set aside in 1942 on which to build a "hideout" for President Roosevelt, which he called Shangri-La, so that he could remain close to Washington during World War II. Later President Eisenhower changed the name to Camp David after his grandson. The remaining 4,329 acres were transferred to the state of Maryland for its state park system.

[2]The National Park Service retained 848 acres to form the Hopewell Village National Historic Site as part of the national park system.

[3]The name was changed to Prince William Park, and the area is part of the Washington, D.C., park system.

center. Other criteria were abundance of good water, available building material, and an interesting environment. We felt water recreation was important and wanted to be sure to have a location where we could build small lakes if a lake was not already there. We had to show that at least a reasonable part of the lands we purchased was submarginal from an agricultural standpoint. All of the areas in this category are attractive for recreation purposes and are by no means submarginal from that standpoint. Originally the idea was to get land that could be purchased for five dollars an acre, though later that was extended to an average price of ten dollars an acre. Of course, buying Theodore Roosevelt's old Elk Horn Ranch, in North Dakota, at two dollars an acre helped balance off some of the more expensive lands acquired in the RDA program.

A lot of startling experiences resulted from the program. In recounting one that was particularly interesting I prefer to leave the location and names out of the story, though the facts are absolutely true. We were trying to buy some ten thousand acres along the waterfront of a reservoir. I was on a field trip elsewhere when I got a call that the man with authority to enter into a contract wouldn't talk to anybody but me. Since the area in question was on the way to my next stop four hundred miles away, I made an appointment for the next afternoon at his office. My companion and I started driving the next morning and got there on time only to find that the man had gone down to the guest house. Although this was out of our way and would require driving at night to get to our next appointment the following day, we decided to go see him. We arrived at the house about 6:30 P.M. He and his guest, an important customer, were drinking and gambling. We stood around for almost two and a half hours without talking business. They offered us a drink or two, which we accepted, but we declined to gamble with them. Finally, I got more than a little annoyed and told the man what was on my mind. His guest took up for us, and so the man we came down to see said, "Well, I haven't time to talk now, but if you had a contract with you all written up, I would sign it." I replied, "Well, I just happen to have a contract in my pocket for 10,000 acres at $5.00 an acre." I sure got a dirty look, but the man's client again stepped in, saying, "If you're a man of your word you'll sign it. You said you would." He signed and we left.

A ten-thousand-acre tract was used as a guideline because a tract of something more than five thousand acres seemed to divide itself readily into two parts, one for an organized camping area and the other for general public use. Each should have available natural or artificial bodies of water. Public use areas generally had a large picnic area for family use and group picnics, and a reasonable number of family campgrounds were planned and constructed. In the organized camping area there could be several projects, each having from three to six organized camps. A camp consisted of a general mess hall, an office, and an infirmary, and it had from three to four units, each unit containing a lodge with six cabins of four beds and a cabin for the leader. Thus, the camp was designed for around 72 to 96 campers and had a total capacity of 98 to 120 people. Most of these camps were built from stone and lumber from the project site and cost from $75,000 to $100,000.

It was our intention from the beginning, even though we had no existing authority at the time, to turn these areas over to the states to add to the state park systems when we were authorized to do so. In cases where the state was not particularly interested, we turned the areas over to counties or metropolitan areas, but most of the states participated in the program. All the plans for land acquisition and development carried both National Park Service and state or county park authority approval. It wasn't until June 6, 1942, that Congress enacted a law that gave the secretary of the interior authority to either deed or lease to the states any lands purchased under the Recreational Demonstration Area program together with all improvements, subject to an agreement that they would be used for public park and recreation purposes for at least twenty years. I believe the last transfer was made to the state of Maryland in 1956.

The RDA program was well under way when the entire Land Program was transferred, May 1, 1935, by executive order to the newly established Resettlement Administration, under Rex Tugwell. This new administration had at least three divisions: one division had to do with the resettlement of families, another concerned itself with the acquisition and planning of the Greenbelt towns, and the third was a land utilization division headed by Dr. L. C. Gray. For a time we were given an office in Gray's division because a good deal of the work of that division was similar to what we were doing in the RDA program. I ended up with an office in the Interior Building for National Park Service planning matters, an office in the Bond Building at New York Avenue and Fourteenth Street to handle the CCC program, and then an office south of the Mall in one of the temporary World War I buildings where Gray had established his headquarters. On November 14, 1936, an executive order was signed by which everything concerning the RDA program was turned over to the National Park Service, and we simply submitted to the Resettlement Administration a request for funds.

The RDA turned out to be a very successful program, and, while the CCC regional offices and their inspectors assisted admirably in all ways, a great deal of credit is due personally to Matt Huppuch, who headed the program, and to his very efficient and hard-working staff, which included Pete DeGelleke, Charlie Gerner, Julian Salomon, Fay Welch, and many others, as well as the professional field people who worked with him. They operated as a separate unit of the service under my general supervision, and they had power to delegate authority that made possible considerable independent action. I look back on the RDA program as one of the really fine accomplishments of the New Deal. It involved practically every new emergency agency that had funds available for land acquisition and development and the authorities in twenty-four states, as well as the old-line bureaus of the federal government that had continuing responsibilities. Considerable ingenuity was required to bring everything together for the common purpose. This feat turned out to be relatively easy, however, because those in charge really believed in the objectives.

HISTORIC AMERICAN BUILDINGS SURVEY

In November, 1933, Charles E. Peterson, a historic architect on Tom Vint's staff, drafted a memorandum recommending a national project for documenting historic buildings. His suggestion was activated as the Historic American Buildings Survey (HABS). The main purpose of the survey was to assemble measured drawings and photographs of America's rapidly disappearing historic architecture. A secondary purpose, which actually made the study possible, was to provide work for unemployed architects and draftsmen.

Charles Peterson was dedicated to the preservation of historic architecture and good craftmanship. He was sometimes so insistent that he was not easy to reason with, but I do not know of anybody ever proving he was wrong. He was well received and highly respected in intellectual circles, and there was no question as to his professional qualifications. Because of the vast amount of historic sites and buildings in the National Park System, Peterson took a very important part in discharging the responsibilities assigned to Tom Vint and his organization. Tom was a canny Scotsman and a master at handling temperamental and creative people and getting everything possible out of their efforts. He and Charlie became very close friends, and the Park Service, the American Institute of Architects (AIA), and the country as a whole are very much indebted to both of them. Peterson not only advanced the idea of the Historic American Buildings Survey but pushed it and kept on urging and demanding perfection in its pursuit. I know because quite a few times I was on the receiving end of his pleas for funds.

Prior to the HABS program there had been small scale recording projects of a similar type successfully carried out as unemployment programs in several cities. Peterson's proposal for documenting historic buildings on a national scale won rapid approval by Secretary Ickes and by the Civil Works Administration, the agency that in the beginning was to provide the major part of the funding. In organizing the project the enthusiastic cooperation of the AIA and the Library of Congress was enlisted. Dr. Leicester B. Holland, who served both as chairman of the AIA's committee on the preservation of historic buildings and as head of the Department of Fine Arts of the Library of Congress, and Edward C. Kemper, the executive secretary of AIA, were instrumental in cementing this cooperation.

The Library of Congress was to serve as the repository for the complete records, and the AIA, through its local chapters, provided the organizational framework for conducting the survey. Administration of the project by the Washington office of the National Park Service was in the hands of a small staff under Tom Vint, including Thomas T. Waterman, John P. O'Neill, and Frederick D. Nichols. The country was divided into thirty-nine districts, each with a district officer who was nominated by the local chapter of the AIA and appointed by the secretary of the interior. These men recruited architects for field work and with the aid of an advisory committee drew up priority lists of the buildings to be recorded. They were also responsible for maintaining the high standards of quality and accuracy set by the national office.

The initial phase of HABS recording lasted from the first of January until the end of March, 1934, when all Civil Works Administration projects were terminated. During this period the program employed 772 persons and produced 5,110 measured drawings and 3,260 photographs of 882 structures. These remarkable results led the National Park Service, Library of Congress, and American Institute of Architects to enter into a formal agreement in June, 1934, to establish the Historic American Buildings Survey as the official national program for the collection and disposition of architectural records.

All through the emergency period up until World War II the National Park Service financed the program with other emergency funds that became available. Just how much was spent on this project from March, 1934, to the beginning of the war is almost impossible to determine. Much funding and help came from the CCC, and the HABS program was broad enough in scope to allow for considerable help from other emergency programs. Park Service general funds were used to a certain extent, as well as allotments of Recreational Demonstration Area funds.

During the war many projects had to be dropped, including HABS, but after the war federal funding was restored. The old agreement between the AIA, the Library of Congress, and the National Park Service again became effective with the same high standards established in 1934 but on a much smaller scale because of the limitation of regular appropriations. The Park Service appropriations had been severely cut during the war. For the years 1942 to 1956 the archives of HABS grew only through donations of records from private individuals and a few from the National Park Service.

In 1956, as part of the service's Mission 66 program, HABS was reestablished as an active recording program. The survey programs continued much as before, directed by a small national staff. The field teams, however, are now composed of architectual students and historians under the direction of a professor of architecture, and a much greater emphasis is placed on documentation by photographs and written data. As of January 1, 1974, HABS archives contained records of over 16,000 buildings, including 34,000 measured drawings, 44,000 photographs, and 13,000 pages of written data. This collection provides basic reference material for architects and historians on some of our greatest historic buildings that have been lost to the bulldozers, and it continues to be, as it has been for 40 years, one of the most popular collections in the Library of Congress.

SEASHORE AND LAKESHORE STUDIES

One of the most interesting and worthwhile of the New Deal conservation programs was the shoreline study that set out to preserve miles and miles of Atlantic, Gulf, and Pacific coastlines for the use and enjoyment of people from all parts of the country. Although full emphasis was not given to shoreline preservation until the fifties, the fact that private development was consuming this resource and leaving less and less of it available for public use was recognized even before the New Deal. Very little had been done, however, to reserve seashore areas for public use. The rush for seashore summer homesites had got well under way during the prosperous early and middle twenties. There had been a big land boom in Florida and along the Gulf coast and up the eastern shore, and the first thing a subdivider, or even individuals would do, would be to level off the dunes to build houses. Of course, during the depression a good deal of this work stopped, but the previous boom had taken its toll. It was most suitable therefore to include seashores in the overall conservation and recreation planning made possible through funds from the PWA, the WPA, and especially the CCC.

In 1934 and 1935 the National Park Service, using its regionalization setup for handling state park work, launched a study of the seashores along the Atlantic coast and the Gulf of Mexico. The service received fine cooperation from the Coast Guard and other agencies that had personnel they wanted to keep busy in order to justify their permanent appropriation base, and their technical knowledge provided very important factual information for our investigations. The study was broken down into several parts but had two main emphases: first, those areas of outstanding importance from the national standpoint that might be considered as additions to the national park system, and second, those that were outstanding from the state standpoint and that were needed primarily for active recreation purposes. Shortly after the study was started it was felt that, though the Atlantic and Gulf shorelines were in the greatest danger and in need of protection, the study should be extended to include the Pacific coast as well. This was done approximately six months later.

These studies resulted in the selection of about fifteen areas for possible inclusion in the national park system, and about thirty areas for state park systems, although our proposals were not developed to a stage that justified funding. One particular shoreline, however, Cape Hatteras, had attracted a lot of attention—first, because of the importance of old Cape Hatteras Lighthouse on this stretch of coastline known as "the graveyard of the Atlantic" and, second, because there are several small towns on the outer sandbar inhabited by Coast Guard people and commercial fishermen. Some 1,200 of the First World War veterans who joined the bonus march on Washington in 1932 and who were moved out of the capital area by General Douglas MacArthur were settled in camps at Cape Hatteras so that the men could be employed on a project to reestablish sand dunes that had been overgrazed by cattle and left vulnerable to wind and wave erosion. The veterans were housed on barges on Pamlico Sound, which lies between Cape Hatteras and the mainland. We had also established a couple of CCC camps on the cape, which was a North Carolina state park.

Lindsay Warren was the representative in Congress for that district, and his administrative assistant was Herbert Bonner. Warren succeeded in getting legislation through Congress authorizing the establishment of over seventy miles of public seashore from Nags Head southward to the cape and from the cape over to Ocracoke Inlet. The law provided that sufficient lands would be included within the fishing communities for overnight accommodations for seashore visitors. The law also provided that the state-owned part of the area be turned over to the federal government and that the state would buy and donate all the remaining land necessary to create the Cape Hatteras National Seashore as authorized. This bill became law on August 17, 1937, but the state never got around to fulfilling its commitment.

I mention Cape Hatteras because it was the first national seashore to be authorized. Without the help of both Lindsay Warren, who later became United States comptroller general, and Herb Bonner, who succeeded to his place in Congress, and without the Mellon funding that stimulated state appropriations, Cape Hatteras National Seashore might never have been established—certainly not within its present boundaries. (In Chapter 3 is an account of the part that the Mellon family foundations played in its establishment.) Furthermore, but for this accomplishment, another seashore study made during Mission 66 in the middle fifties might never have got started or might have been delayed so long that many areas that have since been authorized would have been lost to public ownership.

Establishing the boundary of Cape Hatteras National Seashore was no easy task. It was necessary to protect shorelines and sand dunes and preserve the natural wildlife habitat while at the same time providing public use areas and allowing space for reasonable growth of existing communities. There were seven small communities on the outer banks on Pamlico Sound. Most of the oceanfront and the waterfowl hunting area was owned by northern interests, yet the local people felt it was their land because they had been using it for years. In order to satisfy the local people, when we started planning in detail we divided the entire project into seven or eight sections and prepared detail maps for each section. Victor Mekins, editor of the local weekly newspaper at Manteo that serves the whole cape, said he would print a special edition with our maps and statements and see that every family within the project, whether a subscriber of the newspaper or not, got a copy. We also announced that the week after the special edition we would visit each community to answer questions and receive suggestions. We knew that some of the people were for the project and that some had strong feelings against it, but many wanted to know more about it before they made up their minds. The main stumbling block was the group of some fifteen or twenty caretakers of the several hunting clubs owned by well-to-do northern people. Fully aware that misunderstandings and lack of information cause most of a public official's troubles, we felt that public airing of the proposal with full explanation of all its aspects was the only way to win local public support.

Representative Bonner, who had succeeded to Warren's seat in Congress, Clark Stratton, our very able young project manager, and I started on our rounds on a Wednesday at the far end of the project at the town of Ocracoke, then moved east to the town of Frisco in the afternoon, and then to Hatteras for an after-dinner public meeting and to spend the night. Everything went along very well during the day. We didn't get too many strong objections, and we accepted several reasonable requests for adjustments in boundary location. But we had gotten indications that we were going to have some trouble that night at the meeting at the schoolhouse in Hatteras.

We arrived at the schoolhouse shortly before eight and discovered that the only people there were the hunting club employees. It turned out that the other townspeople didn't show up because they knew what might happen and didn't want to be a part of it. Clark Stratton made a few opening remarks, got a few Bronx cheers, and introduced me. I started right in to tell them about the project as authorized and the boundary we had worked out around the town of Hatteras, but I didn't get very far. They really went at me. I would stop talking until they quieted down and then try to go on, but to no avail. This went on for about ten minutes, although it seemed longer, and I was about to blow my top when Representative Bonner got up and told me to sit down, that he wanted to take over. He proceeded to tell them in no uncertain terms that he didn't care what they wanted, that the area was going to be established the way the Park Service wanted it, and that they and their New York bosses could go to hell. He told them that they had acted in a way that was a disgrace to the South and that they were just a bunch of puppets for the Yankees. Further, he stated that the Cape Hatteras National Seashore would be a great thing for the cape, the state, and the entire country, and that he intended to see it through to completion. Finally, he said that we didn't want their kind of support and that he had more votes in his backyard than they could deliver on the whole cape. With that he turned to Clark and me and

Sleeping Bear Dunes National Lakeshore has 71,105 acres of native sand dunes, forests, and lakes on two offshore islands and a section of Lake Michigan shoreline. *Courtesy National Park Service.*

said, "Let's get out of here; it stinks." We walked out and left them sitting there.

We spent the night in the town of Hatteras and the next morning met with a few people at Buxton. We were disappointed that we had not been able to speak to the people of Hatteras and that not many turned out at Buxton. But at the next town, Avon, low and behold we were received like heroes! A lot of the Hatteras and Buxton people were present, and they had joined with Avon's people to arrange an old-fashioned fish fry. They knew full well what had happened at Hatteras and were pleased with what we had done and what Herb Bonner had said, and believe me, we were pleased that they were pleased.

Point Reyes National Seashore, California, is noted for its beaches backed by tall cliffs, lagoons and esteros, and offshore birds and sea lion colonies. The author made the basic field study for this area in the CCC period. *Courtesy National Park Service.*

The war clouds were gathering in the late thirties, and by 1939 and 1940 legislation authorizing additional seashore areas seemed impossible. The next national seashore was established in 1961, twenty-four years after the authorization of Cape Hatteras. In the intervening years the war had come and gone, and the cold war had set in and was tapering off. The time seemed right to get back to progressive and much needed conservation programs. Though included in the Park Service's Mission 66 planning program, the new seashore studies were actually started with donations from foundations estab-

Cape Cod National Seashore, Massachusetts, was the first national seashore established as the result of the shoreline studies made during Mission 66 and the first area in the history of the national park system for which Congress authorized funds to purchase the land. *Photo by M. Woodbridge Williams, courtesy National Park Service.*

lished by Paul Mellon and his sister, Mrs. Ailsa Bruce, while Mission 66 was being prepared. Many of the areas that had been favored for preservation in the studies of the thirties had disappeared or had been destroyed for park use beyond redemption. The new seashore studies program was broad in its objectives, following closely the principle of the earlier studies and including areas of either national or state significance. This time the studies covered not only the shorelines of both oceans and the Gulf of Mexico but also those of the Great Lakes.

The first postwar seashore legislation passed by Congress as a result of these studies was for Cape Cod. That legislation caused a great deal of difficulty when it came to convincing the good people of Massachusetts that the cape should be made a national seashore. Long hours were spent in meetings with townspeople and with conservation groups. I believe the secret of our success was that we had the strong backing of President John F. Kennedy, Senator Leverett Saltonstall, of Massachusetts, and the state conservation commissioner, Francis Sargent, who later became governor. As with the Cape Hatteras project, the local newspaper, *The Cape Coder*, was our big supporter, and without the devotion of its editor and his wife, Mr. and Mrs. Frank Burling, I don't know what we would have done. The legislation proved to be a milestone in the history of the national park system, because Congress created a precedent by authorizing federal funding to buy the necessary land and all such bills passed by Congress since then have authorized appropriations for land purchase. Until then legislation adding areas to the national park system had required that the lands be either federally owned or given to the government. It was what we often called the beg, borrow, or steal system.

The Cape Cod bill authorized sixteen million dollars for land acquisition, only half the amount we asked for. The foundations that had matched the state funds to buy Cape Hatteras, while not making a definite commitment, had led me to believe they would put up the other half of the Cape Cod funds. Arrangements were made to have a luncheon meeting between the executive officer of the foundations and me at the Cosmos Club in Washington; I invited the secretary of the interior to participate, and he accepted. Toward the end of the meal I opened the discussion with the remark that it was going to cost at least thirty-two million dollars to buy all the land needed for the Cape Cod National Seashore and that Congress had authorized only sixteen million dollars in federal funds. At this point the secretary stated that he didn't think we would have any trouble getting additional funds for this particular project because it was in Massachusetts, the home state of the president. He had in mind another project he felt was very important and needed some funds. I didn't feel I should try to contradict the secretary. The executive officer was a very good listener, but the secretary did not get his money. The result was that in order to get the necessary funding for the Cape Cod project we had to go back to Congress several times for additional authorization and funds for land purchase.

The Cape Hatteras and Cape Cod national seashores opened up a whole new phase of conservation. And Cape Cod is a real landmark in that it set a precedent whereby it is now a policy of Congress to provide funds for the purchase of land needed for the national park system. The seashore conservation studies were the forerunners of the policy of preserving shorelines of various bodies of water, including our free-flowing rivers. The shoreline areas in the table that follows were established during the sixties and seventies and are the result of the study made in the fifties; but it was the seashore studies of the thirties, the CCC, and the Cape Hatteras authorization by Congress that initiated the program under which they were established. The table lists the national seashores and national lakeshores, showing the dates they were authorized or established, miles of shoreline, and acreage. Only seven in the list were recommended in the CCC study. The other eight that had been recommended in the thirties no longer qualified by the time funds were available.

Area	Date Authorized or Established
Cape Hatteras National Seashore, North Carolina	
70 miles of Atlantic Ocean seashore and 28,500 acres	Aug. 17, 1937
Cape Cod National Seashore, Massachusetts	
40 miles of Atlantic Ocean seashore and 44,600 acres	Aug. 7, 1961
Point Reyes National Seashore, California	
45 miles of Pacific Ocean seashore and 64,500 acres	Sept. 13, 1962
Padre Island National Seashore, Texas	
80 miles of Gulf of Mexico seashore and 133,900 acres	Sept. 28, 1962
Assateague Island National Seashore, Maryland and Virginia	
35 miles of Atlantic Ocean seashore and 39,630 acres	Sept. 21, 1965
Fire Island National Seashore, New York	
32 miles of Atlantic Ocean seashore and 19,300 acres	Oct. 9, 1965
Cape Lookout National Seashore, North Carolina	
58 miles of Atlantic Ocean seashore and 24,500 acres	March 10, 1966
Pictured Rocks National Lakeshore, Michigan	
35 miles of Lake Superior shoreline and 67,000 acres	Oct. 15, 1966
Indiana Dunes National Lakeshore, Indiana	
13 miles of Lake Michigan shoreline and 8,720 acres	Nov. 5, 1966
Apostle Islands National Lakeshore, Wisconsin	
140 miles of Lake Superior shoreline and 42,825 acres	Sept. 26, 1970
Sleeping Bear Dunes National Lakeshore, Michigan	
64 miles of Lake Michigan shoreline and 71,000 acres	Oct. 21, 1970
Gulf Islands National Seashore, Florida and Mississippi	
87 miles of Gulf of Mexico seashore and 125,000 acres	Jan. 8, 1971
Cumberland Island National Seashore, Georgia	
19 miles of Atlantic Ocean seashore and 41,600 acres	Oct. 23, 1972

TOTALS: 718 miles; 711,075 acres.

It took from March 1, 1872, the date Yellowstone National Park was established, until August 7, 1961, the date of authorization of Cape Cod National Seashore—a period of eighty-nine years—to recognize that the preservation of our national heritage for the benefit of the people, present and future, is an important federal responsibility that deserves spending federal money to buy the land that will make such preservation possible. Admittedly, I take pride in pointing out that the shoreline preservation program sprouted from the

National Park Service CCC program of the thirties and came into full bloom in the Mission 66 period in the late fifties and early sixties. Perhaps more important is the fact that the shoreline program set the policy for the Park Service to assume its full responsibilities as defined by Congress, which backed the program by providing legislative assurance of proper funding.

My pride is expressed on behalf of all those who fired up the shoreline concept and saw it through to completion. I include the United States Coast Guard and the many state park people, as well as our friends in Congress, especially Chairman Wayne N. Aspinall, of Colorado, and John P. Saylor, of Pennsylvania, both of the Interior Affairs Committee of the House; Chairman Clinton P. Anderson, of New Mexico, and Senator Henry C. Dworshak, of Idaho, both of the Senate Interior Committee; and of course Senator Carl Hayden, of Arizona, and Representative Mike Kirwan, of Ohio, chairmen, respectively, of the appropriations committees of the Senate and the House that handled our requests for appropriations. Without their deep interest in and support of the National Park Service objective, our efforts would have amounted to naught.

SHANGRI-LA

When President Franklin D. Roosevelt was asked during a press conference in the spring of 1940 where he had mysteriously spent the better part of a day away from the White House with only a minimum Secret Service escort, he smiled and replied simply, "Shangri-La." No one knew then that he referred to the mountain spot a short distance north of Washington that he had selected as a presidential hideaway for weekend relaxation.

Around the latter part of March, Roosevelt sent a communication to National Park Service Director Newton B. Drury indicating that he would like to find a place fairly close to Washington where he could have a cabin or a small lodge for occasional use. The war in Europe was causing more and more concern in this country, and the president couldn't risk being as far away from the capital as Hyde Park or the Little White House in Georgia. His advisers did not want him to use the presidential yacht because of the dangers involved. Of course, President Herbert Hoover's camp on the Rapidan River in Shenandoah National Park was available, but President Roosevelt was not a fly fisherman, and the damp valley aggravated his asthmatic condition.

At that time I was in charge of Recreation and Land Planning, and Director Drury called me to his office to discuss the matter. He told me the president was looking for a place at an elevation of about 1,500 to 2,000 feet and within an hour or an hour and half from Washington by car. He had already checked out Sugar Loaf Mountain, a short distance from Washington, in Maryland, and found that under no circumstances would the owner make it available. In the course of our discussion two or three places came to mind almost immediately, but all of them needed checking out on the ground. The director emphasized that the matter should be kept confidential.

The following day a small group of us, including Harry Thompson, a very capable landscape architect with the National Capital Park System, and Ab Good, an excellent architect and author of the book *Park and Recreation Structures*, started investigating some seven or eight places in Maryland and Virginia. We checked every conceivable place within reasonable distance of the necessary utilities and satisfactory roads. We ended up with three sites to suggest to the president. One was Comers Deadening, a mile or so from Skyland in Shenandoah National Park, in Virginia, at an elevation of 3,300 feet. It was about a hundred miles from Washington and could be reached by car easily in two and a half hours. To build the camp would require two or three months and approximately $150,000. We had a preliminary layout plan prepared to go with a memorandum. The second site was known as campsite number four in the Catoctin Recreational Demonstration Area, in Maryland. It was about sixty miles from Washington, at an elevation of 1,700 feet, and would require approximately one and a half hours of travel time over good roads. It was one of the four group campsites called for in the Catoctin Recreational Demonstration Area master plan, but construction had not been started. The cost here would be approximately the same as at Shenandoah—$150,000. The third suggested site was also in Catoctin Recreational Demonstration Area, about a half mile from the number four campsite. At this site the group camp had already been constructed, but with certain revamping it would meet the requirements of the president and would cost in the neighborhood of $25,000.

On April 22 the director went to Catoctin with the president for a look at the two proposed sites. The following day the director indicated that he was quite sure the president wanted site three, which we had estimated would cost around $25,000 to alter and make suitable for his use. By April 25 we had a memorandum prepared for Director Drury to send the president that outlined what we proposed to do and that included a cost estimate, which came to $18,650, and a floor plan showing the proposed alterations and additions to the lodge. It stated that if these funds were made available immediately and if we could obtain the necessary wartime construction priorities, we could proceed at once.

There was some slight delay, but soon I was asked to go with the president on another visit to Catoctin, and I took along Ab Good, the architect. In looking over sites three and four again, the president indicated that he was more interested in number four. Site four had a one-room mountain cabin about one hundred feet back from the breaking line on Military Crest, where the mountain starts to get very steep. The vacant cabin had a full length porch facing the distant view to the east and south. The floor of the porch was well pitched to provide for quick runoff of rainwater. The president was fascinated with the view from this cabin and wanted to sit a while; so RDA Project Manager Mike Williams went down to his office at the foot of the mountain and brought back his desk chair—the only chair he thought would be comfortable for the president—and put it on the porch. Two Secret Service men lifted the president out of his car and placed him in the chair. As soon as they let go the chair stated rolling toward the edge of the porch, where there was a drop of two or three feet to the ground. The Secret Service men dove and caught the chair before the president went off the porch. It was a narrow escape, but the president was all laughter and said he realized that somebody might try to get him someday, but he never suspected his own boys.

Number four was the site he wanted, and that was the one he got. It required a great deal more than the $18,000 we had estimated as the cost of remodeling camp number three. The president and the Secret Service had in mind accommodations for some forty-five guests and staff, in addition to servants and Secret Service men. Further, the area would have to be completely enclosed with a heavy mesh wire fence out of sight of the president and his guests. All utility wires would have to be underground. A special building would be needed for the telephone operators with quarters for four because they would maintain twenty-four-hour service. Fortunately, we had some CCC barracks we could make over into a dormitory for the Secret Service men. After the camp was completed and occupied, the Marines came in for security purposes and had to have quarters, but they took care of that themselves.

We informed the president that we would have to revise our original figures of $150,000 upward, but before we could say anything more he told us laughingly that the Congress would never give him $150,000 for such a purpose. He said that he wanted the camp nevertheless and that we should be able to reduce the cost in some way. All he could give us was $15,000, and he wanted to have the place ready by June 1. Well, we started in, and there was hardly a day when somebody from the Washington office was not at Catoctin. Harry Thompson and Ab Good spent a great deal of time there with Project Manager Williams, who was a hard-working man who knew how to get things done. The job was finished about two weeks late, but the president was very much pleased with it.

President Roosevelt took great pleasure in going up to Shangri-La during construction, and it wasn't uncommon for the telephone to ring and the operator to say the president was leaving in a half hour for Shangri-La and would like me to join him. On one of these outings we stopped on the way to pick up Queen Wilhelmina of the Netherlands. At Catoctin the three of us sat on a car robe spread out on the ground right in front of the lodge under construction to have lunch and look out over the beautiful rolling Maryland farmland. Altogether, I believe, it was about as nice an assignment as a person could have had.

The navy had been of great help to us, getting various supplies on priorities that we could not touch. Everything had to be electrified including the protective fence, and I don't know how many miles of underground cables we had to put in. The captain of the president's yacht, who enjoyed going to Catoctin, got the cable for us and charged it to maintenance of the yacht. One day the admiral in command of the navy yard called the captain into his office and wanted to know what he was trying to do with all that cable on the yacht, "sink it?" The captain had previously told him about helping us to get the president's camp in shape, charging certain things to the yacht, but apparently the admiral had forgotten. So the captain said, "Well, Admiral, you know the yacht is at Shangri-La." The admiral looked blank for a minute, then said, "Oh hell, all right." A good deal of the furniture from the president's yacht was also moved to Shangri-La.

The incident of President Roosevelt's near tumble from the cabin porch the day he inspected the site of his future Shangri-La was a relatively minor one compared with the tragedy that almost happened one night that he spent there. That evening the president sat playing cards with some friends at a table directly beneath a chandelier made from an old farm wagon wheel fitted with wrought iron electric light fixtures. The next morning the table was found crushed under the heavy wooden part of the wheel. Apparently it had been gradually drying and shrinking and had slipped out of its suspended iron rim some time during the night, after the people who had been sitting under it had left. Roosevelt was not told of this, nor have I seen the story published heretofore. We rushed up to the camp early the next morning and saw to it that the table was repaired and light fixtures put together again. This time the wooden part of the wheel was securely bolted to the iron rim.

Shangri-La is still there and apparently being well used by our presidents. It is not an elaborate place but very comfortable and attractive. President Dwight D. Eisenhower changed the name to Camp David, as he had a right to do, though I wish he had kept the name Shangri-La. Additions made to it: instead of the screened porch that FDR had, there is now an enlarged, glassed-in porch; President Eisenhower added two tees and small fairway and a green so that he could practice golf; FDR had a swimming pool built, and I understand that it is still there and used. The property is still the responsibility of the National Park Service, as is the White House. Having had the responsibility of building the presidential retreat and not having been back since 1942 or early 1943, I was curious to see it again. So, once when I was in the White House going over plans for LBJ State Park near the Johnson Ranch in Texas, I asked Lady Bird Johnson whether she could arrange for Mrs.

Wirth and me to go up and take a look at it. She talked to the president, and I got word back that they would like very much for us to spend the night there. We declined the overnight invitation but did go up with our friends Mr. and Mrs. Roger Ernst and had a fine day and a nice lunch at Camp David.

PARK STRUCTURES AND FACILITIES

One of the most important accomplishments of the Civilian Conservation Corps was the contribution and recording of good park architecture. At the beginning of the CCC, Dorothy Waugh prepared several small publications on suggested facilities, with special reference to design and the kinds of materials to be used. Dorothy is a daughter of Frank A. Waugh, my landscape architecture professor back in Massachusetts, and she had done illustrations for several books her father published. Her work was very good, but as work programs developed we had to get out more complete information of this kind for distribution to the camps and to state and metropolitan park offices.

We were very fortunate in having on our Washington office staff a very fine architect, Albert H. Good, who came to us highly recommended by an outstanding landscape architect and park manager, Harold S. Wagner of the Akron, Ohio, metropolitan park system. Ab, as he became familiarly known, produced a compilation of successful park and recreation structures. This extremely valuable work was published in 1938 through the Government Printing Office under the main title *Park and Recreation Structures.* It was printed in three parts, "Administrative and Basic Service Facilities," "Recreational and Cultural Facilities," and "Overnight and Organized Camp Facilities." Each part was a separate paperback volume of large dimensions, and its sewn binding allowed the book to be opened flat and used on a drafting table. Each volume was generously illustrated with photographs and architectural drawings.

Perhaps the best way to explain Ab Good's professional approach to preparing *Park and Recreation Structures* is to quote from his Apologia:

> A cherished dictum of the many friends of the natural park concept through its formative years has been that structures must be regarded as intrusions in areas set aside to be conserved in their natural state. This unequivocal pronouncement indeed nourished the budding park idea, and has been a favorable and protective influence in its flowering. General acceptance of the principle has so held in check structural desecration of parks that few persons have been moved to brand the statement a half truth, standing very much in need of qualifying amendment to suit today's many-sided park concept. To do so will doubtless be received as a minority report, if not as shameless heresy; nevertheless, the case will be here argued.
>
> Time was when only areas of superb scenery, outstanding scientific interest, or major historical importance held interest for the sponsors of natural parks. There was proper concentration on saving the outstanding natural wonders first, and it was

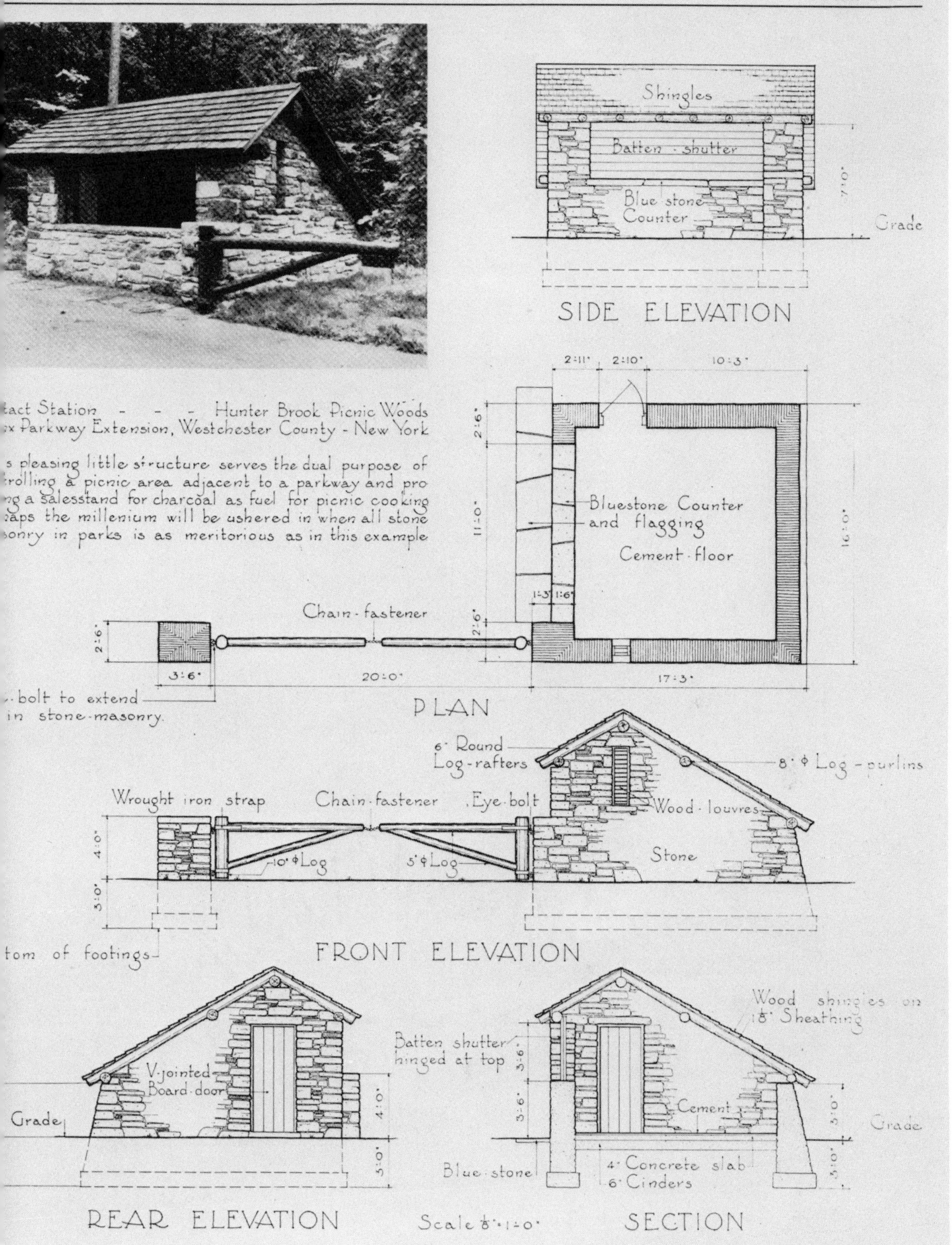

Contact Station, Bronx Parkway, Westchester County, New York. *From* Park and Recreation Structures *by Albert H. Good, 1938.*

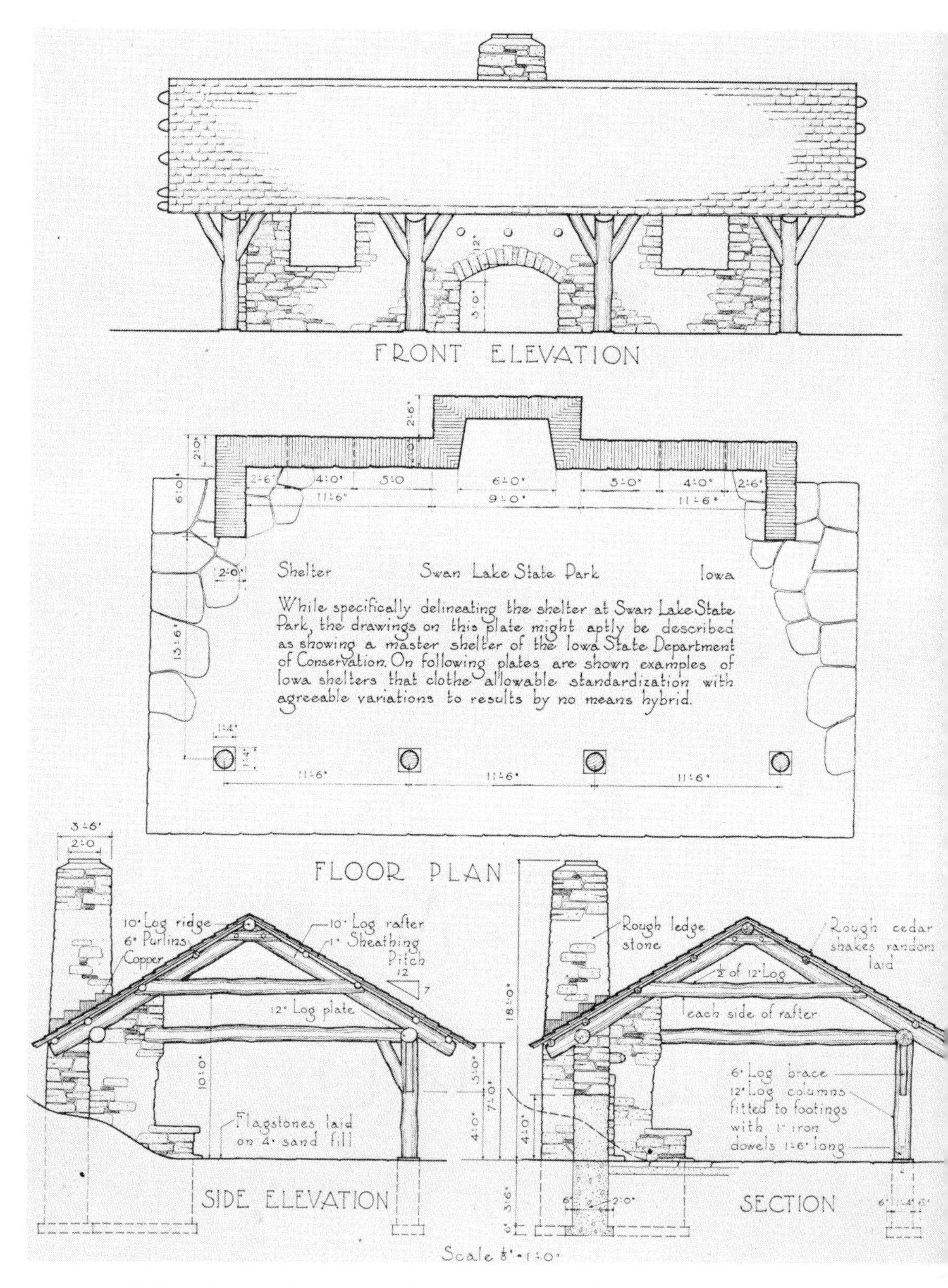

Shelter, Swan Lake State Park, Iowa. *From* Park and Recreation Structures *by Albert H. Good, 1938.*

probably along with the acquisition of the first superlative areas that structures in parks came to be frowned on as alien and intrusive. . . . Now and forever, the degree of [man's] success within such areas will be measurable by the yardstick of his self-restraint. . . .

The fact that superlative Nature was beyond gunshot of concentrations of five or ten million people happily did not result in these populations being denied the recreational and inspirational benefits that subsuperlative Nature can provide. It was wisely reasoned that there is more nourishment in half a loaf in the larder than a full loaf beyond the horizon—or no loaf at all. . . .

Tracts, admittedly limited or even lacking in natural interest, but highly desirable by virtue of location, need, and every other influencing factor, bloom attractively on every side to the benefit of millions. It is inexact to term these, in the accepted denotation of the word, parks—they are reserves for recreation. More often than not their natural background is only that contrast-affording Nature which makes other areas superlative. Does such a background warrant the "no dogs allowed" attitude toward structures so fully justified where Nature plays the principal role? Does it not rather invite structures to trespass to a fulfillment of recreational potentialities and needs, and to bolster up a commonplace or ravaged Nature? It seems reasonable to assert that in just the degree natural beauty is lacking structures may legitimately seek to bring beauty to purpose.

Those who have been called on to plan the areas where structural trespass is not a justifiable taboo have sought to do so with a certain grace. We realize that the undertaking is legitimatized or not by harmony or the lack of it. We are learning that harmony is more likely to result from a use of native materials. We show signs of doubting the propriety of introducing boulders into settings where Nature failed to provide them, or of incorporating heavy alien timbers into structures in treeless areas. . . .

As we have vaguely sensed these things, we . . . become aware of the unvoiced claims of those long-gone races and earlier generations that tracked the wilderness, plains, or desert before us. In fitting tribute we seek to grace our park structures by adaptation of their traditions and practices as we come to understand them.

Thus we are influenced by the early settlers, English and Dutch, along the Atlantic seaboard; something of Old France lingers along the trail of Pere Marquette and the fur traders. Reaching up from New Orleans, Florida, and Old Mexico, Spanish traditions and customs rightfully flourish. . . . The habits and primitive ingenuity of the American Indian persist and find varied expression over wide areas. Interpreted with intelligence, these influences promise an eventual park and recreation architecture, which, outside certain sacrosanct areas, need not cringe before a blanket indictment for "unlawful entry."

DIGEST OF LAWS RELATING TO LOCAL PARKS AND RECREATION

Another very important accomplishment of the CCC days was a digest of the laws relating to local parks and recreation activities in every state and the territories of Hawaii and Alaska. This book was prepared by a CCC staff lawyer, Roy A. Vetter, and was published in 1940. Roy advised on the many legal matters that began cropping up every day once the CCC got under way, providing the legal opinion needed to make administrative decisions. He was a hard worker, and we were very fortunate to have him on our staff.

Secretary Harold Ickes wrote the foreword for the *Digest of Laws*, explaining why it was a necessary and important publication: "Everything that a public agency does has its basis in legislation. In the past, government agencies and other bodies responsible for or interested in promoting the park and recreation movement have been impeded to no inconsiderable degree by the lack of any reference source to the laws relating to the subject matter. This digest is intended to fill that need."

Roy Vetter's preface stated that, "This digest is the result of an effort to bring together in a single volume an abridgement of the general laws of the several States and Territories relating to local parks and recreation. It reflects an examination of the laws enacted through the 1939 legislative sessions."

The book is written in such a way that an administrator can use it without too much specific legal advice, and it includes legal citations so that the reader can find the complete text of the laws. No doubt many of these laws have been changed and new ones have been enacted. Still, I feel certain that the book, as printed in 1940, has many references that would be of help today to a planner or an administrator trying to work out a park program. There is no question, however, that a book of this kind ought to be brought up to date every few years to be of real usefulness, and, to the best of my knowledge, that is not being done.

All housing accommodations were removed from the rim of Yellowstone Canyon during Mission 66, restoring the full beauty of the canyon. Relocation of the accommodations at Canyon Village a few miles away was a joint project of the National Park Service and the concessionaire. *Photo by Joseph Scherschel, courtesy National Geographic Society*

The quiet coves, blue-green waters, white sands, and coral reefs of Virgin Islands National Park are unmatched in the national park system. Under water "hiking" is a unique experience. This park was made possible by a gift from Laurance S. Rockefeller. *Photo by James Stanfield, courtesy National Geographic Society*

The highest elevation on the eastern seaboard and a rugged shoreline set the mood of Acadia National Park in Maine, a gift to the nation by John D. Rockefeller, Jr., and friends. *Photo by Robert E. Gilka, courtesy National Geographic Society*

Thomas A. Edison's home, library, papers, workshops, and models of his inventions are preserved at Edison National Historic Site, West Orange, New Jersey, the gift of former Governor and Mrs. Thomas A. Edison, Jr. This is a view of the library. *Photo by Victor Boswell, courtesy National Geographic Society*

In this house, within Appomattox Court House National Historical Park, Virginia, two graduates of the United States Military Academy at West Point met April 9, 1865, when General Robert E. Lee surrendered the Confederacy's largest field army to Lieutenant General Ulysses S. Grant. *Photo by Bruce Dale, courtesy National Geographic Society*

The Elizabeth Park Rose Garden, designed and built by the author's father, Theodore Wirth, when he was superintendent of parks in Hartford, Connecticut, has been credited as the first municipal park rose garden in the country. *From Conrad L. Wirth Collection*

The White House in Washington, D.C., has been the official residence of the presidents of the United States since 1800. Its maintenance and care are assigned to the National Park Service. *From Conrad L. Wirth Collection*

One of the 10,000 geysers in Yellowstone National Park, Wyoming, pours its steaming hot water into the Firehole River. *From Conrad L. Wirth Collection*

Old Faithful Geyser is seen by all visitors to Yellowstone National Park. Features such as this and the Grand Canyon of the Yellowstone River led Congress to set aside over 2,200,000 acres in the northwest corner of Wyoming as the world's first national park in 1872. *From Conrad L. Wirth Collection*

Two enormous canyons of the Kings River and the summit peaks of the High Sierra dominate the wilderness embraced in Kings Canyon National Park, California. *From Conrad L. Wirth Collection*

Canyonlands National Park in Utah is a true geological wonderland of rocks, spires, and mesas seen in every direction. Each turn along the trails provides a different picture. This is Angle Arch. *From Conrad L. Wirth Collection*

Active volcanism continues in Hawaii Volcanoes National Park on the island of Hawaii. In contrast, at lower elevations luxuriant vegetation provides food and shelter for a variety of animal life. *From Conrad L. Wirth Collection*

Distant views into four states are gained from the top of the mesa that shelters these pre-Columbian cliff dwellings and other works of early human occupancy in Mesa Verde National Park, Colorado. *From Conrad L. Wirth Collection*

Unique and fragile ecosystems of the Kipahulu Valley, scenic pools along Oheo Gulch, and many rare and endangered species are preserved in Haleakala National Park on the island of Maui, Hawaii. *Courtesy National Park Service*

Mountain scenery contrasts with desert along the Rio Grande in Big Bend National Park, Texas, where a variety of geological structures contain six of the earth's seven life zones. In this view of Santa Helena Canyon, Mexico, is on the left and the United States on the right. The park was given to the nation by the state of Texas. *Courtesy National Park Service*

Carved by erosion, the scenic landscape of Badlands National Monument in South Dakota contains animal fossils forty million years old. Prairie grass supports bison, bighorn sheep, deer, and antelope. *Courtesy National Park Service*

Surf casting is a favorite form of recreation at Cape Hatteras National Seashore on the North Carolina coast. The old lighthouse overlooks the "graveyard of the Atlantic," where many ships have foundered. The area was acquired with state funds matching a donation from the Mellon Foundations. *Courtesy National Park Service*

A Danish colonial sugar plantation on Saint John Island was restored to illustrate the history of Virgin Islands National Park. *Courtesy National Park Service*

Not a sunset glow, but the natural color of this volcanic crater formed in A.D. 1100 suggested the name of Sunset Crater National Monument in Arizona. *Courtesy National Park Service*

Mabry Mill illustrates the mountain culture preserved along the Blue Ridge Parkway, which connects Shenandoah National Park in Virginia and Great Smoky Mountains National Park in North Carolina, a distance of 469 miles. *Courtesy National Park Service*

Pictured Rocks National Lakeshore on Lake Superior, Michigan, contains multi-colored sandstone cliffs and other natural features as well as numerous birds and animals. *Courtesy National Park Service*

The birthplace and early childhood home of the famous black leader and educator who founded Tuskegee Institute in 1881 is preserved as Booker T. Washington National Monument in Virginia. *Courtesy National Park Service*

Storming across the "rude bridge that arched the flood," the "embattled farmers" turned back a British column with shots "heard round the world" in the opening battle of the American Revolution at Concord, Massachusetts, on April 19, 1775. Minute Man National Historical Park includes four miles of Battle Road between Lexington and Concord. *Courtesy National Park Service*

Lake Mead National Recreation Area, Nevada and Arizona, the first of its classification established by Congress, is administered under a cooperative agreement between the National Park Service and the Bureau of Reclamation. *Courtesy National Park Service*

Francis Scott Key was held aboard a British vessel as a representative of the United States on a peace mission when he witnessed the successful defense of Fort McHenry at Baltimore in 1814 and was inspired to write the "Star Spangled Banner." The flag saluted with fireworks at Fort McHenry National Monument and Historic Shrine bore forty-nine stars, marking the addition of Alaska to the Union. *Courtesy National Park Service*

The site of the Continental Army's bitter winter encampment of 1777–78 has become Valley Forge National Historical Park, Pennsylvania. The park contains General Washington's headquarters and re-creations of log buildings and cannon used by the troops. *Courtesy National Park Service*

Dunes of glistening white gypsum, ten to sixty feet high, are home to small, light-colored animals that have adapted to the harsh environment at White Sands National Monument, New Mexico. *Courtesy National Park Service*

Many recreation opportunities are provided along the twenty-seven-mile segment of the Saint Croix National Scenic Riverway in Wisconsin and Minnesota. *Courtesy National Park Service*

Isle Royale National Park, the largest island in Lake Superior, was given to the nation by the state of Michigan. It is distinguished by its forested, wilderness character and pre-Columbian copper mines. Timber wolves and moose live on the island. *Courtesy of National Park Service*

The largest single unit of the national park system, Glacier Bay National Monument covers over 2,800,000 acres of Alaska wilderness. It contains great tidewater glaciers, plant communities that range from rocky terrain vegetation recently covered by ice to lush temperate rain forest, and a variety of wild animals, fish, and birds. *Courtesy National Park Service*

8

War: Hot and Cold

By 1941 the oncoming war had affected all activities in the National Park Service and in many other bureaus of the government as well. Although a bill had been introduced in Congress to abolish the CCC, many of us were still clinging to the hope that it could be sustained at a low ebb for at least a few years. In December, Secretary Ickes wrote to the president regarding a letter the president had sent to Social Security Administrator Paul V. McNutt that called for gradual elimination of the army from the operation of the Civilian Conservation Corps and that requested that legislation be framed to consolidate the corps with the National Youth Administration. The secretary stated that he was in full accord with the removal of the army from the CCC, but he concluded with this appeal: "I strongly urge that instead of transferring all War Department duties in the CCC administration to the Federal Security Agency you consider a plan which would transfer the bulk of these duties to the Departments of Interior and Agriculture, leaving with the Federal Security Administrator responsibility for determination of general policies and for program coordination." He reported that the Department of Agriculture fully agreed with his recommendations. That letter was forwarded to the White House on December 6, 1941.

The next day, Sunday, December 7, the Japanese bombed Pearl Harbor, and we were at war. The United States declared war on Japan on December 8, and on Germany and Italy on December 11. There was no doubt then that we were through with the CCC; it was no longer a question of reorganizing it but rather of disbanding it. Every emergency program began to dry up, and by the next fiscal year—July 1, 1942, to June 30, 1943—the only funds available for CCC operations were a few thousand dollars to take care of the transfer of equipment and materials to other jurisdictions.

Meanwhile, orders came for the National Park Service, along with two other bureaus of the Department of the Interior, to move to Chicago and make their Washington space available for war activities. With the splendid cooperation of all concerned, all arrangements were handled smoothly. Associate Director Arthur Demaray, his secretary, and three or four staff members remained in Washington to carry out the service's responsibilities there and to act as liaison for the Chicago headquarters. An office and a secretary

Director Newton B. Drury and Elizabeth Drury attending a fortieth class reunion at the University of California in 1952. They saw the National Park Service family safely through the trying years of the move to Chicago and back during the World War II and cold war periods of restricted operations, 1940 to 1951.

also were maintained in the capital for Director Newton B. Drury, who often had to visit Washington.

August 8, 1942, was our moving day. Assistant Director Hillory A. Tolson was assigned full responsibility to organize the move. Many railroad cars were required to transport the service's furniture and equipment to Chicago. Arrangements had to be made to temporarily house the service's staff in hotels and motels there until houses and apartments could be found to rent. Quite a few of us found living quarters along the north shore of Lake Michigan. The offices were in the Merchandise Mart, within walking distance from the station for me; though there were winter days when, walking into the icy wind blowing off Lake Michigan, I didn't think I'd make it.

Those were very discouraging and trying times. Many of our best people were the first to leave for military service, and because of family ties many could not go to Chicago with the Park Service. Further, the call to military service affected the individual parks almost as much as it did the Washington office. With gasoline rationing, travel to the parks went down. Funds for maintenance and care of facilities were cut below the minimum needed for preservation alone. Our appropriations in 1940—regular funds together with the cost of the CCC camps in national parks—amounted to $33,577,000, but during the war years they were rapidly reduced. The low point was reached in the 1945 fiscal year, when funding for the service amounted to only $4,740,000. After V-E Day our budget began to pick up until it reached $30,111,000 in 1950. But the damage had been done so far as maintaining park roads and structures was concerned. Moreover, our organization had been greatly reduced, and not all who had left came back.

In June, 1945, the secretary of the interior was asked to send representatives of the department to Berlin, Vienna, and Rome to advise the military government on matters in which the department was interested. I was selected to go to Berlin, but since no definite date was set, the director sent me to the West Coast on an inspection trip. I received word while in Yosemite that I should return immediately and get ready to leave for Europe. I returned to Chicago, having taken some of the necessary inoculations before I left Yosemite, and made arrangements to move my family back to Minnesota, the home of both our parents. We stored our furniture in Chicago and found a small furnished bungalow in Minneapolis.

On September 21, 1945, I left Minneapolis, spent a day in Chicago, and then continued to Washington. I was transferred to another payroll but retained my civil service status and grade. I was told that I would have to be in uniform, as were all Americans in the foreign theater at that time, but that I would have no military rank. I was also told the kind and amount of clothes I would need in Berlin, and I bought them right away. But the urgency apparently was over, because I sat in Washington checking every other day on when I was supposed to leave and how. I found out that special planes would be provided to take us over. The wait proved to be a long one, keeping me in Washington until October 28. I helped Demaray around the office and renewed contact with my brother, who was then a captain in the navy. He had been through the Pearl Harbor attack, the Battle of the Coral Sea, and Guadalcanal, and he had been wounded. During the month I was in Washington there was a change in plans; on October 22 I received word that I would be sent to Vienna, Austria, instead of Berlin.

I departed on the twenty-eighth and, after stopovers in Bermuda, the Azores, and overnight in Paris, then proceeding via Frankfort and Salzburg, I arrived in Vienna at 5:15 P.M. October 31. There were about seven of us in the party, and we were the first group of American civilians to arrive in Vienna. We were met by several officers, including Colonel Wm. E. Caraway and General L. (Les) D. Flory. General Flory was on General Mark Wayne Clark's staff and was handling the military government part of Clark's command in Vienna. We all had dinner together that evening. It was unusual for a general to meet a group of civilians, but General Flory explained that he wanted very much to meet me. In the late thirties, as a captain, he had been

Civilian advisers to the World War II United States military command in Vienna, Austria, wore officer's uniforms without military insignia. Photographed at Kahlenberg the winter of 1945–46 were, *left to right*, Conrad L. Wirth, Walter Armstrong, and Fred Meyer.

in charge of a National Park Service CCC camp on the historic site near Fredericksburg, Virginia, where several major Civil War battles had been fought, the Battle of the Wilderness among them. He had read many of the instructions the Park Service had sent out regarding the CCC work program on the battlefield sites, and most of them had been signed by me. We became very good friends, and I enjoyed my stay there very much. It turned out that I was the ranking civilian, with a civil service grade that gave me the general's commissary privileges.

One thing I learned in Vienna was what it meant to be on the losing side in the war. The Austrians were taken over by Hitler against their will before the war really started, and then they were subjected to the pounding forces of our side in driving Hitler out. After our victory, the occupation of their country by the fighting forces of the Allies wasn't any too pleasant for them, either, though I believe it was absolutely necessary during the reorganization of local government. After years of occupation by troops of several nations, people get to the point where they give a wide berth to anybody in uniform. My little apartment in Vienna belonged to an Austrian family of four that had to move out so that I could live there. I found out who they were and where they were staying and invited them over several times. The first time they came their attitude was a little cold, although they did say they were glad to see the Americans. Before they left I invited them to come again and asked whether the wife would cook dinner for the five of us if I furnished the materials. This offer was accepted with pleasure, and we did it several times.

I had greater difficulty establishing rapport in another instance. After I left for Austria, my wife went to the University of Minnesota to brush up on conversational German in anticipation of joining me in Vienna. Her professor happened to be from Vienna, and when he found out that I was there, he told Helen that none of his letters had gotten through to his mother since the Germans took over and that he had not received any news from her. He gave Helen a letter addressed to his mother in the hope that I could find her and deliver it.

I took my trusted jeep and followed his directions until I came to a big, heavy wooden gate between two four-story buildings that were joined together as one building above the gate. The only way to get to any of the apartments in that city block was through those solid wooden gates. All the apartments faced inward, away from the four surrounding streets, and there were no side street entrances. It was after dark, and through a very small crack I could see a dim light on the other side. I pulled the rope that rang a low-pitched bell inside, and I knocked hard on the gate. I was about to give up when I heard somebody coming down some wooden steps. Soon a male voice at the gate asked what I wanted. I explained, and he told me to push the letter through a little slot he would open. I objected, saying I wanted to see the lady and give her the letter in person and explaining why. After a few more words he told me to wait a few minutes. About five minutes later I heard the footsteps of two people coming. They opened the gate to let me into the courtyard, closed and locked it after I got inside, and told me to follow them. We went up some outside stairs to the second floor, then along a porch, and finally to a door. They knocked and were told to come in. They didn't leave me alone for a minute. There in the room was a very dignified, nice-looking lady sitting on a plain wooden chair beside a large round table. She was smoking a cigarette, and beside her was a plate containing some small cigarette butts.

I introduced myself and asked her if she had a son in the United States. She said yes, told me his name, and said she had not heard from him for years. I gave her the letter, and she asked me to sit down. As she read it she tried very hard not to show any emotion. When she finished she could hardly speak, but she passed me the plate and asked if I would like a cigarette. I took one of the butts and lit it. We talked a little, and she offered me a glass of wine. Then she asked me if I would mail a letter to her son. I said I would and gave her my office address. The next day one of the men who had let me in brought me the letter. And so I became her letter carrier.

Before I left that night, I gave her a couple of packages of cigarettes, two bars of soap, and a half dozen bars of candy that I had carried in my overcoat pocket. She was very grateful, because soap and cigarettes were very hard for them to get. The cigarette butt she had offered me had undoubtedly been picked up on the street after some GI discarded it. In those times if you were walking along a street smoking, pretty soon you would hear footsteps behind you, and when you threw away your cigarette it would be picked up as a collector's item. Later her son sent a box of food which I delivered to her.

I was assigned to work with a Colonel E. A. Norcross, who was responsible for dealing with land matters and conservation of natural resources. As a part of my orientation program I made a trip by jeep to Salzburg, headquarters of the American army in the American sector of Austria under the command of General Harry J. Collins. On my return I wrote a memorandum on what I thought ought to be done in and around Salzburg. It was a relatively short report and didn't say a great deal other than that I objected very strenuously to the troops painting the letters and numbers of their units in bright colors on old, historic buildings. Norcross handed my report to General Flory, who called me in to see him. He suggested that I delete from my report the part that was critical of the field troops under General Collins, explaining that one never criticizes a general in the field with the fighting troops. I understood his point of view, but I told him that I had been sent over to represent Secretary Ickes and his department, that the department considered painting on the walls of historic buildings to be vandalism as well as poor public relations, and that I wanted to have that viewpoint on the record. (Actually I was serving as policy adviser to the United States Allied Council.) Flory implied that he'd send the report through if I wanted him to but that it might result in my being sent back to the States. I replied that, though I was enjoying my duty there, I would take the risk.

I had arrived in Vienna on October 31, handed in my Salzburg report on December 8, and got my first paycheck on December 10. On December 21 I was told that I was to be transferred to the executive division directly under General Flory, and I moved there on December 27. Apparently I had been on the State Department payroll and now, in the executive division, I was transferred to the War Department payroll with the same civil service classification. The executive division coordinated the work of the several divisions responsible for the military government under the command of General Clark. The command of the military government was changed every month amongst the four allies—the United States, England, France, and Russia. Every time the command was changed, the chairmen of the divisions were likewise changed. Consequently, toward the end of the month, each of the various divisions going out of office had a farewell party, and, the first few days of the following month, the divisions taking over would have their incoming receptions. As a member of the executive division, I was invited to eight or ten parties a month.

Toward the end of February it became clear that the ranking officers would soon be able to bring their families over, and so I notified my wife and began to look for a house. In March the ban was lifted, and I filed a request to bring over my wife and our son Pete. General Clark approved my request, and I selected a nice villa not far from General Flory's home. On March 28, General Flory showed me a wire received from the War Department to the effect that the Interior Department was requesting my return. I knew that Secretary Ickes had resigned, and I had heard that Oscar Chapman was the new secretary. I wired the secretary's office for information, and on April 4 I received a wire from Under Secretary Chapman saying it was important that I return soon. General Flory and General Tate agreed that I should be released from duty as requested by the Department of the Interior. All approvals were in from Washington—the State Department, War Department, and Interior Department—by April 10. I wanted to leave the several assignments I was working on in good order, and this task took me about two weeks. One of my main assignments was working with two colonels on drafting an American version of a treaty with Austria.

I finally got things straightened around so that I could leave on April 26. I left Vienna on the Mozart at 7:35 P.M., and the commander of the train gave me his bed, or bunk, since there were no other sleeping accomodations. I arrived in Linz at 2:25 A.M. and transferred to the Orient Express, which left at 6:30 A.M. We passed over the Austrian-German border at 9:55 A.M. and over the French-German border at 10:20 P.M., arriving in Paris on Sunday, April 28, at 9:00 A.M. The first ship I could get back was the *General Brooks*, which was to sail at 4:00 P.M. on May 4. I was assigned to share a room with seventeen army officers. The ship was a regular navy transport, and I was the only civilian in the officers' quarters. Everything was crowded, because of all the military personnel heading back home, but nevertheless it turned out to be a very enjoyable voyage. After letting the captain know I was the brother of Turk Wirth, Naval Academy Class of 1921, I received a much-coveted invitation to dinner in the captain's cabin, an honor usually reserved for ranking officers. The ship docked in New York at 11:00 A.M. on May 13.

The next morning my wife and I took the train back to Washington and started hunting for a furnished house, because Chapman's wire had indicated I would be stationed in Washington and our furniture was stored in Chicago. The reasons why I was in Washington were a little vague to Helen and me, and finally I came to the conclusion that the department must be planning to bring the whole Park Service back to Washington within the year. The war was over, and the pressure for space was easing. When I reported at the Washington office on the morning of Wednesday, May 15, I found that they had no money to pay my salary until the beginning of the next fiscal year, July 1. So I stayed on the War Department payroll until then.

I was informed several years later by Horace Albright that Oscar Chapman had been told that he was going to be appointed secretary of the interior and that he was calling me back to appoint me assistant secretary; but at the last minute President Harry Truman changed his mind and instead appointed Julius A. Krug secretary. By that time it was too late to change the orders returning me from Austria. I told Horace that, while I would have been very appreciative of the high honor, I would have turned it down, preferring to remain with the Park Service. But as I look back, it is possible that on the spur of the moment I would have accepted.

The National Park Service made a very important contribution to the war effort, although we had to assume a defensive attitude. We wanted to cooperate to the fullest extent possible with the military and other federal agencies involved in war activities without allowing the national park system to deteriorate. Many of the facilities, especially those that belonged to the concessionaires, were made available to the military as rest areas for recuperation of injured men. Some park areas were used for mountain maneuvers and for training ski troops. Others were used to train paratroopers and men who would work as saboteurs behind the enemy lines.

All of this was good, and we were happy we had facilities and personnel to be of help, but we did not lose track of the fact that the national park system was a heritage that should not be destroyed, except as a very last resort. The service's main problem was with those who wanted to exploit the resources that were being conserved in the national parks. Some thought the sitka spruce in Glacier Bay National Monument, in Alaska, should be cut for airplane construction or for the use of other countries, even though they had far more sitka spruce than we had. There were situations where certain minerals in a park were closer to manufacturing centers than the source of minerals the manufacturers were using, and therefore they wanted to take minerals from the park. Many applicants would not take no for an answer but would apply all the pressure they could muster. Although the pressures on Director Drury were tremendous, he approached all the problems in a very practical way. In a few places where no appreciable harm could be done, he allowed certain surface minerals to be used if they were in short supply. I know of one case in particular in which a valuable source of a mineral that was in very short supply was located in one of our big parks way up on a mountain and very close to the park boundary. No permit was granted, but under our close supervision we allowed the mineral to be removed. For convenience of reference and analysis, the various kinds of proposals and authorizations have been broken down into ten major classifications. These and the number of authorizations issued in each classification for all areas administered by the National Park Service, except the National Capital Parks, are as follows:

Newton B. Drury, director of the National Park Service from August 20, 1940, to March 31, 1951.

Classification	Number of Authorizations
Permanent transfer of jurisdiction	4
Temporary transfer of jurisdiction	6
Utilization of minerals, timber, forage, water, etc.	31
Occupancy and use, involving construction or appreciable modification of landscape features or both	71
Occupancy and use of existing facilities	73
Exclusive occupancy of operators; facilities	5
Field exercises, maneuvers, overnight bivouacking	162
Temporary rights-of-way	26
Loan or transfer of materials or equipment	27
Miscellaneous	58

I am certain that nothing was done in the parks that was permanently detrimental to them. When the war was over, however, we realized very vividly what had happened. The lack of maintenance—preventive maintenance as it is called—had caused deterioration of roads, buildings, and other facilities to such an extent that they could not be repaired but had to be replaced. The asphalt pavement on roads, for instance, had dried out and cracked in many places, and, as traffic began to build up, the road surfaces began to crumble. Patching a dried up and crumbling road is not feasible. Buildings that had been used for a number of years without maintenance had also deteriorated.

The appropriation of less than $5 million in 1945 was barely enough to keep the heart of the park organization intact and could not provide even ordinary protection of some 180 parks. Some units in out-of-the-way places, especially, were left unattended. Although there was a gradual buildup after 1945, by 1950, with 21 additional parks and twice as many visitors as we had in 1940, the Park Service funds were 25 per cent less than in 1940. And things were getting worse. The shooting war was over, but the cold war and grants in aid to nations throughout the world—allies and former enemies alike—left very little funding for the National Park Service. The number of visitors to the parks had grown from 33.2 million in 1950 to 56.5 million by 1955, while our appropriations had increased from $30.1 million to only $32.9 million. It got so bad that conservation writer Bernard De Voto wrote a very strong column urging that half of the parks be closed and that all funds be devoted to those left open to the public. It was quite evident that the cold war was damaging our parks more than the war itself had. We coined such expressions as "the people are loving the parks to death," and "patch on patch is no longer possible," to describe the seemingly hopeless situation in 1955. Something drastic had to be done to protect the parks and keep them in condition for the amount of use that people were entitled to give them. Many natural, scientific, and historic areas that should have been added to the national park system were being gradually destroyed and lost forever. The seashores that were studied and recommended for parks in the thirties were disappearing; they were no longer available. It was most discouraging.

Looking back, suppose we had got double the appropriations we were given between 1950 and 1955. Could we possibly have done enough to heal the damage suffered during the stagnant war years? What would have happened had we carried out Bernard De Voto's suggestion and used the money we had for operating half of the parks, letting the rest go to seed? I know, of course, that De Voto didn't really mean that; it was just his way of saying how bad things were. We were, however, in a situation where something spectacular had to be done to awaken Congress and the administration to what

On an inspection trip to Big Bend National Park, Texas, before its dedication were, *left to right*, Assistant Director Conrad L. Wirth, Regional Director Miner Tillotson, Pedro, and Director Newton B. Drury.

A committee from Texas and a congressional delegation called on President Harry Truman to invite him to attend the dedication of Big Bend National Park in 1950. Director Newton B. Drury of the National Park Service, *second from right*, and the author, *second from left*.

had actually happened, to rouse everybody to roll up their sleeves and go to work.

The damage to parks during World War II was going to require a big sum of money to bring all the various elements back into full bloom to be of service to the public. The fact is that even twice the amount of funds that we were getting at that time would not have provided the answer. It was not alone a question of repairing what existed; it was a question of rebuilding both the national park system and the National Park Service. Conditions got so bad that greater amounts of money, up to an average of $100 million a year for ten years, would have to be provided to do the job right. The Park Service was ready and willing to roll up its sleeves and go to work if the administration and Congress would only give the word. And under the Mission 66 program, they did.

9

Mission 66 and the Road to the Future

The National Park Service's Mission 66 might be fairly described as a renaissance. From the time that automobile travel began to build up in the 1920s following World War I until driving was curtailed by gasoline rationing in World War II, visitor use of the national and state parks increased tremendously. Moreover, the types of facilities preferred by people visiting the parks in their own cars were different from the kind formerly provided for those who traveled by train and took coach tours. Annual appropriations had been sufficient to protect park areas and develop the necessary facilities for this increased use. During World War II attendance dropped sharply, and a number of the national parks were made available to the military both as training grounds and as rest areas for troops suffering from combat fatigue. In view of the need to pour funds into all phases of the war effort, appropriations for administration of the park system were sharply curtailed. But ten years after the war the park system was still short of funding, in spite of a resurgence of visitation and the problems of inadequate maintenance, protection, and development during the war and postwar years. Mission 66 was conceived in 1956 and was designed to overcome the inroads of neglect and to restore to the American people a national park system adequate for their needs. This was to be accomplished within ten years, by 1966.

A lot could be written on the conditions that existed in the areas of the national park system in 1955, but an article in *The Reader's Digest* described them bluntly:

> One out of three persons in the United States will visit some part of our national-park system during 1955. To these visitors I must pass along a warning: Your trip is likely to be fraught with discomfort, disappointment, even danger.
>
> This warning, the result of a year-long investigation which included an 8000-mile inspection tour, is borne out by the director of the National Park Service (NPS) himself, Conrad L. Wirth. Says Mr. Wirth:
>
> "It is not possible to provide essential services. Visitor concentration points can't be kept in sanitary condition. Comfort stations can't be kept clean and serviced. Water, sewer and electrical systems are taxed to the utmost. Protective services to safeguard the public and preserve park values are far short of requirements. Physical facilities are deteriorating or are inadequate to meet public needs. Some of the camps are approaching rural slums. We actually get scared when we think of the bad health

conditions." [Charles Stevenson, "The Shocking Truth About Our National Parks," *The Reader's Digest*, January, 1955. Quoted by permission.]

Mission 66 required a lot of helping hands in its formulation and execution. A group of Park Service professionals started with nothing but an idea and put together a program of such comprehensive proportions and solid design that it attracted nationwide attention and received the full backing of the Department of the Interior, the president, and Congress. The service developed an *esprit de corps* and a determination in this endeavor that were wonderful to behold. Mission 66 influenced the activities of several other federal and state agencies and even attracted the interest of the White House in favor of other conservation studies and projects. Roy E. Appleman, the Park Service historian, had a very important part in working up the program and later compiled the history of organizing and launching Mission 66. I am indebted to his report for much of what follows in this chapter.

One weekend in February, 1955, I was pondering the reason the Park Service couldn't get the money we needed for the national parks. In 1940, when there were 161 areas in the system, totaling 21 1/2 million acres, with close to 17 million park visitors, total funds available were $33,577,000, including funds for some 109 national park CCC camps. In 1955, with 181 areas totaling 23 7/8 million acres and visitation more than tripled to a total of 56,573,000, the appropriation of $32,525,000 was approximately $1 million below the 1940 level. Moreover, our appropriations had been cut drastically during the war—down to a low of $4,740,000 in 1945—and we were in desperate need of extra money to repair the damage that wartime neglect had wrought. I had been in the director's chair for three full years, during which we had presented the government with some very strong arguments for what we felt were reasonable requests for funds. We had also submitted two-, three-, and four-year programs as requested by the Bureau of the Budget. But nothing happened. A few minor increases were approved, but even those were knocked out by the committees of Congress.

As I pondered our dilemma, I asked myself, "What would I want to hear from the Park Service if I were a member of Congress?" The answer to this question was a series of new questions: What would be the total amount of work required to bring the whole park system up to a satisfactory condition after the lean years of funding? How much would it cost? What would be the most economical way of getting this job done? How long would it take the service to do this on a reasonably economic basis? I envisioned not a crash program but a long-range one. As I went along with my cogitations, the various aspects of the problem began to clear up and make sense. I also realized that this kind of program would be difficult to set up, and I began to have strong doubts. Perhaps it would not clear the department, not to mention the Budget Bureau. Two- or three-year programs were all they were ever willing to consider, and even then they would make no commitment beyond the first appropriation year.

I spent several hours the next day, Sunday, working up some notes and making estimates based on figures I remembered—they were more "guesstimates" than estimates—and my thinking began to crystalize. I reasoned that other bureaus, such as the Bureau of Public Roads, the Bureau of Reclamation, and the Army Corps of Engineers got money year after year. They had big projects, such as dams and long highways, to construct that couldn't possibly be completed under a single annual appropriation or even in two or three years. That was it. Our projects were all relatively small ones that could be cut out of the budget because they were not sufficiently appealing to the committees that reviewed our request. But if we submitted one all-inclusive, long-term program for the entire park system, it would mean a complete review and some major policy changes by Congress. The whole program could be so arranged that if it were stopped halfway through, for example, half of the parks would be in good shape and the other half would be in poorer shape than ever. If we requested funds for a specific segment of a complete package program and all the congressmen knew that the parks in their states were part of the package and would be similarly taken care of within a given time, it seemed that once the overall program got started it would be hard to stop. Further, by letting larger contracts to do all the work necessary in an area and finishing the job instead of doing a little bit at a time, the project would in the long run be more economical and would interfere less with management and public use.

On Monday morning, February 7, I expounded my ideas to my branch heads. I proposed that we set up a special staff, selected from personnel in the Washington office, and put this group in the conference room, with no telephone, to work exclusively on the plan. They would be relieved of all their regular duties and would devote full time to the plan until it was completed, even if that took a year. These Mission 66 committee members would be selected so as to represent the major functions of the service, and they would be people who were so important in their regular assignments that they would be sorely missed.

The branch heads favored the proposal with enthusiasm. Although my original thought provided for only one Mission 66 committee, they suggested that a steering committee be set up consisting primarily of the bosses of the members of the main committee. Both were under my general supervision. The steering committee was to meet with the Mission 66 committee at regular intervals to review the work and make suggestions. The two committees worked well together and came up with an outstanding report and program that were the envy of other bureaus of the federal government. The members were:

Steering Committee	Mission 66 Committee
Lemuel A. Garrison, Chairman Chief, Conservation and Protection Branch, Operations Division	William G. Carnes, Chairman Chief Landscape Architect, Division of Design and Construction
Thomas C. Vint Chief, Division of Design and Construction	Harold G. Smith Assistant Chief, Programs and Plans Control Branch, Operations Division
Henry Langley Chief, Programs and Plans Control Branch, Operations Division	Robert M. Coates Chief, Economics and Statistical Section, Conservation and Protection Branch
John E. Doerr Chief, Natural History Branch, Division of Interpretation	Howard N. Stagner Principal Naturalist, Natural History Branch, Division of Interpretation
Donald E. Lee Chief, Branch of Concessions Management, Operations Division	Jack B. Dodd Assistant Chief Forester, Conservation and Protection Branch
Keith Neilson Finance Officer, Administration Division	Roy E. Appleman Staff Historian, History Branch, Division of Interpretation
Jackson E. Price Chief, Branch of Lands, Operations Division	Raymond L. Freeman Assistant Chief, Branch of River Basin Studies, Division of Cooperative Activities

We realized from the beginning that if the program was to be successful we would have to have a title that was short, expressive, easy to remember, and provocative. We spent some time on the problem of the title at our first meeting, and our discussions concerning a title helped us to form a better understanding of our total objective. We felt a sense of "mission" in the program and listed all that we hoped to accomplish. We talked about the time needed to do all that had to be done. We felt we had to allow enough time to make certain that what we did would be economically sound and well executed, and we finally decided that ten years was the length of time to "try on for size." Further, 1966 would mark the fiftieth anniversary of the establish-

The Mission 66 committee, whose members devoted full time, including after hours, to setting up the program. *Left to right:* Howard Stagner, naturalist; Bob Coates, economist; Jack Dodd, forester; Bill Carnes, landscape architect and chairman; Harold Smith, fiscal; Roy Appleman, historian; Ray Freeman, landscape architect–land planner. 1956. *Courtesy National Park Service.*

ment of the National Park Service, and it would be a good golden anniversary if the park system was in acceptable condition by that time. We reasoned that everything we had in mind was contained in two words, *Mission 66.*

Roy Appleman's account describes the temper of the Washington office after the staff meeting on February 7: "Excitement ran through the Park Service offices just before noon that Monday as word passed around that a special study group had been formed to inquire into possible changes in the service's policies and to plan for the future. Members of the staff received news of their selection for the work with a mingled feeling of surprise, uncertainty, and anticipation. But all looked forward to the afternoon meeting when they would learn more about the task ahead."

At that meeting I emphasized two things: one, a reasonable objective for the service over a long period; and, two, a program to accomplish that objective. I told them they wouldn't find the answers in any book, regulation, or even in legislation, but we had to find the answer, whatever it might be, because the public was not satisfied with the condition of the national park system and was calling on us to say what must be done, and why, to correct that condition; the public wanted to see our cards. I handed down two deadlines. I informed the staff that I wanted the program outline available for presentation at the Public Services Conference at Great Smoky Mountains National Park on September 18, 1955. I also got very emotional and told them that I would give them until Friday, February 11, to prepare a memorandum that I could send to the field and the personnel in the Washington office informing them of the service's Mission 66 project and what we hoped to accomplish.

The Mission 66 staff and the steering committee started right to work. The memorandum was prepared and went out on time. It stated in part:

> The year 1966 will mark the Golden Anniversary of the National Park Service. In an effort to solve, by that time, the difficult problem of protecting the scenic and historic areas of the National Park System from over-use and, at the same time, of providing optimum opportunity for public enjoyment of the parks, I have initiated a project which we are calling MISSION 66. . . .
>
> The purpose of MISSION 66 is to make an intensive study of the problems of protection, public use, interpretation, development, staffing, legislation, financing, and all other phases of park operation, and to produce a comprehensive and integrated program of use and protection that is in harmony with the obligations of the National Park Service under the Act of 1916.
>
> The *immediate* objective of MISSION 66 is the development of a dynamic program to be presented to the Secretary for consideration by the Bureau of the Budget and the Congress beginning with the 1957 fiscal year estimates. The *ultimate* objective is the complete execution of the program by the time the Service celebrates its Golden Anniversary in 1966.

In the first two or three weeks the staff delved into a considerable amount of history, policy, and legislation, going back to the establishment of Yellowstone, the Antiquities Act, the founding of the Park Service, the presidential reorganization orders of 1933, the Historic Sites Act of 1935, the Park, Parkway, and Recreational-Area Study Act of 1936, and the CCC program. As an axiom of intent and purpose, the committee adopted for its own, a statement that was made by Justice Mathew W. Hill in the case of *Dexter* v. *Washington* and that was delivered in the Washington Supreme Court on February 18, 1949 (202 Pacific reporter, 2d series): "Edmund Burke once said that a great unwritten compact exists between the dead, the living, and the unborn. We leave to the unborn a colossal financial debt, perhaps inescapable, but incurred, none the less, in our time and for our immediate benefit. Such an unwritten compact requires that we leave to the unborn something more than debts and depleted natural resources. Surely, where natural resources can be utilized and at the same time perpetuated for future generations, what has been called "constitutional morality' requires that we do so."

Each person within the Mission 66 staff and steering committee was free to question anything he thought could be done in a better way. Nothing was to be sacred, except the ultimate purpose to be served. Men, method, and time-honored practices were to be accorded no vested deference. Old traditions seem to have determined standards far beyond their time; for instance, the distance a stagecoach could travel in a day seemed to have been a controlling factor in establishing public facilities in some parks.

By the end of February the Mission 66 committee had started collecting detailed material in order to develop the program for Mission 66. A request for factual information was sent to each division and branch of the service, and a questionnaire was sent out to the parks. (The term *parks* was to be common to all classifications of areas in the system for the purposes of Mission 66.) The office in Washington, the regional offices, and the field offices were instructed to give high priority to any request that came from the Mission 66 committee or the steering committee. A list of twenty-eight items that should be looked into in each park was tabulated. The Mission 66 staff reviewed the Mount Rainier National Park master plan and asked for a pilot study of Mount Rainier. The superintendent, Preston P. Macy, came to Washington for five days. Macy was a man with many years of very successful park administration experience. They had a lot of good "skull practice" with Macy, with excellent results.

By March 17 work had progressed far enough that the steering committee and Mission 66 staff felt a second memorandum should go to the field. The memorandum reviewed the work done by the committees, clarified certain of the earlier directives, summarized some of the more troublesome problems, and outlined the steps yet to be taken. It firmly requested suggestions and recommendations from the field. Part of the memorandum was a questionnaire to be answered by each park superintendent, outlining a course of action for the Mission 66 program in the park under his administrative control. All replies were to be sent to the Mission 66 staff by April 11. Finally, the memorandum also invited all employees to send any suggestions or thoughts they might have to the Mission 66 staff in Washington. The responses were many and good.

During the week of April 11 a meeting of regional directors was held in Shenandoah National Park and attended by representatives of the steering committee and the Mission 66 committee. In view of the findings of the Mount Rainier National Park pilot study, it was decided at that meeting that pilot studies should be carried out on a variety of other areas. The parks selected constituted a good cross section of the service's administrative, preservation, protection, development, and visitor-use problems. They were Yellowstone National Park, in Wyoming, Chaco Canyon National Monument, in New Mexico, Shiloh National Military Park, in Tennessee, Adams Mansion National Historic Site, in Massachusetts, Fort Laramie National Historic Site, in Wyoming, and Everglades National Park, in Florida.

The Mission 66 staff placed on my desk once a week a brief of their accomplishments on the subjects they were currently pursuing or would be taking up the following week, together with a statement on the decisions they had reached the past week. Copies of this report went to key people in the Washington office. It reminded all of their responsibility to speak out with suggestions or objections as the work progressed and not to wait until the report was completed. I quote from Roy Appleman's notes:

As often as his duties would permit, Mr. Wirth stepped through the side door of his office to join the Staff informally for a few minutes. He would comment on some aspects of the work or pass on to the Staff members some bit of information he had just received. He cut through the confusion that often seemed to overwhelm the Staff and helped to keep its work on course by advice and criticism. Above all, his optimism on the outcome of the Staff's work was of immeasurable value.

As this indicates, everybody had a responsibility to help put Mission 66 together. We were not going to have time for long reviews after the committee finished its report which, when finished, was to be final.

The service's field forces had conducted several visitor polls during the summer at the request of the Mission 66 committee, and the results followed very closely those of a poll made by an outside organization that was not financed by National Park Service funds. Of approximately 1,750 persons interviewed, a total of 718 had visited national parks in the preceding five years. Of those, 69 per cent had complaints of one kind or another. Many complaints concerned the facilities available in a park and the general condition of the parks; there were very few complaints against Park Service personnel. About one-third mentioned overcrowding, and about one-half referred to overnight accommodations. Practically all park visitors wanted either cabin or motel accommodations. Very few wanted hotel accommodations, and only 14 per cent wanted campgrounds. Seventy per cent visited a park for one day or less, and only 29 per cent stayed overnight.

In 1952, my first full year as director, we had a field meeting in Glacier National Park. At that time we got a lot of complaints from the ladies about living conditions for the staff in the parks. I had seen some of the housing, and it was terrible. At that time I asked Herma Baggley, wife of George Baggley, then superintendent of the Lake Meade National Recreation Area, in Arizona and Nevada, if she would head a committee made up of a Park Service wife from each park to get pictures and make a report with recommendations on the condition of their housing. Tom Vint was to work with them in drawing up standard floor plans for new housing. Besides the terrible condition of the buildings, the rooms and windows were of different sizes in different parks so that when a family moved from one park to another such items as furniture, rugs, and curtains did not fit. The ladies did a great job, and their final two-volume report, with pictures and descriptions, came in just about the time Mission 66 got started. It fitted right into the scheme of things. The report contained standard floor plans for two- and three-bedroom houses. The exterior architectural appearance of these more or less uniform houses could be varied and suited to a particular locality. This study made a great impression on the Bureau of the Budget and the committees of Congress and resulted in the building of thousands of new homes for our field people.

We confronted another specific problem in Yellowstone National Park. In

Some ranger housing in areas of the national park system before 1950 was grossly inadequate. Shown here is a wooden shack with outside "convenience." *Courtesy National Park Service.*

The view was the only superlative feature of this wood and canvas ranger quarters complex. *Courtesy National Park Service.*

Living was rugged in ranger quarters such as these. *Courtesy National Park Service.*

This square adobe house had seen its better days.

Two Bedroom Duplex

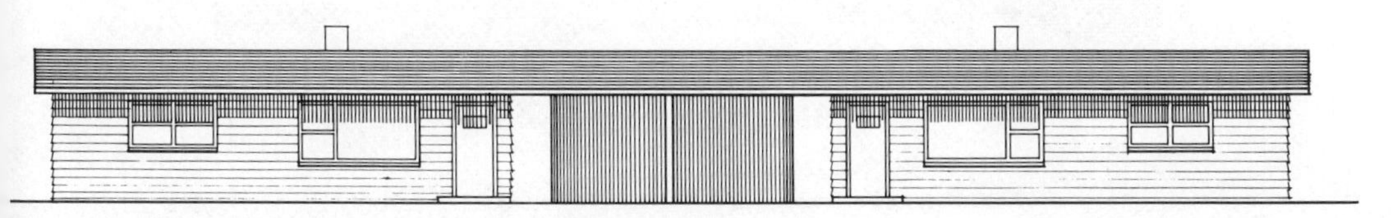

Front elevation

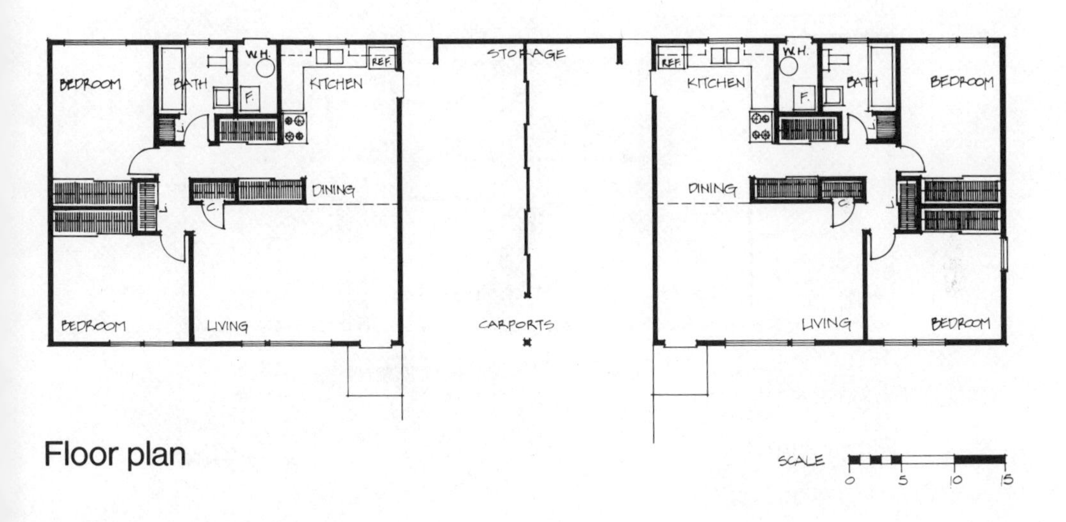

Floor plan

PLAN • D 920 sq. ft. each

BUREAU BUDGET (NORMAL) 1000 sq. ft.

New ranger housing was designed in several standard sizes and room arrangements, with exteriors modified to conform to the prevailing architecture of the area of location. This is a two-bedroom duplex.

Three Bedroom Standard

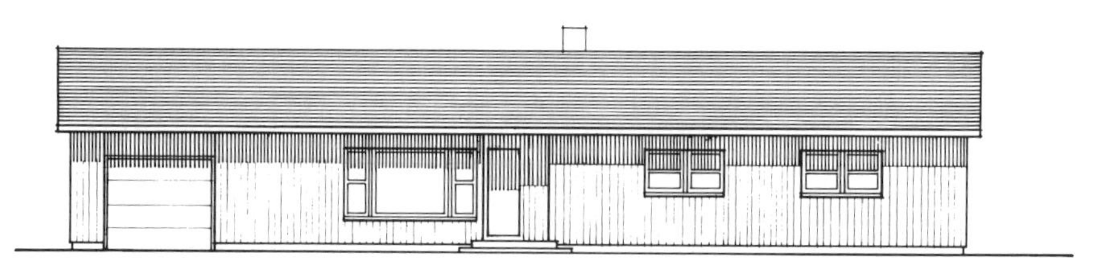

Front elevation

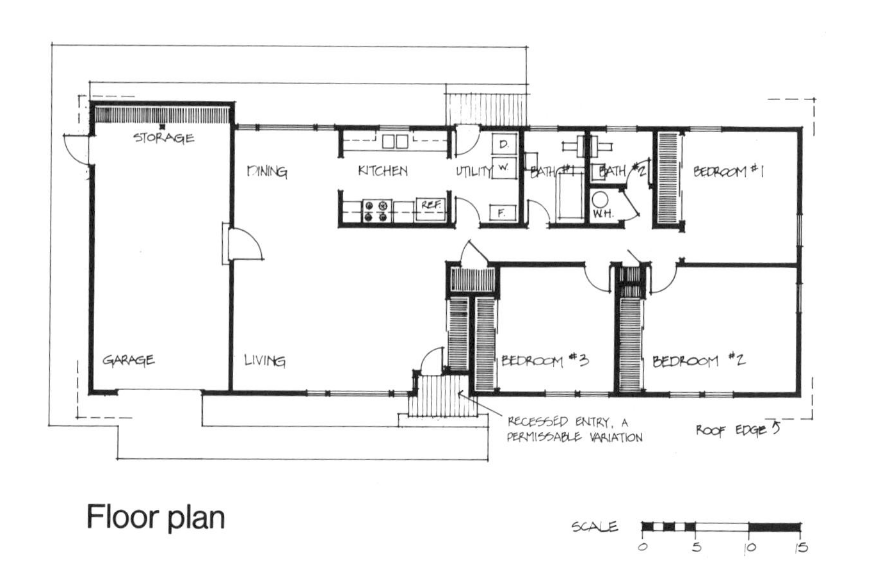

Floor plan

FLOOR AREA	1240 sq. ft.
BUREAU BUDGET (NORMAL)	1415 sq. ft.

A three-bedroom standard floor plan.

1955 the twenty-year concession contracts were soon to expire, and new contracts would have to be negotiated. If we were going to make any changes that might affect the concessionaires, this was the time to consider them. It also presented an opportunity to make sure the plans of the concessionaires and those for the park itself would be in harmony. Arrangements were made for Yellowstone's Superintendent Edmond B. Rogers, its resident landscape architect, Frank Matson, Chief Ranger Otto Brown, and Chief Naturalist Dave Condon to come to Washington and spend a full week with the Mission 66 committee to examine in detail the Yellowstone master plan.

By the first part of April, 1955, it became evident from correspondence received from personnel in the regional offices and the parks that it would be advisable to send Garrison and Carnes, the chairmen of the steering committee and the Mission 66 committee, into the field to give a thorough explanation of Mission 66 and to answer questions. Their schedule included all of the regions and the eastern and western design offices. This tour cleared away many misunderstandings and also created a great deal of enthusiasm among the field people. Appleman wrote of the results: "After these meetings, the several Regional Offices established MISSION 66 Committees within their own organization and scheduled a series of meetings with Park Superintendents and their staffs. In this way, by the end of June, a rather complete indoctrination of the purposes and scope of MISSION 66 had been spread throughout the personnel of the Service. With very few exceptions, Service personnel, from the Director's office to the smallest park staff, proceeded to give their best efforts and thoughts to the project."

On June 27 a third memorandum was sent to the field and set the stage for the next big step of the Mission 66 plan: the preparation of the individual Mission 66 park prospectuses. It outlined some eight other pilot studies to be undertaken, reviewed the work already accomplished, set forth further procedures to be carried out, and described the current activities of the staff. It directed, based on the master plan and further material that had been gathered, that each park staff prepare its own prospectus with whatever assistance it needed from the regional offices and that these drafts be delivered to the Washington office not later than July 20. Because of the difficulty involved in the Everglades National Park prospectus, a Washington conference was arranged as in the case of Yellowstone.

These pilot studies made it clear to us that, despite guiding principles and precepts, people were going to have diverse ideas of what constituted the best and most suitable plan for park development and public use. And each thought that his plan promised the best protection of the parks' unique resources and would provide the most enjoyment for the people. These studies also pointed up again how important the master plans were in drawing up the Mission 66 program, for without them it would have been impossible to organize a sound program. The detail and the in-depth factual material contained in the master plans made it possible for us to formulate policy, administrative, interpretive, and developmental decisions. The main thing we had to do to get Mission 66 on the track was to review these master plans and bring them up to date, since many had not been kept current during World War II and the cold war. (For an account of the master plan conception see Chapter 3.)

On June 30 I told the staff I wanted eight pilot studies finished, legislation blocked out, principles guiding the study written out, and a balanced program drafted and ready for the Public Services Conferences at Great Smoky Mountains September 20. By the time of the meeting we would need an all-inclusive statement and budget for the plan written and reproduced in the form of a brief, popular-style book. It would have to include charts and tables summarizing the more important statistics on visitor use, needs, proposed facilities, and costs; a pictorial presentation of some of the more widespread problems; and a review of the status of Mission 66 and what still had to be done. In July we had a meeting to discuss the nature and format of the Mission 66 report for presentation at the conference. We agreed that we wanted chapters on employee housing, visitor housing, concessions, camping, roads, and administrative facilities and that the document should be a sort of "Bible" for Mission 66 thereafter. We also discussed the task of getting the program ready for submission to Congress by January 1, 1956. Further, we needed a performance-oriented report that would give the total cost of various units of construction. We also needed to prepare legislation to (1) help finance concession activities, principally for providing overnight accommodations; (2) inquire into the feasibility of a contractual authorization for constructing buildings and utilities in the parks; and (3) inquire into the feasibility of establishing a revolving fund for erecting employee housing.

The original concept was to get an omnibus bill introduced in Congress to take care of all Mission 66 needs; however, after much discussion the omnibus bill idea was abandoned in favor of an individual bill for each subject heading so that if one failed all would not be lost. That first year we were to concentrate on several of the small park areas as well as some of the big ones. We figured that if we could get a considerable amount of funding for a small area and complete everything in one year—housing, visitor centers, roads, trails, campgrounds, whatever was necessary—we would demonstrate what we were trying to do.

In our discussions the question of park use fees came up, and I decided against camping fees and stated that I objected also to entrance fees, even though we had been collecting them for years. Fees charged in the parks now for camping and other things are later innovations. At the time Mission 66 began the only fees enforced were entrance fees. We all realized that there was a certain psychological advantage in having people pay a reasonable entrance fee, for it placed a token value on what the visitor was going to see, use, and enjoy—a value that would, we hoped, encourage him to use the park and facilities with care. Further, we reasoned, a person who can afford to drive across the continent should be able to pay a dollar or so as a car entrance fee.

As we went along we were becoming more and more confident that Mission 66 would be a success. By late summer Assistant Director Hillory A. Tolson and I felt we should begin to include some of our first-year estimates for Mission 66 in our 1957 fiscal year appropriation request, which had to be prepared and clear the department and the Bureau of the Budget by the end of 1955 and be submitted to Congress in January, 1956. Our hearings before the congressional committees would start in January or February and we hoped that Congress would act on our request by June 30, because fiscal year 1957 started on July 1, 1956. We just could not wait for the final approval of Mission 66.

By September 15 the staff had completed in time for distribution and use at the Great Smokies conference a twenty-two-page illustrated popular book on Mission 66 entitled *Our Heritage* and a fifty-three-page Mission 66 report. The first agendum of the conference was a summary of the major purposes of Mission 66. It was emphasized that there were three underlying assumptions: (1) that the service must plan for a total of eighty million visits by 1966; (2) that this visitor load must be accommodated without undue harm to the parks; and (3) that planning for the future must include all existing facilities that were usable. The presentation became the basis for a slide talk with a tape recording that was produced in quantity for circulation in the parks in order to acquaint not only the park staffs but also the public with the plan. The journalists covering the meeting did a very good job of reporting on Mission 66 in influential newspapers throughout the country, including *The New York Times*. Because of the constant reference to Mission 66 in the daily press, readers were rapidly becoming aware of it and of the National Park Service's plans for the future.

On the evening of May 12, 1955, I received a call at home from Harry Donohue, an assistant to Assistant Secretary Orem Lewis, telling me of a possibility for the Mission 66 plan to be presented to the president at a cabinet meeting. The next day I called the Mission 66 staff together, and told them that there were indications that we would be called upon in the near future to present the whole Mission 66 concept at a cabinet meeting and then later in the fall to present our program of implementation. Our first reaction to the request from the White House was that Mission 66 was a Park Service project, we wanted to do it ourselves, and we did not want higher authorities to lay down any requirements for us. We relied on our own professional ability and judgment. We did keep the department posted on our general progress, but I asked Secretary Douglas McKay and Assistant Secretary Orem Lewis to give us a free hand in this matter, and they did except toward the end.

We were all very curious about how the idea of a cabinet presentation originated. Actually it wasn't until several months after the presentation had been made that anyone in the National Park Service learned just how the whole thing came about. Maxwell M. Rabb, secretary to the cabinet, conceived the idea. He had read an editorial in the *Saturday Evening Post* describing the deplorable condition of the national parks and the need for improvement and modernization of visitor accommodations. He mentioned it to his assistant, Bradley H. Patterson, Jr., and said he was wondering if the national parks would not be a good subject for cabinet discussion. Patterson volunteered to work on the suggestion with the Interior Department. It soon became apparent that the White House had not known there was such a plan as Mission 66 being prepared.

The preparations for the cabinet presentation took months. As we continued to have one postponement after another, we began to wonder whether we would have to appear before Congress before the president had seen the plan and spoken out on it. We had submitted to the Bureau of the Budget in the late fall of 1955 a supplemental request for funds primarily to get an early start on Mission 66, even though the plan was not completed. We were turned down. The Bureau of the Budget was not against our program but felt that anything pertaining to Mission 66 should be held up until the president had an opportunity to review it and express himself.

In October the budget people were howling for information because they were preparing our 1957 request. We decided that we would go full blast for 1957 as the first year of Mission 66. We needed ten fiscal years to complete Mission 66, and we had to start with the 1957 fiscal year, beginning July 1, 1956, if we were going to get through by 1966, our fiftieth anniversary.

We were planning three Mission 66 documents: (1) a popular-style booklet for general distribution; (2) a detailed official report with statistics, charts, graphs, an explanation of the proposed development and operation program, work load figures, funding requirements, and a format used for appropriation estimates; and (3) a final prospectus for each park. All park officials were requested to begin preparing the data and have them in Washington no later than November 15. Days and nights were spent going over the vast amount of material available, adjusting some of it, eliminating, and adding. We agreed on a brief report—one that could be presented to the public—and gave it the title *Our Heritage*. It was in color and brief but all-inclusive, with charts. The Creative Arts Studio had the contract and did a good job; however, it was difficult for them to get the feeling, in a few words, of what we were trying to

Bradley H. Patterson, Jr., assistant secretary to the cabinet in the Eisenhower administration, is on the left of this group attending a luncheon of the Potomac Corral of the Westerners at the Cosmos Club in Washington, D.C. On Patterson's left are the author and Roy E. Appleman, historian of the National Park Service.

say. In the end, our own Herb Evison worked with a rewrite man for several weeks and got the text into better form. This booklet was not to be released until after our meeting with the cabinet.

On January 5, 1956, the president included a statement on the parks in his message to Congress on the State of the Union. Very seldom has the Park Service been mentioned in so important a document. The president said: "During the past year the areas of our national parks have been expanded and new wildlife refuges have been created. The visits of our people to the parks have increased much more rapidly than have the facilities to care for them. The administration will submit recommendations to provide more adequate facilities to keep abreast of the increasing interest of our people in the great outdoors." We interpreted his words to mean that we no doubt would get favorable action, and we began to breathe a little easier.

Our material for presentation to the president was carefully reviewed with Brad Patterson, who had visited many of the parks and knew our problems. We made several dry runs of the cabinet presentation, and Patterson was a great help to us. It was unanimously agreed that Secretary McKay would open the presentation with a statement of two or three minutes, after which I would present Mission 66, the problem and the solution. Assistant Secretary Wesley A. D'Ewart would then take two or three minutes to point out the political value of such a program and how it would be received by Congress. As it finally turned out, the Mission 66 presentation was on the cabinet meeting agenda for January 27. In all honesty I don't think any presentation has ever been made before the cabinet, or perhaps anywhere else, that had received so much preparatory attention by so many people as this one.

Sam Dodd, a hearing officer in the Bureau of the Budget, was able to help Bradley Patterson secure Bureau of the Budget approval of Mission 66's fiscal provisions in advance of the cabinet meeting. No one in the Park Service knew of this, however, until everything was over. Patterson had felt that, when the Mission 66 program came before the cabinet, the president would turn to Director of the Budget Roland R. Hughes and ask his opinion of it in relation to the administration's budget. If Hughes had expressed doubt or outright opposition to it, the program in all probability would have come under a cloud in the president's view.

The agenda for the cabinet meeting of January 27 were published at the White House on January 25 and listed four topics for the cabinet's consideration. On Friday, the twenty-seventh, starting at 9:30 A.M., the first item was "The National Parks Mission 66—CP-43/1," and it listed Secretary of the Interior McKay, Assistant Secreatary D'Ewart, and Director Wirth as those giving the presentation. The brief prepared by Patterson and distributed by Max Rabb to the cabinet members was seven pages long on legal-size paper, and two and a half pages of it summarized the projected ten-year program of Mission 66, the needs, and the proposed accomplishments.

I asked Lon Garrison, Bill Carnes, and Howard Stagner to accompany me to the meeting. Stagner was proficient with slide and movie projectors and on him would fall the responsibility of preventing any malfunction of the equipment during my talk. Everything was in order when the cabinet members started arriving around 9:25. I overheard Harold E. Stassen's remark to Henry Cabot Lodge, the ambassador to the United Nations who had come down from New York for the cabinet meeting, "What is this Mission 66—Davy Crockett in Yellowstone?"

Punctually at 9:30 the door to the president's office was opened, and President Eisenhower entered the room. He took a seat at the center of the conference table and the others took their seats. As soon as everyone was seated, the president asked for a moment of prayer. Promptly after this Secretary McKay made his opening statement on Mission 66. Then I outlined the existing problems and set forth the program we proposed to meet them. I spoke for about sixteen minutes and used slides to illustrate the crowded conditions in the parks. Following the slides I showed a three-minute color movie taken in some of the larger parks in June of the preceding summer, illustrating the same theme. After the film I referred to large charts showing the financial schedule and the legislative needs for the program I had just outlined. When I finished Assistant Secretary Wes D'Ewart, drawing on his ten years' experience in Congress, stated that he felt the Congress would support such a program because all its members were concerned with the problem. Then Secretary McKay turned to the president and asked, "Mr. President, and gentlemen of the Cabinet, are there any questions?"

The president spoke up right away and said, "Yes, I have a question. Why was not this request made back in 1953?" The secretary explained that there had been a tight budget that couldn't include it then, but the time was right now to move forward. Some discussion went on about the concessionaires, then cabinet members asked questions about revenues, park fees, matching park development cost, and so forth. One of the members of the cabinet asked why there should not be a charge of $1.00 per visit, which would produce an estimated revenue of $80 million a year. At this point President Eisenhower interjected that he did not think it right to charge visitors fees to the historical and patriotic shrines of the nation, even though it might be justified in a large park in the West. Then he asked how much money we were collecting in entrance fees and we told him it was approximately $5 million a year. President Eisenhower commented that that kind of money didn't mean anything to a program of this kind. He went so far as to suggest that our people should not be bothered with collecting fees. He mentioned Gettysburg National Military Park with all of its entrances and how much it would cost to collect the fees.

After the discussion of about twenty minutes President Eisenhower asked the secretary if he could start the Mission 66 program of improvement for the parks at once. The secretary answered that he could start it as soon as we got the money. The president then said that he approved of the Mission 66 program as a basis for an expanded ten-year development of the national parks and historic sites. He said he would sign a letter to Congress recommending the program but that Secretary McKay would be responsible for presenting and supporting the program before the Congress. That finished up our Mission 66 presentation, and we were escorted out of the room and asked to wait until the cabinet meeting was adjourned, at which time we were to make another presentation to the department cabinet assistants who were regularly called together after each cabinet meeting for an oral briefing by Rabb and Patterson in order to insure full and immediate staff follow-through on cabinet decisions. So we gave a second presentation in the cabinet room at 11:30.

Although the president had indicated that he was in favor of Mission 66, a closing remark he made before going on to the next item on the agenda removed any possible doubt about his approval. He said "This is a good project; let's get on with it." During the discussion following the presentation there was no criticism of Mission 66 whatever, and no reluctance to accept it was expressed by anyone.

The president's letter went forward in the usual way and was received in Congress a few days after the cabinet meeting. Several members of the Senate and House had followed the progress of the Mission 66 study for several months and had taken a very active interest in it. But we had not released to members of Congress any of the plans before the presentation to the president and the cabinet, and so they did not know specifically what the program called for. There had been intimations: Secretary McKay at the dedication of Big Bend National Park, Texas, in November, 1955, had spoken glowingly about Mission 66 and what it would do to help park development, especially at Big Bend. The president's approval removed any question of support by any executive department or agency of the government and provided solid administration endorsement of the Mission 66 program.

When we appeared before the Bureau of the Budget and the committees of Congress, we told them very frankly that our estimates were based on the prices of the day and were believed to be sound but that we reserved the right each year to increase them by the percentage of increase in the cost of labor and materials and that, of course, the overall budget would be increased if and when new areas were added to the park system and therefore became Mission 66 projects. They understood and agreed. Each year we would revamp our estimates based on increased cost data furnished by the Departments of Labor and Commerce. Our total ten-year budget estimate for Mission 66, exclusive of cost increase and the addition of new areas, was $786,545,600. The actual cost of Mission 66 during the ten-year program amounted to over $1 billion. I'm sorry to say we did not complete the program as originally planned because of the growth in the park system during this ten-year period.

As soon as the rush for the White House presentation was over we proceeded to review all the master plans and all the proposed projects and to start a schedule of operations. On February 8 the American Pioneer Dinner was held in the cafeteria of the Interior Department. Approximately sixty members of the Senate and the House of Representatives and their wives accepted the invitation. All the members of the Board of the American Plan-

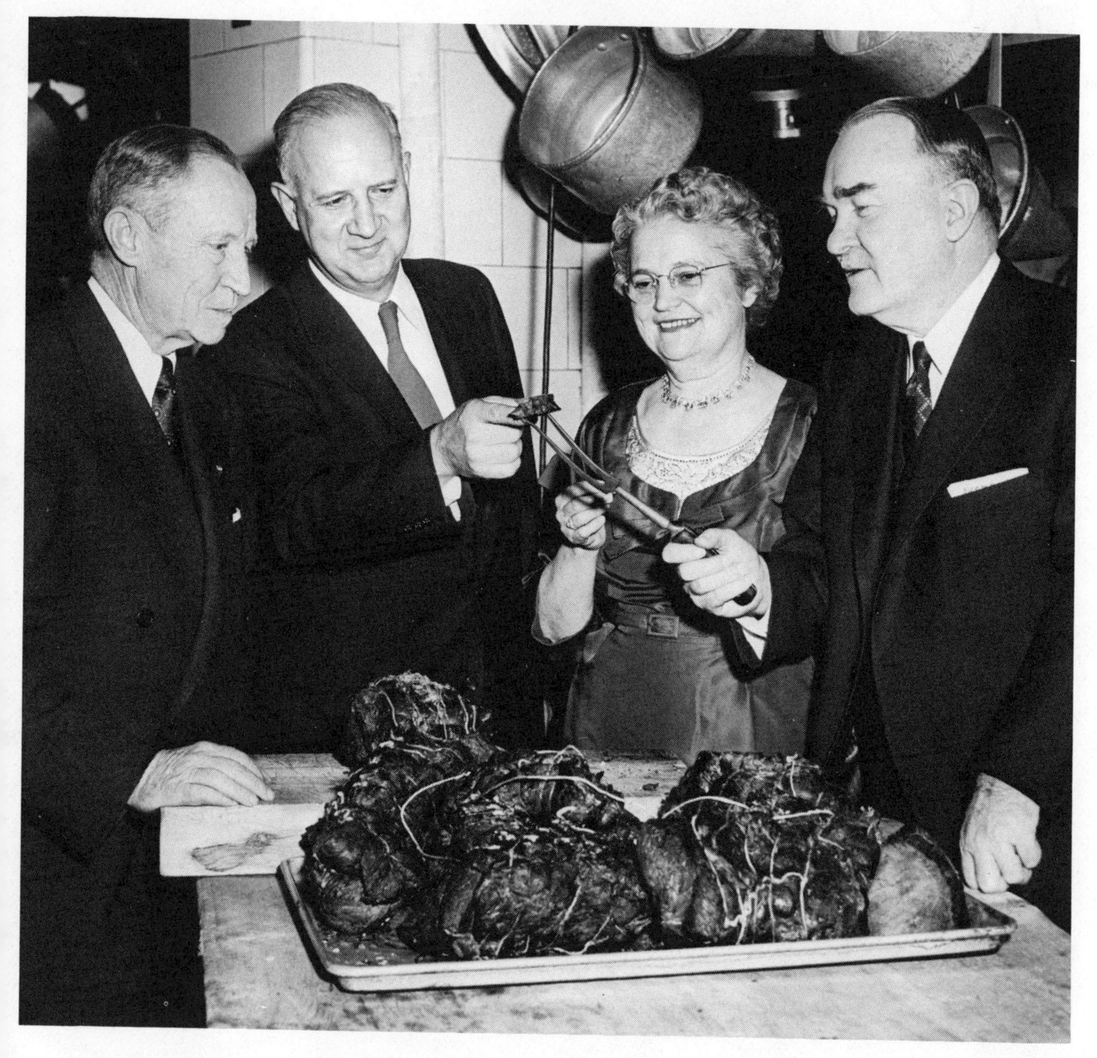

Some of the bison and elk meat donated by the state of South Dakota for the Pioneer Dinner at the Interior Department was checked in by Under Secretary Clarence Davis, Director Wirth, and Mrs. Singer and Russell Singer, executive vice-president of the American Automobile Association. *Photo by Abbie Rowe, courtesy National Park Service.*

ning and Civic Association attended. Officials of conservation groups and others influential in the conservation field were also invited. The dinner was sponsored jointly by the secretary of the interior, the National Park Service, and the American Automobile Association. The menu featured bison and elk meat furnished by the state park authority of South Dakota. After dinner we

presented the Mission 66 program and showed a film entitled "Adventures in the National Parks" that had been prepared for this occasion by Walt Disney. At this meeting we made our first distribution of the booklet entitled *Our Heritage*, which served as a popular presentation of Mission 66.

With the highly successful Pioneer Dinner over, the Mission 66 committee was relieved of its duties as rapidly as odds and ends could be cleared up. The steering committee was reorganized and enlarged as the advisory committee for Mission 66. This committee of ten members, with Lon Garrison as chairman, had six field members and its job was to monitor the Mission 66 program. An increased appropriation in 1956 fiscal year had got Mission 66 off to a flying start and that, combined with an increased appropriation of over $19 million for 1957 fiscal year propelled us forward. Our appropriation had been increased from $32,915,000 in 1955 to $68,020,000, a total increase of about $35.5 million, which more than doubled our 1955 budget. In round figures the increase represented $4.25 million in operation funds and $30.75 million in capital improvement funds. This put a heavy burden on our relatively small organization, and the Bureau of the Budget as well as the committees of Congress and the department were watching us very closely. If we failed or didn't produce as we had promised, there was no doubt in my mind that our well-laid plans would be suspended. They might well look for a new director, too.

The Department of the Interior was extremely pleased with what the service had done and awarded the departmental unit award for meritorious service to the Mission 66 committee. The secretary of the interior also presented me the Department of the Interior's Distinguished Service Award.

The guidelines that had been worked out by the Mission 66 committee were revamped slightly as time went along. They were as follows:

1. Preservation of park resources is a basic requirement underlying all park management.
2. Substantial and appropriate use of the National Park System is the best means by which its basic purpose is realized and is the best guarantee of perpetuating the System.
3. Adequate and appropriate developments are required for public use and appreciation of an area, and for prevention of overuse. Visitor experiences which derive from the significant features of the parks without impairing them determine the nature and scope of developments.
4. An adequate information and interpretive service is essential to proper park experience. The principal purpose of such a program is to help the park visitor enjoy the area, and to appreciate and understand it, which leads directly to improved protection through visitor cooperation in caring for the park resources.
5. Concession-type services should be provided only in those areas where required for proper, appropriate park experience, and where these services cannot be furnished satisfactorily in neighboring communities. Exclusive franchises for conces-

The author receiving the Department of the Interior Distinguished Service Award from Secretary Douglas McKay and Assistant Secretary Wes D'Ewart. *Photo by Abbie Rowe, courtesy National Park Service.*

sioners' services within a park should be granted only where necessary to insure provision for dependable public service.

6. Large wilderness areas should be preserved undeveloped except for simple facilities required for access, back-country use and protection, and in keeping with the wilderness atmosphere.

7. All persons desiring to enter a park area may do so; however it may be necessary to place a limit on the number of visitors who may enter certain prehistoric and historic ruins and structures because of limitations of space or because only a restricted number may safely pass over or through them at one time. Lodging, dining, and camping facilities cannot be guaranteed every visitor.

8. Operating and public-use facilities of both government and concessioners which encroach upon the important park features should be eliminated or relocated at sites of lesser importance, either within or outside the parks.

9. Where airports are needed they should be located outside the park boundaries;

and use of aircraft within the areas of the System should be restricted to investigations, protection, rescue, and supply services.

10. Camping is an appropriate and important park visitor use in many parks, and every effort should be made to provide adequate facilities for this use.

11. Picnic grounds should be provided in areas where picnicking is an important element in the visitor day-use pattern.

12. A nation-wide plan for parks and recreation areas as envisioned in the Park, Parkway, and Recreational Area Study Act of 1936 should be completed and implemented as promptly as possible so that each level of government—local, State, and Federal—may bear its share of responsibility in the provision of recreation areas and services.

13. Adequate and modern living quarters for National Park Service employees should be provided when required for effective protection and management. Living quarters for government and concessioner employees, when located within the park, should be concentrated in a planned residential community out of public view.

14. The use of a park for organized events, organized competitive sports, or spectator events which attract abnormal concentrations of visitors and which require facilities, services, and manpower above those needed for normal operation should not be permitted except in the National Capital Parks.

The table on page 261 shows the growth of the national park system over a forty-three-year period. In examining the columns of the table starting with the numbers of areas, it should be noted that in the ten-year period of fiscal years 1957 through 1966 the areas increased by 78, from 180 to 258, or about 42 per cent. The rapid increase in areas actually started around 1961, because the earlier years of Mission 66 were devoted to planning and carrying out the necessary field studies. As these were completed, legislation was submitted to Congress for approval. Many of the areas studied and selected as additions to the national park system as a result of Mission 66 did not get acted upon until several years after Mission 66 had expired. In the five years following the end of Mission 66 another 26 areas were established or authorized, 23 of which were the result of studies started during Mission 66. These areas added up to over 2,600,000 acres, and amongst them were the Seashore and Lakeshore National Recreation Areas, a new classification.

The actual acreage owned by the federal government shows an increase of 1,653,000 acres during the Mission 66 period. Acquiring funds for land acquisition had always been a problem for the service. Traditionally, areas set aside as units of the national park system had to be taken from lands already owned by the federal government or given to the government by other public bodies or by private interests. This policy was often referred to by members of the service, unofficially and off the record, as the "beg, borrow, or steal" method. The land purchase authorization for Cape Cod National Seashore in 1961 changed that policy. Since then all legislation authorizing new areas of the national park system have included land purchase. With the establishment of the Bureau of Outdoor Recreation in 1964, hundreds of millions of

Fiscal Year	Number of Areas	Federal Acres (000)	Visitors (000)	Operation Funds (000)	Capital Improvement Funds (000)	Total Funding (000)
1930	55	10,963	3,265	$ 2,174	$5,716	$ 7,890
1935	130	15,286	7,676	6,799	5,000	11,799
1940	161	21,551	16,755	13,036	8,062	21,098
1945	168	20,473	11,714	4,736	4	4,740
1950	182	23,882	33,253	15,157	14,954	30,111
1955	181	23,889	56,573	18,697	14,218	32,915
1956	181	24,898	61,602	20,781	28,079	48,860
1957	180	24,410	68,016	22,976	45,056	68,032
1958	180	24,398	65,461	27,605	48,400	76,005
1959	183	24,497	68,900	29,963	50,000	79,963
1960	187	25,704	79,229	32,682	47,000	79,682
1961	192	25,158	86,663	37,876	51,528	89,404
1962	191	26,003	97,045	42,224	67,976	110,200
1963	201	25,859	102,711	48,017	72,776	120,793
1964	203	26,102	111,386	51,386	61,697	113,083
1965	214	26,549	121,312	56,199	71,987	128,186
1966	258	26,551	133,081	61,380	66,380	127,760
1967	263	27,187	139,676	67,743	55,323	123,066
1968	273	27,971	150,836	78,572	49,612	128,184
1969	277	28,460	163,990	81,674	21,958	103,632
1970	282	28,543	172,005	96,450	28,627	125,077
1971	284	28,731	200,543	120,244	36,707	156,951
1972	297	28,850	211,621	133,133	99,460	232,593
1973	298	28,937	222,376	170,661	51,087	221,748

dollars of federal funds were made available for land purchases not only for the National Park Service but also for other federal agencies engaged in conservation and recreation programs, as well as for state and metropolitan park areas. From 1965 through 1973 the service received over $440 million from this source, which is not shown in the table.

The column on visitation is interesting because the Mission 66 program was built on the estimated 80 million visits by 1966. That estimate turned out to be off by better than 53 million, or 66 per cent. The visits in 1966 totaled 133 million, an increase of more than 71 million, or 116 per cent, over 1956.

The columns on appropriations show that operation funds increased by over $40 million in the ten-year period, or 200 per cent; and capital improvements funds increased by $38 million, or approximately 136 per cent. We had estimated that for the ten-year period we would need $310,385,600 for operation and $476,160,000 for capital improvements, or a total of $786,545,600. The actual costs of Mission 66, including the head start funds of

$15,945,000 that we got in 1956 and the $26,172,000 that we got in 1965 and 1966 for land purchases from the Bureau of Outdoor Recreation, amounted to $412,392,000 for operation and $622,833,000 for capital improvements, or a total of $1,035,225,000. The Bureau of Outdoor Recreation contribution is not shown in the table.

It is interesting to note that there was a considerable jump in funding in fiscal year 1956, a year before Mission 66 officially started. That increase of some $17 million was due to anticipation of Mission 66. The Mission 66 request was completed by January, 1956, and the House Appropriations Committee and the Bureau of the Budget, after presidential approval, wanted to get the program started as soon as possible; so they made a supplemental allotment to our 1956 appropriation. But Mission 66 itself officially started on July 1, 1956, the beginning of fiscal year 1957.

There is an interesting sidelight about how we got the first $17 million the year before Mission 66 actually was scheduled to start. We had submitted a supplemental request to the Bureau of the Budget in the fall of 1955 in order to get an early start on Mission 66, but this was held up by the budget authorities. A day or two after the cabinet presentation we appeared before Representative Mike Kirwan's Subcommittee on Interior Appropriations. Mike opened the meeting by saying he had heard about Mission 66, that it sounded good to him, but that he saw nothing in the budget about it. He then asked me, "If I added $5 million to your 1956 appropriation for Mission 66, could you get started?" All I said was, "Yes, sir." A few days later we got a call from the Bureau of the Budget asking us to send them a justification to submit to Congress requesting a $10 million supplement for Mission 66. I told them that they had our request for $12 million that we had sent over in the fall of 1955 and that they could use all or any part of that. About two weeks later I got a call from Mike Kirwan, who wanted to know what I was trying to do to him. He called my attention to his promise to give us $5 million to get started on Mission 66 and asserted that now we were sending up a request for $12 million. I told him what had happened but that I had not seen the request before it went up and really didn't know the Bureau of the Budget had sent it until I got his call. He was very disturbed and told me that if they wanted to play poker that was all right with him. He said he would allow the $12 million they requested but was going to raise them another $5 million. I was not to say anything to anybody about it until the bill was reported out. This was certainly a bit of plain good luck, and of course I did as the chairman requested.

Following is a quick checklist of construction accomplishments of Mission 66:

Park roads—1,570 miles of reconstructed roads, 1,197 miles of new roads, mostly in new areas, or a total of 2,767 miles.

Examples of the kinds of construction undertaken to provide services to the public and protection for the parks. Amphitheater at Camp 7, Yosemite National Park, California.

Marina at Camp Grant on Yellowstone Lake, Yellowstone National Park, Wyoming.

Visitor center, Death Valley National Monument, California.

Utility building at Panther Junction, Big Bend National Park, Texas.

Bridge across the Snake River at Moose in Grand Teton National Park, Wyoming. *Courtesy Philip Hyde.*

Drinking fountain at Saint Mary Lake picnic area, Glacier National Park, Montana.

Administration building, Glacier National Park, Montana.

Trails—359 miles of reconstructed trails, 577 miles of new trails, a total of 936 miles.

Airport runways—30 miles of runways, all outside the parks.

Parking areas—330 parking areas with a total vehicle capacity of 10,868 were reconstructed and repaired. 1,502 new areas with a capacity of 49,797 vehicles were added, giving us a total of 155,306 vehicle capacity in the national park system.

Campgrounds—575 new campgrounds increased camping facilities by 17,782 campsites, giving a total, as of 1966, of 29,782 campsites.

Picnic areas—742 new picnic areas, which included 12,393 new picnic sites, were added, and thousands of old picnic sites were reconstructed and improved.

Campfire circles and amphitheaters—82 campfire circles and amphitheaters with a seating capacity of 30,252 were built, and 6 older campfire circles and amphitheaters with a seating capacity of 4,645 were reconstructed, making a total available seating capacity, in all the areas, of 41,037.

Utilities—535 additional water systems, 521 new sewer systems, and 271 power systems were provided. Additions were made to 301 old water systems, 223 old sewer systems, and 126 old power systems. This makes a total of new or additional for the concessionaires of 836 water systems, 744 sewer systems, and 397 power systems.

Administrative and service buildings—221 new administrative buildings were constructed, making a total of 1,917 available. Also 36 new service

The approach to Grand Teton National Park, Wyoming, from the north, a Mission 66 project. It has since been named the John D. Rockefeller, Jr., Parkway.

buildings were constructed, making a total of 164, or a total of all administrative and service buildings in the service of 2,081.

Utility buildings—218 new utility buildings were constructed, making a total of 1,152.

Historic buildings—458 historic buildings were reconstructed and rehabiltated, costing a total of $15,100,954.

Employee residences, dormitories, apartments, etc.—743 additional single and double housing units and 496 multiple houses, or a total of 1,239 structures, were constructed.

Comfort stations—584 new comfort stations were built, and 17 were rehabilitated, for a total of 601.

Interpretive roadside and trailside exhibits—we built new, replaced, or rehabilitated a total of 1,116 roadside or trailside exhibits.

Marina improvements—50 marinas, boat launching ramps, and beach facilities were built and boat docks were constructed or reconstructed.

Other facilities—9 new fire lookout towers, 39 new entrance stations, and 37 new trailer sanitation disposal systems were built.

The dedication ceremony at the Horace M. Albright Training Center, Grand Canyon National Park, Arizona, a Mission 66 project.

Training facilities—We established two training centers, one on the south rim of Grand Canyon and one at Harper's Ferry, West Virginia. The one at Harper's Ferry, named the Stephen T. Mather Interpretive Training and Research Center in honor of the service's first director, not only is a training center for rangers and administrative employees but recently has been enlarged to include offices and shops for the planning and construction of interpretive services and devices. The main building is part of the old Stover College, which had been closed for several years before it was purchased and developed for its present purpose. The Horace M. Albright Training Center, named in honor of the service's second director and located in Grand Canyon National Park, was built at a cost of $331,000 primarily for the training of new rangers, though it is also used for advanced training of rangers and other personnel.

Visitor centers—Mission 66 studies indicated that the museums that existed in the parks were not adequately serving the public. The Park Service decided to change its visitor facilities from small, museum-type buildings to structures of open design that would include information and interpretive

This visitor center in Sitka National Historic Park, Alaska, tells the story of the battle in 1804 between the Tlingit Indians and the Russians, as well as about the Indian culture. It also has several rooms where Indian handicraft is made and shown. The superintendent is a very capable lady of the Tlingit tribe. *Photo by John M. Morse, courtesy National Park Service.*

Visitor center, Logan Pass on Going-to-the-Sun Highway, Glacier National Park, Montana. *Photo by Keller, courtesy National Park Service.*

Visitor center, Cape Cod National Seashore, Massachusetts. *Photo by Jack Boucher, courtesy National Park Service.*

facilities, exhibits, and rest areas. The resulting "visitor center" concept is being used widely in the parks. It has been adopted by a number of federal and state agencies and also by private enterprises, such as power plants, to inform the public of their services. The more elaborate centers in larger parks have souvenir sales, food services, and complex audiovisual equipment; a few have small auditoriums. In some instances the visitor center and park administrative offices are under one roof. During Mission 66, 114 visitor centers were built.

Generally speaking, we greatly improved the operation of parks by giving them adequate facilities and by giving maintenance high priority. Further, Mission 66 was able to stimulate better cooperation between the concessionaires and the government through such arrangements as providing utilities on a rental basis. The concessionaires invested more than $33 million of private funds during the Mission 66 period for new and improved cabins, lodges, motels, stores, curio shops, service stations, marinas, and other instal-

Breaking ground for Canyon Village to replace the old developments on the canyon rim in Yellowstone National Park, Wyoming, that should not have been built there in the first place. *Left to right:* Billy Nichols, president, Yellowstone Park Company; Director Wirth; Charles A. Hamilton, president, Hamilton Stores Company; and Jack Haynes, president, Haynes Studios. *Courtesy J. E. Haynes.*

lations. An example was the building of the new Canyon Village and Grant Village in Yellowstone National Park and removal of the Old Canyon Lodge Hotel and cabins from the rim of the colorful Grand Canyon of the Yellowstone.

One of the major projects undertaken by Mission 66 was the 469-mile Blue Ridge Parkway, connecting Shenandoah National Park, in Virginia, with Great Smoky Mountains National Park, in North Carolina and Tennessee, via North Carolina. This project was suggested by the late Senator Harry F. Byrd, of Virginia, early in 1933 when President Roosevelt made his first inspection of some of the CCC camps in the national forests and national parks of Virginia. Roosevelt thought well of the parkway idea, and shortly

Linville Falls on the Blue Ridge Parkway, purchased and given partly to the U.S. Forest Service and partly to the National Park Service by John D. Rockefeller, Jr., is administered by both agencies within their jurisdictions on the basis of a master plan approved by both. *Photo by Ralph H. Anderson, courtesy National Park Service.*

Construction detail of a bridge on the Blue Ridge Parkway. *Courtesy National Park Service.*

Tunneling for the Blue Ridge Parkway was difficult and expensive, but necessary in mountain country. *Courtesy National Park Service.*

afterwards construction was started under the National Industrial Recovery Act of June 16, 1933. Specific legislative authority was enacted by Congress in 1936. Work proceeded as the land was acquired, all through the thirties, with Public Works Administration funds. As World War II approached, funds were diverted to needs related to the war. By the time Mission 66 was started only about one-third of the distance of the parkway had been completed and made usable. Most of the work had been in places where construction was less difficult. Under Mission 66 funds were included to complete the parkway. The Forest Service worked in cooperation with the National Park Service on this project. We fully intended to complete the Blue Ridge Parkway during Mission 66 and came very near doing it, even though some of the contracts were not completed until a few years after 1966. The one unresolvable issue was a ten-mile stretch on the slopes of Grandfather Mountain for which the state could not get the right-of-way. The owner, Hugh Morton, was quite a political power in North Carolina, and he did not want us to scar up the mountain. We and the state spent a lot of time negotiating with him, to no avail. In the end, Mission 66 provided better than 75 per cent of the cost of construction of the entire Blue Ridge Parkway.

An extremely important area that benefited from Mission 66 was Independence National Historical Park, in Philadelphia. The story about Independence would fill a book in itself. It was authorized on June 28, 1948, and from March 16, 1959, through August 21, 1964, there were nine amendments extending the boundary lines. Independence Hall and the square on which it stands belong to the city of Philadelphia and are assigned to the federal government for the purpose of restoration, preservation, interpretation, and management. The hall contains the chamber in which the Declaration of Independence was signed and Congress Hall. Independence Hall was in such bad condition that it was unsafe for public visitation. We removed and stored much of the flooring and paneled inside walls. Then we built a steel frame and floor beams and actually fastened the outside walls to this frame and replaced the panel walls and the floors. We used donated and Mission 66 money, and some specially appropriated funds. We and the nation as a whole should be particularly grateful to Judge E. O. Lewis, of Philadelphia, who got some ten bills through Congress and helped on appropriations that made the project possible. Without doubt, Independence National Historical Park is one of our most important historic sites if not the most important.

Another very fine project carried out during Mission 66 was the new visitor center at Gettysburg, Pennsylvania. We had a cyclorama that we acquired when Gettysburg National Military Park was transferred to the National Park Service by the army in 1933. It was a big painting on canvas some twenty feet wide and more than two hundred feet long, and it was poorly displayed in an old building and rapidly going to pieces. We built a circular room in the

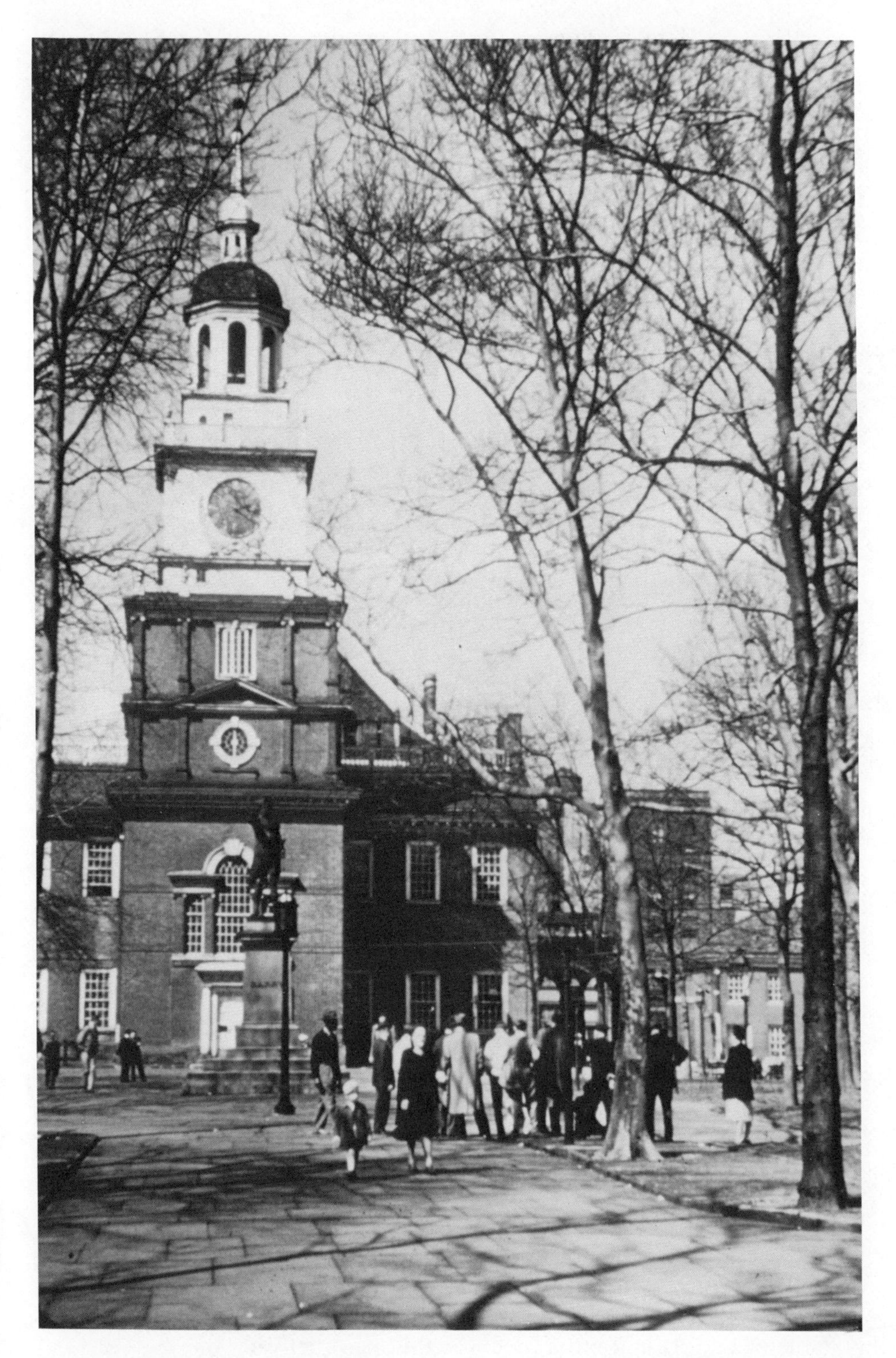

The buildings of the Independence Hall complex in Philadelphia were greatly strengthened during Mission 66 to preserve the site where many very important matters were worked out in establishing our nation.

The Jefferson National Expansion Memorial National Historic Site was a long time in coming, but it is a very attractive, well-designed memorial commemorating the Louisiana Purchase. *Photo by M. Woodbridge Williams, courtesy National Park Service.*

visitor center of such a size that the cyclorama could be spread all the way around the inside wall and thus depict the whole battle of Gettysburg in this single enclosure. It took over a year to restore the canvas, which had to have several sections replaced.

Also a great pride and joy to us was the archaeological work we did on Jamestown Island and in Yorktown, Virginia, which are connected by the Colonial Parkway through Williamsburg. We built a visitor center at Jamestown to tell the stories of the first permanent English settlement there and one at Yorktown to tell of the culminating battle of the American Revolution. Another eastern project was carried out at the Statue of Liberty in New York harbor. While it wasn't completed during Mission 66, it was started and well along by 1966. We removed the fill inside an old fort that serves as a setting for the Statue of Liberty and put a roof over the space between the walls of

The Gateway Arch, key symbol of the Jefferson National Expansion Memorial in Saint Louis, was "topped off" when the final section was inserted on October 28, 1965. *Photo by Robert Arteaga, courtesy National Park Service.*

the old fort and the pedestal of the statue, giving us a big room all around the pedestal, which now is the Museum of Immigration.

Still another big project was the Jefferson National Expansion Memorial, in Saint Louis. It was authorized in 1935, but construction was not started until Mission 66. We received $15 million for the total development, which among other things included a 630-foot high stainless steel arch designed by architect Eero Saarinen to commemorate the spirit of the pioneers and western expansion of the nation. It was under construction when I left office in 1964. The big arch contains conveyances to carry people to the top of the structure. When the plans and specifications were drawn up and let for bid, the lowest acceptable proposal came within a few hundred thousand dollars of our total authorization. Inasmuch as this type of construction had never before been attempted, I felt we couldn't take a chance on anything going wrong that might require additional funds easily exceeding our balance. I informed Representative Clarence Cannon of Missouri, chairman of the Appropriations Committee of the House of Representatives, that I could not go ahead with such a small margin of reserve funds unless I had some real assurance from the Missouri delegation that they would protect the service if anything went wrong. In a meeting with the Missouri congressmen we explained that we felt that the bid was a good one from a good firm but that the small balance in the authorization set by Congress was not enough to cover an emergency if one should arise, which was a possibility in the type of construction we were undertaking. The only thing we wanted was to lay the problem before them, explaining that if they agreed to back us and help to bail us out if necessary, we would consider going ahead with the contract. They voted unanimously to back us and requested us to sign the contract. Although our money held out, we had to go back and seek further authorization to cover the rest of the improvements.

One more project should be mentioned, the Stevens Canyon road in Mount Rainier National Park, in the state of Washington. In Horace Albright's time, about 1928, the service started building a road from Paradise down Stevens Canyon so as to approach Paradise from the east as well as the west and to have a connection with Yakima Park without driving half way around Mount Rainer outside the park. This project had been receiving small amounts of funds when available year after year since 1929, with only about three months of work possible each season before everything was snowed in. Every spring when the workmen started in again, they spent half of the time first cleaning out the rock slides caused by the spring thaw. By 1956 the road was about one-third finished, and the worst part was yet to be done. With Mission 66 we let a much bigger three-year contract that permitted working from both ends and storing big equipment near the job. The three-year contract finished the job with the exception of some wall construction that could not be properly estimated until the road was built.

During Mission 66 definite steps were taken to move as many of the administrative, government housing, and utility buildings and shops as possible out of the national parks to reduce their interference with the enjoyment of park visitors. In Yosemite a new employee residential and service area was established outside the park at El Portel. The concessionaires were moved from the center to one side of Yosemite Valley, thus restoring the meadows and greatly improving both service to the public and the scenic values. At Mount Rainier National Park the headquarters area was moved out of the park to a location below the heavy snow line and closer to public facilities, such as stores, churches, and schools. The general policy of moving business

The Tioga Road in Yosemite National Park is seen here going over toward the headwaters of Tenaya Creek, a branch of the Merced River. It is one of the most scenic roads in the country. *Courtesy National Park Service.*

Looking down Tenaya Creek from Tioga Road in Yosemite National Park, with Half Dome in the distance. *Courtesy National Park Service.*

Village store in Yosemite Valley. Mission 66 called for moving all development out of the meadows in the valley. With ready cooperation from the concessionaires, the buildings were removed and new ones erected in the village on the side of the valley. *Courtesy National Park Service.*

and administrative activities out of the parks when possible is a sound one. A great deal was done, but a lot remains to be done. If this policy is fully carried out, the parks will be much better protected from overcrowding and will better serve the visiting public, and the living conditions of the government employees will be substantially improved.

Five years after the Mission 66 program was launched at the conference in the Great Smoky Mountains, we met at Grand Canyon to reexamine it. We concluded that the concept was sound and had found immediate support at the higher levels of government and with people in general. In the beginning we actually thought we were being too bold, but now, seeing what we had done and what we had yet to do, we realized that we had not planned big enough. Although Mission 66 had been revised and brought up to date each year to meet changing conditions, we found that instead of having the urgency behind us, we were facing a new dimension—an action program was required that would dwarf the first five years of Mission 66. In the past we had been permitted the luxury of a time lag between recognition of our needs and their ultimate realization, but no longer was that the case. We realized that we were getting ever closer to our very last chance to round out the park system as a whole. Time was going against us. Our new additions to round out the system were beginning to come in faster than we could plan for their protection, development, and management. There was another factor to consider. In the beginning we were pioneers. We launched a very popular program, and we accomplished a lot. But by the time of our meeting at Grand Canyon, we realized that we had company, that many other federal bureaus had come forward with similar programs to meet the challenges of the sixties—the population explosion and the social and cultural developments.

The degree to which subsequent developments in the nation's park and recreation movement were stimulated by the success of Mission 66 should not be underestimated. In the fall of 1957 President Eisenhower sent a message to Congress calling for the establishment of the National Outdoor Recreation Resources Review Commission to study the nation's recreation resources, and the legislation was approved by Congress and signed by the president on June 28, 1958. Though not connected to the Park Service, this act nevertheless embodied several basic principles that the National Park Service had followed through the years, including those provided in the Park, Parkway, and Recreational-Area Study Act of 1936. The 1936 act was the best we could get at the time, but it did not provide us basic authorization to do a complete job; whereas the 1958 act established a commission to look into the overall national recreation requirements and make definite recommendations on ways to implement a plan for nationwide park and recreation programs at all levels of government. I am egotistical enough to feel that the presentation of Mission 66 at President Eisenhower's cabinet meeting and the success of the program somewhat influenced the president's desire to go forward with a broad, all-inclusive national program. It is interesting to note that the bureaus that were connected with the CCC program in the thirties had continued an informal committee discussion group that was still operating at the time the Outdoor Recreation bill was introduced in Congress. Also, in the winter of 1956–57, municipal, state, and national park people had organized the Committee of Fifteen, consisting of five persons from each level of government, who were meeting under the auspices of the 1936 act for the purpose of drawing up legislation that would provide funds for the study and implementation of a nationally coordinated system of parks and recreation areas at all levels of government to be financed through federal aid on a matching basis. The legislation would also provide in its draft form an outline of standards of professional qualifications for park and recreation administrators.

Several functional aspects of the president's new committee were difficult for me to understand. For instance, the ORRRC used some forty contractors to do various studies, including thirteen universities and seven bureaus of federal departments. Two of the bureaus were in the Department of the

President Dwight D. Eisenhower cuts the ribbon to open the Virginia section of the George Washington Parkway from Key Bridge over the Potomac River to the Beltway, November 3, 1959. With the president, *left to right:* Harry Thompson, regional director, National Capital Parks; National Park Service Director Conrad L. Wirth; Representative Joel T. Broyhill, of Virginia; and Assistant Secretary of the Interior Roger Ernst. *Photo by Abbie Rowe, courtesy National Park Service.*

Interior, namely the Geological Survey and the Bureau of Sport Fisheries and Wildlife. Why not the National Park Service? I must say, however, that a good many of the contractors came to the service for information and help, for we were the only ones who had the facts they needed without their spending a great deal of time and money. Again, only once was I invited to attend one of the ORRRC meetings, and that was after I had complained because they were considering recommending the establishment of a new bureau, the Bureau of Outdoor Recreation (BOR), to plan and finance a national recreation program. We felt that a new bureau was not necessary; it was our responsibility. When I went to the meeting I found that they had already decided on the new bureau, and I didn't have a ghost of a chance to change their minds. I was even bucking our own secretary. Possibly they reasoned that a separate planning agency would do a better job. I do want to say in all sincerity that ORRRC did a very good job and should receive the everlasting gratitude of everybody. Its success can be traced to the deep feeling, active interest, and sound judgment of its chairman, Laurance S. Rockefeller. He possessed the talent and wisdom to solicit diverse opinions and put them and his own thinking together before reaching a conclusion.

Just before our meeting at the Grand Canyon in 1961, President John F. Kennedy had sent a message to Congress dealing primarily with conservation, with special reference to parks. In it he said:

America's health, morals, and culture have long benefited from our National Parks and Forests and our fish and wildlife opportunities, yet these facilities and resources are not now adequate to meet the needs of the fast-growing, more mobile population, and the millions of visitor days which are now spent in federally owned parks, forests, wildlife refuges, and water reservoirs will triple well before the end of this century. To meet the Federal government's appropriate share of the responsibility to fill these needs, the following steps are essential:

A. To protect our remaining wilderness areas, I urge Congress to enact a wilderness protection bill along the general lines of S174.

B. To improve both the quality and quantity of public recreational opportunities, I urge Congress to enact legislation leading to the establishment of seashore and shoreline areas such as Cape Cod, Padre Island, Point Reyes, for the use and enjoyment of the public. Unnecessary delay in acquiring these shores which are vital to an adequate public recreational system will cause tremendously increased costs.

C. For similar reasons I am instructing the Secretary of the Interior in cooperation with the Secretary of Agriculture and other appropriate Federal, State, and local officials and private leaders to formulate a comprehensive federal recreation land program, conduct a survey to determine where additional national parks, forests, and seashore areas should be proposed. Take steps to assure that land acquired for the construction of Federally financed reservoirs is sufficient to permit future development for recreation purposes, and establish a long-range program for planning and providing adequate open spaces for recreation facilities in urban areas.

The Wilderness Bill, of course, was about to be enacted; and reports of the Outdoor Recreation Resources Review Commission were soon to be issued that recommended the establishment of the Bureau of Outdoor Recreation which would be provided with funds to acquire lands needed for federal park and recreation purposes and to aid the states and their political subdivisions in the planning, acquisition, and development of parks and recreation areas. Cape Cod was authorized by Congress in August, 1961, and Padre Island and Point Reyes national seashore areas in September, 1962.

Although Mission 66 may not have been the action that triggered a general reawakening of government to its responsibilities in the field of conservation and recreation—a responsibility I believe was being neglected—it certainly was the first program of its kind and generated many similar programs by other bureaus, commonly referred to as multiple land-use programs. Secretary of the Interior Fred A. Seaton, in a letter to me of November 21, 1959, wrote: "Mission 66 has provided the conservation movement of the entire nation with renewed vigor. It has inspired similar long-range conservation programs by other federal agencies and by state and country organizations." I believe that Mission 66 had an effect on the entire country almost as great as the CCC program had in the thirties. Conservation as a whole took a big step forward in both the CCC and Mission 66 periods.

10

The Winds of Change

Late in the fall of 1950 some vague rumors were circulating that Newton Drury was considering going back to California. Then, in February, Associate Director Arthur Demaray disclosed that he was thinking of retiring in April. He had spent some forty years in government service, including thirty-four years with the National Park Service, of which he had been associate director for eighteen years. But before Demaray had a chance to retire, Director Drury announced his decision to resume his work with the Save-the-Redwoods League and to accept appointment as director of the state parks of California, which had been offered him by Governor Earl Warren, a classmate of his and of Grace and Horace Albright's at the University of California. Secretary of the Interior Oscar L. Chapman informed me that he was planning to appoint me director of the National Park Service but wanted to offer the job first to Arthur Demaray if he would stay on. He asked me if I would talk to Demaray to see if he would defer retirement if appointed director. Chapman wanted to honor Demaray by giving him the directorship before he retired. I too felt Demaray deserved the position and urged him to accept the appointment, and he agreed to stay on for a short time. Newton Drury's resignation took effect on March 31, 1951, and Demaray took office the following day. I was appointed to succeed him as associate director.

Demaray had done a considerable amount of work in connection with budget and legislative matters and had represented the director on the planning and zoning commissions for the city of Washington. When he became director he assigned many of these responsibilities to me. As associate director I began to appreciate the tremendous amount of work that the Administrative Branch under Assistant Director Hillory Tolson did in preparing the budget and justifications.

In October, Director Demaray announced that he was going to retire on Friday, December 7. I entered on duty as director on Saturday, and my first day in the director's office was Monday, December 10, 1951.

Chapman and Demaray had timed their moves in accordance with the fact that 1952 would be an election year. Though the Park Service was a career service, there was always the chance that a new secretary might try to change that status. I'm very sure that Chapman and Demaray both felt that the new

Arthur E. Demaray, director of the National Park Service from April 1, 1951, to December 8, 1951.

director should be in office at least a year before the beginning of the term of the next secretary of the interior, and that was expected to be January, 1953, whether the Democrats or Republicans won the 1952 election. In other words, I had a year to prove my capability in order to avoid the possibility of the director's position becoming a political appointment.

As it turned out, Secretary Chapman left office January 20, 1953, when the Eisenhower administration came in. Oscar was a politician and a very, very good one. He was a strong believer in the principles of conservation and in what we in the Park Service were doing. He went out of his way to be helpful. I'm sure he felt that the profession of politics required many of the qualities that a good administrator should have. He believed strongly that a good job well done was the best politics. He was always courteous, smiling, and reasonable, and I developed a personal affection for him. I may be a little biased, because it was he who promoted me to the directorship of the National Park Service.

I will confess that nearly every day since my talks with Secretary Chapman and Arthur Demaray in March I could not help but think and plan for the

A statesman-politician in the finest sense of the term, Oscar L. Chapman served ten years as assistant secretary, two years and eight months as under secretary, and three years and eight months as secretary of the interior. *Photo by Abbie Rowe, courtesy National Park Service.*

time when I would be director, and as I did my self-confidence got stronger and stronger. I analyzed my abilities and considered what things should be done differently—not that the way they had been done in the past was wrong but that my own approach would be different. Of one thing I felt certain: if my administration was to be a success, it must earn the full support of the park people in the field. True, I was a civil service career person with a good background and considerable experience, but all of my twenty years with the National Park Service had been in the Washington office. I had had a lot of contact with the field people and had spent much time in the field, but I felt very strongly that I needed a well-qualified, highly respected field man to share in policy-making and administrative responsibilities if my administration was to be strong and responsive to the field forces. They were the real troopers in the front-line trenches who protected the parks and gave the kind of service the people had a right to expect.

During the eight months of Demaray's incumbency as director I had given considerable thought to several other things that seemed very important to me. First, and of utmost importance, as director I wanted to know the Washington office personnel intimately. I wanted to hear them express themselves on various problems and subjects pertaining to management of the National Park Service. In order to do that I established, starting in February, 1952, a regular squad meeting every Monday morning. The squad consisted primarily of branch chiefs, together with one or two other special assistants to the director. At these meetings we discussed general policy, work accomplished, and important matters that should be handled and who was to handle them. I also set up staff meetings for the first and third weeks in each month. The purpose of these sessions was to let the staff—the branch heads and their division chiefs and any special assistants they would like to have present—tell in their own way of their accomplishments and express any ideas they wished to expound. The meetings took on a seminar quality and were very enlightening to me. They gave us all better insight into the various problems encountered from day to day—problems that we perhaps would never have heard about if it were not for those meetings.

Second, I wanted to reestablish what was known as the superintendents' meetings, and I wanted these meetings held in the parks and not in Washington. We had discontinued them during the war and the following cold war period because of lack of funds. Although they were called superintendents' meetings in the thirties, they were organized by the Washington office, and the papers given were prepared mostly by the Washington office staff. The field staff found this disturbing. I felt that the superintendents should organize their own meeting, subject to review in the director's office, that papers given by the Washington staff should be limited to very important policy subjects, and that the rest of the session should be an open forum, sort of an old-fashioned town meeting.

Third—and very important—the Park Service ever since the Mather and Albright days had paid a great deal of attention to budget and legislative matters and to relationships with members of Congress, and I wanted to be sure that there was no slippage in these efforts and try if possible to improve them. The Park Service had a lot of friends on the Hill: the result of good service, sound budgets, and carefully drawn and reasonable legislation. Quite a few people on the Washington staff knew various congressmen personally, and we encouraged them to increase and enhance these friendships wherever possible. For instance, on the House Appropriations Committee the chairman, Mike Kirwan, was a very good friend of mine, and Ben Jensen, of Iowa, the minority leader of the subcommittee handling Park Service work, was a very close friend of Hillory Tolson's. A few days before our hearings on the budget, Mike Kirwan and I would discuss our request in his office. These talks gave me an opportunity to indicate to him both the needs that we were unable to include under our budget ceiling and, if the committee felt they had to reduce our request, which items we considered absolutely essential. I'm sure that Hillory Tolson did the same with Ben Jenson, especially when Ben was chairman. On the Senate Appropriations Committee we had Carl Hayden, of Arizona, and Guy Cordon, of Oregon. Most of our matters before the legislative committees had to do with special items, and nine times out of ten these matters applied to a state, or maybe two or three states, for establishing new park or recreation areas. In cases where the representatives and senators from the states involved wanted a bill reported favorably the committee usually did so.

The first superintendents' meeting in the new style was held in the fall of 1952 in Glacier National Park. We discussed it in advance in the squad meeting and selected two superintendents to organize the meeting. We suggested that at least two or three afternoons be set aside as discussion periods in which people from the floor could address the director and his staff, outline problems, and ask for clarification or change of policy. The meeting in Glacier was a lively one, and we gave answers to questions right on the spot whenever possible, confirming them in writing within two weeks after the meeting. Written response was given as promptly also to questions that could not be answered from the platform. There were only about four or five out of some forty or fifty issues raised that we had to delay answering until we got back to Washington and checked the law or the administrative policies of the secretary.

The last night of the superintendent's meeting there was a banquet. Howard Hayes, who was president of the Glacier Park Company, the National Park Service concessionaire for Glacier National Park, had arranged with the Blackfoot Indians to make the new director an Indian chief. Two of the biggest, huskiest Indian chiefs I had ever seen, all decked out in ceremonial dress with strings of beads, feathered bonnets, and what not, came to the platform along with an interpreter. They talked to me in their native language while the interpreter translated their words into English and my replies into the Blackfoot language. They finally put a headdress on me with the finest colored Indian feathers I'd ever seen. I was told that I was a "blood brother" and that my new name as a chief of the Blackfoot Indians was Curly Bear. I thanked them, and then in a facetious way I told them I had read in the newspapers that *we*—the Blackfoot—had struck oil on the reservation and that now as a blood brother I assumed I would share in the profits. Before the Indian translator could pass this along, one of the chiefs turned to me and said, "Hell no!" in very good, loud English accompanied by a scowl that led me to believe he didn't think I was kidding. He snatched the Indian bonnet from my head, we shook hands, and the Indians left the stage. Mike Mansfield, then the congressional representative from that district, was present and was highly amused.

All told, the meeting was a howling success. One of the greatest benefits of a meeting of this kind was getting people together where they could talk things over and get to know and understand one another better. We decided that future meetings should be held in odd-numbered years to avoid national election years, when political candidates might seek to get good local exposure. For the Glacier meeting we had received a letter from the headquarters of one of the major political parties offering to place a speaker on our program, but of course we declined. The next meeting was therefore held one year later, in 1953, in Yosemite National Park, and from then on the meetings took place every two years.

These meetings paid big dividends; they were great for morale building, and they provided every superintendent, from the smallest park to the largest, equal opportunity to bring up any problems he felt ought to be discussed. They were a service not only to the superintendents but also to the branch chiefs in the Washington and regional headquarters. They gave all those attending a far clearer idea of the workload and the requirements of the field and the problems of the Washington and regional offices. But the biggest dividend as far as I was concerned was the firsthand insight I got into the ability, character, and habits of the key people of the service, which was particularly helpful in selecting people for promotion.

Knowing that I was to become director a number of months before I was actually appointed enabled me to give considerable thought to the selection of an associate director, the number two man. I knew that from the standpoint of service morale as a whole a field person should be selected for that position if at all possible. Had it seemed otherwise, the logical choice would have been Hillory Tolson; but although Hillory was a sincere, very capable, and loyal National Park Service man, he had been pretty well fastened to the Washington office during his entire service, as I had been, except for the short time he had been regional director in Santa Fe.

By the time I took office I had made up my mind that I needed a park superintendent as associate director—a person with a good record who would be thoroughly acceptable to the field forces. He also had to be a person who could work with both Hillory Tolson and me. The one field man who came to mind almost every time I started thinking about filling the job was Eivind T. Scoyen. Although getting close to retirement, he was held in high regard by everyone. He had been superintendent of Sequoia and Kings Canyon national parks in California since 1947 and had literally spent his whole life in the national parks. He was born in Old Fort Yellowstone at Mammoth Hot Springs, headquarters for Yellowstone National Park before the National Park Service was established, and had been a ranger in the early Mather days. In length of service and field experience, he was senior to both Tolson and me. I finally selected him, and he entered on duty in Washington on January 17, 1956, just as Mission 66 was getting under way. I could not have made a better choice. He had everything I needed in that position and fitted right into the Washington office.

When Dwight D. Eisenhower took office as president of the United States in 1953, he appointed Douglas McKay, former governor of Oregon, as secretary of the interior. I liked him from the day I met him. I went to him with a memorandum about the National Park Service and told him that I was the director, that I liked working at that job, and that I thought I could do a good job for him, but that if he felt somebody else in the Park Service would make a better director, I would step aside and would appreciate getting my old job back in the Park Service. He smiled and said he had given some thought to that and had come to the conclusion that I had to stay in the job and he wouldn't think of replacing me under any circumstances. He believed strongly in the career service, and while I had been in the job as director for only a year, he had nothing but good reports about the Park Service. It was in Doug McKay's term of office that we came up with Mission 66, and he certainly supported that program—every feature of it.

I learned a lot from Doug McKay, and there is one incident I like to tell about because it illustrates a sound principle. The National Press Club in Washington had a luncheon for McKay shortly after he took office, and some of the bureau chiefs of the department were invited over to hear him speak. The press club dining room was crowded. The secretary was given fifteen minutes to make a statement, after which he was plied with questions. The first reporter asked him what he thought of Oscar Chapman's water policy. McKay answered something like this:

> Well, Oscar Chapman is my friend, and I am not going to say anything about his water policy. . . . I have the Chevrolet agency in Salem. I have been in business for quite a few years and I learned a long time ago to tell a customer coming into my shop about Chevrolet, all the good parts at least, and never tell him what's wrong with the Ford because there is a Ford agency down the street and I know he would be pretty sure to go down there and check me out and I'd have a good chance of losing a sale. So if you want to know about my water policy I'll be glad to tell you, but you'll have to talk to Oscar Chapman about his water policy.

When President Eisenhower asked McKay to run for the Senate from Oregon, the president appointed Fred Seaton as secretary of the interior. He was an excellent man, in my opinion, who left it pretty much up to the Park Service personnel to do a good job but to keep him posted. In fact, he practically took me in as an adopted member of the secretarial staff, inviting me to their parties when other bureau chiefs were not included. I did the same thing with Fred Seaton as I had done with Doug McKay when he came into office: I called on him, presented him with a résumé on the Park Service, and expressed my hopes that he would still want my services as director. Fred Seaton felt the same way about the Park Service as Doug McKay. Seaton had been an assistant to President Eisenhower and was at the cabinet meeting when we presented Mission 66 to the president.

The superintendents' meetings in the field provided an effective way of developing comprehensive policies and plans, and the early meetings contributed to the formulation of Mission 66. The 1952 meeting in Glacier did a great deal to breach the change in directorship and develop amongst us a better understanding of each other: we saw that each man's job, each area of the system, each office was very important to a successful total operation. The 1953 meeting in Yosemite brought out the importance of the concessionaires as a part of the team. And it got us thinking of trying to find some way out of our quandry over financing a reconstruction program. It emphasized the need of working out new concession contracts and mending the bad feeling that had developed when in the forties the department's solicitor had told the concessionaires that when their contracts were up, all their investments accrued to the federal government. The Public Lands Committee of Congress then put on record the term "possessory interest" so that the concessionaires' investments in the parks placed on government property in accordance with the terms of their contracts had the same legal status as improvements on private properties. Both the Glacier and Yosemite meetings set the stage for a united effort that resulted with the development of Mission 66. By the time of the Great Smokies meeting of 1955, Mission 66 was presented in nearly final form (as described in Chapter 9).

On June 1, 1954, we were finally able to establish western and eastern design and construction offices as recommended by Tom Vint, with Sanford (Red) Hill in charge of the San Francisco office and Edward S. Zimmer heading the Philadelphia office. The regional offices retained a liaison officer who could go out and help the small areas on minor matters, and each of the larger parks had its own professional planners. But the design offices, in accordance with Tom Vint's recommendation and my concurrence, were to handle all design and construction work. In winter the field men would be pulled into the central offices at San Francisco and Philadelphia, and there the landscape architects, engineers, and architects would meet and talk over the past summer's accomplishments and plan the next year's work. This procedure helped greatly in devising detailed master plans. The eastern design office handled almost everything east of the Mississippi, and the western office covered the parks west of the Mississippi.

The spirit was running high, and by 1957 when we had our meeting in Yellowstone and Teton I'm sure we all had the feeling that nothing could stop

Three horsemen start out on a seven-day trip to the Two Ocean Plateau and Heart Lake Basin of Yellowstone National Park; Associate Director Eivind Scoyen, Director Conrad L. Wirth, and Superintendent Lemuel A. "Lon" Garrison. *Courtesy National Geographic Society.*

us. We were in our 1958 fiscal year, the program called for $73,794,500, and Congress had given us $76,005,000 in accordance with our adjusted request.

I arrived in Yellowstone early to work on an article for the National Geographic Society (*National Geographic*, May, 1958) and one of their writers, Nat Kenney, was with me. We were going on a five-day pack trip. I got sick the second day out and had to turn back. I was laid up in the hospital for several days, and Senator Byrd found out about it. One morning while still confined to bed, I looked out the window and saw the senator and his old friend, Blackburn Moore, the speaker of the House of Delegates of Virginia, coming across the lawn from the hotel carrying a big covered platter. They came right to my room, and on the platter was a Yellowstone Lake Cutthroat they had caught the day before, all fixed up for my breakfast. It was at that time that I prevailed upon Senator Byrd to attend the meeting and say a few

"Ranger Onelick Evergreen," who mysteriously showed up at the superintendents' conference in Grand Teton National Park in 1959, is greeted by Director Wirth and ordered to return to his ranger district as fast as he can.

words. He told the meeting that his Committee on Finance had made a study of the National Park Service and had come to the conclusion that the service was getting $1.10 out of every dollar appropriated by Congress. That statement was transmitted by both the United Press International and Associated Press and was also printed in the *Congressional Record*.

The meeting that started in Yellowstone and ended in Teton was a hard working session. We had some in-house matters to straighten out and we cleaned them all up before the meeting was over, including the problem of housing needs presented by the wives of the superintendents. They were very happy to know that in accordance with their recommendations new houses were being built and many more were financed. We ended the meeting with a skit featuring Ranger "Onelick Evergreen" played by Superintendent John G. Lewis of Isle Royale National Park, Michigan.

Also at that meeting I was presented with a scroll signed by over six hundred people. I consider it the nicest thing anybody could have received, because it expressed so well the spirit of unity that prevailed.

The National Park Service Family
Assembled at the
Park Development Conference

September 10–17, 1957

Yellowstone National Park
Grand Teton National Park

Hereby subscribe their names for themselves, and for the National Park Service employees they represent

in honor of
CONRAD L. WIRTH, DIRECTOR

With unswerving devotion to the principles of conservation, together with perception of the needs for greater public use and enjoyment of the National Park System, you have given unsparingly of your energy and enthusiasm, and through your MISSION 66 Program, have awakened and sustained the interest of the public and their elected representatives to the need for action and appropriations to preserve and develop the NATION'S HERITAGE.

Your determination, strength and belief in PARK IDEALS, your unfailing recognition of work well done, your friendly manner and good humor, have won for you and your park family, respect and acclaim. The recognition you have received in the form of Trusteeships, Doctorates, Citations, Distinguished Service Awards, Gold Medals, and other honors are all well deserved. We take pride in their bestowal.

By this means, we wish to express our continued ADMIRATION and APPRECIATION, and give you our pledge of FULL COOPERATION in future years. May they be golden years, rich in the rewards of public benefits from the good you are accomplishing.

WELL DONE, CONNIE!

Another honor came my way that year. I had been a member of the National Geographic Society for many years. In 1957 Melville Bell Grosvenor was elected to the presidency and editorship of the society. About two months after his election, he called me and said he wanted to come over with Thomas W. McKnew, then vice-president and secretary, to discuss an important matter. At the meeting they told me they were considering filling a vacancy on the society's Board of Trustees and wanted to know whether I would accept the position if elected. I didn't take more than a split second to say yes and that I would consider it a high honor. Apparently I was elected at the next board meeting, because within thirty days I was informed of the date and time of the first meeting I would attend as a trustee. I consider being elected to the Board of Trustees of the National Geographic Society a great distinction, affording, as it does, a close association with an organization whose purpose and activities I wholeheartedly endorse. I learned after I was on the board that I was filling the vacancy created by the death of Admiral Richard E. Byrd, the renowned explorer and brother of my good friend Senator Harry F. Byrd. I am now also on the society's Executive Committee and its Research and Exploration Committee.

The 1959 field meeting was held at Williamsburg, the heart of Colonial National Historical Park. There Bill Carnes and his group gave a résumé of the progress in Mission 66 and how it looked to the future. Our good friends the glassmakers, who contributed greatly to the reproduction of the old colonial glass furnaces of 1608 on Glass House Point at Jamestown, were present, including Carl Gustkey, president of the Imperial Glass Company in Wheeling, West Virginia. Carl had provided glasses with the Park Service emblem and Mission 66 on them for each field meeting starting in 1953.

At the meeting in 1961, at the Grand Canyon, we were working under a new secretary, Stewart Udall, and this was his first exposure to many of the Park Service people, though as a congressional representative from Arizona he had served on the Public Lands Committee, and so he was no stranger to us. We felt sure that what we were doing met with his approval. I had received my appointment as a career employee under a Democratic administration from Secretary Chapman and had gone through two terms of Republican secretaries, Doug McKay and Fred Seaton, with no problems whatsoever. While Mission 66 had been started when Secretary McKay was in office, we had taken great pains not to allow party politics to enter our operations. Things went along very quietly with the change of administration, and we soon learned that we were going to get very good support from Udall. I was just a little bit concerned about my status, because although Stew had practically assured me that all was well, he wanted to talk to the president. About two weeks after taking office, however, President John F. Kennedy came out with a statement to the effect that he was not going to make any changes in the National Park Service. Of course the president had been a senator, and while I had had no direct contact with him I'm sure he knew of our activities in Massachusetts, which included the Cape Cod National Seashore Area and the famous Minute Man National Historical Park, between Lexington and Concord.

It was at the Grand Canyon meeting that I began to think about the inevitable close of my Park Service career. I was in my sixties, and it seemed to me that I should either retire late in 1963 and give the new director a year to get settled in the job before the presidential election year in 1964, or plan to stay on until late 1965 or perhaps to the end of Mission 66, which would be June 30, 1966. By the late fall of 1961, I began to give retirement more serious thought. In October, Eivind Scoyen, Ronnie Lee, and three others who would not be in the running for the directorship because of their health or their age met with me in a motel near Annapolis. I told them that I planned to retire about a year before the 1964 presidential election and wanted to talk with the secretary about my replacement. I asked them to help me select at least five men in the service who would make a good director. I wanted to make a very strong appeal for the appointment of somebody from within the service. We discussed many candidates and selected five.

Nineteen sixty-two was a very busy year. Scoyen retired the first week in January, and I did not appoint a new associate director because I wanted to get the secretary committed on the next director. I would appoint as my associate director the man he selected to succeed me. I wished that Eivind had stayed on for another year, but I never asked him to because he had stayed on four years longer than he had originally agreed. In 1962 I was chairman of the board of the National Conference on State Parks, and in the fall I was elected president of the American Institute of Park Executives. The AIPE was the oldest park and recreation organization, having been founded in 1898, and it had a membership of some four thousand city park people.

The eighteen months between June, 1962, and the end of 1963 brought one problem after another in rapid succession. It all really started with an interview I gave to the *U.S. News & World Report*, which I thought was pretty good. I had notified the department of the magazine's request, saying that unless they objected I was going to grant the interview. The interview took place about ten days before the first world conference on national parks held in Seattle, Washington. It is the policy of *U.S. News & World Report* to send the transcript to the interviewee for review before it is printed. The magazine sent the transcript by air mail to Seattle, where I was attending the conference, and asked me to return it in four days. I spent the night going over it, and it read very well. Two of the department's public relations men were at the conference, and I asked them to go over it. They made only two or three suggestions, which I accepted. Secretary Udall was there, and I asked him whether he wanted to read it. He said, "No, if they have gone over it it's okay." So I sent it back to the publishers and told them it was all right with the changes I had indicated. The article appeared in the August issue. A few days after it came out I received a letter from the secretary that startled me, and I feel even today that he never actually wrote it, nor did those who reviewed the transcript in Seattle.

August 15, 1962

Dear Connie:

I have just finished reading the interview with you which appeared in the current issue of the *U.S. News & World Report*. To be quite candid, I must report that I read this article with amazement and chagrin. Your reappointment as Director was announced by President Kennedy; you also head a Service which is an integral part of the Department of the Interior—but any reader would inspect this article in vain for evidence that you are aware of any ties to this Administration, or that you have any serious interest in the new programs which it has presented to the Congress and the American people.

If this article reveals your true state of mind, I would suggest that you get aboard—QUICK!

Sincerely,
Stewart L. Udall
Secretary of the Interior

I replied to these surprising remarks with the following letter:

August 17, 1962

Dear Stew:

This is in reply to your "QUICK" note of August 15.

I question whether anybody has tried harder to stay in the background, or to carry out your wishes, than I have. I believe the record will show this, and we can do more if given a chance.

I can make mistakes like anyone else, but when one's loyalty and motives are questioned in a note like yours of August 15, it cuts pretty deep. I sincerely hope that my interpretation of your note in this respect is wrong.

Briefly, the Department knew of this informal interview in advance. The transcript was mailed to me in Seattle and I was requested to return it in four days. I asked Dick Rodgers and Jim Faber to look it over, which they did. They made suggestions, which were accepted, and I feel sure they thought it was a pretty good interview. I asked you whether you wanted to see it, but your time was so limited that you had to pass it up. I quoted you in one place because I had heard you express yourself on that particular subject. I am sorry they did not indicate in the introduction that the National Park Service is a Bureau of the Department of the Interior—they should have.

What I said I believe in very sincerely, and I believe it is not in variance to your beliefs to any great degree even though you no doubt would have expressed your opinions in a different way.

I should like to have talked to you about this in person; however, you are out of town and your note requires an early reply. I leave Wednesday, August 22, for an extended field trip to check on our operations; something I have put off for two years. If you will have time to see me on Monday or Tuesday, I will appreciate it very much.

Sincerely yours,
Conrad L. Wirth
Director

My letter was never answered or acknowledged either in writing or orally. I could understand the secretary's concern, but I resented his threat and his implications. I agree that the magazine's introduction should have indicated that the Park Service was a bureau of the Department of the Interior: we're just as proud of the department as are the secretaries who come and go.

Further, there is one error in his letter. He mentions that President Kennedy reappointed me as director, whereas the only appointment as director that I received, and all that was necessary, was the appointment by Secretary Chapman. I never received an appointment to the directorship of the National Park Service from any president, nor did I receive one from Secretaries McKay, Seaton, or Udall. President Kennedy did announce that he wanted me to stay on, and I appreciated that very much because I imagine he could have done the same thing that President Richard Nixon did January 1, 1973, when he removed Director George Hartzog, a career man, and put in a political appointee. But he didn't, and neither did Eisenhower or Johnson.

Another unfortunate occurrence of 1962 ought to be recorded. In the 1930s there was a need, which continues today, to preserve a fairly large tract of long grass prairie land as it existed before the arrival of white settlers. In Kansas, near Topeka, there are thousands of acres of long prairie grass that would make a very fine prairie national park. A careful analysis of the local situation was made, and we gained fairly good support from people in Kansas. We kept the secretary informed of our activities, and he expressed a desire to see the area. We got the cooperation of all the landowners concerned, state and Kansas University officials, and the local newspapers in a plan to take the secretary on a three-hour helicopter trip over the proposed park, making several stops. We made a dry run, without the secretary, which went smoothly.

On the first setdown on the secretary's trip, however, there was a man waiting for us. Secretary Udall was first out of the plane and went right over to shake his hand. The man ordered him off the property. The secretary, without saying anything more or giving us a chance to straighten the matter out, returned to the helicopter and canceled the rest of the trip. I talked to the man and found that he was not the owner but a tenant farmer. The owner had in fact given us permission to land on the property at this precise location, but apparently the tenant disagreed with the owner and decided to exercise a little authority of his own. Anyway, the secretary returned to Washington. I went on with the trip and spoke at a public hearing and at the university and got a good reception. I also gave a tape-recorded interview to a newspaper reporter and got a nice write-up from that. While I was with the tenant farmer, however, I was photographed talking to the man by a newspaper photographer. It was cold and windy, and the noise of the helicopter was so disturbing that we had to shout at each other to make ourselves heard, which made it look in the picture as though we were almost coming to blows. That picture went all over the country; in fact, I got word from my younger son, who was a major in the Air Force then stationed in Germany, that it had appeared in the military newspaper with some comment about the government seizing private property. It did not appear in the Topeka paper, which was owned by the former secretary of the interior under the Eisenhower administration, Fred Seaton.

Back in Washington I got a memorandum dated December 6 from the assistant to the secretary. It read in part as follows:

> It appears to me that insufficient planning went into the preparation for the Secretary's visit to the site of the proposed Prairie National Park. Neither the temper of the residents nor the political realities were taken into consideration adequately.
>
> First, to me there is no excuse for exposing the Secretary to the kind of treatment and publicity he received from the irate rancher. Advance checking with owners or operators of the ranches where stops were planned would have avoided this.
>
> Second, this is a Democratic Administration, and we are not going to leave arrangements in the hands of Republicans. If the Republican is so minded, he can easily arrange incidents like the one in Kansas, which made most of the newspapers. At best, he can be interested only in his own publicity and his own aims—not those of the Secretary or the Administration. Further, if there is any political advantage to accrue to local politicians, we are not playing fair with people who support us if we let a member of the opposite party "grab the glory."
>
> Apart from the primary subject of this memorandum, I don't believe the incident with the rancher particularly improved the chances of getting this park established.
>
> I do not propose to cooperate in future park inspection trips unless there is assurance of better and more realistic planning. You, Assistant Secretary Carver, and I have the only three copies of this memorandum.

I went up to the assistant's office with his memorandum after checking the record to be sure of myself. In answer to his second paragraph I told him the record was clear that all property owners had been approached and had given their approval. Further, I reported that two Park Service planners had flown in the army helicopter and set down at every stop that we planned to make with the secretary a week before the secretary's trip and had encountered no trouble. I also informed him that the man who talked to the secretary was not the property owner. In answer to the third paragraph I assured him we were not playing party politics. The secretary's office had been in touch with the only Democratic representative from the western part of the state and also with the Republican representative in whose district the proposed national park was located and had been given the green light for a visit and inspection. I told him that we understood politics and knew that Kansas was a Republican state; also, that former Secretary Fred Seaton owned at least one paper in the nearby community and that his paper supported the project, as did the local representative and the university. I told him that if he or Carver released his memorandum while I was director and the secretary was in office I would have to answer it in full.

Now, because this is the kind of a book it is, I feel I can include this incident to illustrate what one is apt to run into in government service. Both

Udall and I are out of office, as are Carver and the writer of the memo. Whether I convinced the assistant that the secretary's trip was carefully and prudently planned, I don't know. So far as I know Udall is not aware of the memorandum I got from his assistant.

It was the first part of August, 1962, when, in anticipation of retiring at the end of 1963, I felt it would be well to organize a task force to review Mission 66 and lay the groundwork for a program to follow it. They were to analyze very carefully what we had done and weigh the changes that had taken place in travel habits of the people; increased travel impact on the parks; types of equipment being developed for recreational use, especially camping; and everything that might affect the policies we should consider for future programs. We named this study and report "The Road to the Future." While I had it in mind to have this material ready for the new director if I retired, I did not say so. I stated that the main purpose of this examination was to give us at least two years to prepare a program that we could put into effect starting July 1, 1966, so that there would be no lag in our progress after Mission 66.

In January, 1963, I had lunch with Secretary Udall in his private dining room and showed him a draft of my letter requesting retirement (pages 302–303). I also told him the next Park Service field meeting was set for the fall in Yosemite and that we had a task force making a study of past accomplishments and changing conditions that could be the basis for a planned program after Mission 66, hence the theme of the conference would be "The Road to the Future." I said I would like very much for him to come out for the last day of the meeting and address us, at which time I would give him my letter requesting retirement. I also gave him the list of the five people in the service whom I hoped he would consider in selecting the next director. Secretary Udall was most agreeable; he understood my reasoning and thought the procedure I suggested was well planned. He told me he would be glad to have me stay on as director but would respect my wishes.

Two weeks later the secretary telephoned to say he had gone over the list of five names and had in mind selecting George Hartzog, who had been superintendent of Jefferson National Expansion Memorial in Saint Louis. George had left the service on August 21, 1962, to take a job with a businessmen's organization in Saint Louis as their executive officer, but both the secretary and I felt that the few months he had been out of the service presented no disadvantage. He was still a man with fifteen or sixteen years of Park Service experience, including several years in the Washington office handling concession contracts and land and legislative matters; field service in Rocky Mountain National Park as assistant superintendent and in Great Smoky Mountains National Park in the same capacity; and, of course, his three and a half years as the superintendent of Jefferson National Expansion

U.S. DEPARTMENT OF THE INTERIOR,
NATIONAL PARK SERVICE,
WASHINGTON, D.C., OCTOBER 18, 1963.

Hon. Stewart L. Udall
Secretary of the Interior,
Washington, D.C.

Dear Mr. Secretary:

As you know, I have been considering retirement since 1962. In February of this year, I submitted to you the names of five Park Service people that I felt were well qualified to fill the associate director position which had been vacant since Mr. Scoyen's retirement. Mr. Hartzog was selected from this list, and appointed. At that time, I indicated that I intended to retire in about a year, and gave you my reasons. While neither you nor Mr. Carver agreed that I should consider retirement, you indicated that you would respect my wishes. My reasoning has not changed since then.

You and the President have committed yourselves to further the development of a strong career service. Well-trained employees with an opportunity for advancement is basic to a strong career service. It is good government; it is good business. The National Park Service is a career service and, in my opinion, a very good one. It is a vigorous, capable, aggressive, and loyal organization, dedicated to serving the public in accordance with the objectives enacted into law by the Congress and the policies established by the administration and the Secretary of the Interior. These are traits that were built into it by its first directors, Stephen T. Mather and Horace M. Albright, and maintained down through the years by the directors who have followed them—Arno B. Cammerer, Newton B. Drury, and Arthur E. Demaray.

From my observations in over 35 years of Government service, I believe that if the integrity of career service is to be maintained and strengthened, three basic principles should be recognized:

1. Opportunity for advancement: There should be a general rule that key personnel subject to day-to-day pressures should retire in the early 60's, and younger, well-trained individuals advanced into the administrative and policymaking positions. This will result in quicker reactions to changes caused by our fast-growing national economy and the resulting increased needs of our people.

2. Use of knowledge and experience: There should be established within the framework of the civil service regulations a method for the retention of a reasonable number of senior employees as advisers, who would not be subject to day-to-day routine and pressures. This would bring better balance and stability into the organization. Today private business is picking up many of these well-trained Government employees on that basis.

3. Elimination of incentive distractions: The schedule C Classification should be abolished insofar as it is applied to the operating and technical career bureaus. I don't know of anything that has discouraged career employees more than the establishment of schedule C.

There is little that I can do about items 2 and 3, but knowing your strong feelings with reference to a better career service I could not help but express my thoughts. I can do something about item 1. Therefore, I respectfully request your approval of my retirement, to be effective after the close of business on January 11, 1964.

I shall always be proud and grateful for the opportunity afforded me by Directors Albright and Cammerer, and Secretary of the Interior Harold L. Ickes, to play an important role in the CCC program in the thirties, working with many bureaus of the Department and the leaders in the State Park field; and to Secretaries McKay, Seaton, and you for supporting the Mission 66 program during my tour of duty as the sixth director of the National Park Service. Of course, I have a warm spot in my heart for Secretary Oscar L. Chapman, for it was he who gave me my promotion to director of the National Park Service on December 9, 1951. I sincerely hope that I have lived up to his expectations. And you, Secretary Udall, have sparked and brought into focus the building of a national park system worthy of the American people. Certainly there is much yet to be done but the fact remains that the surge forward is underway, due largely to your efforts and leadership.

I believe we often forget the important contributions by our lawmakers, the elected representatives of the people, to the park and recreation programs. I have appeared before the committees of Congress for over 30 years and I have nothing but admiration, respect, and sincere appreciation for their helpful and thoughtful consideration of our requests and reports. I number many of them among my very best friends.

There are also the conservationists, individuals, and associations, as well as various civic minded people, many of whom have been of tremendous help to the Service and to me personally, for which I am most grateful.

And last, but most important next to Mrs. Wirth who has shared my ups and downs and is my greatest critic and by far my strongest supporter, are the employees of the National Park Service. I have known all of the five previous directors of the National Park Service, and worked on the staff of four of them. They taught me much and helped me greatly, and they know my deep appreciation. But, I also know that they would understand and agree when I say that I owe the greatest debt of gratitude to the many loyal and devoted associates of mine in the National Park Service. Many of them have retired since I joined the Service in 1931, and those that are still in the Service I grew up with. No bureau chief could ever have had a more devoted, hard-working, and loyal organization than the people that make up the National Park Service. I shall never be able to adequately express to them my heartfelt appreciation. I commend them to you, and to the new Director.

Sincerely yours,
Conrad L. Wirth
Director

Memorial, where he did an excellent job. I called George and offered him the job. He accepted and reported on duty as associate director on February 18, 1963.

That year, 1963, saw many Mission 66 projects completed and dedicated. I took part in nine dedications and gave seventeen talks. The visitor center at Chancellorsville Battlefield near Fredericksburg, Virginia, was scheduled for dedication on May 4, and I was to be master of ceremonies. We invited Assistant Secretary John Carver to give the dedication address. He accepted, and although we were usually asked to help prepare a suitable draft for such an occasion, we got no such request from John. He was a lawyer by profession and very opinionated, dictatorial, and demanding at times. If he didn't get just what he wanted, he would flare up and become very critical, and then he would cool off. On May 1, I received word from the design and construction office that Carver had asked to see the plans for the visitor center. They sent him the only plans they had, which were construction drawings. I called the assistant secretary, telling him I felt the detailed plans would not give him a very good idea of what the building would look like, and I asked whether we could help him. He said he could write his speech without any help and added that perhaps I would not like what he intended to say. He said that when it was finished he would send me a copy so that I could read it if I wished. I received it the next day and read it that night. The whole gist of his talk was a running critique of the building itself, the arrangement, and the architectural treatment. It was hard for me to believe that anybody, especially someone on the secretarial level, would accept an invitation to be the principal speaker at a public dedication and then be critical of the project and of one of his own agencies. I knew the building—I had approved the plans.

The next morning I called John and told him I disagreed with his remarks about the building and that I hoped he would not use them, adding that if he saw the building he would feel better about it. He said he was going to give his talk as he had prepared it. I couldn't believe my ears. I told him that if he gave that speech I would have to reply to his criticism on the spot. I further told him I couldn't believe that an administrative officer would criticize his own organization in public as he was proposing to do. That night I spent considerable time making notes for my rebuttal. I realized that to carry out my intention would constitute good grounds for dismissal, but I felt I could not live with myself or my associates if I didn't take a positive stand. I also knew that he was so far wrong and that public reaction would be so great that a dismissal would not stand up.

When I saw the finished building on the day of the dedication, it looked even better than I had envisioned. I asked whether Carver had arrived, and the ranger informed me he had taken the assistant secretary through the building and that he had seemed pleased and had gone off into the woods to finish preparing his remarks. The time for the dedication arrived. I got up on the platform and John followed, and in passing me he said, "Connie, I have changed my talk." I said, "I'm glad to hear that, John." He gave a very good talk. I thanked him for his speech and adjourned the dedication ceremonies. He never said another word to me about the occasion, and I never brought up the matter. I was very pleased that he had abandoned his original intention.

When in the fall of 1962 I was elected president of the American Institute of Park Executives, one of the first things I did was to appoint a committee to look into the advisability of trying for the fourth time in thirty-five years to bring together in some kind of a federation the five or six different organizations then supporting the park and recreation movement. The committee was asked to have its report ready for consideration at the 1963 AIPE meeting in Washington, D.C. We felt that a federation would bolster each group's particular field of park and recreational activity without disrupting its primary purpose, provide a channel for interchange of professional experience and a planning interchange at all levels of government, and manage the administrative overhead common to all at considerable savings. These savings could be used for research and planning and thus provide the professional park and recreational men with the tools to carry out their responsibilities.

The joint meeting of the American Institute of Park Executives and the National Conference on State Parks in the fall of 1963 was the next big event as my retirement grew closer. The meeting started on Sunday, September 22, and ran through Friday, the twenty-seventh. As president of the AIPE and chairman of the board of the National Conference on State Parks, I was very busy. On Wednesday I was presiding over the joint meeting, the main subject of which was the report of the committee on the matter of consolidation. Vice-president Lyndon B. Johnson, an old friend of mine of some thirty years, was not on our program, but I had asked him to drop in at one of our afternoon general joint meetings, and he said he would try. That Wednesday he did, and the visit was a real surprise to our group. Charles K. Boatner, our information chief at the time, had been on the vice-president's staff when Johnson was in Congress and knew him well. He had prepared a very nice one-page statement that I could use to introduce the vice-president. Johnson was escorted by several secret service men, some of whom came in beforehand and placed themselves so that they could get a good view of the whole assemblage of over a thousand people. I stopped the proceedings, but before I could announce what was happening, the vice-president came through the door and headed straight for the podium. I gave my short introduction, and then he took over.

He spoke first of the importance of preserving our natural heritage and then talked at some length about our American values, concluding with this personal anecdote:

One of the first projects I got for my district was a conservation project—a soil conservation project with CCC labor. One of the next things was a WPA project that extended running water to our school for the first time. We had to dig through the soil with picks. We had a new teacher at our little school. He was very proud of the fact that the Congressman had graduated from it, so he was introducing me down the line to all these people who had been raised with me and my father and my grandfather in this little town of Johnson City named after my grandfather. He introduced me to Mr. Smith and to Mr. Brown and each time he said, "Do you know our new Congressman?" (He was a little pompous.) Every one of those old fellows looked up. They did not want to be deterred from their jobs by meeting a boy they grew up with, and of course all of them knew me—knew me too well, perhaps. When I was a youngster, nine years old, I had a shoeshine parlor. There was a man named Earl Haley. He went off to war, and when he came back on furlough we would shine his shoes and his leggings. He would come in every Saturday, and he had more money than the locals did. He made $30 a month in the Army, and he would always give us a dime tip—a dime to shine his shoes and a dime tip.

After the war, Earl wound up on the WPA, and he was out with his pick and he was digging. The school superintendent said: "Mr. Haley, do you know our new Congressman?" Earl had a chew of tobacco in his mouth. He spat it out and said: "Know him? I reckon I know him. He used to shine my shoes." I wonder how many shoe shine boys we have in the audience this morning. But that is the strength of America. Here in America boys who shine your shoes have a chance to rise to the highest offices in the land, and we really mean what we say in our Declaration of Independence and in our Constitution about equality. We really proved last election that you can elect a man from the north who is a Catholic and a man from the south who is a Protestant.

Although we have always had with us some prejudice and some bigotry, we are proving every day that we love this country and we are going to preserve it and we are going to protect it and we are going to do what we think is best for it. That is why you are here today, and I prize my association with you.

Our final meeting was to be a banquet at the Sheraton Park Hotel. The secretary of the interior and Assistant Secretary John Carver and their wives were invited to attend as our guests, along with the chiefs of the various bureaus with which we did business and other government officials. The day before the banquet Dick Rogers, an assistant to John Carver, contacted me to say that Carver, who was acting secretary, wanted me to put the director of the Bureau of Outdoor Recreation at the head table. I told Dick this couldn't be done because the committee had already made all the table arrangements and had provided special tables right in front of the podium for the chiefs of the bureaus, and I couldn't put one of them at the head table if I wanted to. I emphasized that this meeting was not sponsored by the Park Service or the Interior Department but by an association of federal, state, and local park people who had their own rules to which we adhered. Although I happened to be president, I was not going to try and tell the banquet committee what to do. His reply was that he would report that to the acting secretary, but he would rather be out of town. I told him I'd be glad to call Carver myself, but resignedly he said, "No, I'll do it." I heard no more that night.

The next morning I was sitting at a desk in the hotel convention office making some notes with some dozen people standing close by. The whole convention was about to leave by bus for Arlington National Cemetary to place a wreath on the Tomb of the Unknown Soldier, followed by a tour of the Washington park system. There were some two thousand people in all. In walked one of our park police sergeants who came up to me and said, "Director Wirth, Secretary Carver sent me here to bring you down to his office right away." Everybody turned and looked at me. I thought for a moment and then said, "Well, Sergeant, will you please tell the Acting Secretary that I can't come right now because we are about to leave to place a wreath on the Tomb of the Unknown Soldier, and after that is over I will be happy to come to his office—and I can do so under my own power." The sergeant looked at me and smiled and said, "Mr. Wirth, that is what I had hoped you would say." And he left.

After the ceremony in Arlington I proceeded to the Interior Department and went up to my office. Associate Director George Hartzog was there and suggested I be conciliatory in this case to satisfy Carver and avoid an argument. I told him no, I would not do that, that I would tell Carver frankly why I could not respond to his request and he should be smart enough to understand. I went to Carver's office, and he showed me the draft of a wire he intended to send Laurance Rockefeller. It asked Rockefeller not to give his scheduled talk that night at the banquet. I told John to go ahead and send it, but I suggested he dispatch it to the hotel because Rockefeller was already there and had given me the pleasure of reading his talk, which I thought was an excellent one. I also reminded him that the invitation to speak had been extended by the AIPE and the NCSP, not by the department or the service. He took back the wire, and as far as I know he never sent it. He then said he was thinking of calling off the Park Service's field meeting in Yosemite National Park that was to start on October 13, a little more than two weeks off. He said he would do it on the basis of cost, and that he had asked the Park Service budget office to give him a detailed report on the total cost of the proposed meeting.

I told Carver that he should have asked me for this information because I already knew how much it would cost, that in fact this was our regular biennial meeting year and the necessary funds were included in our budget which the department had approved and Congress had appropriated. I told him that each park and office would have representatives at the meeting, that the money had already been allotted to them for their expenses, and that the total cost would be approximately $25,000. He said, "Well, I'm thinking of calling the meeting off." I said, "John, you have the authority to do it, but I suggest you let us know before people start traveling to the meeting." Then I said, "John, why do you do these things? Why can't you be reasonable and understand that this meeting now going on in Washington is not a federal meeting; there are over 2,000 people attending and only about one per cent of them are federal government employees. This is their meeting, not yours or mine, and I think you're making a very unreasonable request and you can't give me one good reason why the director of the Bureau of Outdoor Recreation should be at the head table and not the head of the Fish and Wildlife Service, the head of the General Land Office, or the representatives of the Reclamation Service, the Forest Service, the Public Health Service, or the Bureau of Public Roads." He didn't say a word; his face was red, and I think mine must have been too. Neither of us had anything more to say and I left.

We had a very good banquet. Mark Evans, of Metromedia, and later ambassador to Finland, was master of ceremonies. Representatives were present from the Department of the Interior, Agriculture, Health, Education, and Welfare, and Commerce. Laurance Rockefeller gave a very fine talk and it was well received. The evening was really a gala affair. There were two tables up front for bureau chiefs and all were introduced. John Carver did not show up, and I did not see him again until the Yosemite meeting.

Mrs. Wirth and I arrived in Yosemite on Friday, October 11. Others started coming in on Saturday, and the field meeting started with reunions, committee meetings, and social functions on Sunday. On Monday "The Road to the Future" was presented with slides and sound, and this presentation together with the discussions that followed took up most of the day.

At breakfast on the second day Hillory Tolson gave me a sealed envelope that contained his request for retirement as of December 31, 1963. I felt sure he didn't know that I was going to retire, and he had certainly kept his own plans secret until then. Here we both were, announcing our retirement at the Yosemite meeting. It was short notice, but I talked it over with George Hartzog and we decided it should be made public. Wednesday at the noontime stop at Wawona, on a trip through the park, we had a little ceremony for Hillory. I don't think we did very well, but it was the best we could do under the circumstances.

The next day John Carver came in shortly after noon, addressed the conference, and left right afterwards for Washington. He had kept secret what he was going to say, and I guess the 1963 meeting in Yosemite could be called the "meeting of secrets." Carver lashed out at the Park Service in no uncertain terms. He picked on picayune things that had crept into some correspondence and on job descriptions that, taken out of context, were misleading, especially to those looking for things to crab about. The tenor of his remarks is illustrated by the following excerpts:

> . . . I sometimes have the feeling that the entire Park Service is resolutely shutting its eyes to the fact of the creation of the Bureau of Outdoor Recreation, and to the

Laurance S. Rockefeller addresses a banquet audience at the joint meeting of the American Institute of Park Executives and the National Conference on State Parks in Washington, D.C., in 1963. Ambassador Mark Evans, master of ceremonies, is seated next to Director Wirth, with Mrs. Rockefeller at the left. *Photo by Abbie Rowe, courtesy National Park Service.*

nature of the functions assigned to it. Particularly do I have the feeling that the Secretary's order creating the Bureau and the subsequent act of Congress (not to say the specific directions of the appropriations committees contained in their reports) are regarded as idle conversation. Perhaps if you don't think about such things they will go away. But I don't think so.

At this conference you are going to discuss the Long Range Plan. I would advise you constantly to bear in mind that you can't bootstrap your way into ascendancy in functions which have by Secretarial order and by law been transferred to another bureau.

Which leads to my third point. When all else fails, the Park Service seems always able to fall back upon mysticism, its own private mystique. Listen to this sentence: "The primary qualification requirement of the Division Chief position, and most of the subordinate positions . . . is that the employees be . . . imbued with strong convictions as to the 'rightness' of National Park Service philosophy, policy and purpose, and who have demonstrated enthusiasm and ability to promote effectively the achievement of National Park Service goals."

This has the mystic, quasi-religious sound of a manual for the Hitler Youth Movement. Such nonsense is simply intolerable. The National Park Service is a bureau of the Department of the Interior, which is a Department of the United States government's executive branch—it isn't a religion, and it should not be thought of as such.

Of course you should have strong convictions, but you are expected also to have discipline. The sentence I've read is from a proposed submission to be made to the Civil Service Commission, which reached my desk last month. Taken by itself, it might be interpreted not to have the connotation I've given it.

But read on with me. Later in the report there is singled out a truly classic case, admirably suited to emphasize the mystical nature of your jobs. That was the famous "hunting in the parks" statement of September 14, 1961, issued without Departmental clearance, and leading to a crisis in public relations the like of which had not been seen up to that time. The Secretary was made to look foolish; I was caught in a vicious crossfire, and the whole thing was a fiasco.

Out of it, eventually, came the Leopold Report, the solid backing for a good position, but to credit the Park Service with the Leopold Report is like crediting a collision at sea for a dramatic rescue effort—the captain of the offending ship is hardly likely to get a medal for making the rescue effort possible.

His points were essentially confined to one theme: "You didn't say anything about me;" but they further revealed a lack of understanding of nationwide comprehensive planning plus a flair for poor judgment, the same trait Carver showed at Chancellorsville and the banquet in Washington a few weeks earlier. Surely the BOR never expected that it would be required to plan all the parks, recreation fields, and open spaces for all the federal agencies and the political subdivisions of the nation, nor did Congress, nor the secretary of the interior. That bureau is responsible for putting together an overall plan and reporting on the park and recreation system of the nation as a whole, but the only way they can do that is to collect information from the state and federal agencies handling park and recreation work. If the Bureau of Outdoor Recreation were given enough money I am sure that they would be highly successful, and the nation would be much better off if they followed the same principle as the Public Roads Administration, that is, working with the state and federal agencies. The basic studies must be done by those in charge of managing the parks. Further, neither the secretary nor Congress has transferred the responsibility of the National Park Service to the BOR; the service is required by law to think and plan to better carry out its responsibility to the country. Not only does this *not* interfere with the BOR, but it actually makes it possible for the BOR to better carry out its own responsibility to develop a national comprehensive outdoor recreation plan that will include all governmental agencies that deal with parks and recreation.

As to the primary qualifications of a division chief in the Park Service: believe me, if he is not interested in the parks and loyal to his objectives he shouldn't be there. Anyone in any agency, public or private, who doesn't feel that he can carry out its policy and be a part of the team should seek other employment. Further, all the "philosophy, policy, and purpose" of the National Park Service was established by law and the department. When Carver calls loyalty "mystique" and implicates it with the Hitler Youth Movement, all I can do is apply his own words to his attitude and reasoning: "Such nonsense is simply intolerable."

The last item he brings up is about "hunting in the parks" and the "Leopold Report." As I recall the policy he refers to had been followed through the years with the approval of the department secretaries long before Carver took

The meeting in Yosemite National Park in October, 1963, at which Assistant Secretary of the Interior John Carver delivered his "National Park Service mystique" remarks. *Courtesy National Park Service.*

office, and everybody knew it. The Leopold Report, as he indicated, substantiates the policy. Our basic act states that we are to preserve the parks "and the wildlife therein," but there are many things that experts like Leopold, in and out of the service, have worked on through the years that make it possible for us to mandate and at the same time meet the problems caused by the changes in the habits of the creature called man. I am sorry that John got caught in "a vicious crossfire." It was of his own making.

That auditorium was full of very angry people after Carver's speech. He left immediately, handing Tom Flynn a bundle of copies of his speech and telling him to distribute them. (Tom had been in Carver's office before joining the service as chief of the office that administered our concessions.) He came to me and asked what he should do. The speech was terrible, and so I told Tom to go ahead and distribute them. When Carver got back to Washington he held a press conference. The next day *The New York Times* reported that I was being fired. This news hit Yosemite the morning of the day that Secretary Udall arrived. George Hartzog and I met the secretary at El Portal early in the afternoon, and I gave him my letter requesting retirement. It was unchanged from the draft he had seen some nine months earlier. The conference was all settled in the assembly room when we arrived at Camp Curry in Yosemite Valley. I introduced the secretary, and he announced that I had given him my request to retire and read my letter. Eivind Scoyen was at the meeting and told how several of us had met over a year earlier to make recommendations on the upcoming retirements, and that the secretary had accepted our suggestions. The secretary, after praising me and mentioning how everything had been handled in accordance with my long-standing requests and suggestions, announced the appointment of George Hartzog as director effective January 9, 1964, the date of my retirement, and of Clark Stratton to succeed Hartzog as associate director. There was no doubt in my mind that Udall had learned of what Carver had done and was trying to smooth things over without mentioning the subject.

I have described these events to serve as a warning, because such things are bound to happen to others, and the worst part of it is that one is almost helpless to defend himself. Now, years later, many of my friends have urged me to tell what happened and clear the record, and to do so complies with one of the basic purposes of this book, namely to expose life as a career civil servant.

On Monday, October 28, 1963, Senator Harry F. Byrd, of Virginia, placed a speech in the *Congressional Record* defending my reputation as former director of the National Park Service. Included in the speech were a letter from Secretary Udall and also an editorial from the *Washington Evening Star*. The *Washington Evening Star* editorial was from the October 22, 1963 issue:

October 22, 1963

Mr. Horace Albright,
Los Angeles, Calif.

Dear Horace:

Needless to say, I share your concern over the items which appeared in the press which implied that Director Connie Wirth's retirement was a result of some policy crisis or personality conflict within my Department. Nothing could be more untrue—of more unfair to Connie.

You know the high esteem that I have for him and I attempted to convey this at the Yosemite conference when I stated that his contribution has given him a place on the highest honor roll of those in this century who have done the most to preserve a rich outdoor legacy for the American people.

In order that you will have the true facts concerning the leadership transition in the National Park Service I want to recite them again:

(1) At the time Associate Director Eivind Scoyen retired in early 1962 it was my feeling, and I expressed it to Director Wirth, that he should be replaced with a career man who would be selected and groomed to become the next director;

(2) Connie concurred, and late last year he submitted to me a list containing the names of five career Park Service employees whom he recommended for consideration for appointment as associate director;

(3) After much discussion and evaluation we decided to ask George Hartzog—who

George B. Hartzog, Jr., director of the National Park Service from January 8, 1964, to December 31, 1972.

was then employed by downtown St. Louis—to come to Washington for a special interview, and at that time we persuaded him to return to the Park Service and accept the associate director's position;

(4) Later, in February or March Connie indicated that he intended to retire about January 1, 1964, and stated that he would like to announce his retirement at the Biennial Conference of Superintendents at Yosemite in October. At that time I agreed to attend this conference and we also decided to make a final decision during the intervening period on his successor and to announce his appointment simultaneously.

As you observed at Yosemite, the arrangements we made were carried out and it gave me the highest pride and satisfaction to note the deep affection and loyalty felt for Connie by his associates in the Park Service, and the warm and enthusiastic reception given to the announcement of the Hartzog appointment.

The public should know the facts I have outlined here and I am confident that you and other friends of Director Wirth and of the Park Service will help to see that the truth is disseminated and any misapprehensions are dispelled.

Sincerely,
Stewart L. Udall
Secretary of the Interior

We have sometimes been critical, even strongly critical, of the stiffnecked attitude of the National Park Service. When it stands like Horatius at the bridge, blocking some project vital to the emerging new Washington, patience runs low.

On the other hand, if it had not been for the National Park Service, Washington might well have lost, or perhaps never have acquired, what amounts to one of the finest park systems in the world.

Since 1951, Conrad L. Wirth has been Mr. Park Service to us.

Connie Wirth's retirement as Park Service Director was announced last Friday, 4 days after Assistant Secretary of the Interior Carver made a speech to park superintendents that was highly critical of the organization's attitudes and contained the implication that the Interior Department high command had lost patience with Mr. Wirth.

Among other things Mr. Carver charged the Service with resorting to a semireligious mystique to thwart Interior Department policies. He said it fostered a public-be-damned attitude and was not cooperating with the Department's new Bureau of Outdoor Recreation.

Mr. Wirth denies that his retirement was hastened by his superiors. And Interior Secretary Udall, since Mr. Carver's speech, has taken pains to praise Mr. Wirth's record and to disavow to Mr. Wirth's subordinates Mr. Carver's implied slap. It is now clear that George B. Hartzog, who is to succeed Mr. Wirth as Director, was one of five men recommended for the post by Mr. Wirth. His selection does not presage an aboutface in the national park policy.

We are glad that this is the case. For to sacrifice to expediency or popular demands of the moment the basic policy of conserving natural America for generations yet unborn could have tragic consequences.

The men who fathered the park movement were zealots. They were missionaries. Without these qualities the movement never would have got off the ground. The men who continue their work must have the same basic zeal.

While we intend to continue to argue the merits of specific decisions on the use of park land, we do not believe that a "soft" policy concerning such use should be adopted. We congratulate Connie Wirth on 32 years of dedicated service to the Nation and especially to its Capital. If his successor does as well, we will all have been very ably served.

The banquet on the last night of the Yosemite meeting in the Ahwanee was one the like of which could not ever be repeated. The Ahwanee's big dining room was full; the dinner was great; my brother, the admiral, and his wife had come up from San Francisco; the park people and concessionaires put on a skit; and the ovation I got was tremendous. Udall, who sat next to me, turned to me after the applause and remarked, "That was a tremendous ovation they gave you, you've got a lot of loyal friends." The secretary, who said a few nice words, seemed hurt, I thought, by what Carver had done the day before. At any rate, it was a gala affair and we all had fun. Helen and I greatly appreciated the demonstration. What crowned the evening as far as I was concerned was what Helen Wirth did. She stood up and asked for the floor and got it and gave one the nicest short talks I've ever heard, thanking everybody for all they had done for us over the years. It was absolutely perfect. She did something that I could not do, and I felt very proud to be her husband. The meeting had come to a pleasant finish, and a couple of days later we left for a meeting with the secretary's advisory board on national parks and the dedication of the Horace M. Albright Training Center at Grand Canyon National Park.

11

Congressional Relations: Official and Personal

Now that I have retired from the government and have a chance to look back objectively on thirty-six years in the federal service, I have a desire to express some of my thoughts about the Congress of the United States. I have a very high regard and deep appreciation for Congress, both the House and the Senate. The members represent a cross section of the people of the United States and are well qualified to make the laws for our country. They are often maligned and referred to as "politicians" as if that were something bad. We are a democracy, and our form of government requires politicians or statesmen—whichever you wish to call them. We, the people, select them and can remove them if they do not serve us well. Consequently I've always felt that derogatory references to them are not fair. A congressman must be prudent, shrewd, artful, expedient, and judicious to survive in political life. These attributes make up the science or art of politics. If he has these qualifications he'll be in Congress for a long time, to the benefit of the country.

As a government employee my direction and responsibilities were derived from the laws of our land, which were enacted by Congress. My actions were subject to review and approval by both Congress and the secretary of the interior. I have been critical of Congress at times because my judgments did not prevail, and I have also criticized higher administrative authority for the same reasons. On looking back, though I think I was right in most cases, I do recognize the possibility that I may not always have presented my thinking effectively and that there is always the chance of an honest difference of opinion. When something positive was accomplished, we in the bureaus of the departments have, more often than not, taken credit for a job well done and neglected to share it with committees of Congress. In many cases, without the backing of Congress, which provided authority and financing, we could not have been successful. Mission 66 is a good example. I say "thank you" to the Congress of the United States for the support it has given the National Park Service through the years in carrying out our assigned duties and responsibilities.

In mentioning some of the members of Congress who have been particularly helpful, I know I will leave out some very important friends, not intentionally, but nevertheless unfortunately. I know that the committee and subcommittee chairmen are very important and powerful individuals, but I also know that they derive their power from the members of their committees and that their leadership stems from their statesmenship. Committee members, if they read these pages, should know that my expressed appreciation is intended for all.

THE HOUSE APPROPRIATIONS COMMITTEE

When I first arrived in Washington in 1928, Representative Louis C. Cramton, of Michigan, was chairman of the Subcommittee on Appropriations for the Department of the Interior. His committee also processed appropriations for the Office of Public Buildings and Grounds and the National Capital Park and Planning Commission. At that time I was an assistant to Lieutenant Colonel U. S. Grant III, engineer in charge of Public Buildings and Grounds and executive officer of the planning commission. In a minor way I helped with appropriation and legislative matters, mostly in connection with the development of the park system of the city of Washington. Cramton along with Senator Arthur Capper, of Kansas, had introduced the bill that would authorize an appropriation for park land acquisition in the District of Columbia and, on a matching basis, for acquisition and development of the park system beyond the district line into Maryland and Virginia. The authorization included funds to buy the land for the George Washington Memorial Parkway. I got to know the congressmen very well.

When I transferred to the National Park Service, I found that Representative Cramton was almost like one of the Park Service family. He was a very good friend of Director Albright's and was included in many of the Park Service social gatherings. His advice on legislative matters, apart from his function as chairman of the Appropriations Subcommittee, was highly respected and greatly appreciated. He was defeated when he ran for reelection in 1932, went back to Michigan, and a few years later was elected to the state legislature. He died in 1966, the year the National Park Service celebrated its fiftieth anniversary.

The 1932 election gave control of the House of Representatives of the Seventy-second Congress to the Democrats, and Representative Edward T. Taylor, of Colorado, took over as chairman of the Subcommittee on Appropriations for the Interior Department. Here again we were most fortunate in having a good friend and a strong supporter of the National Park Service. I won't attempt to enumerate the many things Representative Taylor did with far-reaching effect on the responsibilities of the entire Interior Department. He had become a highly respected leader in Congress. He was on the Appropriations Committee as early as 1928 and served as chairman of the Subcommittee on Interior Appropriations from 1933 to 1943. His congressional

House Subcommittee on Interior Appropriations

ngress	Fiscal Year Appropriation	Chairman, Majority Leader		Ranking Minority Leader	
9th	1928	Louis C. Cramton	Michigan	Charles D. Carter	Oklahoma
0th	1929	″	″	Edward T. Taylor	Colorado
	1930	″	″	″	″
1st	1931	″	″	″	″
	1932	″	″	″	″
2d	1933	Edward T. Taylor	Colorado	Frank Murphy	Ohio
	1934	″	″	″	″
3d	1935	″	″	W. P. Lambertson	Kansas
4th	1936	″	″	″	″
	1937	″	″	″	″
5th	1938	″	″	Robert F. Rich	Pennsylvania
	1939	″	″	″	″
6th	1940	″	″	″	″
	1941	″	″	″	″
7th	1942	″	″	″	″
	1943	Jed Johnson	Oklahoma	″	″
8th	1944	″	″	Albert E. Carter	California
	1945	″	″	″	″
9th	1946	″	″	Robert F. Jones	Ohio
	1947	″	″	″	″
0th	1948	Robert F. Jones	Ohio	Michael J. Kirwan	Ohio
	1949	Ben F. Jensen	Iowa	″	″
1st	1950	Michael J. Kirwan	Ohio	Ben F. Jensen	Iowa
	1951	″	″	″	″
2d	1952	″	″	″	″
	1953	″	″	″	″
3d	1954	Ben F. Jensen	Iowa	Michael J. Kirwan	Ohio
	1955	″	″	″	″
4th	1956	Michael J. Kirwan	Ohio	Ben F. Jensen	Iowa
	1957	″	″	″	″
5th	1958	″	″	″	″
	1959	″	″	″	″
6th	1960	″	″	″	″
	1961	″	″	″	″
7th	1962	″	″	″	″
	1963	″	″	″	″
8th	1964	″	″	William Henry Harrison	Wyoming
	1965	″	″	″	″
9th	1966	Winfield K. Denton	Indiana	Ben Reifel	South Dakota
	1967	″	″	″	″
0th	1968	Julia Butler Hansen	Washington	″	″
	1969	″	″	″	″
1st	1970	″	″	″	″
	1971	″	″	″	″
2d	1972	″	″	Joseph M. McDada	Pennsylvania
	1973	″	″	″	″

district took in all of Colorado west of the Rocky Mountains, an area that included two national parks and five national monuments. By 1937, Representative Taylor had become chairman of the Appropriations Committee, but he retained the chairmanship of the subcommittee on the Interior Department through 1942, when he was followed by Representative Jed Johnson, of Oklahoma, who had been a member of the subcommittee since 1935.

At the meeting of the Subcommittee on Appropriations for Interior on March 17, 1943, Chairman Jed Johnson welcomed as new members, Michael J. Kirwan, and Ben F. Jensen. Those men, the first a Democrat and the second a Republican, turned out to be two of the best supporters we had on the Appropriations Committee over a period of seventeen years.

Jed Johnson, the Oklahoma Democrat, remained as chairman through to 1948. While I knew Johnson quite well from CCC days, I had practically no contact with him when he was chairman of the Appropriations Subcommittee. He served during the difficult war years. In 1945 the total appropriation for the Park Service was only $4,740,000, which is less than the service had in 1930 and $28,800,000 less than in 1940. Representative Robert Jones, of Ohio, followed Johnson as chairman for one session of Congress and in turn was followed by Ben Jensen, of Iowa, for the 1949 appropriations bill. Both were Republicans.

In 1949, Jensen was the ranking Republican on our subcommittee, and Mike Kirwan the ranking Democrat. Whenever the party majority changed in the House of Representatives, one or the other of them became chairman of the subcommittee. During that period, between 1949 and 1965, the Democrats had a majority in the House of Representatives for fourteen years, and consequently the chairmanship fell into Mike Kirwan's hands more often than into Ben Jensen's. Ben and Mike worked together, however, and if they had any disagreements over our budget because of political differences they never displayed them during committee hearings. I am most familiar with this period because it is the period that I was director and appeared before the Appropriations Committee to justify the service's requests for funds.

I should explain that it is customary in the National Park Service for the director and the assistant director for administration to defend the service's request for appropriations and legislation before the committees of Congress. It is the responsibility of the service's Branch of Administration to collect the necessary data for preparation of the budget request. All branches and offices of the service cooperate in reviewing and making recommendations concerning items that pertain to their respective operations in the field as well as in the Washington office. The responsibility for preparing the budget for the service, however, belongs to the assistant director of the Branch of Administration subject to the final approval of the director. When the director and assistant director of the Branch of Administration attend the congressional appropriation hearings, they are usually accompanied by fiscal and other technical staff people who can help justify the request.

Hillory Tolson was the assistant director in charge of the Branch of Administration while I was director, as he had been for a number of years. Tolson was a good administrator and had handled the preparation of budgets under the directorships of Cammerer, Drury, and Demaray. He had developed a very efficient staff, and the two on that staff that I most often dealt with were Clarence Montgomery and Harold Smith, both outstanding men.

During the dozen years that I was director of the National Park Service, the two key members of the House Appropriations Subcommittee were Ben Jensen, the Republican, and Mike Kirwan, the Democrat. They, and in fact the whole committee, were most considerate and favorable toward our Mission 66 program, and it can certainly be said that without their help and understanding Mission 66 could not have succeeded. But I am also certain that a lot of the confidence and support that we received resulted from the way in which our budgets were prepared, justified, and presented to Congress. Many times we were complimented on this by the Congress and the Bureau of the Budget, and I know that much of the credit for this was owing to Hillory Tolson and his boys, whose aim in their work was perfection.

I must relate an incident involving Mike Kirwan that illustrates his character. (I have told the story about the first money we got for Mission 66 in Chapter 9 on that program.) After I retired in 1964 I wanted in some way to show Congressman Kirwan my appreciation for all he did for the service while I was its director. On Laurance Rockefeller's suggestion I took Mike and his wife to Virgin Islands National Park. The three of us had a very enjoyable time at Caneel Bay for a little over a week. The last night there, while I was getting ready for dinner after having cocktails in Mike's room, he came in and sat down and said, "What can I do for you Connie?" I told him absolutely nothing, that the purpose of this trip was to express thanks for all he had done to help me while I was director and that Laurance had made this trip possible. He repeated several times, "Are you sure there is nothing I can do for you?" I said no. He then said, "I'm glad to hear you say that, because when you are a congressman most people are nice to you because they want something, but you have never asked for anything except those things in line with your government responsibilities." Then he said that he never had received much schooling because his family was very poor. He had had to go to work when he was still a young boy, and he knew what it was to be hungry and knew the value of money. He was interested in the parks because they brought a lot of people enjoyment that they could not get in any other way. That tied right into his reasoning expressed during committee hearings when he kept wanting us to put in more picnic and camping areas so that the low income people would have places to go and enjoy themselves.

Mike Kirwan was a good representative of the people who elected him. As far as I know he never went back to his district to campaign for office; but it seemed that in every succeeding election he would get a larger percentage of the vote. He said that if he went back to campaign he would have to promise the people a lot of things he couldn't deliver.

THE SENATE APPROPRIATIONS COMMITTEE

The Constitution requires that all appropriation bills originate in the House and then go to the Senate. Often disagreements are resolved in conference between the House and Senate committees. Bureaus that suffer budget cuts in the House usually try to get them restored in the Senate. As far as the Park Service is concerned, I would say we were successful in this maneuver 75 per cent of the time, although whenever the House and Senate committees go into conference to iron out their differences it seems that more often than not the House view prevails.

In 1928 Senator Reed Smoot, of Utah, was chairman of the Senate Subcommittee on the Interior Appropriations. I really never knew him. He was chairman until 1934, when one of the great men of the Senate, Carl Hayden, became chairman. Hayden was chairman over a period of thirty-one years, from 1934 through 1968, with only two breaks of two years each—in 1947 and 1948, when Kenneth S. Wherry, of Nebraska, was chairman, and in 1953 and 1954, when Guy Cordon, of Oregon, held the chair.

Once when Mission 66 was under way and Hayden was chairman, we had several requests for funds to restore some of the old Civil War battlefields and to establish visitor centers to help interpret the engagements. Most of the battlegrounds are in the southern states, and four or five southern senators came in to urge that the appropriations be granted. Chairman Hayden was the only member of the committee present; perhaps it was just as well because, even though the other members relied almost entirely on his judgment, when they were present the hearings took a great deal longer. After the southern senators had left, Hayden said, "Off the record, Connie, I thought the South lost the war between the states." And I replied, "Yes, Senator they did, but they didn't lose a battle."

At one of the hearings when Senator Cordon, also a supporter and friend of the service, was chairman, he asked me a question and before I had an opportunity to answer it, Carl Hayden spoke up with the answer. Whereupon the chairman turned to me and said jokingly, "Connie, I think you'd better let Carl Hayden defend your budget; he knows as much about parks as you do." I answered, "I'd be very glad to let our case rest with Carl Hayden any time, providing it had the chairman's approval also." Carl Hayden retired at the end of the session of Congress in 1968. He had been in Congress first as a

gress	Fiscal Year Appropriation	Chairman, Majority Leader		Ranking Minority Leader	
9th	1928	Reed Smoot	Utah	William J. Harris	Georgia
0th	1929	"	"	"	"
	1930	"	"	"	"
1st	1931	"	"	"	"
	1932	"	"	"	"
2d	1933	"	"	Kenneth McKellar	Tennessee
	1934	"	"	"	"
3d	1935	Carl Hayden	Arizona	Gerald P. Nye	North Dakota
4th	1936	"	"	"	"
	1937	"	"	"	"
5th	1938	"	"	"	"
	1939	"	"	"	"
6th	1940	"	"	"	"
	1941	"	"	"	"
7th	1942	"	"	"	"
	1943	"	"	"	"
8th	1944	"	"	"	"
	1945	"	"	"	"
9th	1946	"	"	Chan Gurney	South Dakota
	1947	"	"	"	"
0th	1948	Kenneth S. Wherry	Nebraska	Carl Hayden	Arizona
	1949	"	"	"	"
st	1950	Carl Hayden	Arizona	Kenneth S. Wherry	Nebraska
	1951	"	"	"	"
d	1952	"	"	Guy Cordon	Oregon
	1953	"	"	"	"
d	1954	Guy Cordon	Oregon	Carl Hayden	Arizona
	1955	"	"	"	"
th	1956	Carl Hayden	Arizona	Karl E. Mundt	South Dakota
	1957	"	"	"	"
th	1958	"	"	"	"
	1959	"	"	"	"
th	1960	"	"	"	"
	1961	"	"	"	"
th	1962	"	"	"	"
	1963	"	"	"	"
th	1964	"	"	"	"
	1965	"	"	"	"
th	1966	"	"	"	"
	1967	"	"	"	"
th	1968	"	"	"	"
	1969	"	"	"	"
st	1970	Alan Bible	Nevada	"	"
	1971	"	"	"	"
d	1972	"	"	Charles H. Percy	Illinois
	1973	"	"	Ted Stevens	Alaska

representative and then as a senator ever since Arizona had become a state in 1912, a total of fifty-six years.

The senator who followed Hayden as chairman was Alan Bible, of Nevada, who retired at the end of the 1974 session of Congress. I never had an opportunity to appear before the committee while he was chairman, but I know him well. He also served for many years on the Interior and Insular Affairs Committee, the legislative committee of the Senate, and helped to pull our irons out of the fire many times. We always found him to be an upright, thoughtful, pleasant, intelligent, helpful senator, and a gentleman.

LEGISLATIVE COMMITTEES

There are hundreds of bills introduced in every session of Congress that if enacted would establish additional activities, effect changes in policies, or introduce new controls or regulations that might affect an agency either directly or indirectly. The legislative committee that handles National Park Service bills in the House is called the Public Lands Committee and in the Senate is called the Interior and Insular Affairs Committee. The committees hold hearings, and the agencies affected are required to submit reports and to provide witnesses to testify and answer questions from committee members. The public is usually invited, and individuals are given an opportunity to make statements or submit reports on behalf of themselves or as representatives of organizations. Presentations to legislative committees become difficult at times—even disastrous. Both the legislative and appropriations committees meet in executive session after hearings and make their decisions, commonly referred to as "marking up the bill," after which the staff prepares the reports. At times there are strong disagreements within the committee, and when that happens both majority and minority reports are prepared and find their way to the floor of the House or Senate.

When we started Mission 66 we had several pieces of legislation we wanted enacted that would have helped us or at least cleared up any doubts as to our legal rights. One of these would have let us spend some of our money to build facilities (campgrounds and maintenance facilities, for example) on federal lands outside the parks, provided the administering agency involved agreed, in order to avoid encroaching on scenic areas of the national parks. We prepared bills and they were introduced, but try as we might they were never called up for hearings. Consequently we did the best we could without them. In 1962 at one of the hearings before the Public Lands Committee of the House, we were asked what right we had to move certain government facilities out of a park even though they were put on federally owned land. The member asking the question stated that the legislation to authorize such action had not been acted upon by the committee. We told him that our legal adviser in the solicitor's office had indicated that if the federal agency that had

gress		Chairman, Majority Leader		Ranking Minority Leader	
)th	1927	Nicholas J. Sinnott	Oregon	John M. Evans	Montana
	1928	Addison T. Smith	Idaho	"	"
st	1929–30	Don B. Colton	Utah	"	"
2d	1931–32	John M. Evans	Montana	Don B. Colton	Utah
3d	1933–34	René L. DeRouen	Louisiana	Harry L. Englebright	California
4th	1935–36	"	"	"	"
5th	1937–38	"	"	"	"
6th	1939–40	"	"	"	"
7th	1941–42	J. W. Robinson	Utah	"	"
8th	1943	"	"	"	"
	1944	J. Hardin Peterson	Florida	James W. Mott	Oregon
9th	1945–46	"	"	Karl M. LeCompte	Iowa
0th	1947–48	Richard J. Welch	California	Andrew L. Somers	New York
1st	1949	Andrew L. Somers	New York	Richard J. Welch	California
	1950	J. Hardin Peterson	Florida	Fred L. Crawford	Michigan
2d	1951–52	John R. Murdock	Arizona	"	"
3d	1953–54	A. L. Miller	Nebraska	Clair Engle	California
4th	1955–56	Clair Engle	California	A. L. Miller	Nebraska
5th	1957–58	"	"	"	"
6th	1959–60	Wayne N. Aspinall	Colorado	John P. Saylor	Pennsylvania
7th	1961–62	"	"	"	"
8th	1963–64	"	"	"	"
9th	1965–66	"	"	"	"
0th	1967–68	"	"	"	"
1st	1969–70	"	"	"	"
2d	1971–72	"	"	"	"
3d	1973	James A. Haley	Florida	"	"

jurisdiction over the site was agreeable and we had justified the appropriation adequately before the Appropriations Committee, the question of basic legislation was purely academic and we could proceed without it. Apparently the answer was satisfactory, because nothing further was said.

THE HOUSE PUBLIC LANDS COMMITTEE

When appearing before committes of Congress, especially the legislative committees, a few simple, reasonable things should be borne in mind: (1) Develop the attitude that if they give of their time to consider your legislation you, the bureau chief, should be glad to testify. (2) Don't try to play party politics, especially if you are a career civil servant. Let the politicians do that. You want all of their votes regardless of party affiliation. (3) Don't overdo it, but show your appreciation for their consideration of your problems. (4) Learn as much as you can about all of your committee members. (5) Be factual and forthright in your presentations and in your answers to their questions. (6) Get to know the committee staff members and avoid running around their ends. (7) Last but very important, don't get long-winded, and know enough to stop when you think you have the necessary votes. You can usually get a reading on how things stand by observing the chairman or the sponsor of the bill.

One of the first congressmen I got acquainted with was a person I had known slightly in New Orleans in 1927. His name was Rene L. DeRouen, and he was chairman of the House Public Lands Committee. We had met when we were both members of the New Orleans Young Men's Business Club. I will confess I never did like strong Louisiana coffee, but every time I called on Rene, I had to have a cup. I took my medicine like a man, and I really enjoyed being with him. He was chairman up through the third session of the Seventy-sixth Congress in 1940. He held that position when the Historic Sites and the Park, Parkway, and Recreational-Area Study acts went through Congress, and I must not forget the act of August 10, 1937, that enlarged Chalmette National Monument, in Louisiana, and gave it national historical park status.

DeRouen was followed by J. W. Robinson, who was quiet and soft spoken but determined and helpful. He was chairman for the two years—1943 and 1944—of the Seventy-eighth Congress. Chairman Robinson was followed by J. Hardin Peterson, of Florida, better known to us as Congressman Pete. Congressman Pete and I became very good friends, and he was a strong supporter of the national park system. We had absolutely no differences on that score, and most anything we needed he would work for.

In the twelve years from 1947 through 1958, there were six different chairmen as shown on the chart on page 323. Congressman Pete was back for one session in 1950. These gentlemen were all fine people, always very considerate and interested. It was during Clair Engle's chairmanship that we started Mission 66, although without any basic legislation. While Congress may not have been opposed to the legislation we sought, it did nothing about it, and even though we got along without the legislation, it would have helped if Congress had approved it.

Beginning with the Eighty-sixth Congress, in 1959, through the Ninety-second Congress, which ended in December, 1972, the chairman of the House Public Lands Committee was Wayne N. Aspinall, of Colorado, with John P. Saylor, of Pennsylvania, as ranking minority leader. The record of the committee during that period is outstanding from a Park Service point of view. I don't recall a park bill reported out of committee that ever failed to pass once it was called up in the House for consideration. There was occasional criticism of the length of time it took to get certain bills out of committee, but Wayne Aspinall wanted to be sure that a clear majority of the committee was supporting a bill by the time it got to the floor of the House, and he would keep his bills in hearings until he was sure of that advantage. Certainly he encountered serious opposition to some bills; he even had to accept some amendments from the floor. But be that as it may, they got through. The record was so overwhelming that I obtained the following list of the major bills related to park matters that were enacted during Aspinall's chairmanship. Many of these acts of Congress provided new units to the park system, and the rest concerned such things as boundary adjustments, and policy and administrative matters. By far the majority of these acts were the result of studies carried out during Mission 66 under the general supervision of the Branch of Lands headed by Ben Thompson and by Ted Swen after Ben's retirement. Long as this list is, I know that it is not complete.

Eighty-Fifth Congress 1957–1958

Fort Clatsop National Memorial	Oregon
General Grant National Memorial	New York
Grand Portage National Monument	Minnesota
Independence National Historical Park	Pennsylvania
Cowpens National Battlefield Site	South Carolina

Eighty-Sixth Congress 1959–1960

Arkansas Post National Memorial	Arkansas
Bent's Old Fort National Historic Site	Colorado
Haleakala National Park	Hawaii
Minute Man National Historical Park	Massachusetts
Wilson's Creek National Battlefield	Missouri

Eighty-Seventh Congress 1961–1962

Cape Cod National Seashore	Massachusetts
Point Reyes National Seashore	California
Padre Island National Seashore	Texas
Fort Davis National Historic Site	Texas
Fort Smith National Historic Site	Arkansas and Oklahoma
The White House	District of Columbia
Piscataway Park	Maryland
Lincoln Boyhood National Memorial	Indiana
Hamilton Grange National Memorial	New York
Theodore Roosevelt Birthplace and Sagamore Hill National Historical Site	New York
Frederick Douglas Home	District of Columbia

Eighty-Eighth Congress 1963–1964

Ozark National Scenic Riverways	Missouri
Fire Island National Seashore	New York
Canyonlands National Park	Utah
Lake Mead National Recreation Area	Arizona and Nevada
Fort Bowie National Historic Site	Arizona
John Muir National Historic Site	California
Fort Larned National Historic Site	Kansas
Saint Gaudens National Historic Site	New Hampshire
Allegheny Portage Railroad National Historic Site	Pennsylvania
Johnstown Flood National Memorial	Pennsylvania
Roosevelt Campobello International Park	New Brunswick, Canada
Ice Age National Scientific Reserve	Wisconsin

Eighty-Ninth Congress 1965–1966

Delaware Water Gap National Recreation Area	Pennsylvania and New Jersey
Assateague Island National Seashore	Maryland and Virginia
Whiskeytown-Shasta-Trinity National Recreation Area	California
Cape Lookout National Seashore	North Carolina
Bighorn Canyon National Recreation Area	Montana and Wyoming
Guadalupe Mountains National Park	Texas
Pictured Rocks National Lakeshore	Michigan
Wolf Trap Farm for the Performing Arts	Virginia
Indiana Dunes National Lakeshore	Indiana
Agate Fossil Beds National Monument	Nebraska
Pecos National Monument	New Mexico
Alibates Flint Quarries and Texas Panhandle Pueblo Culture National Monument	Texas
Nez Perce National Historical Park	Idaho
George Rogers Clark National Historical Park	Indiana
San Juan Island National Historic Park	Washington
Golden Spike National Historic Site	Utah
Herbert Hoover National Historic Site	Iowa
Hubbell Trading Post National Historic Site	Arizona
Roger Williams National Memorial	Rhode Island
Chamizal National Memorial	Texas
Fort Union Trading Post National Historic Site	North Dakota and Montana

Ninetieth Congress 1967–1968

Redwood National Park	California
North Cascades National Park	Washington
Ross National Recreation Area	Washington
Lake Chelan National Recreation Area	Washington
Biscayne National Monument	Florida
John Fitzgerald Kennedy National Historic Site	Massachusetts
Saugus Iron Works National Historic Site	Massachusetts
Carl Sandburg Home National Historic Site	North Carolina

Ninety-First Congress 1969–1970

Voyageurs National Park	Minnesota
Florissant Fossil Beds National Monument	Colorado
Chesapeake and Ohio Canal National Historic Park	Maryland
Apostle Islands National Lakeshore	Wisconsin
Sleeping Bear Dunes National Lakeshore	Michigan
Gulf Island National Seashore	Mississippi and Florida
William Howard Taft National Historic Site	Ohio
Eisenhower National Historic Site	Pennsylvania
Lyndon B. Johnson National Historic Site	Texas
Fort Point National Historic Site	California
Andersonville National Historic Site	Georgia

Ninety-Second Congress 1971–1972

Fossil Butte National Monument	Wyoming
Hohokam Pima National Monument	Arizona
Buffalo National River	Arkansas
Cumberland Island National Seashore	Georgia
Golden Gate National Recreation Area	California
Gateway National Recreation Area	New York and New Jersey
Glen Canyon National Recreation Area	Utah and Arizona
Lower Saint Croix National Scenic River	Wisconsin and Minnesota
Lincoln Home National Historic Site	Illinois
Puukohola Heiau National Historic Site	Hawaii
Grant-Kohrs Ranch National Historic Site	Montana
Longfellow National Historic Site	Massachusetts

Mar-A-Lago National Historic Site	Florida
Thaddeus Kosciuszko Home National Memorial	Pennsylvania
Benjamin Franklin National Memorial	Pennsylvania
John D. Rockefeller, Jr., Memorial Parkway	Wyoming

I know that Aspinall and committee Minority Leader John Saylor worked together on park legislation. They both thought highly of the National Park Service and tried to help it in every way they could because they felt that the preservation and interpretation of our natural and historic heritage for the use and enjoyment of the people was one thing the nation needed if it was to remain sound and prosper. True, they would not hesitate to let us know if they felt we were doing something they thought was not right. The nation and the service owe them and their committee a great debt of gratitude.

I'm placing special emphasis on these two men, especially the chairman, for several reasons. As will be noted, I have included in the list of bills not their numbers but the areas or subject matter involved and the location by state if applicable. On that list is a bill that radically changed the procedure in developing the national park system. This bill, which became the act of the Eighty-seventh Congress, established Cape Cod National Seashore and authorized sixteen million dollars for purchase of the lands, thus creating the new policy of acquiring park lands by government purchase. Under the chairmanship of Wayne Aspinall the Land and Water Bill also became law. That act provides funds for land acquisition for the national park system as well as for conservation measures administered by other federal agencies. It also—and this is very important—provides funds to aid the planning, purchase, and development of parks and recreation areas for state and metropolitan park systems. The funds available for these purposes now amount to hundreds of millions of dollars a year. The act establishing the Bureau of Outdoor Recreation to administer these funds and to see that comprehensive planning is undertaken before the funds are allocated also came out of Wayne's committee. It should be noted that both Wayne Aspinall and John Saylor were members of the Outdoor Recreation Resources Review Committee that Laurance Rockefeller chaired and that recommended the establishment of the BOR. Also not mentioned in the list is passage of the Wilderness Act, a most important piece of legislation affecting all landholding agencies of the government, including the National Park Service.

Wayne Aspinall had served as an assistant to Representative Edward T. Taylor, of Colorado, and he later represented Taylor's old district in Congress. Toward the end of Aspinall's service in Congress the district was extended to include some heavily populated areas in northeastern Colorado, and Wayne was defeated in the primaries by an individual from the urban areas who in turn was defeated in the final election in 1974. I know that some special interest groups outside Wayne's congressional district exerted considerable pressure to defeat him, and I'm sorry to say that one of those special interest groups is called conservationist. Certainly there were some things that Wayne Aspinall and his committee did that I objected to, but in my opinion and in the opinion of many others Aspinall, John Saylor, and their committee deserve a place of high honor for their accomplishments in providing for the conservation of our heritage, both natural and historic, and in extending to all levels of government financial and other authorization to develop adequate park and recreation facilities for all people. I am convinced that those who believe in sound, practical conservation and yet voted against Wayne or urged others to vote against him never examined the record.

From a legislative standpoint many people believe that the Wilderness Act, the Cape Cod Act, the Bureau of Outdoor Recreation Act, and the Land and Water Act stand shoulder to shoulder with the Yellowstone National Park Act, the Antiquities Act, the National Park Service Act, the Historic Sites Act, and the Park, Parkway, and Recreational-Area Study Act. They are equally important to the development of a cooperative national system of parks, historic sites, and recreation areas at all levels of government for the people to enjoy and pass on to those who follow.

THE SENATE INTERIOR AND INSULAR AFFAIRS COMMITTEE

From the Seventieth through the Seventy-ninth congresses (1927–46), the Senate Interior and Insular Affairs Committee was called the Public Lands and Surveys Committee. One of our strong supporters in the Senate, Gerald P. Nye from North Dakota, was chairman of that committee through the Seventy-second Congress of 1931–32. Like Louis Cramton on the House Appropriations Committee, Nye was a social friend as well as a sound adviser to the Park Service on legislative matters.

With the advent of the New Deal on March 4, 1933, the Republicans became the minority party and the Democrats took over the chairmanship of the various committees of the Senate. Senator John B. Kendrick, from Wyoming, became chairman of the Public Lands and Surveys Committee at the beginning of the first session of the Seventy-third Congress on March 9. (This session is covered fully in Chapter 4.) The second session began on January 3, 1934, and at that time Key Pittman, of Nevada, became chairman of the committee and was followed on May 4, 1934, by Robert F. Wagner, of New York. The record shows that Wagner was the only man, either Republican or Democrat, on the committee from east of the Mississippi River. His chairmanship therefore presented a somewhat odd situation, because the Public Lands and Surveys Committee at that time was primarily concerned

Senate Interior and Insular Affairs Committee

Congress		Chairman, Majority Leader		Ranking Minority Leader	
70th	1927–28	Gerald P. Nye	North Dakota	Key Pittman	Nevada
71st	1929–30	"	"	"	"
72d	1931–32	"	"	"	"
73d	1933	John B. Kendrick	Wyoming	Peter Norbeck	South Da
		Key Pittman	Nevada	"	"
	1934	Robert F. Wagner	New York	"	"
74th	1935–36	"	"	"	"
75th	1937–38	Alva B. Adams	Colorado	Gerald P. Nye	North Da
76th	1939–40	"	"	"	"
77th	1941	"	"	"	"
	1942	Carl A. Hatch	New Mexico	"	"
78th	1943–44	"	"	"	"
79th	1945–46	"	"	Chan Gurney	South Da
80th	1947–48	Hugh Butler	Nebraska	Carl A. Hatch	New Mex
81st	1949–50	Joseph C. O'Mahoney	Wyoming	Hugh Butler	Nebraska
82d	1951–52	"	"	"	"
83d	1953–54	Hugh Butler	Nebraska	James E. Murray	Montana
84th	1955–56	James E. Murray	Montana	Eugene D. Millikan	Colorado
85th	1957–58	"	"	George W. Malone	Nevada
86th	1959–60	"	"	Henry C. Dworshak	Idaho
87th	1961–62	Clinton P. Anderson	New Mexico	"	"
88th	1963–64	Henry M. Jackson	Washington	Thomas H. Kuchel	Colorado
89th	1965–66	"	"	"	"
90th	1967–68	"	"	"	"
91st	1969–70	"	"	Gordon Allott	Colorado
92d	1971–72	"	"	"	"
93d	1973–74	"	"	Paul J. Fannin	Arizona

with the great masses of western lands belonging to the federal government. During the period beginning with the Seventy-third Congress in 1933 and ending with the Seventy-fourth Congress in 1936, Senator Peter Norbeck, of South Dakota, was the minority leader on the committee. He was a strong supporter of state and national parks. The Historic Sites Act of 1935 and the Park, Parkway, and Recreational-Area Study Act of 1936 were products of this period.

Senator Alva Adams, of Colorado, was chairman during the Seventy-fifth and Seventy-sixth congresses and in the first session of the Seventy-seventh. In the second session of the Seventy-seventh Carl A. Hatch, of New Mexico, took over and carried on through the Seventy-eighth and Seventy-ninth congresses. And that takes us through 1946. There is little I can say about the Senate committee during this period as my duties were directed to other matters. In the first session of the Eightieth Congress, in 1947, the committee's name was changed to Public Lands Committee; but in the second session, in 1948, it was given its present name, the Committee on Interior and Insular Affairs.

Starting with the Eighty-first Congress in January, 1949, Joe O'Mahoney, of Wyoming, became chairman of the Interior and Insular Affairs Committee and continued in that position until the end of the Eighty-second Congress in 1952. During Joe's chairmanship, and Representative J. Hardin Peterson's chairmanship in the House, one of the real gems of the national park system, Grand Teton National Park, in Wyoming, was extended and established as it now exists. Its completion climaxed an effort that was started before the turn of the century but that really began to take shape in 1929. It involved two acts of Congress, a presidential proclamation, a lawsuit, and more hearings than I care to try to count.

Ronald F. Lee summarized the Grand Teton story in his booklet *Family Tree of the National Park System*:

Jackson Hole had been talked of as a possible addition to Yellowstone as early as 1892, and from 1916 onward the Service and Department actively sought its preservation in the National Park System. . . . It was John D. Rockefeller, Jr., however, who rescued Jackson Hole for the nation after a visit in 1926 left him distressed at cheap commercial developments on private lands in the midst of superlative natural beauty—dance halls, hot dog stands, filling stations, rodeo grand stands, and billboards in the foreground of the incomparable view of the Teton Range.

Rockefeller began a land acquisition program, which he offered as a gift to the United States. Meanwhile, however, bitter opposition developed among cattlemen, dude ranchers, packers, hunters, timber interests, and local Forest Service officials who preferred livestock ranches or forest crops to a National Park, county officials who feared loss of taxes, and members of the Wyoming State administration who were politically concerned. When no park legislation had been enacted by 1943, Rockefeller indicated he might not be justified in holding his property, on which he paid annual taxes, much longer. President Roosevelt decided to act and on March 15, 1943, proclaimed the Jackson Hole National Monument, consolidating 33,000 acres donated by Rockefeller and 179,000 acres withdrawn from Teton National Forest into a single area adjoining Grand Teton National Park.

Roosevelt's proclamation unleashed a storm of criticism which had been brewing for years among western members of Congress. Rep. Frank A. Barrett of Wyoming and others introduced bills to abolish the monument and to repeal Section 2 of the Antiquities Act containing the President's authority to proclaim National Monuments. A bill to abolish the monument passed Congress in 1944 but was vetoed by President Roosevelt who pointed out in an eloquent message that Presidents of both political parties, beginning with Theodore Roosevelt, had established ample precedents by proclaiming 82 National Monuments, seven of which were larger than Jackson Hole. The proclamation was nevertheless also contested in court, where it was strongly defended by the Departments of Justice and Interior and upheld. Finally, a compromise was worked out and embodied in legislation approved by President Harry S. Truman on September 14, 1950. It combined Jackson Hole National Monument and the old Grand Teton National Park in a "new Grand Teton National

Park" containing some 298,000 acres, with special provisions regarding taxes and hunting. It also prohibited establishing or enlarging National Parks in Wyoming in the future except by express authorization of Congress.

During the summer of 1950 while hearings were being held on the park act, Congressman Pete and Senator Joe O'Mahoney decided to conduct a joint meeting of the House and Senate committees in the area to examine the whole matter and listen very carefully to the pros and cons. As the Park Service's assistant director in charge of lands, I was asked by the two chairmen to arrange for them to meet in Yellowstone and then go to the Grand Tetons by automobile. They wanted seating arranged so that there would be one person for the park and one against the park in each car with a member of the committee. Congressman Pete suggested I get in touch with Representative Frank A. Barrett, from Wyoming, who was on the Public Lands Committee and against the park, and get from him a list of people who should represent the opposition.

When a date for the field meeting was set by the two chairmen, I called Frank Barrett. I told him I was going out there at least a day in advance to work out the itinerary. I hadn't quite finished my statement when Barrett proceeded to take me over the coals, informing me in no uncertain terms that I shouldn't go, that people were so angry out there that somebody was liable to be crazy enough to shoot me. I replied that I didn't think I'd get shot, and anyway I'd been asked to go by the chairmen of the House and Senate committees. He bluntly told me he wasn't going to take part in it. The next day, however, he called back. He had cooled off and gave me the names of four people who would represent the opponents.

The controversy over the park was a real hornet's nest, and the expedition of the congressional committees to the site was not without incident. As we came out of Old Faithful Inn to set out for the Grand Tetons, a car drove up, jammed to a halt, and out came Frank Barrett and another opponent, Felix Buchenroth. Barrett rushed up to me and shook his fist in my face, accusing me of trying to run the state of Wyoming. The discussion got a little loud and almost to a pushing stage. The boisterous argument attracted some of the park visitors, and a crowd started forming. Congressman Pete helped break it up and ushered us to our assigned cars.

One of our scheduled stops was an excellent vantage point on Antelope Flat, where we viewed the whole Grand Teton Mountain range to the west, with the Snake River winding its way through Jackson Hole in the foreground after coming around Signal Peak in the north and disappearing some eight miles south near the settlement of Moran. It was a beautiful day and a strikingly beautiful view. We had a geologist from the University of Wyoming with us to tell about the geology of the country. The geologist gave a very fine talk, lasting perhaps ten minutes, in which he spoke of the geological faults and hence the uplift of the Teton Mountains and the sinking of Jackson Hole. But he happened to oppose the park and concluded by saying, "So you see, gentlemen, the land we're standing on really has no scenic value. The only scenery is the mountains, and if you take them away you don't have anything." With that Congressman Pete piped up and said, "If you're going to get rid of those mountains send them down to Florida where we can use them." Everybody laughed as we moved on to the next point of observation.

We ended the day at the theater in Jackson, where a public hearing had been arranged. The theater was full of people, and there was a lot of hooting and hollering. The opposition had a large turnout and was making the noise. But all the hearings on Jackson Hole National Monument were difficult. It seemed that most of the local people wanted the monument abolished. It had been cattle country for years, elk-hunting country always, and they wanted to keep it that way, the opponents contended. On the other side, the scenery in the Teton–Jackson Hole country is tremendous and it belongs to all the people, the proponents countered. I think it was one of the most clear-cut divisions of opinion I have witnessed in any of the proposed national park hearings I've been through.

Several interesting things happened while Grand Teton National Monument was in existence between March 15, 1943, and September 14, 1950, when the national park was extended to include the monument. In order to ridicule the monument's historic values, which constituted some of the justification for the presidential proclamation that established the monument, someone got an old outhouse and put a sign on it that read, "Horace Albright was here." They then took pictures of it and printed post cards and gave them fairly wide distribution. Opponents to the monument also got the famous old movie star Wallace Beery to ride a horse across the monument with a rifle in his arms, supposedly in defiance of the Park Service rangers. This stunt made the pages of *Time* magazine. Of course, there were no rangers on duty because Congress refused to appropriate any funds for the monument, and the service could not spend any funds or assign any personnel there until the monument was abolished and the land made a part of Grand Teton National Park. In one of my later conversations with Felix Buchenroth I told him I understood Wallace Beery had to use a stepladder to get on the horse, and I thought it would be a good idea for them to donate the ladder to the Park Service so we could put it on display in our visitor center. I laughed, and he looked at me with a scowl on his face and then broke into a grin.

Senator Cliff Hansen was one of the opposition's most articulate leaders. A cattle rancher during the park extension controversy between 1943 and 1950, he became governor of Wyoming for four years before he went to Washington as senator in January, 1967. When he was governor he was given a luncheon in New York by officials of several large oil companies, to which Laurance Rockefeller, Kenneth Chorley, a close associate both of Laurance and of John D. Rockefeller, Jr., and I were invited at his request. On that occasion he said: "I fought against the establishment of the Grand Teton National Park as hard as I could and I lost and I want you all to know that I'm glad I lost, because I now know I was wrong. Grand Teton National Park is one of the greatest natural heritages of Wyoming and the nation and one of our great assets." He then thanked us for what we had done, especially Laurance and his father, John D. Rockefeller, Jr.

Looking back at the long struggle that beset the establishment of Grand Teton National Park, I can appreciate how the local people felt. They had settled in that country and developed a cattle business, holding on to a little of the Old West for the benefit of visitors. A change was taking place—a big change—and all they could envision was harm to their livelihood. I think we all learned something from the Jackson Hole experience. I'm glad to say the Park Service's relationship with the people in Teton County is very good. The adjustment made in the legislation seems to have satisfied all points of view to a reasonable degree.

The Republicans became the majority party in the Senate at the start of the Eighty-third Congress in 1953 when President Dwight D. Eisenhower took office. Senator Hugh Butler, of Nebraska, became chairman of the Interior and Insular Affairs Committee. I was director at that time, and we were still under the pressures of the cold war. Our efforts were directed largely toward increased appropriations to build up our maintenance organization in the parks, for they were seriously understaffed. By the Eighty-fourth Congress, in 1955, the Democrats again became the majority party in the Senate. James E. Murray, of Montana, became chairman and served through to the end of the Eighty-sixth Congress, in 1960. The Eighty-sixth was the same Congress in which Wayne Aspinall, from Colorado, took over the chairmanship of the House Public Lands Committee. At that time Mission 66 had completed many of its field studies of proposed new units, the bills were formulated and submitted to Congress, and five new units were added to the national park system. In the Eighty-seventh Congress another twelve were added, and then the number began to increase rapidly. At the beginning of the Eighty-seventh, Senator Clinton P. Anderson, of New Mexico, became chairman for two sessions of that Congress. In 1963, in the Eighty-eighth Congress, the chairmanship went to Henry M. Jackson, better known to many of us as "Scoop" Jackson, for the state of Washington. Senators Murray, Anderson, and Jackson were always very considerate of our needs and worked very closely with Chairman Aspinall on park matters. Senator Murray was not in very good health, however, and retired after the Eighty-sixth Congress.

The Interior and Insular Affairs Committee had several subcommittees, one of which handled national park matters, and we dealt primarily with the chairmen of the subcommittees. Among them were Henry (Scoop) Jackson, Alan Bible, of Nevada, and Frank (Ted) Moss, of Utah. They were all very much interested in the parks and helped greatly. Although I retired on January 7, 1964, the big influx of proposed legislation to add new parks to the system resulting from studies made during Mission 66 lasted some six or seven years beyond the end of Mission 66. I'm glad to say that after Mission 66 the Park Service continued with further studies in an effort to assure that the great heritage of natural and historic areas of this nation will be accorded the stature and given the protection they deserve.

SOME OF THE PRETTY GOOD GUYS

The preceding accounts have given some idea of how things work in legislative circles. I will now relate a few interesting personal experiences and offer observations on some senators and representatives that I think will help fill out the congressional profile for the reader. I am sure the following will show that they are pretty good guys.

Senator Harry Flood Byrd, of Virginia

The late Senator Harry Flood Byrd was one of my very close friends, as well as a good friend of the service. He believed in and supported the concept of the national park system. He was governor of the state of Virginia when Shenandoah National Park was established before the CCC days. He bought the land with state funds—he believed in pay as you go, and there were no state bonds to provide the money—and transferred the acreage to the federal government. He was also the one who suggested to President Roosevelt that the Blue Ridge Parkway be built to connect Great Smoky and Shenandoah national parks.

He was not on any of our committees, but he was nevertheless always a friend of the Park Service. As mentioned earlier, when Senator Byrd visited Yellowstone National Park to give a short talk at our superintendents' meeting, he stated that we got $1.10 out of every dollar Congress gave us. Later I tried to get the senator to raise it to $1.20, but he wouldn't. Some few years later at the dedication of Cumberland Gap National Historical Park, he reported in his talk that his staff had studied the matter again and the very best they could do was to get it up to $1.15.

Senator Byrd paid for the building of six shelters—one a year—in Shenandoah National Park, along the Appalachian Trail. They were properly dedicated, and each was named after a "byrd," as for example Hawks Byrd Nest. They are built of stone, with shake roofs. Each shelter is some twenty feet

Director Wirth and Senator Harry F. Byrd, of Virginia, stop for refreshments the second day out on their hike from Logan Pass on Going-to-the-Sun Road in Glacier National Park, Montana, to Waterton Lake National Park, Canada. *Courtesy National Park Service.*

long and sixteen feet wide, and one long side has been left open facing a beautiful mountain view.

Senator Byrd got a great deal of pleasure from hiking, especially in the mountains. On one occasion we met in Glacier National Park, in Montana, and hiked from Logan Pass, a 6,600-foot elevation, on Going-to-the-Sun Highway up to Waterton Lake in Canada's Waterton National Park. It took us three days and we camped out two nights. Superintendent John (Jack) W. Emmert went with us, as did Chief Ranger Elmer Fladmark, the senator's son Dick, and his longtime friend, the Speaker of the House of Delegates of the state of Virginia, Blackburn (Blackie) Moore. The first day out we stayed in Granite Park Chalet, one of the old mountain lodges now used as a shelter for hikers who bring their own camping gear. After dinner we sat on the second-story porch wrapped in blankets and looked westward out over the

Changing over from a car to a snow-cat on the way up to Tioga Pass in Yosemite National Park, California. *Left to right:* Hil Ohlman, president of the Yosemite Park Company; Superintendent John Preston; Senator Harry F. Byrd, of Virginia; Regional Director Lawrence Merriam; and Director Wirth. *Courtesy National Park Service.*

mountainside. As dusk set in we saw a big mother grizzly bear with two cubs come up to within two hundred feet of the building. We were safe on the second floor, but it was a sight the senator never forgot.

The next day we covered about twelve miles on irregular mountain terrain and camped out that night in tents, sleeping on the ground in sleeping bags. It was porcupine country, and porcupines can always smell leather, which they like to chew because of the salt in it. All night long Fladmark, who was a great big man and an excellent ranger, got up and chased the porcupines away. The next day we could see various pieces of wood around the camp with porcupine quills sticking in them. The senator told his old friend Blackie that there was a porcupine in his sleeping bag. He had placed a piece of firewood in it when Blackie wasn't looking. I never could find out definitely whether Blackie Moore was scared or not, but he acted it out in great shape.

Another time I told Senator Byrd that I was going out west for about four weeks and that I planned to be in Yosemite National Park, in California, over

Easter. We decided to meet there. In Yosemite the district ranger went up the mountain every two or three weeks in a snow-cat to measure the depth and water content of the snow for the irrigation officials in the valley. When we arrived Superintendent John Preston invited us to go along and we accepted. We got to the top, an elevation of above ten thousand feet, about four in the afternoon and opened the ranger's cabin. It was cold but with a warm sun, and the tops of the Sierras were beautiful to behold. There was snow as far as one could see. We cooked ourselves a nice dinner and went to bed around ten o'clock. The next morning we got up just before the sun came up. We raised the American flag at sunrise and stood in silent prayer for fully five minutes. It was a beautiful sight and God's creations were all around us. We then lowered the flag, put it back in the ranger's cabin, locked up, took the snow findings, and went back down the mountain.

One time Senator Byrd called me and said he would like to see the parks in Hawaii, but he had a problem. Hawaii was a congressional issue just then because its statehood was coming up and also because the military had plans for the area. Byrd was opposed to both, and he was sure the people there would be after him and that this would spoil his trip. Yet, he needed a change and wanted to see Hawaii. He always traveled at his own expense, but in this case he needed some guidance. One of our fine naturalists, Dr. George Ruhle, was stationed on the big island of Hawaii, and we supplied the senator with a ficitious name and asked Ruhle to give him an educational tour of the islands. We told Ruhle his guest was interested in plants, geography, and history and did not want to meet people or be entertained in any way. We also told him that he would learn the visitor's true identity when he met him and that his guest would take care of all expenses. Ruhle took annual leave and met his guest, and he and the senator had a very enjoyable time. The day after the senator left Washington with destination supposedly unknown, however, some newspaper reporter called up his home in Berryville, Virginia, and the maid who answered the telephone told him that Senator Byrd was on a trip to Hawaii. It didn't take long for that information to get to Hawaii, and the newspapers, the politicians, and the military began looking for him. The papers printed notices asking anybody who saw Senator Harry Flood Byrd to please notify the military and the governor. But they never found him. The day before the senator was to return home he telephoned the military and the governor that he was leaving and would be at the airport an hour before departure and that if they wished to talk to him they could see him at that time. Byrd had found Ruhle to be a highly learned person so well acquainted with the entire Pacific area and Asia that he later got him to be his guide on a trip through that part of the world.

It was a sad day for the country when Senator Harry Flood Byrd died. He was a descendant of a long line of Virginia Byrds, and their ancestral home is

Senator Harry F. Byrd, of Virginia, with his constant companion.

one of the restored historic buildings in Williamsburg. One of the honors I most highly regard was that of being one of the senator's eight honorary pallbearers. The present Senator Harry Flood Byrd, Jr., is very much like his father: staunch, independent, a true patriot.

Representative Compton White, of Idaho

Representative Compton White, of Idaho, was a member of the Interior Insular Affairs Committee of the House. He had a feeling that the Park Service was always "grabbing land," and if we wanted just a few acres of the public domain in connection with a boundary line adjustment he would give us quite a going over. In one of our planning studies of Joshua Tree National Monument, in California, we decided to eliminate about three sections of land totaling about two thousand acres that we did not need and wanted to return to public land status. A bill was introduced and was called up for a hearing by Chairman Wayne Aspinall. I appeared as a witness and was discussing the bill when White came in to the hearing late. Without checking the text of the proposed legislation, he asked for the floor and started to give the Park Service a lecture on land grabbing. The other members of the committee started to smile, but nobody interrupted him. Finally, Representative John Saylor asked Compton to yield, explaining that the bill before the committee was to eliminate some two thousand acres of land from the Joshua Tree National Monument, not add to it. With that Compton said, "Well, maybe so, but I think they need a talking to like this every once in a while." So we got both the lecture and his vote in favor of the bill.

Senator Milward L. Simpson, of Wyoming

One day I was before the senate committee defending a bill that would allow us to exchange a piece of land that the service had in Maryland for some land that the Potomac Electric Power Company owned on the Virginia side of the Potomac River at Great Falls. The bill provided that any difference in value, as determined by three separately chosen appraisers working together, would require a cash settlement. The land that the power company owned contained an old canal and locks around Great Falls that George Washington had designed and built when he was a young engineer, and to us it therefore had great historical interest.

But Milward Simpson definitely objected to the proposal. Senator Alan Bible, who was then chairman, interrupted the debate and said, "Connie, this piece of land that you are talking about is just outside of Washington. Why don't you take Senator Simpson out and show him the land?" We went the following Sunday, and when we got there Simpson was astounded by what he saw and wondered why such a fine piece of land of such historic value so close to the capital had not been acquired years earlier.

The bill being considered by the committee had been introduced by Senator Byrd at our request, and Senator Simpson wanted to know whether Byrd would object if he helped get the bill enacted. I was sure he wouldn't, and I suggested that Simpson, who had never met Senator Byrd, go and call on him. As I suspected, Byrd was glad to talk with him, for he remembered the trouble the Park Service had with Simpson in establishing Grand Teton National Park. Milward Simpson, as a private citizen and as governor of Wyoming, had been one of the people who toughly opposed establishment of that park. With the help of the two senators, the Great Falls bill went through and the exchange was made, giving the government control of both sides of the Potomac River around the falls.

Representative Charles Bennett, of Florida

In the late forties Representative Charles Bennett approached the Park Service with the proposal to establish a historic site now called Fort Caroline National Memorial, just south of Jacksonville, Florida, on the Saint John's River. It overlooks the site of Laudonnier's Colony of 1564, an early French attempt at settlement within the present United States. The French and Spanish began two centuries of colonial rivalry in North America at this location. Actually, the site of Laudonnier's Colony had been washed away by the river, but the location is known and a replica of the old fort and a visitor center have been constructed overlooking the old site. Although the colony did not survive, it was there fifty years before the first permanent English settlement was established at Jamestown, Virginia.

Legislation authorizing the national memorial was enacted in 1950, and the area was established January 16, 1953. Bennett and his friends put up money to buy the land and some of the authentic antiquities of that period, which were found in Spain and brought back to this country. Most of the development was done during Mission 66. Charles Bennett is a disabled World War II veteran who is deeply interested in early American history. Since the beginning he has donated his regular monthly veteran's disability allowance to the National Park Service for the purchase of meaningful artifacts having to do with our historic heritage.

Senator Ernest Gruening, of Alaska

Ernest Gruening was a delegate to Congress when Alaska was a territory, and then he became one of the first elected senators from the state of Alaska. He was a kindly man and a devoted conservationist, greatly interested in the preservation of our natural resources. He constantly checked with us on all matters he thought would have any effect on our responsibilities and would alert us to coming possible problems. He loved Alaska, the Park Service, and the Fish and Wildlife Service, and there is nothing he wouldn't do to help an agency do its job right. We often consulted him. He didn't always agree with us, but he was nice about it, and I always liked to see his smiling face when he called on me, even though I didn't know what he had on his mind.

Senator Peter Norbeck, of South Dakota

Peter Norbeck was one of the really down-to-earth senators (he owned a well-digging business), and he understood the need for parks at all levels of government. He used to go to all the state park meetings, and in fact was at the meeting in 1921 when the National Conference on State Parks was organized. He was a senator when I first came to Washington in 1928. After I transferred to the National Park Service in 1931, I came into direct contact with him in setting the boundary lines of Badlands National Monument, in South Dakota, before its establishment on January 25, 1939. He was also one of the main supporters of Custer State Park, in the Black Hills of South Dakota. He lived right near that park and devoted a great deal of time to its development and administration. Mount Rushmore National Memorial, also in the Black Hills south of Rapid City, was another project in which he took a great interest.

I do not want to give the impression that Senator Norbeck was interested only in South Dakota. We could call on him for help on any matter affecting the Park Service. Occasionally we had difficulty getting Congress to do anything about small items of legislation that were noncontroversial and important to us. We'd discuss such a proposed measure with him, and when the time seemed right he'd submit it as an amendment to other legislation under consideration and get it accepted, even though it had very little to do with the particular bill before the Senate.

He developed cancer of the jaw, and after one of his treatments at the Mayo Clinic I had an appointment with him in Rapid City. He met me with a car and driver for a journey to Badlands National Monument, where we were going to talk over some boundary adjustments. As we were driving along he told me a little about his life. He had never lost an election but had never carried his home precinct, where, he said laughingly, the people knew him too well. He told me that when he had returned from the Mayo Clinic by train about a week before quite a crowd gathered around the back platform at the Rapid City station to greet him. As he stood looking over the crowd he noticed that a few people were smiling because they thought he looked so well, but the rest seemed sober and disappointed in his appearance. Finally somebody in the crowd shouted, "Senator, why have you been going to the Mayo Clinic?" With a serious expression he answered, "I have a fatal disease." At that remark, those who had looked sad smiled, and those with the smiling faces turned sad. Then somebody shouted, "What is it, Senator?" And he replied, "Old age," and smiled. Then those who were smiling put on their sour faces again, and those who had turned sad smiled once more because they knew he would outlive a good majority of the crowd who had come to meet him. He laughed over this recollection, and we went on about our business, although his recent surgery was very noticeable and he had difficulty talking. He and my father were very good friends, and my father used to drive over from Minnesota to the Black Hills to visit the senator.

Representative William Lemke, of North Dakota

As long as I'm in the Dakotas I should mention Representative Lemke, who was on the Public Lands Committee of the House. He was a typical Dakota farmer and a very pleasant person to be with. In the thirties the Park Service had used some submarginal land funds to buy some 69,000 acres along the Little Missouri River near Medora, North Dakota, which included part of Theodore Roosevelt's Elk Horn Ranch. It was purchased as one of our Recreational Demonstration Areas and our earliest thoughts were to give the land to the state for a state park, but as time went along the historians prevailed and it was retained as a part of the national park system. Representative Lemke wanted it to become a national park, but Director Drury didn't think it qualified, although he considered it a very good sample of the old shortgrass prairies of the West and thought it was well within the national historic site classification. The difference of opinion between Drury and Lemke became very pronounced. Finally an agreement was reached, and a bill went through Congress authorizing the Theodore Roosevelt National Memorial Park, which was established on April 25, 1947.

I never will forget the dedication. I don't remember just how many people came, but they were far greater in number than we had planned for. A platform had been erected for the dedication ceremony, a big field had been set aside for parking, and a hillside that could have taken care of at least two or three thousand people was available. The event had been pretty well advertised. The ceremony was to take place in the afternoon. People started arriving before sunrise; quite a few cars had come in the day before. The private car of the president of the Northern Pacific Railroad was on the track at Medora, where some of us had lunch. By the time the ceremony was to begin the parking area was overflowing, the seats were all taken, and the hillside was crowded. As we drove up for the dedication a state patrolman told us that cars were parked for at least three miles along the road in both directions. North Dakota is not a heavily populated state, but people had also come hundreds of miles from Montana, South Dakota, and Minnesota, and even from Nebraska and Canada. The farmers and ranchers in that great open country will travel untold miles for a get-together like that. The dedication was a highly successful affair.

About twenty of us were guests at a ranch some twenty miles away, and we needed the state mounted patrol escort to get through the crowd on our way back. It was a typical North Dakota ranch. They served a fine family-style dinner. About eight of us, including Representatives Lemke and Compton White, of Idaho, were put up in one of the old bunk houses, which was quite primitive. Compton White was talkative that night. From about ten or ten thirty on, various guests started for their bunks to turn in, all in one big room. Finally just Lemke, White, and I were left, and then Lemke left us around midnight. By a quarter to one I had had all I could take, and, feeling that I had extended all necessary courtesy, I stumbled off to my bunk, tired as could be, leaving Compton White at the table by himself. He had fed us some wild stories of his life as an old prospector in the Idaho mountains. About six o'clock in the morning people began to stir, and as I looked out of the window I saw Compton White over at the well several hundred feet away in his longhandle underwear. With two pails he was fetching water so that the rest of us could wash and shave when we got up. He had also built a fire in the stove. If he had gone to bed at all he couldn't have slept more than a few hours. It was hard for me to realize that Compton was the same Representative White who, back in Washington, would always give us hell.

Representative John P. Saylor, of Pennsylvania

John Saylor was a congressman of great integrity, a firm believer in the national park system and in the Park Service, and one of our most constructive critics. He was a strong supporter of all forms of conservation of our natural resources. At every opportunity he and his wife would visit the national parks. Though they visited many different parks, they would usually try to stop at Yellowstone, where they had many friends. In the committees of Congress, Saylor was a tower of strength and a recognized practical conservationist in the interest of people and their environment. He was a Republican representing a Democratic district, elected to Congress time after time because of his statesmanship.

Once in Yellowstone he was driving between Fishing Bridge and West Thumb when the driver of the car in front of him opened the window and threw out an empty beer can. John Saylor overtook him, forced him over to the side of the road, and told him to get out and pick up that thing and put it in a trash receptacle at West Thumb. The man started to argue but John's voice was firm and loud enough to bespeak his authority and his size—six feet four inches and over two hundred pounds—which didn't leave much to argue about. The man did ask why he should go back and pick up the can, and John said, "Well, I'm a taxpayer and you happened to drop that can on the one square foot of Yellowstone National Park that I own, and I don't want it there and neither does anybody else." John also told him that if he didn't pick it up and put it in the trash he would take him to the ranger at West Thumb and charge him. So the man walked back and picked up the can, and John followed him all the way into West Thumb and saw him dispose of it in a proper manner. He never did tell the man he was a congressman.

Representative Wesley A. D'Ewart, of Montana

John Saylor and Wesley A. D'Ewart, from Montana, were great friends. Wes D'Ewart was a rancher and a strong supporter of Yellowstone. When he went to Congress he was placed on the Public Lands Committee. But in 1954 he gave up his House seat to run against Senator James E. Murray and was defeated. He was appointed assistant secretary of the interior in October, 1955, by President Eisenhower. It was an interim appointment subject to confirmation by the Senate. Senator Murray, chairman of the Interior and Insular Affairs Committee, wouldn't let his committee confirm the appointment, and D'Ewart went back to ranching, leaving the department July 27, 1956. Even Senator Harry Byrd couldn't get Murray to relent and confirm the appointment. D'Ewart was one of the best assistant secretaries as far as the Park Service was concerned. It was Wes D'Ewart who put on the big push at the cabinet meeting when we presented the Mission 66 program.

A lot could be said about our friend Wes, but I will limit it to one story involving D'Ewart and Saylor at a public hearing in Yellowstone. The businessmen of West Yellowstone were pushing for a high-speed road from Livingston, Montana, up to Mammoth and through the park to West Yellowstone. Wes decided to have a hearing at Mammoth, and since John Saylor was in the park he invited him to sit in on the hearing. When the people from West Yellowstone had finished, D'Ewart introduced Saylor and asked him if he wanted to say anything. John asked superintendent Edmund B. Rogers several questions about traffic in the park, the frequency of accidents, and so forth, revealing that there had not been any fatal accidents on the roads for over four years. Then John told how many people were killed on the Pennsylvania Turnpike in a year, saying that hardly a day went by without at least two or three fatal accidents. He ended by telling them they had a good thing going and had better not get greedy and spoil it. I wouldn't put it past John and Wes, in their love for Yellowstone, to have planned the whole setup. Anyway, that was the last we heard of the proposed high-speed road.

Representative John E. Moss, of California

Representative John E. Moss, of California, is chairman of the Subcommittee on Oversight and Investigations. I am including him here because in my entire thirty-six years of experience in the government, including many appearances on the Hill, I had only one serious confrontation with Congress, and that was with Moss and his committee. I had never met Representative Moss until then, nor have I encountered him since, and he may be well qualified to be included in this chapter with "Some of the Pretty Good Guys," although at the time of the investigation I refer to I didn't think so. However, the investigation had to do with land matters in Death Valley, and it all started with a discontented attorney in our San Francisco regional office, Sid McClellan, who nurtured a grievance of some kind to the point that he wanted to get something on the National Park Service and especially Horace Albright. He started digging into the official files and developed what he concluded was a case of conflict of interest. He took it up with the staff of Moss's committee, or possibly with Moss himself, and they also felt he had something. So McClellan resigned from the National Park Service and went to work on the staff of the Moss committee; but of course, that wasn't conflict of interest in his view.

The situation was this: The U.S. Potash Company, of which Horace Albright was vice-president and executive officer, owned land in Death Valley. Much of it consisted of mining claims where the company had in bygone days mined a considerable amount of potash. The company also owned Furnace Creek Inn, the only place to stay in Death Valley. Tom Vint convinced me that our plan for development of the area should be changed; however, there were several questions involved, and so I made a point on my next field trip to go by Death Valley and spend a couple of days there. Lawrence Merriam, the regional director, went with me, as did Vint and some others. On that trip we decided to place the park headquarters building on a piece of property owned by the U.S. Potash Company, contrary to the master plan that I had approved the year before. The state of California, thanks to the Forty-niners, was willing to put up some money to build the new headquarters and visitor center if we could get the land. We consulted Horace Albright, and after some discussion he was able to persuade the U.S. Potash Company to donate the land we wanted. While there we stayed at Furnace Creek Inn for a couple of nights, and of course the regular price of accommodations was considerably more than we were allowed by the government for travel expenses. But the Fred Harvey Company was running the inn for the potash people and also had the concession contract with us at the south rim of the Grand Canyon and at Petrified Forest. The government contracts, which were approved by everybody who wanted to take a look at them (in fact they cleared through the Public Lands Committee of the House of Representatives as well as the

Comptroller General), contain a provision that the park concessionaires shall not charge government people on official business more than their per diem allowance. This rule applied to the members of Congress and their staffs, and of course they took advantage of it. The investigation was based primarily on the issue of a conflict of interest, or, to put it more directly, an alleged sellout on my part. The accusation was that Albright, director of the Park Service in the early thirties, had bought me, the director in the fifties, causing me to move the location of our proposed new building to one more advantageous to Albright's company. During the hearing the question of free or discount hotel accommodations was claimed to be an added incentive for me to sell out.

To tell the truth, I never did really know exactly what they were so bothered about. They had hearings in the field and then they came to Washington. By that time I was out of government service and living in New York. They wanted me to come down to testify but they wouldn't pay my expenses unless they subpoenaed me. I told them in that case to go ahead and subpoena me, which they did, and I got my expenses paid. They wrote a great big, long report. I read only part of it and, since I didn't see anything that bothered me, I told Horace Albright I would put it in "file 13" and wouldn't even try to answer it. It was a waste of money. They were a little hard on Horace, claiming that he had tried to influence a government employee, and of course I've got to admit that I have a lot of respect for him and that I consulted him often when I was director. If I had it to do all over again I would do the same thing. Horace doesn't sell out to anybody, and neither do I.

As far as the per diem is concerned, they said I was there for two nights and I only paid for one—why? What had happened, according to my record, was that I gave the inn all of my per diem for two days, but their bookkeeper credited it all to one day and nothing to the second day. When I told the committee this they went into a long huddle and decided to drop the subject. The committee's investigators, who went to Yellowstone as well as Death Valley, got the same treatment as I had because they were on official business. The committee did suggest that the question of per diem and reduced rates to government people on official business should be looked into and some adjustments or changes made.

I must say that Representative Moss was very considerate of me through the investigation, though some of the staff were not looking for facts as much as they were trying to irritate me. Actually, the investigation and the report never even made the newspapers.

Senator Jennings Randolph, of West Virginia

Jennings Randolph was serving in the House of Representatives when we began to talk about Harper's Ferry as an addition to the national park system. Harper's Ferry is a scenic and historic area at the confluence of the Shenandoah and Potomac rivers in the Blue Ridge Mountains. It is important historically because of events that took place there in colonial times, and of course it is famous as the site of John Brown's raid on the United States Armory in 1859. It was authorized as a National Historical Park in 1944 and established May 13, 1955. Representative Howard O. Staggers followed Jennings Randolph when Randolph took a position as an airline executive for a few years. Randolph returned to West Virginia in 1958 to run for the Senate and is now the senior senator from his state. He is an excellent speaker and a very fine person to have on one's side.

On the hill by the Jefferson Rock in Harper's Ferry, there was an old college for blacks named Storer College. It was closed down in the late thirties. With the advent of Mission 66 we did considerable alteration of the old college buildings and turned the campus into a training center for new rangers. We named it after the first director of the National Park Service, Stephen T. Mather, and the dedication took place shortly after I retired. At the same time the service also named the headquarters of the training center, which had been the main building of the old college, Wirth Hall, which pleased me very much. A couple of weeks later I got a letter from Bob Hall, chief of the eastern office of the Branch of Design and Construction, telling how pleased he was to have his name associated with mine on the headquarters building. I wrote him back and told him he was mistaken, that they had a different Hall in mind.

Several years after retiring I had occasion to appear before the Public Works Committee of the Senate as witness in support of a project. Just as I was finishing my statement Senator Randolph came in to give a statement on the project. The senator first praised me and what I stood for in glowing terms, and then he said he would not read his statement and asked the approval of the chairman to file it as a part of the record. He then went on record as supporting my statement, saying that although he had not heard or seen it he nevertheless had such confidence in me that he felt he was perfectly safe in doing so. Fortunately, his statement and mine pretty well followed the same line of reasoning. You can't help but feel very friendly toward a person who has that much confidence in you.

Senator Henry M. Jackson, of Washington

Senator "Scoop" Jackson came to Congress as the representative of a district that included the Olympic Peninsula and sections of Seattle in the state of Washington. Later he ran for the Senate and has developed into one of the real stalwarts of that body. He threw his hat in the ring for the Democratic nomination for president of the United States in 1976.

Olympic National Park, in Washington, contains 93,000 acres and is truly a mountain wilderness, containing some of the finest remnants of the Pacific Northwest rain forest, active glaciers, and the rare Roosevelt elk herd. We went through a very rough period in the forties getting the boundary lines changed so that we could properly carry out the purpose of the park and insure preservation of the elk herd and the rain forest. It was at that time, while he was in the House of Representatives, that I really got to know Scoop Jackson. Although he came from a section of the state that had a big metropolitan area which depended a great deal on timber products, Scoop nevertheless fought for extensions of the park boundary lines. His deep concern and determined efforts were responsible to a large extent for our success. As a matter of fact, Scoop was very upset with Director Drury and me for being too conservative in recommending a boundary line adjustment, and he had a right to be. We were recommending what we thought we could get Congress to approve and not what we really felt was needed. That was the last time I did that.

I spoke of the growth of the national park system during the years that Wayne Aspinall was chairman of the Public Lands Committee of the House, and it must be noted that Senator Jackson was chairman of the committee of the Senate that handled the same bills. He and his committee also deserve a high rating, because all the bills that I listed for Aspinall had to get through Scoop's committee too, and they did.

Lyndon B. Johnson, of Texas

It is difficult to enumerate all that Lyndon Johnson did for conservationist causes from the time he first went to Congress as a representative from Texas in 1937. In the thirties we had CCC camps in his district. I had several meetings with Lyndon and got to know him very well. Our friendship lasted all through his years in Washington, where he served as representative, senator, vice-president, and president. He was interested in and deeply concerned about people, and consequently he was a strong supporter of the National Park Service and, in fact, of all agencies, both national and state, that were dedicated to providing open space for the people and for the preservation of plant and animal life.

He was ably assisted by his wife, Lady Bird Johnson, the leader in a voluntary national program striving for a more beautiful country. At her request I became a member of the Committee for a More Beautiful National Capital. She is a gracious lady and very active in all conservation and human relations fields. She is a trustee of the National Geographic Society and, with President Johnson, she took part in the dedication of the new National Geographic Building in Washington.

I will not try to recount all the instances when I bothered LBJ during the many years he was in Congress or the fewer occasions when he was president. I have already related in Chapter 10 the courtesy he extended to the American Institute of Park Executives and the National Conference on State Parks in 1963, when as vice-president he appeared as a surprise speaker. By the time he was serving his regular term as president, the National Recreation and Park Association was fully formed, consisting of several societies in the recreation and park fields—among them the American Institute of Park Executives, the National Conference on State Parks, the National Recreation Association, the Recreation Society, the Metropolitan Park Commissioners, and the Military and Therapeutic Recreation Societies. In the early fall of 1967 we were holding our first big meeting in Washington, and I undertook on behalf of the NRPA to get the president to address us at our banquet. There were over 2,500 members of the organization present. The election year 1968 was close at hand, and though I made several contacts with the White House, I could not get any assurance of an acceptance because the president's schedule was packed with speaking engagements. We got the secretary of agriculture to agree to address the banquet if the president was unable to make it.

On the day of the banquet I learned that the president was campaigning in New Jersey but was expected back late in the afternoon and was to leave the following day for Hawaii. But there was still no definite answer as to whether he could come to the banquet. About five o'clock, having heard nothing, I called the White House again. I told them my problem, and although they did not commit themselves, they asked what the president and the first lady should wear, which gave me some encouragement. I answered that they could come any way they wished. The man on the telephone said, "I cannot give you a definite reply, but I suggest that you go to your room in the hotel, get ready for the dinner, and wait there for a definite answer." I did. An hour ticked by, and shortly after six o'clock there was a knock on our door. It was a secret service man who came in and started asking questions. Then there was another knock, and it was a lieutenant of the Washington Metropolitan Police Department. They both were asking questions when a third knock on the door announced the hotel's house detective. I figured we were all set.

The dinner was almost over when we got word from a police officer that the president and first lady were on their way and would arrive very shortly. We met them out on the landing and escorted them to the receiving parlor. They sat down for a minute and President Johnson asked me what he should say. I told him just to be himself and say whatever he wished. We took him on up to the banquet hall, and he got a great ovation. President Johnson was escorted in by Laurance Rockefeller, who was president of the NRPA, and James Evans, a trustee who was master of ceremonies. After the Johnsons had finished their meal, the usual announcement was made: "Ladies and Gentle-

President Lyndon B. Johnson asked me to come over and visit him on my last day in office, January 9, 1964. The conversation wasn't all as serious as it looks. We were very good friends. *Photo by Abbie Rowe, courtesy the White House.*

men, the President of the United States." Johnson's first remark was that Lady Bird and he were going to build a state park on their ranch in Texas, and right there and then he appointed Laurance Rockefeller chairman of the finance committee and me in charge of plans. That came as a big surprise. Anyway, I took his charge seriously. He gave a very good talk, and the evening was a huge success.

I learned later that the president had already had some contacts with the National Park Service through Secretary of the Interior Stewart L. Udall and also with the state park people, asking them to get together on his park project at the ranch; so I was the third party in the picture. I found there was some disagreement between the federal and state groups as to what should be done. Finally, being unable to get the two agencies together, I proceeded to draw up my own sketch. I sent these plans to my son Ted, whose firm of landscape architects and planners is in Billings, Montana. His people put it in finished form. Laurance Rockefeller liked the plan and helped me present it to the first lady. I also sent a copy to the National Park Service and the state park people. With some minor changes it was accepted, although not entirely by all those involved; but at least the president and the first lady thought it was very good, and the park has been built along the lines of those plans.

I will close these reminiscences about the Johnsons with the letter LBJ sent me when I retired from the National Park Service on January 8, 1964.

Dear Connie:

Your decision to retire as Director of the National Park Service is tinged with sadness for me—and I am sure for the many legions of friends that you have made while building the peoples' parks to their present prominence in our scheme of a better life.

It has been a great pleasure to labor with you and others of your dedication and ability in the public's interest, and I am pleased to learn that you have accepted appointment to the Senior Advisory Board of the National Parks. This way your experience and imagination will still be available.

Thank you for your many years of service and friendship dating back to those days, almost 30 years ago, when we first started building a National Park through Civilian Conservation Corps labor. I hope that some day again we have the opportunity to "walk along the river together."

Sincerely,
Lyndon B. Johnson

The river to which the president referred is the Pedernales, which runs through the Johnson Ranch in front of the ranch house.

12

Advice: Good and Bad

Anyone who has worked in government, whether federal, state, or local, will know what I mean when I say that a public servant is subjected to an unlimited amount of unsolicited advice on an unlimited number of subjects. Some of it has value, but much of it is absolutely worthless. In a lower-level job one is spared the brunt of this assault; but as one advances in rank and assumes more responsibility, one not only gets more advice but realizes how valuable it can be when it comes from well-informed, judicious sources. In any case, one has to listen, smile, and thank everyone for the advice offered.

Some of this advice comes via Capitol Hill, which introduces additional complications. I have received telephone calls from members of Congress telling me that they have written me a letter on a certain matter in stronger terms than they wanted to use but that this was necessary because a copy was being sent to a constituent. This kind of letter is not answered in the same vein. It must be answered honestly, expressing a firm stand on what is believed to be right, because the reply is usually sent on to the constituent. The rationale for handling letters received through congressional referral emphasizes the difference between an elected or politically appointed official and a career civil service person. The former is obliged to please his constituents as much as possible, while the latter is charged with administering the laws in accordance with the policies and regulations in his department or agency. When the civil service must give a citizen a negative answer, it must state it firmly but as diplomatically as possible.

I have been involved in a number of politically sensitive situations. Some are recounted elsewhere in this book, but one instance should be related here. A relatively high-ranking politically appointed officer made a definite attack on the Park Service and on me for no really good reason, other than to stimulate his ego. He caused quite a rumpus in the upper echelon of the department, and even though the discussions took place behind closed doors, the information was leaked and came to me loud and clear. For a while it was a question whether the person making the attack should resign. Some time later I had an occasion to write a letter on the subject, and I pinpointed what had happened and cleared several people who were thought to have had something to do with it. Shortly thereafter I got a handwritten note from a highly placed official of the department, part of which stated: "You have been one of the 'magnificent bureaucrats' of our day, and I hope by now that the unfortunate events of last October have been forgotten." I have forgiven the guilty one, but I have not forgotten. One should not forget his experiences no matter how unpleasant, because experiences are the foundation of the road to the future. I believe that ultimately the nasty attack on the service and on me did more good than harm.

A lot can be learned from politicians, and I can't help but repeat a story I heard over the radio a week before the 1976 New Hampshire primary election. Representative Morris (Mo) Udall was running for the Democratic presidential nomination along with some eight or ten others. As he approached a gathering of prospective voters in a meeting room, he heard a lot of laughter. When he got inside he was greeted by the presiding officer, who said, "I was just telling these people that you are running for president." Mo replied with a big smile, "Yes, and I heard all the laughing." That got a loud laugh and a big hand, and it broke the ice. This bit of humor must have got him quite a few votes from the people in that room.

Having written about members of Congress and in-government relationships in other chapters, I will now turn to the activities of individuals and organizations outside of government. About two years after I became director of the National Park Service, I received a letter from an old friend, Joe Prendergast, an official of the old National Recreation Association. At the time he lived in Alexandria, just across the river from Washington. He signed the letter as president of a historical association. He was disturbed about the possibility that the National Park Service would reroute the George Washington Parkway along the Alexandria waterfront. His letter resulted in a meeting in my office, and we talked for about a half-hour. Just before he left I said, "Joe, I haven't heard of your historical association; it's new to me. How many members do you have?" With a smile he told me that he was the only member and that he had the letterhead run off as a gag. He added that he thought it would help him get in to see me so that he could go into detail about preserving the historic Alexandria waterfront. He further said he would be very glad to have me as a member without dues and he could elect me vice-president. I declined.

I don't know how many associations there are in this country, but I dare say we have more organizations concerned with the conservation of natural and historic resources than any other country in the world. As director I took out membership in nearly every organization that might have a bearing on the activities of the National Park Service. My dues amounted to over $1,200 annually, or almost 7 percent of my salary. It was the best way for me to keep tabs on what was going on, and it was educational. I learned a lot about people and their thinking, individually and collectively. Now my memberships are limited to organizations in which I have a very definite professional interest and personal association, though these still number over two dozen.

Private organizations and special-interest groups can bring considerable pressure to bear on a public agency. One of the problems we had on Yellowstone Lake will serve to illustrate. Motorboats of a certain size are permitted on the lake, and all the launching sites are either at the north end or near Fishing Bridge, Bridge Bay, and West Thumb. About 80 percent of the lakeshore is thus left in wilderness. We wanted to keep all motorboats out of the area south of Frank Island, especially the southern half of the Southeast Arm. Several streams flow into the lake at that location, including the Upper Yellowstone River. Over many thousands of years these streams have formed deltas and small, low islands with sandy shores. On the sandbars certain kinds of birds made their nests. Much to our concern *some* people took great delight in speeding their boats by the sandbars to make waves and see the birds fly away, and sometimes the waves would flood the nests. Of course there were other good reasons for keeping motorboats out of such wilderness regions, but this kind of behavior by motorboat users, even if unintentional, left us no alternative but to close the South and Southeast arms to them. Yellowstone Lake is a large lake, and the closing of these two arms—which amounted to 20,000 acres of water surface with 90 miles of shoreline—still left around 90,000 acres of water surface and 110 miles of shoreline open to motorboating. Nevertheless, closing the area below Frank Island to motorboats brought a great deal of pressure on the service from a small but well-organized group of motorboat owners and even from an assistant secretary of the department who came from a nearby state. This pressure made it necessary for the service to hold five public hearings in and around Yellowstone at considerable expense. Thanks to help from several national conservation organizations, we were able to hold our ground. The protesters did not represent anywhere near even 10 percent of the people who lived around the park or a majority of those who owned motorboats.

There was another case where a large commercial company took over a choice camping spot for the entire season, even though camping was limited to two weeks per camper, by using the names of some ten people in the company on different applications for camping permits. They moved in a large, expensive trailer for the summer and assigned it at different times to some of their best customers as a business promotion, thus depriving the general vacationing public of camping opportunities. Of course when the superintendent got wise to what was going on, he put a stop to it but not without protests. We bureaucrats were spoiling their business.

The national park system exists for the benefit of all the people, and it must be so managed that its natural and historic values will be available, let us say, in the year 2066, when Joe Doaks and Agnes Hobbleskirt will be born. Such is the responsibility of the service, or, if you prefer, the bureaucrats. I am sure that the people who objected to restricting the motorboats on Yellowstone Lake and those unscrupulous businessmen with their trailer and political partners blamed the bureaucrats for stopping them. I was a bureaucrat and am proud of it, and furthermore I am sick and tired of hearing everyone who runs for political office blame the bureaucrats for doing what is required of them even when some individuals don't like it.

So much for a very brief analysis of the climate in which a bureaucrat finds himself and which he must accept as a part of our governmental structure. If a career bureaucrat is to be successful he must never forget the right of the people—his fellow citizens and fellow taxpayers—to petition their government. He must listen to all the people, even though he may consider some of their ideas, suggestions, and demands to be more detrimental than helpful to the nation as a whole.

I have never before attempted to classify conservation organizations according to motivation, but on the basis of long experience in dealing with them I find it tempting. Actually, such sociological taxonomy is better applied to individuals than to organizations, because permanent organizations vary in emphasis and approach from year to year depending on their leadership, whereas an individual's thinking and habits don't usually change very much. I would say that conservationists fall into half a dozen classifications: (1) *Pests* are constantly after government about something that is of no importance except to them, and they are never consistent in their demands. They lack experience but feel they have to stick their cotton-picking fingers into everything. They are the hardest ones to avoid and the last to contribute any constructive ideas. (2) *Endrunners* are always running to the congressman, the secretary, the governor—anybody in higher authority—to complain, to ask the authority to overrule an administrator, or to submit a request on almost anything they think the bureaucrats would not approve. They are always on the job. (3) *Followers* will sign any petition. Pests and endrunners circulate petitions for and against projects, and some of the same names will be found on both. The people who sign just don't think, or perhaps they don't even read the petitions; they simply sign when asked. (4) *Constructive thinkers* are usually pretty competent. They will study a problem carefully, and if they feel strongly about it, they will offer constructive suggestions, most of which will usually be helpful. They can be reasoned with because they are invariably kind and courteous and understand when they are told why something can't be done. (5) *Professionals* are good to have around. If highly specialized in their own field, however, they may not understand the necessity of blending the principles of all professional fields to satisfy the requirements and habits of park users and at the same time protect the features of the park. If they had a little broader vision, most professionals would fit in the next classification. (6) *Consultants*, because of their experience, study, and observation, have the ability to analyze a problem from many angles and are willing to sit down and help work out plans for solving it. While a consultant's final analysis of a situation might differ from the administrator's, he will probably introduce new thoughts worthy of consideration and his contribution could have a definite effect on the final solution.

I recall one particular case in which a park superintendent was plagued by the first category of conservationist. Great Smoky Mountains National Park had a fire lookout tower on Clingman's Dome that was old and rickety and hard to climb, yet it was a wonderful place for people to go because they could see for many miles in all directions. It was a replacement item in the Mission 66 program. Fred Overly was park superintendent at the time it was to be replaced. He had previously been superintendent of Olympic National Park in the state of Washington and had been severely criticized by conservation people in the Northwest. I'd known Fred for years: he was high-strung, but he had imagination and ingenuity. At Olympic during the cold war when money was scarce he had conceived an idea—which we all knew about—of taking down trees with dangerous snags in them around the park camping areas as a safety measure for campers. Trees also had to be removed to build roads into a camping area. In letting the contract for the road work, Overly saved money by having the contractor stack stripped-down trees along the roadside instead of hauling them away. He then arranged with lumber mills in Port Angeles to have the trees sawed into boards. The mills gave half of the boards to the park and kept half in payment for their trouble. Then Overly went to the high school and got the manual training teacher to have his classes build a visitor center for the park as a training project. It turned out to be a very nice and useful building. Some conservation-minded people complained, however, that Overly had taken down the trees just to build a visitor center. The pressure on the park superintendent was so great by the time I became director that I reassigned him as superintendent of Great Smokies. When replacement of the old, unsafe iron fire lookout tower on Clingman's Dome was scheduled, it was suggested that we build a concrete spiral ramp instead of stairs up the new tower so that people in wheelchairs or those who could not otherwise manage the steps could enjoy the view and see how the rangers spot forest fires. Well, certain eastern conservationists immediately got after Overly for proposing to build a concrete ramp instead of wooden steps. They pointed out that there was plenty of wood in the park that could be used at a saving. I can just see Fred now as he told me what he said to them. He told them: "I was superintendent of Olympic National Park and people like you complained because I did just what you are suggesting, so I was moved here, and for your information I'm never going to use even a twig in this park. You people complain no matter what we do, and that's that."

According to Fred they did not know what else to say, and so they left and he heard nothing more from them about the tower.

Some organizations are always looking for a fight. They have got to have a cause for raising money. In some conservationist publications I've seen photographs that make it look as though the Park Service were taking a whole mountain down to build a park drive. The organizations may even be in agreement with a project but write up their campaign in their books in such a way as to suggest they fought for a long time, finally forcing the Park Service to take action. They end up taking full credit for the accomplishment. When I retired I wrote a letter to one organization stating that I'd been a member for over thirty years, that I had read its booklets and pamphlets, and that although they had championed the national parks they had never said a kind word about the service or given it credit for anything it did. I never received a reply.

There have been good organizations that supported the efforts of the Park Service but that nevertheless turned against the service when their leadership changed. I can find no better illustration of this than the Sierra Club's views on the planning and construction of the Tioga Road in Yosemite National Park. Before the park was established, this road was a mining wagon road. It is the only road in the national park system that goes over the High Sierra and even now can be used only in the summer months. Its function is twofold: to permit people coming from the east to get into Yosemite National Park without first going far north or far south; and, most important, to provide an opportunity for people who cannot hike or ride horseback to see that most impressive great expanse of the High Sierra.

I crossed the Tioga Road in 1924, before I had any idea of becoming a Park Service man. Then it was a very narrow, winding mountain dirt road, difficult for automobiles to travel. Over the years, to accommodate the gradually increasing automobile travel, the park maintenance program had improved some of the curves and grades, paved the road in some places, and provided turnouts to allow cars to pass each other. But as travel increased and cars got larger, the number of accidents and complaints from visitors skyrocketed. Rangers assigned to this district had to undertake the burdensome chore of listening to unhappy park visitors. No matter how much the park staff improved and patched the old road, the accidents and hazards continued to increase, and it became evident by the late twenties that major reconstruction would be required over the entire route.

When reconstruction was started in the early thirties with PWA funds, the team of engineers and landscape architects worked closely on the location, alignments, grades, cuts, and fills; and all road structures, including bridges, culverts, parking areas, and the like, were blended into the natural landscape. In addition to review and approval within the National Park Service, the Tioga Road project was reviewed and approved on a continuing basis by the Yosemite Advisory Board, a group of citizens prominent in the conservation field. They included such Sierra Club members as Walter Huber, a prominent San Francisco engineer and conservationist; Frederick Law Olmsted, Jr.; and William E. Colby. They and the Sierra Club gave their approval of the project, subject to minor changes, back in the thirties.

By the fifties the most difficult section, some ten miles, had not been completed, and we hoped to finish it under the Mission 66 program. We began to run into trouble, however, with certain conservationists and with the engineers in the Bureau of Public Roads, even though we had decided to proceed on the route that had been selected and approved earlier.

We did make some very minor changes in order to meet improved safety standards. I went to the field and met with our design and construction people and with David Brower and Ansel Adams. Brower, then executive secretary of the Sierra Club, and Adams, the famous nature photographer, were violent protestors. In our discussions I believe we covered nearly every possible objection and suggestion. Their suggestions were feasible from a construction standpoint but not an improvement in any way over the approved alignment. Further, they were more costly. I asked why they had changed their minds, since the Sierra Club had approved the route years before I became director. I also said that I had heard from several officials of the Sierra Club, and, though they wished the road did not have to be built, they felt that the location previously approved would be as good, if not better, than any other. Dave Brower's reply was that it was a different Sierra Club now.

The objection of the Bureau of Public Roads was that road standards had changed considerably since the thirties, and that a wider road with wider shoulders was now required. In high country with steep slopes, every foot extended out from the centerline of the road creates a scar, from both cuts and fills, much greater than on level ground and correspondingly increases the cost. We couldn't settle the question of shoulder width. The Park Service wanted a safe width of road with narrow shoulders and turnouts wherever the terrain would permit. The engineers wanted shoulders that would allow cars to pull off the road when in trouble. They indicated that if I didn't give them the shoulder width they wanted they would not undertake the project.

At this point the Park Service wrote a letter to Walter Huber, sending a copy to the Bureau of Public Roads. Huber, who had built many mining roads in the High Sierra before this part of the park was established, was a past president of the Sierra Club and past president of the American Society of Engineers. He was at that time a member of the secretary's advisory committee on national parks. We wanted to know whether our recommended two-foot shoulders were sufficient to insure structural soundness of the road, which was another objection raised by the engineers, or whether we should go to four feet as the Bureau of Public Roads held was necessary. Huber took the time to go to the road site and study the matter very carefully. He then wrote me a very full letter indicating that our two-foot shoulder was ample for that type of road, with the turnouts we had planned, except for one place of several hundred feet where he felt it would be wise to widen the shoulder to three feet to provide the stability needed for the twenty-foot road. I then wrote to the Bureau of Public Roads, sending them a copy of Huber's reply, and told them that I was accepting his suggestions, that we were determined to go ahead on the basis of Huber's findings, and that we would appreciate reconsideration of their stand. I asked that, if their decision remained unchanged, they transfer to us the basic engineering data that they had prepared and that we had paid for, so that we could proceed with an outside engineering firm. I received a very nice reply from the bureau indicating that they would proceed with the job along the lines that Huber and the Park Service wished. We were both happy that the matter was finally settled.

Our friends in the conservation field, however, kept picking at us, and we heard from many people around the country, which kept us busy writing letters. It took two more years to complete the project. After the new road was dedicated and opened to the public, we got many letters complimenting us on a job well done. Some of the letters were from people who had criticized us but admitted that they had been wrong and now enjoyed the road very much, although they found it did make a large scar on the face of the glacier-polished granite surface.

I have not mentioned all of the people the service called upon to study and review the Tioga Road project. Practically every aspect of the project that affected the natural history of the area was considered and reviewed by a person professionally well qualified to do so. This is the policy the service uses in all its planning. It often calls upon other bureaus of the government and upon universities and professional individuals outside of government for help. Whether a project involves land, plant life, wildlife, water, or air, these consultants are a very important part of the responsibilities assigned to the National Park Service and therefore are fundamental to all the service's planning.

This is not to say, of course, that there are not times when disagreements of various kinds occur between professional people. Disagreements can be stimulating and constructive and can lead to better understanding of the issues involved. In that spirit I would like to correct here one such misunderstanding of an important matter. In the American Forestry Association's publication of January, 1976, there was an article by Richard McArdle, retired former chief of the United States Forest Service, on the history of the Wilderness Bill. It stated that the National Park Service was against this

President Lyndon B. Johnson greets conservation people and presents pens after signing the Land and Water Bill and the Wilderness Bill in the Rose Garden at the White House on September 3, 1964.

legislation. The Park Service was not against the bill; we were for it. We were opposed, however, to being included in it because the protection section of the original bill was not as protective for national parks wilderness as our own basic legislation. When we convinced the mastermind behind the bill, Howard C. Zahniser, of that fact, he readily adjusted the wording so that the basic standards already established for us by Congress would prevail in the national parks, and we supported the revised bill. I should explain that Dick McArdle is an old friend of mine. He and I received the Rockefeller Public Service Award the same year, and he convinced me to write this book.

One of the greatest interagency programs was, of course, the CCC. To expound on this subject of cooperation and exchange of knowledge just a little further, I quote from a letter that Secretary of the Interior Harold L. Ickes received from Fred Morrell, the representative of the Department of Agriculture on the CCC Advisory Council:

> The CCC was, as you know, a large-scale social conservation undertaking that attracted world-wide attention. Its administration necessitated interdepartmental cooperation on a scale not previously attempted in the government of this, or perhaps any other country. Departmental interests were continuously in conflict. These dif-

Connie Wirth, of the National Park Service, and Fred Morrell, of the U.S. Forest Service, highly respected each other. They handled the CCC programs for the Departments of the Interior and Agriculture and worked closely together.

ferences had to be adjusted by yielding and compromise, and both Interior and Agriculture had to sacrifice interests and priorities, and work for the good of the Corps as a whole. Never in the nine years that I worked with Conrad Wirth did he violate a pact we made in 1933, that neither would advance the interests of his respective department without first advising the other and giving him an opportunity to present his case if he did not agree.

Mr. Wirth represented Interior's interests with remarkable vigor and ability, but as a part of a national program of conservation and not as an Interior's attorney out to win his case, regardless of its merits.

The interesting thing about this is that I wrote a similar letter to the secretary of agriculture. Both were written and sent at about the same time, and neither of us knew that the other was going to write such a complimentary letter about his colleague. These letters should certainly serve to dispel the general belief that there is a lack of cooperation between bureaus and departments of the government. We do disagree from time to time, but that should not prevent cooperation and the lending of a helping hand where needed.

13

Some Observations from Retirement

Over the last twenty years there have been increased violations of the purpose and intent of the civil service system. Most of them have introduced patronage by changing methods of operation and disregarding the basic principle of a career service embodied in the Civil Service Act. In July, 1975, the comptroller general submitted to Congress a report that criticized actions of the Civil Service Commission and referred to some of the violations of the act.

THE CIVIL SERVICE AND "SCHEDULE C"

Some time in the late forties and early fifties, word came out that some civil service positions of high grade were to be placed in a "Schedule C" classification and that the people in those grades could be reassigned to other positions in the government. This concept has some real merit, provided such changes are based on sound administrative judgment; however, it is easily abused and that abuse has for all intents and purposes grown to the extent that it is destroying the main reason for the establishment of civil service.

Shortly after the beginning of the Eisenhower administration, word came down from Interior Secretary McKay of a proposal to place the positions of director of the National Park Service and some seven top personnel on his staff, together with their secretaries, in "Schedule C." I strongly objected, not only because such a step would forfeit the long years of special training and experience required to develop capable people in the specialities needed to plan, develop, and administer the national park system, but also because it disturbed the general morale of people in the organization who felt that they were going to be traded around like professional ball players. Any one of us could be moved to any other agency, and goodness knows who might be sent in to fill our positions. The National Park Service is a professional career service, and its effectiveness lies in that fact. By the time a person gets into the upper grades of the civil service in the National Park Service, he becomes very valuable to the service. On the average, he will have had about twenty years of administrative experience with national parks and be in his upper forties or early fifties, and it would be rather late for him to start a new career.

After several meetings the secretary approved the placing of only the director's position and that of his secretary under the new schedule. But as years went by more positions were gradually placed in the "Schedule C" category until at the present time, I understand, all or most of the so-called supergrades—16, 17, and 18—are classified in the "Schedule C" designation. An "executive" classification has also been established in which the top supergrade positions have been placed by executive order of the president. At the present time any person who accepts an appointment classified as executive grade must give up his civil service rating and agree to serve at the pleasure of the secretary.

By the last year of the first Nixon term, the National Park Service began to get requests from the White House to give certain people jobs. Many of these applications were returned with the explanation that the individuals were not qualified. Word came back to the Park Service from the White House to put them on because refusal to do so would interfere with the president's program. About that time the director of the National Park Service, a long-term career man in his fifties, was requested to submit his resignation, and it is my understanding that other bureau chiefs of the departments were asked to do the same. Director George Hartzog submitted his resignation under protest. He had to resign because he was in the executive classification. It was accepted, and in 1973 a White House staff man with no experience in the parks was appointed director of the National Park Service. After the new director took over, it wasn't long before some twenty or so additional people were brought into the service with qualifications unrelated to the positions they filled. The new director, Ron Walker, was a nice enough fellow and tried hard, but he was politically motivated and it was this that caused him to do some things that were very detrimental to the national park system. Many of us tried to help him, but it was like putting up a brick building with putty in place of mortar.

By the end of 1974, Walker resigned and Secretary Rogers C. B. Morton made an in-depth study, both inside and outside the service, to find a well-qualified person to be the new director. He ended up appointing a career Park Service man, Gary Everhardt. Here again, Everhardt had to give up his civil service rights because the position is still in the executive classification.

I feel sure that Secretary Morton had nothing to do with the selection of Ron Walker. And I do not wish to imply that the secretary would not have made a good selection of a new director of the Park Service to succeed Walker. But I must say that Gary Everhardt was on a list of five suggested candidates that was drawn up by Park Service retirees ("alumni") at their reunion in Yosemite National Park in the early fall of 1974. Following is the letter to Secretary Morton that the alumni committee asked me to sign on their behalf, along with Morton's reply. I wrote a similar letter to the White

Ron Walker, director of the National Park Service from January 1, 1973, to January 3, 1975.

Gary Everhardt, director of the National Park Service from January 13, 1975, to May 27, 1977.

House and got a reply a long time later; both of these letters are also reproduced below, as is my second letter to the White House.

October 7, 1974

Honorable Rogers C. B. Morton
Secretary of the Interior
Washington, D. C. 20240

Dear Mr. Secretary:

At the meeting of the Old Timers in Yosemite National Park, Sunday, September 29 through October 1, there were over 120 Park Service Retirees present, and the Chairman of the Employees and Alumni Association called a meeting of a special committee to discuss what action or steps, if any, should be taken by the Alumni of the National Park Service in connection with returning the Service to Career Civil Service status. Attached to this letter is a list of those who attended that meeting; and an additional number of the Alumni who had been contacted expressed their support of the committee's deliberations.

One of the decisions reached was that I should address a letter to the President of the United States on the general subject of Civil Service, especially as it relates to the

National Park Service, and a letter to you suggesting individuals presently in the service whom we feel you should consider in selecting the new Director of the National Park Service. In other words, Mr. Secretary, we want to be helpful. Further we can't help but feel deeply concerned about the agency that we spent a lifetime working in, and we're proud of the National Park System and Service. We know full well that the responsibility for the appointment is yours and not ours, but we also believe that we know the career people and how they fit into an organization and whether they would be accepted as the Director by their associates. We feel that these factors of selection can be best communicated to you by those who have been closely associated with the growth and history of the Service. What we're trying to convey to you, Mr. Secretary, is our deep interest and most profound desire to help the National Park Service meet its administrative and assigned responsibility with full adherence to its purpose so ably expressed in the basic legislation. We know this objective is also yours, but I guess what we are trying to say is, "This is a family matter and we think Grandpas are part of the family also."

We are listing five people we feel should be given careful consideration, and we are willing to meet and discuss their qualifications in detail if you so desire. [Identification of the individuals recommended to the secretary is deleted out of consideration for them; obviously, Gary Everhardt was one of them.]

I'm sure the background of each of these individuals is fully exposed in the personnel files of the Department. We feel that the appointment of any one of them would be well received by the field. They have all had a certain amount of administrative work in a central office either in Washington or in the regions.

I would like to say personally a word about Ron Walker, and I think the others on the committee would endorse my statement regarding him. Ron is a likeable person who tried hard. There were several things which some of us objected to or felt were unnecessary, although one very fine thing he did was to move considerable authority to the field. However, we feel that he lacked the qualifications and experience to head up a bureau like the National Park Service, and that's not really his fault. There are quite a few of us, however, who would like to have had a greater opportunity to help more than we did.

We beg of you, Mr. Secretary, to give our suggestions careful consideration. If for any reason these suggestions are not acceptable and you wish to discuss with us other people you have in mind, I'm sure that any individual among us or a group of members of the Alumni Committee will be glad to be consulted.

Sincerely yours,

Conrad L. Wirth
For the Alumni Committee

United States Department of the Interior
OFFICE OF THE SECRETARY
WASHINGTON, D.C. 20240

Oct. 25, 1974

Dear Connie:

I appreciate your October 7 letter regarding the appointment of a new Director of the National Park Service when that position becomes vacant. Would you please also relay my gratitude to the other members of your special committee of the Alumni? I hope that all of you already know I value your counsel.

As you might well imagine, we have received a number of recommendations, not to overlook first person applicants. The qualifications of the five persons of your Alumni Committee selected for specific mention are, of course, well known. The five certainly have every right to be proud of being singled out by such a distinguished group, whose combined public service must total more than three centuries.

When the time comes to make the appointment from among the many names before us, it will be a serious responsibility, hardly to be treated lightly, and I regard your recommendations with gravity.

I know the high standards you and your fellow alumni have in mind. And, surely you understand we will insist upon a selection with the professional skills and managerial talent equal to the position. You have my assurance your recommendations will be given the most thorough consideration.

With best wishes.

Sincerely yours,
(Sgd) Rog
Secretary of the Interior

Mr. Conrad L. Wirth
9633 East Bexhill Drive
Rock Creek Hills
Kensington, Maryland 20795

CONRAD L. WIRTH
9633 EAST BEXHILL DRIVE
ROCK CREEK HILLS
KENSINGTON, MARYLAND 20795

October 7, 1974

The President
The White House
Washington, D.C.

Dear Mr. President:

On Saturday, September 28, while I was in San Francisco on my way to Yosemite National Park, I heard on T.V. your statement on inflation and the economy, and I thought it was a very good one. . . . When I arrived at Yosemite I found I was not the only one that heard your talk, and that it had instilled in people the feeling that a sound plan of attack on inflation would soon be made public. We will all pitch in and help in every way we can.

The meeting I attended in Yosemite was a gathering of some 125 Old Timers—retired Park Service employees—to celebrate the 84th anniversary of the establishment of Yosemite and to do honor to John Emmert and James Lloyd who were the first two rangers in Yosemite when the National Park Service was established as a career organization in 1916. . . .

Mr. President, the Alumni and employees of the National Park Service want most sincerely to have the Service restored to the status of a career service. It had always been a career service until 1973 when, for the first time, the President requested the Director to submit his resignation and then appointed a person who knew nothing about parks. Director Ron Walker did the best he could, worked hard, and is a friendly person; however, he resigned as of January 1, 1975, and the professional park people most sincerely request that the Service be returned to career Civil Service status.

Mr. President, there were distributed copies of the article by Carol Kilpatrick in the *Washington Post* of September 21 and we like very much what you said about the Civil Service. We must report that the National Park Service has suffered from the strong assault on the federal career system. We have been informed that in the last several years over 50 career positions in the Service have been taken over by non-Civil Service people whose qualifications are questionable. Well qualified and trained career people, whether in government or private enterprise, can produce the best job, and the best job is the best politics in the long run. We urge most strongly that the present Administration return the National Park Service to its career Civil Service status. We also strongly believe that the national policy must be determined and defined by the Administration and the Congress, and that the professional career personnel are subservient to the Secretary in carrying out the policies of the Government.

The National Park Service down through the years starting with the Mather-Albright period has been a well trained, hard working, progressive organization always willing to work with and carry out the policies of the Government. The "C" classification imposed on the three highest grades of Civil Service has been destructive of the intended Civil Service as originally established. It has weakened the Civil Service structure and lowered the morale of many agencies of government. Under these conditions highly trained professional employees have left their jobs at the first opportunity.

Mr. President, we urge that as part of your anti-inflation effort you return to a sound quality employment program. We feel that such a move will produce better work, at less cost.

This letter and a letter to Secretary Morton have been written under instructions and on behalf of a Committee of Alumni appointed by the Chairman of the Employees and Alumni Association of the National Park Service. Attached is a list of the Committee. The active employees who are members of the Association have had no part in the actions taken by the Committee, and as far as I know have no knowledge that this letter and the letter to the Secretary are being written. We retirees want to be helpful, and in as much as this switch over to political appointment of a Director took place during a Republican Administration we are hopeful that "an in house" correction can be made. We are of a definite feeling that Ron Walker's appointment came out of the White House, hence this letter to you. A copy of this letter is being sent to Secretary Morton so that he will be fully advised of our feelings.

We join with you and all Americans in our prayers for the First Lady.

Sincerely yours,

Conrad L. Wirth
For the Alumni Committee

THE WHITE HOUSE
WASHINGTON

November 8, 1974

Dear Mr. Wirth:

On behalf of the President, thank you for your October 7 letter with its generous compliments on his remarks at the closing of the summit conference on the economy, and your pledge to pitch in to do your part to help whip inflation. Your support of his September 20 memorandum on the Civil Service is also appreciated very much. It was most kind of you to add your good wishes for the First Lady's rapid recovery.

We note with interest your request that the National Park Service "be returned to career Civil Service status". It has remained in the career Civil Service without interruption, and shall continue. An agency's Civil Service status is in no way destroyed by requiring the agency's uppermost officials to be directly and personally responsible to those who in turn supervise them.

We regret that we cannot agree with your assessment that the Civil Service structure has been weakened by non-career classifications placed upon some positions in the three highest Civil Service grades.

You may be aware that legislation has been introduced which would make a number of additional agency positions subject to Senate confirmation. Indeed, the Congress recently wrote into law a requirement that the Director of the Park Service's sister agency in the environmental field, the Fish and Wildlife Service, be a Presidential appointee subject to Senate confirmation.

If Cabinet and sub-Cabinet officers are to have adequate direction over the bureaus they are charged with supervising, then they must have control over the appointment of the top bureau administrators. It seems abundantly clear that, regardless of which Administration holds office, the Legislative Branch agrees with the Executive Branch on that point.

In this same regard, I understand that 26 members of the House Committee on Interior and Insular Affairs have signed a letter to Secretary Morton stressing that his search for a new Director should not be limited to present or former employees of the National Park Service. Unquestionably, there are men and women without prior Park Service affiliation whose qualifications ought to be considered.

We appreciate your continuing support of the National Park Service, and can assure you of the President's commitment to the selection of qualified personnel.

Sincerely,

Norman E. Ross, Jr.
Assistant Director
Domestic Council

Mr. Conrad L. Wirth
9633 East Bexhill Drive
Rock Creek Hills
Kensington, Maryland 20795

CONRAD L. WIRTH
9633 EAST BEXHILL DRIVE
KENSINGTON, MARYLAND 20795

November 18, 1974

Mr. Norman E. Ross, Jr.
Assistant Director
Domestic Council
The White House
Washington, D.C.

Dear Mr. Ross:

I must answer your letter of November 8th. It is hard for me to believe that such a letter as yours could come out of the White House. Further, it is my firm belief that it doesn't exemplify the *present* administration.

Your attitude, as expressed in the second paragraph, is destructive of the Civil Service. The National Park Service, like many of the other Bureaus, is composed of professional people, and when you put a political staff of some twenty-five people or more in the top jobs you destroy the agency's character and morale. The Administration's policies and major administrative control rest in the hands of the Secretary and his Assistant Secretariate staff. The present Director is a nice enough fellow, but when he was sent over from the White House he was not equipped by training or experience to be Director. The NPS has, down through the years, done a good job, in my opinion, and supported the Administrative policies. It is hard for me to see why the change was made in January 1973. I am inclined to believe that it was a White House, rather than a Department decision.

As to your third paragraph, you do not seem qualified to make such a statement. Enclosed are some newspaper articles on the subject.

Regarding your fourth paragraph, yes, I know of this, but it never would have happened except for the things that have been taking place in the last six years, especially since January 1973. However, if the C classifications are going to provide the requirement of confirmation by the Senate of future Directors, this is the only sure means left to guarantee the appointment of qualified people. Such appointments will call for public hearings.

I agree with the statement in your fifth paragraph, the Director of the NPS has always been appointed by the Secretary. However, six of the first seven Directors and their staffs were career people, and the other one was an excellent conservationist and well qualified. It was at the beginning of the second Nixon administration that not only the Park Service but other Bureaus as well found non-qualified political personnel taking over.

As to your sixth paragraph, I agree it is quality that is needed, if you are going to do a good job. Further, when you pick quality for a Civil Service job you strengthen the Career Service. On the other hand, there are a lot of well qualified and loyal people in the National Park Service that could help the Administration in office. Remember, it has been proven, time and again, during the two hundred years of our Republic, that the good job is the best politics, and that can't be done without qualified people. We have left the old ward-heeling type of politics far behind.

I have answered your letter at length, because it needed an answer. I get the feeling from your letter that whoever prepared it had neglected his research.

I assume you know I am a retired government employee with 35 years of Federal service. I started during the Hoover administration and retired in the early part of the Johnson administration. The last twelve years I was Director of the National Park Service, including eight years of the Eisenhower administration. It was President Eisenhower's approval of the National Park Service, Mission 66 program at a Cabinet meeting presentation arranged by Max Rabb that pre-dated the national upsurge in the park and recreation programs. The President shortly thereafter established the Outdoor Recreation Resources Review Commission which resulted in the establishment of the Bureau of Outdoor Recreation and their nationwide programs. I am an independent, and voted for President Nixon in 1972. I like President Ford, and like very much his selection for Vice President.

I'm telling you this because I want you to know I am not a nut. I want to be constructive and I dislike seeing a lecture-type letter such as you signed come out of the White House, especially while President Ford is there. It is very poor politics.

Sincerely,
Conrad L. Wirth

Ross never replied to this letter, nor did anyone else.

The June, 1973, issue of the *National Park Courier*, the newspaper published by the Employees and Alumni Association of the National Park Service, printed an editorial I had written on this subject. I sent a copy of it to several senators. Senator Jacob K. Javits, of New York, thereupon wrote a letter to the Civil Service Commission referring to my published views and requesting a statement of the commission's position on the issues I had raised. Following are the commission's reply to Senator Javits, a letter which I addressed to the commission in 1975 raising new questions, and the commission's response to me.

UNITED STATES CIVIL SERVICE COMMISSION
BUREAU OF EXECUTIVE MANPOWER
WASHINGTON D.C. 20415

4 Sep. 1973

Honorable Jacob K. Javits
United States Senate
Washington, D.C. 20510

Dear Senator Javits:

This is in response to your letter of August 9, 1973, asking our views on the allegation regarding politicizing of civil service positions in the National Park Service, as stated by Mr. Conrad S. Wirth in an editorial in the June issue of the *National Park Courier*. Mr. Wirth expresses his feeling that the position of Director and other top-level positions in the National Park Service have become political positions and the filling of these positions by nonprofessional appointees has a deleterious effect on the morale of career employees.

The position of Director, National Park Service, was placed in Executive Level V of the Executive Schedule by Executive Order 11189, effective August 15, 1964, and upon recommendation of the Secretary of the Interior it was excepted from the competitive service. The position of Deputy Director, National Park Service, was abolished July 9, 1971 and has not been reestablished. Prior to that date it was filled by noncareer executive assignment since it was first established in January 1967. Noncareer executive assignments are authorized by the Civil Service Commission when the incumbent will be deeply involved in the advocacy of Administration programs and support of their controversial aspects; participate significantly in the determination of major political policies of the Administration; or serve principally as a confidential assistant to a Presidential appointee.

Since it was established in 1967 until it was abolished in 1971, the position of Deputy Director was filled by long-term career employees of the National Park Service, serving under noncareer executive assignments. Since the position is noncareer, the incumbents have had to voluntarily relinquish their career tenure to accept the Deputy Director assignment. The position of Director, National Park Service, has been filled historically by career employees, who likewise voluntarily relinquished career status.

The vast majority of supergrade positions are filled on a career basis by career employees. Each request from an agency for excepting a position from the competitive service and placing it in the excepted service receives a most careful scrutiny prior to approval by the Civil Service Commission and every effort is made to keep the number of such positions to an absolute minimum. In fact, the number of noncareer supergrade positions declined from 579 on June 30, 1972, to 536 on June 30, 1973. We can assure you that there has been no wholesale movement of career jobs into the excepted service.

The qualifications of all appointees to supergrade positions, career and noncareer, is by law within the jurisdiction of the Civil Service Commission and each appointment must have the prior approval of the Commission. This enables us to effectively monitor the qualifications of all individuals moving into supergrade positions.

We are not aware of any impropriety in appointments to various supergrade positions in the National Park Service. Neither do we find anything in Mr. Wirth's editorial or letter that requires any action by the Civil Service Commission at this time. We see no threat to the normal goals and aspirations of the career professionals of the National Park Service.

In addition, we are not in receipt of any complaints from employees of the National Park Service reflecting a deteriorating morale of the work force. Complaints, if received, would be referred, as a matter of course, to our Bureau of Personnel Management Evaluation for exploration during their visits to evaluate personnel management practices. A copy of your inquiry and a copy of Mr. Wirth's editorial has been forwarded to the Director, Bureau of Personnel Management Evaluation, for appropriate consideration.

We hope this information has been responsive to your request. Please do not hesitate to call upon us if we can be of any further assistance.

Sincerely yours,

Joseph U. Damico
Director

CONRAD L. WIRTH
9633 EAST BEXHILL DRIVE
ROCK CREEK HILLS
KENSINGTON, MARYLAND 20795

September 16, 1975

Director Joseph U. Damico
Bureau of Executive Manpower
U.S. Civil Service Commission
Washington, D.C. 20415

Dear Mr. Damico:

I have a copy of your letter of September 4, 1973 to Senator Jacob K. Javits in answer to his letter to you dated August 9, 1973 in which he transmitted to you an editorial I wrote that appeared in the National Park Courier. I did not bother writing further on the subject because your letter made it quite clear that you were not going to do anything about it and it was clear that other steps were necessary.

Now that the matter has been at least temporarily straightened out I would like to ask you a question and to point out where the information contained in your letter of September 4, 1973 to the Senator is not correct.

1. Did the Civil Service clear Ronald Walker as being qualified to be Director of the National Park Service?

2. Do you honestly think that an employee in a career appointment is going to go to the Civil Service Commission and file a complaint about its selection of an unqualified political appointment to head up a major bureau of the Federal Government?

3. You sent the Senator's letter and my editorial to your Bureau of Personnel Management Evaluation; that was a complaint. Did they do anything about it and if so what?

4. For your information the position of Deputy Director was not abolished in 1971. There is now and there has been a Deputy Director ever since 1967.

5. You state that "The position of Director, National Park Service, has been filled historically by career employees, who likewise voluntarily relinquished career status." I can only speak for myself when I tell you that I am a retired National Park Service career employee with 36 years of service of which 33 years have been with the Park Service and with better than 12 years as its Director. During my term as Director I served under four secretaries, two of whom were Republicans and two were Democrats and I had just one appointment and I never gave up my Civil Service status and I never was asked to resign as was Director Hartzog.

Mr. Damico, I am not trying to be mean, but there is a large group of retired career service people as well as employees who believe in training and improving oneself to do the best job possible for our government and our country and this can't be done if we and Civil Service don't do our thing. Certainly you must admit that asking Hartzog to resign, which I understand he did under protest, and appointing Ronald Walker, with no knowledge or training in park administration, is not the right way to get the best results and the most out of the tax dollar.

I assume that Executive Order 11189 is still in effect. Would it be possible for you to send me a copy? I would appreciate it very much.

Sincerely yours,
Conrad L. Wirth

UNITED STATES CIVIL SERVICE COMMISSION
BUREAU OF EXECUTIVE MANPOWER
WASHINGTON, D.C. 20415

Oct. 06, 1975

Mr. Conrad L. Wirth
9633 East Bexhill Drive
Rock Creek Hills
Kensington, Maryland 20795

Dear Mr. Wirth:

This is in reply to your letter of September 16, 1975, in which you posed questions concerning the top management of the National Park Service.

The position of Director, National Park Service was established in 1964 at Level V of the Executive Schedule and excepted from the competitive service under Schedule C. The Civil Service Commission was not involved in the selection or approval of Mr. Ronald Walker for that position because we are not involved in the selection and approval of the qualifications of candidates for positions in the Executive Schedule. In case you are not aware of it, Mr. Walker resigned as Director of the Park Service in January 1975 and was succeeded by a former career employee of the National Park Service, Mr. Gary E. Everhardt.

Procedures exist for Federal employees to complain to the Civil Service Commission about all types of personnel actions, including political appointments, which they view as improper. The Civil Service Commission Complaint Office here at our 1900 E Street address handles written, telephone, and walk-in complaints. Employees contacting that office may complain anonymously or request that their complaint be maintained confidential. The system, thereby, allows employees to point out seeming irregularities when they otherwise would not for fear of reprisal.

The Bureau of Personnel Management Evaluation follows up on complaints with a prompt inquiry to the agency concerned and/or by flagging the complaint for investigation during a general evaluation of personnel management in the agency. Your complaint, which was referred to them as a result of your previous letter, was flagged for future investigation and should be considered in the evaluation of top managerial positions currently underway in the Department of the Interior.

Our records indicate that the position of Deputy Director, National Park Service was established in grade GS-17 on January 30, 1967, upgraded to grade GS-18 on January 14, 1971, and canceled on July 9, 1971. In August 1972 the Department of the Interior requested our approval of their proposal to reestablish the position of Deputy Director, National Park Service in grade GS-18 and requested concurrent approval of the qualifications of the proposed appointee. These requests, however, were not approved and the position was not established and filled again at the supergrade level until October 12, 1973. At the time of our response to your letter to Senator Javits in September 1973 the position of Deputy Director, National Park Service had not existed at the supergrade level for more than two years.

The position of Director, National Park Service was in the career service when you were appointed to it in December 1951. However, it was converted to be excepted service under Schedule C in August 1953 and continued under Schedule C when it was upgraded to grade GS-18 in November 1957. Since you were a career employee when you entered the position you retained your career status when the position was converted to Schedule C. If the position had been excepted under Schedule C prior to your appointment to it, you would have relinquished your career status in accepting it and would have served at the pleasure of the Secretary of Interior as did Mr. Hartzog.

Executive Order 11189 is still in effect and a copy is enclosed per your request. I appreciate your concern for the well-being of career employees and the career service and hope this letter has amply responded to your questions.

Sincerely yours,
Joseph U. Damico
Director

If it is true that the Civil Service Commission is "not involved in the selection and approval of the qualifications of candidates for positions in the Executive Schedule," then the National Park Service is no longer a *career* service. Further, the commission's admitted ignorance of Ron Walker's qualifications—or lack of them—for the position of director of the Park Service removes all authority from Damico's statement to Senator Javits that "the position of Director, National Park Service, has been filled historically by career employees." If I am right in believing that civil service employees are selected on the basis of their qualifications, then the executive classification positions are no longer civil service positions. (Regarding the position of deputy director, Damico is intentionally misleading. The position was not canceled, although there was a seesaw game of shifting it from grade 17 to 18, back to grade 17, and up again to 18.)

I must note, however, that of the eight directors of the National Park Service—from the appointment of Stephen T. Mather with the establishment of the service on May 16, 1917, to the end of Gary Everhardt's tour of duty as director in May, 1977—all but one, Ron Walker, were well qualified to fill the position. But that one illustrated the dangers of the new system.

The secretary of the interior, the under secretary, and the assistant secretary are all political appointees charged with seeing that the policy of the administration is carried out. Most of them are new to government, and they come and go. Some don't like it and want to go back to private business; others have been let go for political reasons. The secretary of the interior stays in office for an average of 4.4 years. The under secretary, second in command of the department, has an average longevity of 1.7 years. The assistant secretaries average 2.2 years in office. How could they possibly operate with businesslike efficiency—and government is big business—without well-trained and experienced career personnel to carry out the integral details of government responsibility?

In the twelve years that I was director of the National Park Service there were eight assistant secretaries to whom I reported at different times. In that

1929 to 1977
SECRETARIES OF THE DEPARTMENT OF THE INTERIOR

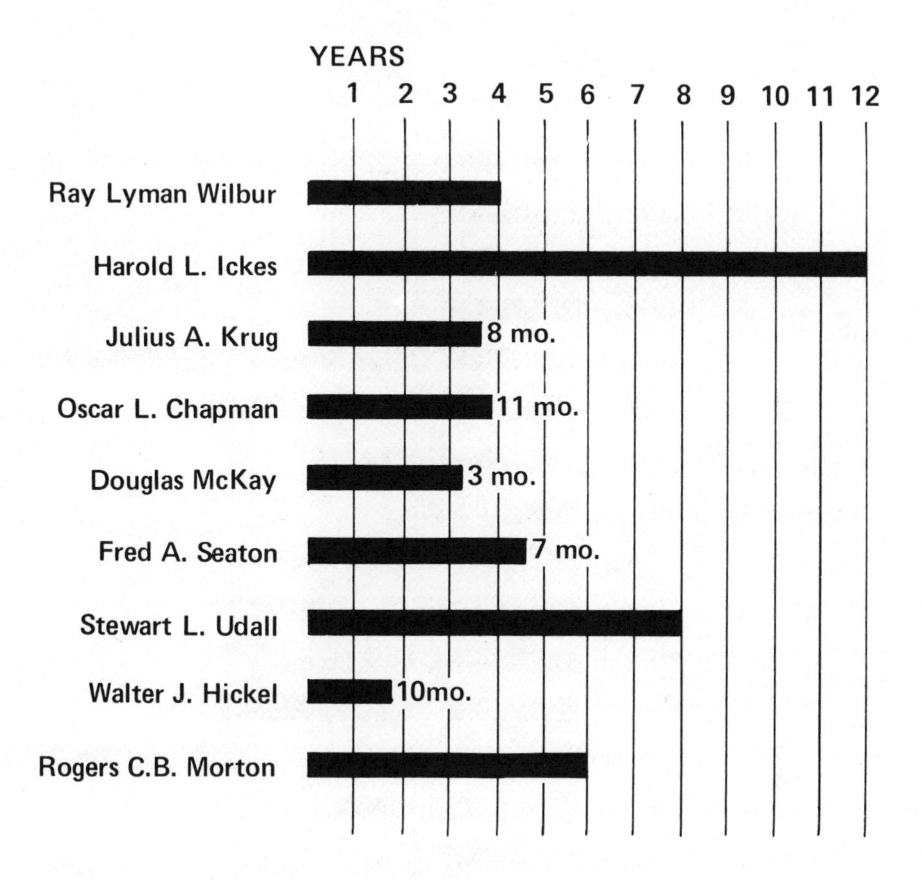

9 Secretaries in 47.3 years; average 5.2 years.

1 Secretary Harold Ickes held office for 12 years.

8 Secretaries, after removing Ickes because it was an unusual case and unlikely to happen again held office for 35.3 years, or average of 4.4 years.

1935 to 1975
UNDER SECRETARIES OF THE DEPARTMENT OF THE INTERIOR

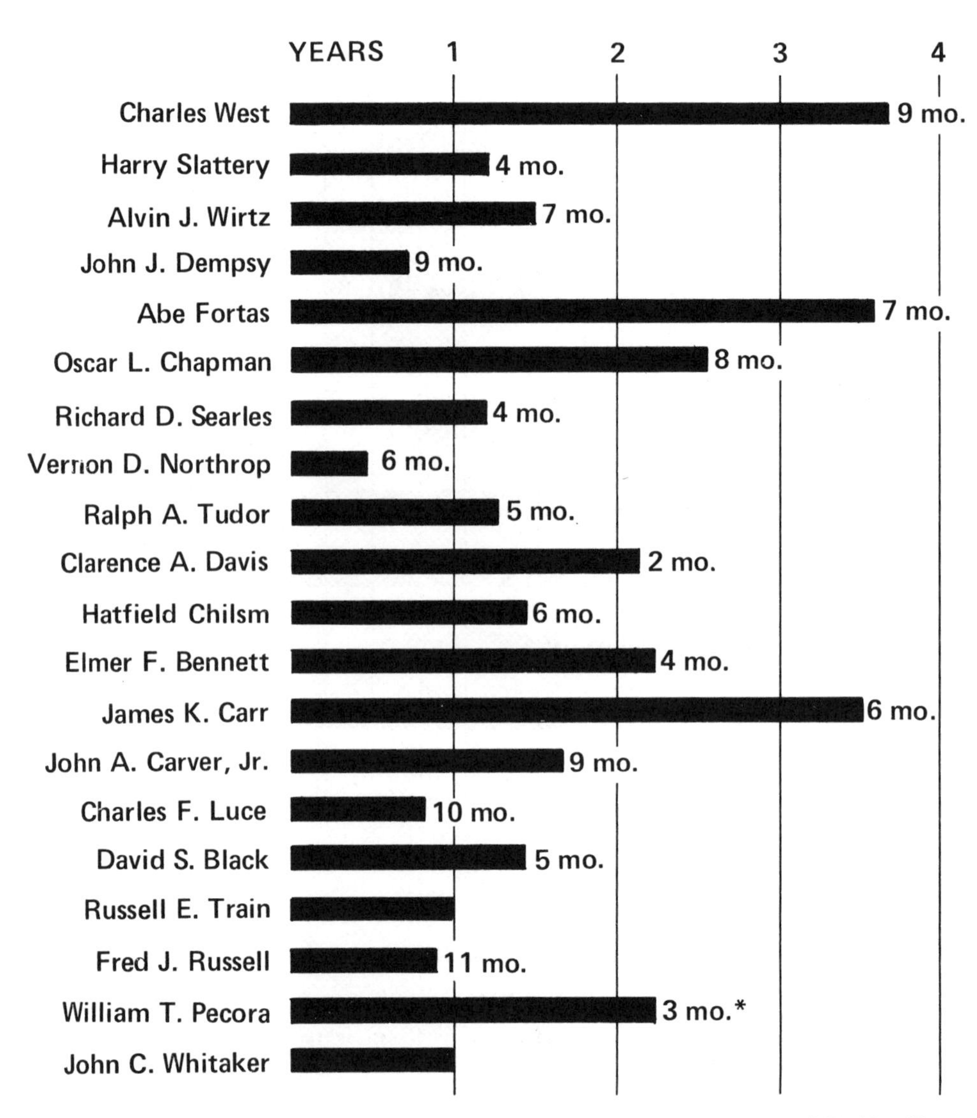

UNDER SECRETARIES started in the Interior Department in 1935 carried through to Jan. 1, 1975. That is a total of 40 years. During this time there have been 20 Under Secretaries that have held office for 34.6 years on an average of 1.7 years. In the 40 years, the office has been vacant for a total of 5.4 years, or 13.5% of the time.

1926 to 1977
ASSISTANT SECRETARIES OF THE DEPARTMENT OF THE INTERIOR RESPONSIBLE FOR N.P.S.

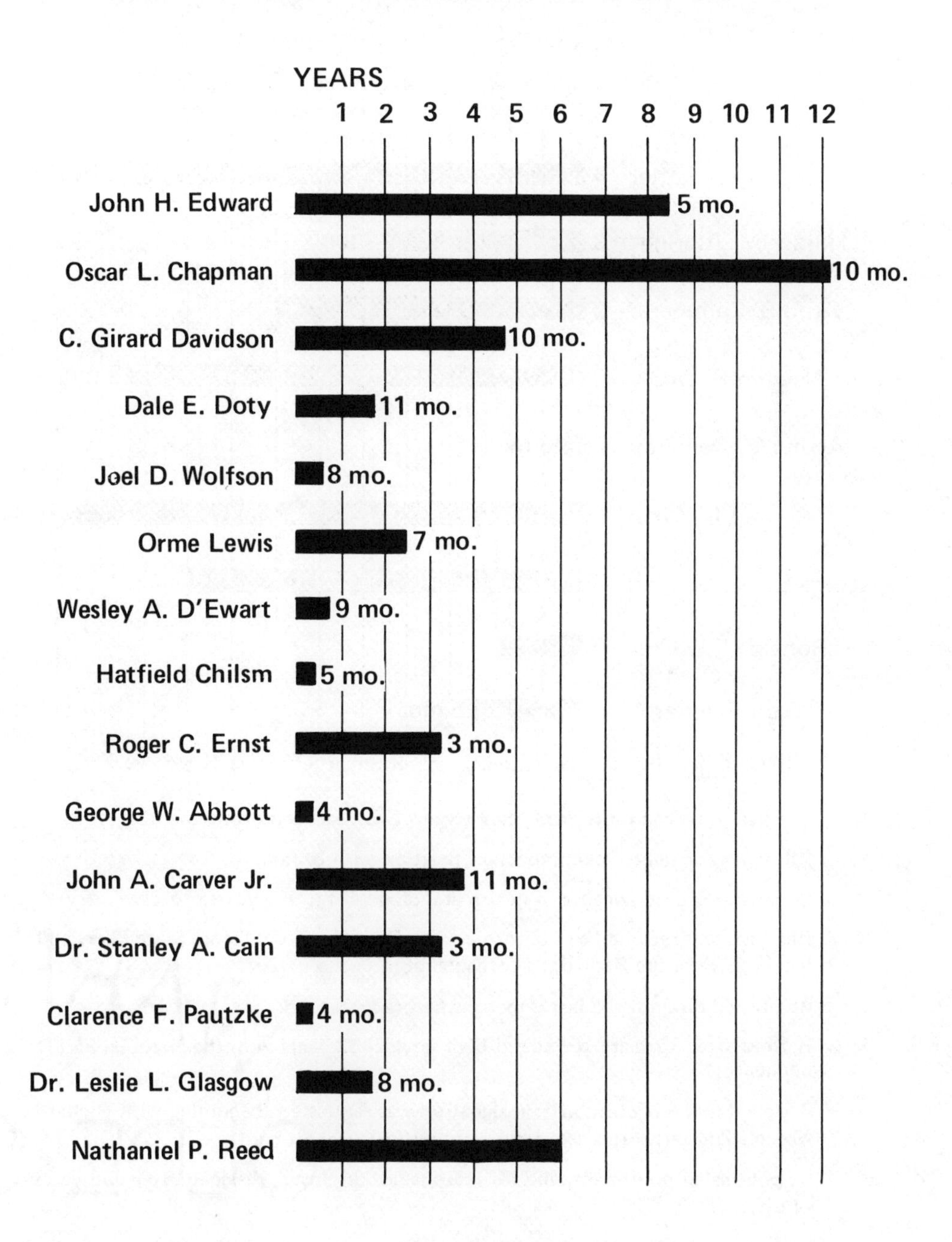

15 Assistant Secretaries over a span of 51.2 years, an average of 3.4 years.

Edwards and Chapman were in office 21 years and 3 months, an average of 10.7 years.

13 Assistant Secretaries, after removing the unusual cases of Edwards and Chapman, in office a total of 28 years and 11 months, an average of 2.2 years. The office has been vacant only .7 of a year in 50 years.

1917 to 1978
DIRECTORS OF THE NATIONAL PARK SERVICE OF THE DEPARTMENT OF THE INTERIOR

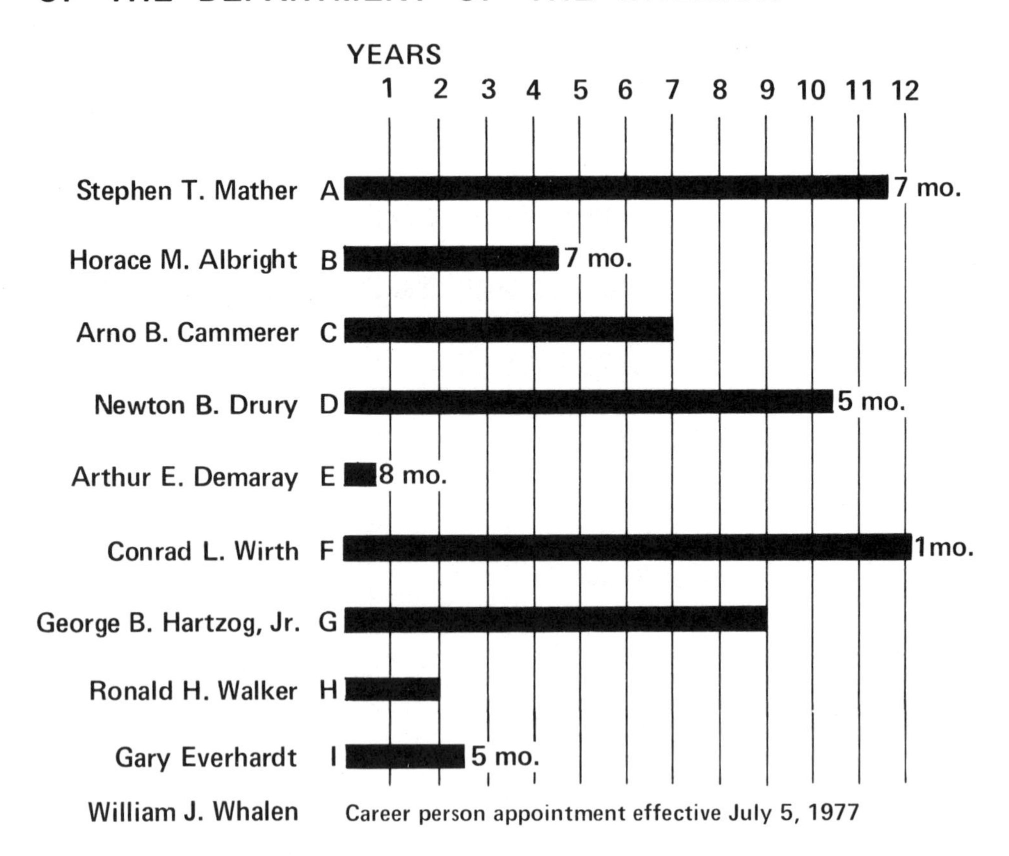

A. Bad health forced retirement, died within two years after retirement.

B. Albright resigned to take important position with Borax.

C. Cammerer retired because of health and died within two years.

D. Resigned and returned to California to be Director of California State Parks and head up "Save the Redwoods" organization.

E. Appointed director the last 8 months before he retired.

F. Retired after 36 years of Federal Civil service, 33 years with the National Park Service.

G. Resigned under protest, after resignation was requested (beginning with Richard Nixon's 2nd term) to make room for political appointment.

H. 1st political appointment, and for reasons not disclosed, resigned after two years of office.

I. Resigned to take an appointment as Superintendent of the Blue Ridge National Parkway.

9 Directors in 59.7 years, or an average of 6.6 years.

7 Directors in 57.1 years, after removing Demaray because it was an unusual case, and Walker because it was an unusual political case and hopefully will not occur again, for an average of 8.2 years.

William J. Whalen, director of the National Park Service from July 5, 1977, to the present.

same period there were eight under secretaries to whom the assistant secretaries reported, and four secretaries. Now what could be expected to happen if a political appointee takes over a bureau, as when the Nixon administration moved Ron Walker into the directorship?

I can't help but draw the conclusion that everything possible should be done to insure that the bureaus have well-trained career people to head them, people with a desire to devote their entire lifetime to getting the job properly done. I know it has been said that a man may be doing a good job, though not carrying out policy established by the political party in power, and that it is difficult to fire civil service people. The solution, in my opinion, is to establish rules and regulations that will allow the replacing of such a person. But he must be replaced by a person with experience and know-how if the job is going to be done and done right.

It is perfectly evident that the civil service structure has already been broken down by executive classification of the upper grades, and, in fact, the Civil Service Commission claims it has nothing to do with the appointment or separation of executive grade classification personnel. The executive grades are established by presidential order. If that regulation prevails the only recommendation I can make is that all such appointments be confirmed by Congress subject to public hearings. This procedure would at least provide an opportunity to examine the qualifications of the nominees.

POLITICAL ACTIVITY OF GOVERNMENT EMPLOYEES

A number of years back the federal government established a law called the Hatch Act that provided a protective blanket for civil servants so that they could devote their talents to the jobs assigned to them free of political influence. That was a big step forward. Recently Congress has been considering various proposals that, if enacted, would weaken the Hatch Act and allow civil servants to take an active part in party politics, even to the extent of running for elective office. If that comes about it will destroy one of the most important bases of a sound civil service system. And I see no reason for the proposed changed. Any career person can run for his boss' job now, except that he can't do it while working for that boss. The government employee has the same rights that all citizens have, or should have, except that he can't go out and campaign for or against a candidate. Any weakening of the Hatch Act would be a terrible blunder.

GOVERNMENT AND THE GOVERNED

In a speech in December, 1971, a department-level government official said that in his long career as a public servant he could not recall a time when the public demonstrated less faith in their government that it had done over the previous decade. In good form he went on to say that he was supporting the administration in its effort to bring the government at all levels closer to the people and to lessen the gap between the government and the governed. I agree wholeheartedly with his stated objective (though I must add that conditions didn't really improve during several years following his statement). It is most important that the governed and their government at all levels understand each other and work for the good of the nation. It is true that as the population multiplies and as its culture and scientific knowledge advance, more and greater differences of opinion develop, and these differences are apt to create voids between people and between the people and their government. A government cannot ignore widespread doubts concerning its credibility, and it is equally important that those in the governed category try to better understand the problems of government. Government career people are charged with the responsibility of carrying out policies, sometimes against their personal inclinations, and they must understand that basic policies are established by the elected or duly appointed representatives of the people.

There is an old saying that is more often true than not: "It *is* the squeaky wheel that gets the grease." On the other hand, there is a modern expression, or a political term, if you please: the "silent majority." When the "silent majority" is favored, it means that we are not going with the minority opinion, even though it is "squeaking." Nevertheless, a well-organized minority very often has its way, and we do not hear from the masses, the "silent majority," until the project or action has been completed, and then often it is too late. The best political administration is one that can identify and understand the needs of the silent majority and then effect the objective with the least irritation of the minority. To the degree it can do that, it will remain in office and accomplish much for all of the people it represents. The same is true of the career person who applies these principles within the framework of his authority and responsibilities.

There is not always a clear distinction between what is best and what is not so good, or even bad. The elements of timing, imagination, and good judgment are important in reaching a proper conclusion. It is also important for an individual in authority to resist a natural inclination to play God by deciding what is best because of personal preference rather than real need.

Maybe I am somewhat biased when I state that government employees, by and large, are at least as well, of not better, qualified and as earnest in their endeavors as are people in private enterprise. I agree that some people in the government service do not bring a great deal of credit to their agencies or departments, but the same is true in organizations outside of government—in civic affairs as well as in private enterprise. The big difference is that government employees are always on the public view. They live and work in a fishbowl. Yet, some of the greatest scientists and best administrators this country has ever known have devoted their lives to the service of their government. Civil servants are observed not just by the public but by politicians and various special-interest groups who believe they can be helpful. Often well-meaning friends cause the greatest problem; though more often than not differences of opinion between friends, when a friendly attitude is maintained, lead to the best solutions. If we can direct all government processes so that everything we do is for the betterment of our country and our fellow citizens, it is a good bureaucracy and it is good politics; otherwise, it's terrible and destructive.

The key to the success of any organization is its leadership, which by another name is administration. I believe a few fundamental tenets are worth examining. They were formulated in my mind as my career advanced. Some of them are derived from statements I have read, which I have altered to a considerable extent based on my experiences and observations. As an administrator, one will find that these principles hold true regardless of the size of an organization or whether it is in government or private enterprise. As soon as a person has one employee under his supervision, he assumes a degree of administrative responsibility, and the following tenets become more important.

(1) Accept yourself and go on from there. Don't be afraid to be different and to set your own pattern. Be gentle to yourself, for only insofar as you have the right attitude toward yourself can you have the right attitude toward others.

(2) Be humble. Humility begins with the recognition of your dependence on others—and an appreciation of their accomplishments and help to you. A person becomes humble only when aware of the enormous debt owed to others and when he realizes how little he knows of all there is to know.

(3) You can be courteous and still be firm. Go forward with warmth and a gracious, hospitable spirit. A firm, courteous request is far more effective than an order, and it produces better results.

(4) You must be adventurous, opening doors to new experiences and constantly on the lookout for better ideas to improve results, including morale. An imaginative and adventurous administrator must develop a sound philosophy through discussion and reasoning. He should share it with the staff and should be willing to test suggested changes. He should have the fortitude to adopt or to drop suggestions and ideas, according to whether or not they promise desirable results. Remember the tortoise: it can go nowhere without sticking its neck out (of course it should know when to pull it in, too).

(5) Look for and recognize your weaknesses, and build your organization to compensate for them. In this way you will build a staff that will share responsibilities, for no administrator has the time or ability to be all things to all people. Your entire organization's ability and confidence in achieving goals will intensify as the going gets more difficult.

(6) Always give credit where due. Your success will depend to a great extent on your recognition of good concepts, ideas, and the abilities of many people. Your own credit lies in your ability to put such concepts, ideas, and abilities together to their best use.

Whether in a small or a large organization, it is necessary to plan for the future and to develop a policy that keeps up with progress. But good judgment must be exercised on how much of a plan or policy can be carried out at one time. I believe that Thomas Jefferson advanced this point as well as it can be stated and in as few words as possible. The inscription on a wall at the Library of Congress quotes Jefferson as saying, "Let us then take what we can get, and press forward eternally for what is yet to get. It takes time to persuade men to do even what is for their own good."

CONSERVATION AND WILDERNESS MANAGEMENT

Howard C. Zahniser, in my opinion one of our great conservationists and a leader in the passage of the Wilderness Bill, said: "Wilderness is a natural area where nature is the host and man the guest who doesn't remain." And Howard R. Stagner, one of the great naturalists in the National Park Service, in one of the service's books entitled *The National Park Wilderness*, put it this way: "Wilderness is a physical condition. Wilderness is also a state of mind. Both concepts are important—the former in the matter of protection and management, the latter in evaluating the benefits of wilderness, both in planning for the intelligent and beneficial use of this important cultural and recreational heritage."

These two quotations point to the basic aspects of wilderness: its value, use, and need of careful management. What are the values of wilderness? Why not use the wilderness to provide man with his changing goodies and to serve his expanding desires which are nurtured by his bent for short-term economic enterprise? What bearing did wilderness have on the history of man, and, even more important, what will it contribute to his history yet to be made? Howard Stagner offers these answers: "Wilderness is expanse . . . and each fixed or fleeting form reflects the artistry of nature. Wilderness is a whole environment of living things . . . and the prosperity of its native wildlife . . . measures the perfection of its waters and floral mantle. Wilderness is the beauty of nature, solitude, and music of stillness. Wilderness invites man to adventure, refreshment, and wonder."

These values and the anticipation of the unknown are the backdrop of our great nation. One of the great authors who have contributed much to our national park system is Freeman Tilden. In a little booklet he did for the service a number of years ago (*The Fifth Essence, an Invitation to Share in our Eternal Heritage*, Washington, D.C., The National Park Trust Fund Board), he wrote:

> The early Greek philosophers looked at the world about them and decided that there were four elements: fire, air, water, and earth. But as they grew a little wiser, they perceived that there must be something else. These tangible elements did not comprise a principle; they merely revealed that somewhere else, if they could find it, there *was* a soul of things—a Fifth Essence, pure, eternal, and inclusive.
>
> It is not important what they called this Fifth Essence. To modern science, weighing and measuring the galaxies with delicate instruments, the guesses of the ancient thinkers seem crude. Yet these men began a search that still goes on. Behind the thing seen must lie the greater thing unseen.
>
> "Heard melodies are sweet, but those unheard are sweeter."
>
> It is true that any thoughtful person may find and meditate upon the Fifth Essence in his own backyard. Not a woodland brook, not a mountain, not a field of grass

rippling in the breeze does not proclaim the existence of it. But here, in this little book which we hope you will enjoy, you will find reference to a consummate expression of this ultimate wealth of the human spirit which lies behind that which may be seen and touched. It is to be found in the National Park System. . . .

There has never in the history of nations been a cultural achievement like this one. We shall not boast. Perhaps no nation has ever enjoyed the peculiar benefits that would make it possible. But, at any rate, we have preserved a part of our precious heritage before it became too little and too late.

Freeman Tilden's book was written before the Wilderness Act became law, but his statements can well apply to wilderness no matter where it is. The preservation and understanding of our wilderness, our open spaces, our free flowing rivers, our seashores, and the history of man are all a part of our conservation of a heritage far more valuable than we realize. I do not believe we fully understand how much we as a nation owe to the generous foresightedness of so many men and women. I think it is well summed up in a statement made by Allan Sproul, at the time he was head of the New York Federal Reserve Bank, in recalling his experience as a young ranger on duty in the Mariposa Grove of Giant Sequoias in Yosemite National Park:

In my present work I am chief executive officer of an institution with over twelve billion dollars of assets, with over five billion dollars of gold belonging to foreign governments and central banks in its custody. I had something more precious in my care when I was the "lone ranger" stationed in the Mariposa Grove. In my ignorance I did not know of it then, but I feel it now when I go back to the Grove to worship in the shade of the Giant Sequoias. I thank God they are still there.

The basic principle contained in the law that established the National Park Service can apply without any difficulty to all widerness areas and parks administered by every level of government (excepting, of course, such intensive-use areas as ball fields and playgrounds). The words in the law I refer to are: "To conserve the scenery and the natural and historic objects and the wildlife therein, and to provide for the enjoyment of same in such manner and by such means as will leave them unimpaired for the enjoyment of future generations." Love of country together with our common need for the benefits derived from wilderness areas demand a nonpartisan approach to conservation. The best learning and wisdom our people have to offer must be devoted to the selection, protection, and management of the resources that are so necessary and beneficial to mankind.

A PERSONAL NOTE

John West was the chief usher at the White House for a great number of years and served under many presidents. The chief usher is the man who supervises the operation and activities of the White House. It is a difficult and very important job. John retired a few years ago and wrote a very interesting book about his experiences. At one place in the book he states that President John F. Kennedy once bawled me out. I don't want to contradict John West; he is a friend and we never had any trouble working out business contacts on matters pertaining to the White House and the White House grounds. But honestly, I don't remember ever having been bawled out by any president. I met and got to know all the presidents in office during my years in the federal service, although I doubt whether Herbert Hoover, Dwight Eisenhower, or Harry Truman really knew me. The ones I knew best were Franklin Delano Roosevelt, John F. Kennedy, and Lyndon Baines Johnson. If John is right, I must be one of the very few bureaucrats who have been bawled out by a president without being fired.

This book is intended to point out what life is like as a federal government civil servant. I have included the reprimands that I have gotten, but one of the nicest things that ever happened to me was to receive a letter from the former first lady, Jacqueline Kennedy. I have her permission to quote the letter. I was contemplating retirement as early as 1962, and on November 22, 1963, President Kennedy was assassinated in Dallas, Texas. I retired in January, 1964, and moved to New York. In late August of that year a special messenger delivered to our home in Bronxville a package and a letter under the seal of the president of the United States. The letter had been written by the former first lady in her own hand and the package contained a gold box bearing the presidential seal and the dates that John F. Kennedy served as president. Below that appeared the engraved signature of Jacqueline Kennedy. Following is the text of her letter:

August 22, 1964

Dear Mr. Wirth:

This little gold box comes with a long story attached to it.

President Kennedy was going to give you the Citation of Merit—this last Fourth of July. He had created it the year before—for people who had done so much for their country—and he was going to award it to a few people each Fourth of July—in his beloved Rose Garden.

He talked to me last summer—about giving it to you. You were retiring as head of the Park Service—and that was sad for him. He was so cognizant of all you had done for so many years. He recognized all the pride and devotion and service that had been such a part of your life—and you were the one who made him see all that the Park Service was—and then in his term—you were retiring—.

That made him so sad—because together you had done something extraordinary. You know how much he cared about the White House and how it looked to the world. His love and care for the grounds were in the tradition of Washington and Jefferson—though he didn't realize that—or consciously strive to emulate them. He just knew that the President's House should live up to an ideal—and you helped him achieve that ideal.

I was always so amazed and touched that with all he had to do—he could find the time to care about the gardens. He loved the Rose Garden so—it brought him such peace—and to gaze out at green lawns instead of crabgrass ones. He was so proud when it looked beautiful—and then he started to receive Heads of State there—instead of at Andrews Air Force Base.

He was so aware that it was *you* who made all that possible. He felt so relieved and sure that the White House would stay the way his vision of it was—once it was safely under the guardianship of the Park Service.

Now he is gone—and you are no longer the head of the National Parks. But the two of you will always be linked together—and you made possible for him some of his happiest hours—for which I am so grateful to you forever.

Once I knew, this winter, that he would never be able to give you the Citation which he wanted to give you so much—I had this little box made.

But I kept putting off giving it to you. It would have revived so many memories.

Now that I am about to leave Washington I feel I must send it to you—as a poor substitute for what you would have had from President Kennedy.

But please accept it with our devotion—and please know that all you did was appreciated more than I could ever express—.

Sincerely,
Jacqueline Kennedy

If I was ever bawled out by President Kennedy, I certainly don't remember it; but if so I must have come back pretty strong, for apparently it didn't linger in the mind of either the president or the first lady. On the other hand, John West has provided me the opportunity to reproduce this beautiful letter from Jacqueline Kennedy expressing her feelings and those of President Kennedy toward the National Park Service and myself. I had hesitated to publish it because it is such a thoughtful and personal thing she did on behalf of the late president and herself. But, John West, your statement and my ego left me no choice, and so I thank you very, very much.

Index